T0197978

Get the eBooks FREE!
(PDF, ePub, Kindle, and liveBook all included)

We believe that once you buy a book from us, you should be able to read it in any format we have available. To get electronic versions of this book at no additional cost to you, purchase and then register this book at the Manning website.

Go to https://www.manning.com/freebook and follow the instructions to complete your pBook registration.

That's it!
Thanks from Manning!

grokking

Deep
Reinforcement
Learning

grokking

Deep Reinforcement Learning

Miguel Morales

Foreword by Charles Isbell, Jr.

MANNING
SHELTER ISLAND

For online information and ordering of this and other Manning books, please visit
www.manning.com. The publisher offers discounts on this book when ordered in quantity. For more
information, please contact

    Special Sales Department
    Manning Publications Co.
    20 Baldwin Road, PO Box 761
    Shelter Island, NY 11964
    Email: orders@manning.com

Manning Publications Co.
20 Baldwin Road
Shelter Island, NY 11964

Development editor: Jenny Stout
Technical development editor: Al Krinker
Review editor: Ivan Martinović
Production editor: Lori Weidert
Copy editor: Katie Petito
Proofreader: Katie Tenant
Technical proofreader: Mayur Patil
Typesetter: Jennifer Houle
Cover designer: Leslie Haimes

ISBN: 9781617295454
Printed in the United States of America

··

For Danelle, Aurora, Solomon, and those to come.

Being with you is a +1 per timestep.

(You can safely assume +1 is the highest reward.)

I love you!

contents

foreword

So, here's the thing about reinforcement learning. It is difficult to learn and difficult to teach, for a number of reasons. First, it's quite a technical topic. There is a great deal of math and theory behind it. Conveying the right amount of background without drowning in it is a challenge in and of itself.

Second, reinforcement learning encourages a conceptual error. RL is both a way of thinking about decision-making problems and a set of tools for solving those problem. By "a way of thinking," I mean that RL provides a framework for making decisions: it discusses states and reinforcement signals, among other details. When I say "a set of tools," I mean that when we discuss RL, we find ourselves using terms like *Markov decision processes* and *Bellman updates*. It is remarkably easy to confuse the way of thinking with the mathematical tools we use in response to that way of thinking.

Finally, RL is implementable in a wide variety of ways. Because RL is a way of thinking, we can discuss it by trying to realize the framework in a very abstract way, or ground it in code, or, for that matter, in neurons. The substrate one decides to use makes these two difficulties even more challenging—which bring us to deep reinforcement learning.

Focusing on deep reinforcement learning nicely compounds all these problems at once. There is background on RL, and background on deep neural networks. Both are separately worthy of study and have developed in completely different ways. Working out how to explain both in the context of developing tools is no easy task. Also, do not forget that understanding RL requires understanding not only the tools and their realization in deep networks, but also understanding the way of thinking about RL; otherwise, you cannot generalize beyond the examples you study directly. Again, teaching RL is hard, and there are so many ways for teaching deep RL to go wrong—which brings us to Miguel Morales and this book.

This book is very well put together. It explains in technical but clear language what machine learning is, what deep learning is, and what reinforcement learning is. It allows the reader to understand the larger context of where the field is and what you can do with the techniques of deep RL, but also the way of thinking that ML, RL, and deep RL present. It is clear and concise. Thus, it works as both a learning guide and as a reference, and, at least for me, as a source of some inspiration.

I am not surprised by any of this. I've known Miguel for quite a few years now. He went from taking machine learning courses to teaching them. He has been the lead teaching assistant on my Reinforcement Learning and Decision Making course for the Online Masters of Science at Georgia Tech for more semesters than I can count. He's reached thousands of students during that time. I've watched him grow as a practitioner, a researcher, and an educator. He has helped to make the RL course at GT better than it started out, and continues even as I write this to make the experience of grokking reinforcement learning a deeper one for the students. He is a natural teacher.

This text reflects his talent. I am happy to be able to work with him, and I'm happy he's been moved to write this book. Enjoy. I think you'll learn a lot. I learned a few things myself.

Charles Isbell, Jr.
Professor and John P. Imlay Jr. Dean
College of Computing
Georgia Institute of Technology

preface

Reinforcement learning is an exciting field with the potential to make a profound impact on the history of humankind. Several technologies have influenced the history of our world and changed the course of humankind, from fire, to the wheel, to electricity, to the internet. Each technological discovery propels the next discovery in a compounding way. Without electricity, the personal computer wouldn't exist; without it, the internet wouldn't exist; without it, search engines wouldn't exist.

To me, the most exciting aspect of RL and artificial intelligence, in general, is not so much to merely have other intelligent entities next to us, which is pretty exciting, but instead, what comes after that. I believe reinforcement learning, being a robust framework for optimizing specific tasks autonomously, has the potential to change the world. In addition to task automation, the creation of intelligent machines may drive the understanding of human intelligence to places we have never been before. Arguably, if you can know with certainty how to find optimal decisions for every problem, you likely understand the algorithm that finds those optimal decisions. I have a feeling that by creating intelligent entities, humans can become more intelligent beings.

But we are far away from this point, and to fulfill these wild dreams, we need more minds at work. Reinforcement learning is not only in its infancy, but it's been in that state for a while, so there is much work ahead. The reason I wrote this book is to get more people grokking deep RL, and RL in general, and to help you contribute.

Even though the RL framework is intuitive, most of the resources out there are difficult to understand for newcomers. My goal was not to write a book that provides code examples only, and most definitely not to create a resource that teaches the theory of reinforcement learning. Instead, my goal was to create a resource that can bridge the gap between theory and practice. As you'll soon see, I don't shy away from equations; they are essential if you want to grok a research field. And, even if your goal is practical, to build quality RL solutions, you still need that theoretical foundation. However, I also don't solely rely on equations because not everybody interested in RL is fond of math. Some people are more comfortable with code and concrete examples, so this book provides the practical side of this fantastic field.

Most of my effort during this three-year project went into bridging this gap; I don't shy away from intuitively explaining the theory, and I don't just plop down code examples. I do both, and in a very detail-oriented fashion. Those who have a hard time understanding the textbooks and lectures can more easily grasp the words top researchers use: why those specific words, why not other words. And those who know the words and love reading the equations but have trouble seeing those equations in code and how they connect can more easily understand the practical side of reinforcement learning.

Finally, I hope you enjoy this work, and more importantly that it does fulfill its goal for you. I hope that you emerge grokking deep reinforcement learning and can give back and contribute to this fantastic community that I've grown to love. As I mentioned before, you wouldn't be reading this book if it wasn't for a myriad of relatively recent technological innovations, but what happens after this book is up to you, so go forth and make an impact in the world.

acknowledgments

I want to thank the people at Georgia Tech for taking the risk and making available the first Online Master of Science in Computer Science for anyone in the world to get a high-quality graduate education. If it weren't for those folks who made it possible, I probably would not have written this book.

I want to thank Professor and Dean Charles Isbell and Professor Michael Littman for putting together an excellent reinforcement-learning course. I have a special appreciation for Dean Isbell, who has given me much room to grow and learn RL. Also, the way I teach reinforcement learning—by splitting the problem into three types of feedback—I learned from Professor Littman. I'm grateful to have received instruction from them.

I want to thank the vibrant teaching staff at Georgia Tech's CS 7642 for working together on how to help students learn more and enjoy their time with us. Special thanks go to Tim Bail, Pushkar Kolhe, Chris Serrano, Farrukh Rahman, Vahe Hagopian, Quinn Lee, Taka Hasegawa, Tianhang Zhu, and Don Jacob. You guys are such great teammates. I also want to thank the folks who previously contributed significantly to that course. I've gotten a lot from our interactions: Alec Feuerstein, Valkyrie Felso, Adrien Ecoffet, Kaushik Subramanian, and Ashley Edwards. I want to also thank our students for asking the questions that helped me identify the gaps in knowledge for those trying to learn RL. I wrote this book with you in mind. A very special thank you goes out to that anonymous student who recommended me to Manning for writing this book; I still don't know who you are, but you know who you are. Thank you.

I want to thank the folks at Lockheed Martin for all their feedback and interactions during my time writing this book. Special thanks go to Chris Aasted, Julia Kwok, Taylor Lopez, and John Haddon. John was the first person to review my earliest draft, and his feedback helped me move the writing to the next level.

I want to thank the folks at Manning for providing the framework that made this book a reality. I thank Brian Sawyer for reaching out and opening the door; Bert Bates for setting the compass early on and helping me focus on teaching; Candace West for helping me go from zero to something; Susanna Kline for helping me pick up the pace when life got busy; Jennifer Stout for cheering me on through the finish line; Rebecca Rinehart for putting out fires; Al Krinker for providing me with actionable feedback and helping me separate the signal from the noise; Matko Hrvatin for keeping up with MEAP releases and putting that extra pressure on me to keep writing; Candace Gillhoolley for getting the book out there, Stjepan Jureković for getting me out there; Ivan Martinovic for getting the much-needed feedback to improve the text; Lori Weidert for aligning the book to be production-ready twice; Jennifer Houle for being gentle with the design changes; Katie Petito for patiently working through the details; Katie Tennant for the meticulous and final polishing touches; and to anyone I missed, or who worked behind the scenes to make this book a reality. There are more, I know: thank you all for your hard work.

To all the reviewers—Al Rahimi, Alain Couniot, Alberto Ciarlanti, David Finton, Doniyor Ulmasov, Edisson Reinozo, Ezra Joel Schroeder, Hank Meisse, Hao Liu, Ike Okonkwo, Jie Mei, Julien Pohie, Kim Falk Jørgensen, Marc-Philippe Huget, Michael Haller, Michel Klomp, Nacho Ormeño, Rob Pacheco, Sebastian Maier, Sebastian Zaba, Swaminathan Subramanian, Tyler Kowallis, Ursin Stauss, and Xiaohu Zhu—thank you, your suggestions helped make this a better book.

I want to thank the folks at Udacity for letting me share my passion for this field with their students and record the actor-critic lectures for their Deep Reinforcement Learning Nanodegree. Special thanks go to Alexis Cook, Mat Leonard, and Luis Serrano.

I want to thank the RL community for helping me clarify the text and improve my understanding. Special thanks go to David Silver, Sergey Levine, Hado van Hasselt, Pascal Poupart, John Schulman, Pieter Abbeel, Chelsea Finn, Vlad Mnih, for their lectures; Rich Sutton for providing the gold copy of the field in a single place (his textbook); and James MacGlashan, and Joshua Achiam for their codebases, online resources, and guidance when I didn't know where to go to get an answer to a question. I want to thank David Ha for giving me insights as to where to go next.

Special thanks go to Silvia Mora for helping make all the figures in this book presentable and helping me in almost every side project that I undertake.

Finally, I want to thank my family, who were my foundation throughout this project. I "knew" writing a book was a challenge, and then I learned. But my wife and kids were there regardless, waiting for my 15-minute breaks every 2 hours or so during the weekends. Thank you, Solo, for brightening up my life midway through this book. Thank you, Rosie, for sharing your love and beauty, and thank you Danelle, my wonderful wife, for everything you are and do. You are my perfect teammate in this interesting game called life. I'm so glad I found you.

about this book

Grokking Deep Reinforcement Learning bridges the gap between the theory and practice of deep reinforcement learning. The book's target audience is folks familiar with machine learning techniques, who want to learn reinforcement learning. The book begins with the foundations of deep reinforcement learning. It then provides an in-depth exploration of algorithms and techniques for deep reinforcement learning. Lastly, it provides a survey of advanced techniques with the potential for making an impact.

Who should read this book

Folks who are comfortable with a research field, Python code, a bit of math here and there, lots of intuitive explanations, and fun and concrete examples to drive the learning will enjoy this book. However, any person only familiar with Python can get a lot, given enough interest in learning. Even though basic DL knowledge is assumed, this book provides a brief refresher on neural networks, backpropagation, and related techniques. The bottom line is that this book is self contained, and anyone wanting to play around with AI agents and emerge grokking deep reinforcement learning can use this book to get them there.

How this book is organized: a roadmap

This book has 13 chapters divided into two parts.

In part 1, chapter 1 introduces the field of deep reinforcement learning and sets expectations for the journey ahead. Chapter 2 introduces a framework for designing problems that RL agents can understand. Chapter 3 contains details of algorithms for solving RL problems when the agent knows the dynamics of the world. Chapter 4 contains details of algorithms for solving simple RL problems when the agent does not know the dynamics of the world. Chapter 5 introduces methods for solving the prediction problem, which is a foundation for advanced RL methods.

In part 2, chapter 6 introduces methods for solving the control problem, methods that optimize policies purely from trial-and-error learning. Chapter 7 teaches more advanced methods for RL, including methods that use planning for more sample efficiency. Chapter 8 introduces the use of function approximation in RL by implementing a simple RL algorithm that uses neural networks for function approximation. Chapter 9 dives into more advanced techniques for using function approximation for solving reinforcement learning problems. Chapter 10 teaches some of the best techniques for further improving the methods introduced so far. Chapter 11 introduces a slightly different technique for using DL models with RL that has proven to reach state-of-the-art performance in multiple deep RL benchmarks. Chapter 12 dives into more advanced methods for deep RL, state-of-the-art algorithms, and techniques commonly used for solving real-world problems. Chapter 13 surveys advanced research areas in RL that suggest the best path for progress toward artificial general intelligence.

About the code

This book contains many examples of source code both in boxes titled "I speak Python" and in the text. Source code is formatted in a `fixed-width font like this` to separate it from ordinary text and has syntax highlighting to make it easier to read.

In many cases, the original source code has been reformatted; we've added line breaks, renamed variables, and reworked indentation to accommodate the available page space in the book. In rare cases, even this was not enough, and code includes line-continuation operator in Python, the backslash (\), to indicate that a statement is continued on the next line.

Additionally, comments in the source code have often been removed from the boxes, and the code is described in the text. Code annotations point out important concepts.

The code for the examples in this book is available for download from the Manning website at https://www.manning.com/books/grokking-deep-reinforcement-learning and from GitHub at https://github.com/mimoralea/gdrl.

liveBook discussion forum

Purchase of *Grokking Deep Reinforcement Learning* includes free access to a private web forum run by Manning Publications where you can make comments about the book, ask technical questions, and receive help from the author and from other users. To access the forum, go to https://livebook.manning.com/#!/book/grokking-deep-reinforcement-learning/discussion. You can also learn more about Manning's forums and the rules of conduct at https://livebook .manning.com/#!/discussion.

Manning's commitment to our readers is to provide a venue where a meaningful dialogue between individual readers and between readers and the author can take place. It is not a commitment to any specific amount of participation on the part of the author, whose contribution to the forum remains voluntary (and unpaid). We suggest you try asking him some challenging questions lest his interest stray! The forum and the archives of previous discussions will be accessible from the publisher's website as long as the book is in print.

about the author

MIGUEL MORALES works on reinforcement learning at Lockheed Martin, Missiles and Fire Control, Autonomous Systems, in Denver, Colorado. He is a part-time Instructional Associate at Georgia Institute of Technology for the course in Reinforcement Learning and Decision Making. Miguel has worked for Udacity as a machine learning project reviewer, a Self-driving Car Nanodegree mentor, and a Deep Reinforcement Learning Nanodegree content developer. He graduated from Georgia Tech with a Master's in Computer Science, specializing in interactive intelligence.

Introduction to deep reinforcement learning | 1

. . . .

In this chapter

- You will learn what deep reinforcement learning is and how it is different from other machine learning approaches.

- You will learn about the recent progress in deep reinforcement learning and what it can do for a variety of problems.

- You will know what to expect from this book and how to get the most out of it.

. . . .

       66 *I visualize a time when we will be to robots what dogs are to humans, and I'm rooting for the machines.* **99**

                             — CLAUDE SHANNON
                   FATHER OF THE INFORMATION AGE
       AND CONTRIBUTOR TO THE FIELD OF ARTIFICIAL INTELLIGENCE

Humans naturally pursue feelings of happiness. From picking out our meals to advancing our careers, every action we choose is derived from our drive to experience rewarding moments in life. Whether these moments are self-centered pleasures or the more generous of goals, whether they bring us immediate gratification or long-term success, they're still our perception of how important and valuable they are. And to some extent, these moments are the reason for our existence.

Our ability to achieve these precious moments seems to be correlated with intelligence; "intelligence" is defined as the ability to acquire and apply knowledge and skills. People who are deemed by society as intelligent are capable of trading not only immediate satisfaction for long-term goals, but also a good, certain future for a possibly better, yet uncertain, one. Goals that take longer to materialize and that have unknown long-term value are usually the hardest to achieve, and those who can withstand the challenges along the way are the exception, the leaders, the intellectuals of society.

In this book, you learn about an approach, known as deep reinforcement learning, involved with creating computer programs that can achieve goals that require intelligence. In this chapter, I introduce deep reinforcement learning and give suggestions to get the most out of this book.

What is deep reinforcement learning?

Deep reinforcement learning (DRL) is a machine learning approach to artificial intelligence concerned with creating computer programs that can solve problems requiring intelligence. The distinct property of DRL programs is learning through trial and error from feedback that's simultaneously sequential, evaluative, and sampled by leveraging powerful non-linear function approximation.

I want to unpack this definition for you one bit at a time. But, don't get too caught up with the details because it'll take me the whole book to get you grokking deep reinforcement learning. The following is the introduction to what you learn about in this book. As such, it's repeated and explained in detail in the chapters ahead.

If I succeed with my goal for this book, after you complete it, you should understand this definition precisely. You should be able to tell why I used the words that I used, and why I didn't use more or fewer words. But, for this chapter, simply sit back and plow through it.

Deep reinforcement learning is a machine learning approach to artificial intelligence

Artificial intelligence (AI) is a branch of computer science involved in the creation of computer programs capable of demonstrating intelligence. Traditionally, any piece of software that displays cognitive abilities such as perception, search, planning, and learning is considered part of AI. Several examples of functionality produced by AI software are

- The pages returned by a search engine
- The route produced by a GPS app
- The voice recognition and the synthetic voice of smart-assistant software
- The products recommended by e-commerce sites
- The follow-me feature in drones

Subfields of artificial intelligence

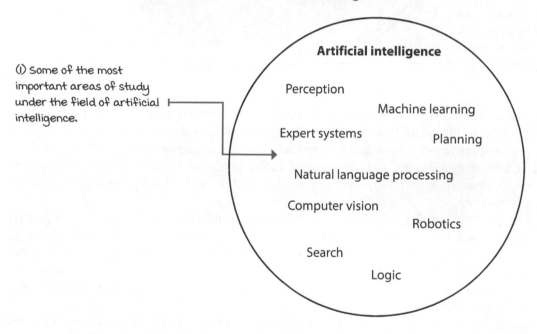

(i) Some of the most important areas of study under the field of artificial intelligence.

Artificial intelligence

Perception

Machine learning

Expert systems

Planning

Natural language processing

Computer vision

Robotics

Search

Logic

All computer programs that display intelligence are considered AI, but not all examples of AI can learn. *Machine learning* (ML) is the area of AI concerned with creating computer programs that can solve problems requiring intelligence by learning from data. There are three main branches of ML: supervised, unsupervised, and reinforcement learning.

Main branches of machine learning

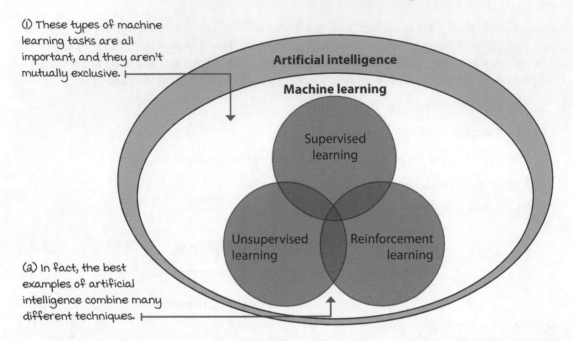

(1) These types of machine learning tasks are all important, and they aren't mutually exclusive.

Artificial intelligence

Machine learning

Supervised learning

Unsupervised learning

Reinforcement learning

(2) In fact, the best examples of artificial intelligence combine many different techniques.

Supervised learning (SL) is the task of learning from labeled data. In SL, a human decides which data to collect and how to label it. The goal in SL is to generalize. A classic example of SL is a handwritten-digit-recognition application: a human gathers images with handwritten digits, labels those images, and trains a model to recognize and classify digits in images correctly. The trained model is expected to generalize and correctly classify handwritten digits in new images.

Unsupervised learning (UL) is the task of learning from unlabeled data. Even though data no longer needs labeling, the methods used by the computer to gather data still need to be designed by a human. The goal in UL is to compress. A classic example of UL is a customer segmentation application; a human collects customer data and trains a model to group customers into clusters. These clusters compress the information, uncovering underlying relationships in customers.

Reinforcement learning (RL) is the task of learning through trial and error. In this type of task, no human labels data, and no human collects or explicitly designs the collection of data. The goal in RL is to act. A classic example of RL is a Pong-playing agent; the agent repeatedly interacts with a Pong emulator and learns by taking actions and observing their effects. The trained agent is expected to act in such a way that it successfully plays Pong.

A powerful recent approach to ML, called *deep learning* (DL), involves using multi-layered non-linear function approximation, typically neural networks. DL isn't a separate branch of ML, so it's not a different task than those described previously. DL is a collection of techniques and methods for using neural networks to solve ML tasks, whether SL, UL, or RL. DRL is simply the use of DL to solve RL tasks.

Deep learning is a powerful toolbox

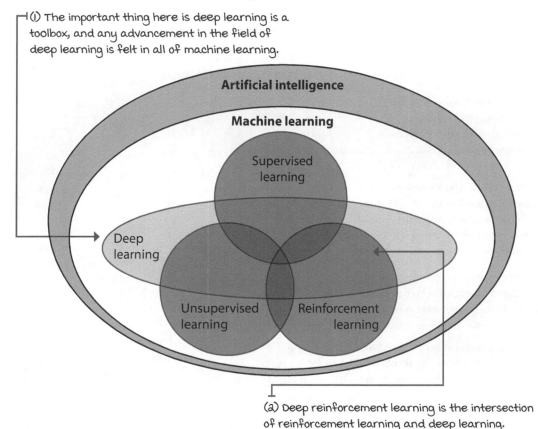

(1) The important thing here is deep learning is a toolbox, and any advancement in the field of deep learning is felt in all of machine learning.

(2) Deep reinforcement learning is the intersection of reinforcement learning and deep learning.

The bottom line is that DRL is an approach to a problem. The field of AI defines the problem: creating intelligent machines. One of the approaches to solving that problem is DRL. Throughout the book, will you find comparisons between RL and other ML approaches, but only in this chapter will you find definitions and a historical overview of AI in general. It's important to note that the field of RL includes the field of DRL, so although I make a distinction when necessary, when I refer to RL, remember that DRL is included.

Deep reinforcement learning is concerned with creating computer programs

At its core, DRL is about complex sequential decision-making problems under uncertainty. But, this is a topic of interest in many fields; for instance, *control theory* (CT) studies ways to control complex known dynamic systems. In CT, the dynamics of the systems we try to control are usually known in advance. *Operations research* (OR), another instance, also studies decision-making under uncertainty, but problems in this field often have much larger action spaces than those commonly seen in DRL. *Psychology* studies human behavior, which is partly the same "complex sequential decision-making under uncertainty" problem.

The synergy between similar fields

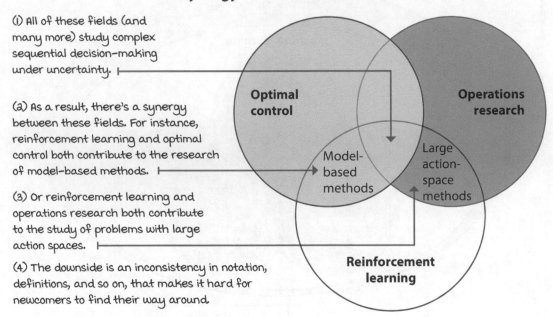

(1) All of these fields (and many more) study complex sequential decision-making under uncertainty.

(2) As a result, there's a synergy between these fields. For instance, reinforcement learning and optimal control both contribute to the research of model-based methods.

(3) Or reinforcement learning and operations research both contribute to the study of problems with large action spaces.

(4) The downside is an inconsistency in notation, definitions, and so on, that makes it hard for newcomers to find their way around.

Optimal control

Operations research

Model-based methods

Large action-space methods

Reinforcement learning

The bottom line is that you have come to a field that's influenced by a variety of others. Although this is a good thing, it also brings inconsistencies in terminologies, notations, and so on. My take is the computer science approach to this problem, so this book is about building computer programs that solve complex decision-making problems under uncertainty, and as such, you can find code examples throughout the book.

In DRL, these computer programs are called *agents*. An agent is a decision maker only and nothing else. That means if you're training a robot to pick up objects, the robot arm isn't part of the agent. Only the code that makes decisions is referred to as the agent.

Deep reinforcement learning agents can solve problems that require intelligence

On the other side of the agent is the **environment**. The environment is everything outside the agent; everything the agent has no total control over. Again, imagine you're training a robot to pick up objects. The objects to be picked up, the tray where the objects lay, the wind, and everything outside the decision maker are part of the environment. That means the robot arm is also part of the environment because it isn't part of the agent. And even though the agent can decide to move the arm, the actual arm movement is noisy, and thus the arm is part of the environment.

This strict boundary between the agent and the environment is counterintuitive at first, but the decision maker, the agent, can only have a single role: making decisions. Everything that comes after the decision gets bundled into the environment.

Boundary between agent and environment

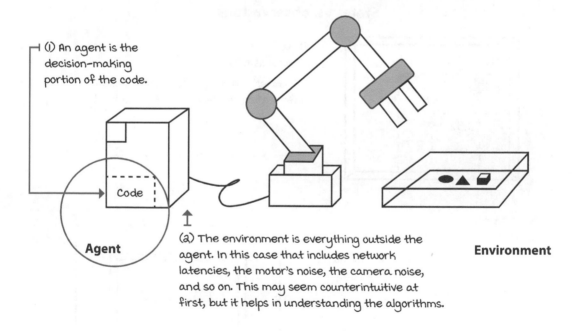

(1) An agent is the decision-making portion of the code.

Code

Agent

(2) The environment is everything outside the agent. In this case that includes network latencies, the motor's noise, the camera noise, and so on. This may seem counterintuitive at first, but it helps in understanding the algorithms.

Environment

Chapter 2 provides an in-depth survey of all the components of DRL. The following is a preview of what you'll learn in chapter 2.

The environment is represented by a set of variables related to the problem. For instance, in the robotic arm example, the location and velocities of the arm would be part of the variables that make up the environment. This set of variables and all the possible values that they can take are referred to as the *state space*. A state is an instantiation of the state space, a set of values the variables take.

Interestingly, often, agents don't have access to the actual full state of the environment. The part of a state that the agent can observe is called an *observation*. Observations depend on states but are what the agent can see. For instance, in the robotic arm example, the agent may only have access to camera images. While an exact location of each object exists, the agent doesn't have access to this specific state. Instead, the observations the agent perceives are derived from the states. You'll often see in the literature observations and states being used interchangeably, including in this book. I apologize in advance for the inconsistencies. Simply know the differences and be aware of the lingo; that's what matters.

States vs. observations

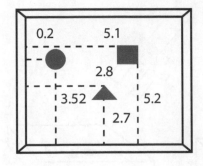

State:
true locations

(1) States are the perfect and complete information related to the task at hand.

Observation:
just an image

(2) While observations are the information the agent receives, this could be noisy or incomplete information.

At each state, the environment makes available a set of actions the agent can choose from. The agent influences the environment through these actions. The environment may change states as a response to the agent's action. The function that's responsible for this mapping is called the *transition function*. The environment may also provide a reward signal as a response. The function responsible for this mapping is called the *reward function*. The set of transition and reward functions is referred to as the *model* of the environment.

The reinforcement learning cycle

① The cycle begins with the agent observing the environment.

Observation and reward

Transition

Environment

State

Agent

Improve

(4) Finally, the environment transitions and its internal state (likely) changes as a consequence of the previous state and the agent's action. Then, the cycle repeats.

Action

(3) It then sends an action to the environment in an attempt to control it in a favorable way.

(2) The agent uses this observation and reward to attempt to improve at the task.

The environment commonly has a well-defined task. The goal of this task is defined through the reward function. The reward-function signals can be simultaneously sequential, evaluative, and sampled. To achieve the goal, the agent needs to demonstrate intelligence, or at least cognitive abilities commonly associated with intelligence, such as long-term thinking, information gathering, and generalization.

The agent has a three-step process: the agent interacts with the environment, the agent evaluates its behavior, and the agent improves its responses. The agent can be designed to learn mappings from observations to actions called *policies*. The agent can be designed to learn the model of the environment on mappings called *models*. The agent can be designed to learn to estimate the reward-to-go on mappings called *value functions*.

Deep reinforcement learning agents improve their behavior through trial-and-error learning

The interactions between the agent and the environment go on for several cycles. Each cycle is called a *time step*. At each time step, the agent observes the environment, takes action, and receives a new observation and reward. The set of the state, the action, the reward, and the new state is called an *experience*. Every experience has an opportunity for learning and improving performance.

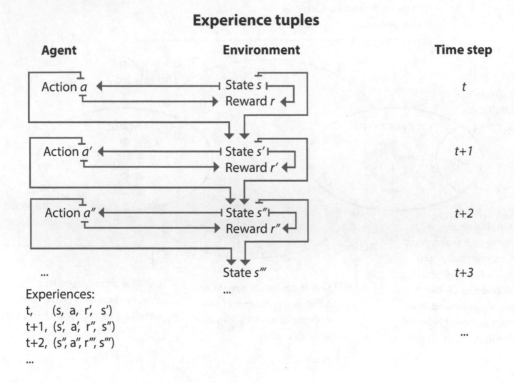

Experience tuples

The task the agent is trying to solve may or may not have a natural ending. Tasks that have a natural ending, such as a game, are called *episodic tasks*. Conversely, tasks that don't are called *continuing tasks*, such as learning forward motion. The sequence of time steps from the beginning to the end of an episodic task is called an *episode*. Agents may take several time steps and episodes to learn to solve a task. Agents learn through trial and error: they try something, observe, learn, try something else, and so on.

You'll start learning more about this cycle in chapter 4, which contains a type of environment with a single step per episode. Starting with chapter 5, you'll learn to deal with environments that require more than a single interaction cycle per episode.

Deep reinforcement learning agents learn from sequential feedback

The action taken by the agent may have delayed consequences. The reward may be sparse and only manifest after several time steps. Thus the agent must be able to learn from sequential feedback. Sequential feedback gives rise to a problem referred to as the *temporal credit assignment problem*. The temporal credit assignment problem is the challenge of determining which state and/or action is responsible for a reward. When there's a temporal component to a problem, and actions have delayed consequences, it's challenging to assign credit for rewards.

The difficulty of the temporal credit assignment problem

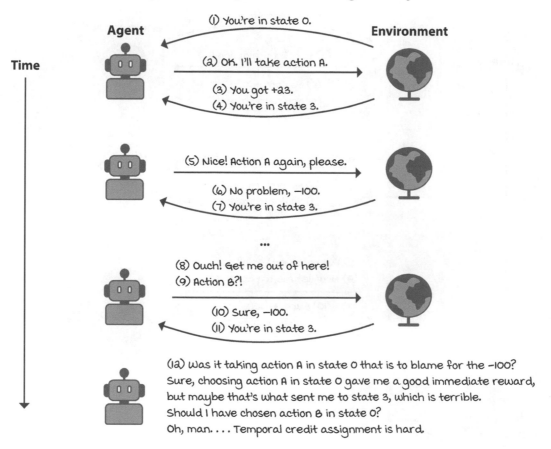

In chapter 3, we'll study the ins and outs of sequential feedback in isolation. That is, your programs learn from simultaneously sequential, supervised (as opposed to evaluative), and exhaustive (as opposed to sampled) feedback.

Deep reinforcement learning agents learn from evaluative feedback

The reward received by the agent may be weak, in the sense that it may provide no supervision. The reward may indicate goodness and not correctness, meaning it may contain no information about other potential rewards. Thus the agent must be able to learn from *evaluative feedback*. Evaluative feedback gives rise to the need for exploration. The agent must be able to balance the gathering of information with the exploitation of current information. This is also referred to as the *exploration versus exploitation trade-off*.

The difficulty of the exploration vs. exploitation trade-off

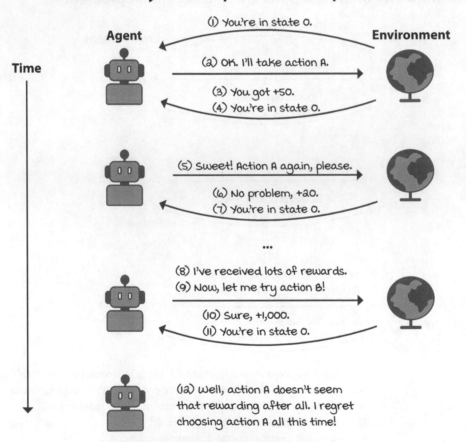

In chapter 4, we'll study the ins and outs of evaluative feedback in isolation. That is, your programs will learn from feedback that is simultaneously one-shot (as opposed to sequential), evaluative, and exhaustive (as opposed to sampled).

Deep reinforcement learning agents learn from sampled feedback

The reward received by the agent is merely a sample, and the agent doesn't have access to the reward function. Also, the state and action spaces are commonly large, even infinite, so trying to learn from sparse and weak feedback becomes a harder challenge with samples. Therefore, the agent must be able to learn from sampled feedback, and it must be able to generalize.

The difficulty of learning from sampled feedback

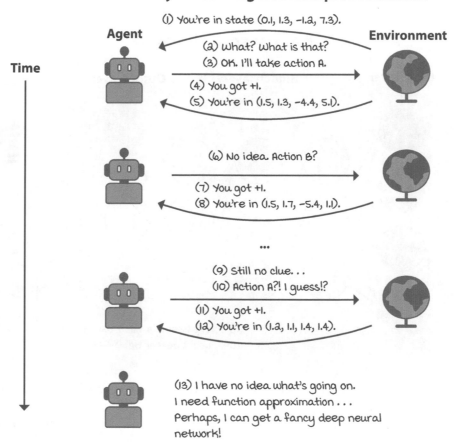

Agents that are designed to approximate policies are called *policy-based*; agents that are designed to approximate value functions are called *value-based*; agents that are designed to approximate models are called *model-based*; and agents that are designed to approximate both policies and value functions are called *actor-critic*. Agents can be designed to approximate one or more of these components.

Deep reinforcement learning agents use powerful non-linear function approximation

The agent can approximate functions using a variety of ML methods and techniques, from decision trees to SVMs to neural networks. However, in this book, we use only neural networks; this is what the "deep" part of DRL refers to, after all. Neural networks aren't necessarily the best solution to every problem; neural networks are data hungry and challenging to interpret, and you must keep these facts in mind. However, neural networks are among the most potent function approximations available, and their performance is often the best.

A simple feed-forward neural network

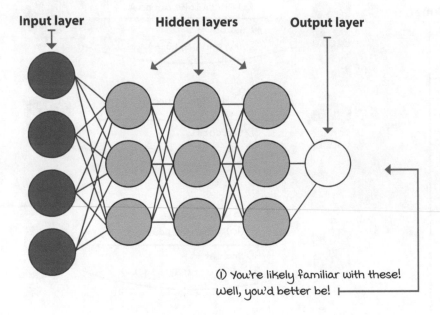

① You're likely familiar with these! Well, you'd better be!

Artificial neural networks (ANN) are multi-layered non-linear function approximators loosely inspired by the biological neural networks in animal brains. An ANN isn't an algorithm, but a structure composed of multiple layers of mathematical transformations applied to input values.

From chapter 3 through chapter 7, we only deal with problems in which agents learn from exhaustive (as opposed to sampled) feedback. Starting with chapter 8, we study the full DRL problem; that is, using deep neural networks so that agents can learn from sampled feedback. Remember, DRL agents learn from feedback that's simultaneously sequential, evaluative, and sampled.

The past, present, and future of deep reinforcement learning

History isn't necessary to gain skills, but it can allow you to understand the context around a topic, which in turn can help you gain motivation, and therefore, skills. The history of AI and DRL should help you set expectations about the future of this powerful technology. At times, I feel the hype surrounding AI is actually productive; people get interested. But, right after that, when it's time to put in work, hype no longer helps, and it's a problem. Although I'd like to be excited about AI, I also need to set realistic expectations.

Recent history of artificial intelligence and deep reinforcement learning

The beginnings of DRL could be traced back many years, because humans have been intrigued by the possibility of intelligent creatures other than ourselves since antiquity. But a good beginning could be Alan Turing's work in the 1930s, 1940s, and 1950s that paved the way for modern computer science and AI by laying down critical theoretical foundations that later scientists leveraged.

The most well-known of these is the Turing Test, which proposes a standard for measuring machine intelligence: if a human interrogator is unable to distinguish a machine from another human on a chat Q&A session, then the computer is said to count as intelligent. Though rudimentary, the Turing Test allowed generations to wonder about the possibilities of creating smart machines by setting a goal that researchers could pursue.

The formal beginnings of AI as an academic discipline can be attributed to John McCarthy, an influential AI researcher who made several notable contributions to the field. To name a few, McCarthy is credited with coining the term "artificial intelligence" in 1955, leading the first AI conference in 1956, inventing the Lisp programming language in 1958, cofounding the MIT AI Lab in 1959, and contributing important papers to the development of AI as a field over several decades.

Artificial intelligence winters

All the work and progress of AI early on created a great deal of excitement, but there were also significant setbacks. Prominent AI researchers suggested we would create human-like machine intelligence within years, but this never came. Things got worse when a well-known researcher named James Lighthill compiled a report criticizing the state of academic research in AI. All of these developments contributed to a long period of reduced funding and interest in AI research known as the first *AI winter*.

The field continued this pattern throughout the years: researchers making progress, people getting overly optimistic, then overestimating—leading to reduced funding by government and industry partners.

AI funding pattern through the years

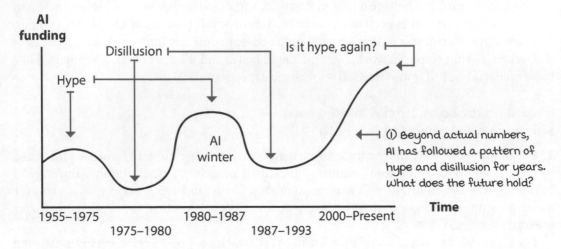

The current state of artificial intelligence

We are likely in another highly optimistic time in AI history, so we must be careful. Practitioners understand that AI is a powerful tool, but certain people think of AI as this magic black box that can take any problem in and out comes the best solution ever. Nothing can be further from the truth. Other people even worry about AI gaining consciousness, as if that was relevant, as Edsger W. Dijkstra famously said: "The question of whether a computer can think is no more interesting than the question of whether a submarine can swim."

But, if we set aside this Hollywood-instilled vision of AI, we can allow ourselves to get excited about the recent progress in this field. Today, the most influential companies in the world make the most substantial investments to AI research. Companies such as Google, Facebook, Microsoft, Amazon, and Apple have invested in AI research and have become highly profitable thanks, in part, to AI systems. Their significant and steady investments have created the perfect environment for the current pace of AI research. Contemporary researchers have the best computing power available and tremendous amounts of data for their research, and teams of top researchers are working together, on the same problems, in the same location, at the same time. Current AI research has become more stable and more productive. We have witnessed one AI success after another, and it doesn't seem likely to stop anytime soon.

Progress in deep reinforcement learning

The use of artificial neural networks for RL problems started around the 1990s. One of the classics is the backgammon-playing computer program, TD-Gammon, created by Gerald Tesauro et al. TD-Gammon learned to play backgammon by learning to evaluate table positions on its own through RL. Even though the techniques implemented aren't precisely considered DRL, TD-Gammon was one of the first widely reported success stories using ANNs to solve complex RL problems.

TD-Gammon architecture

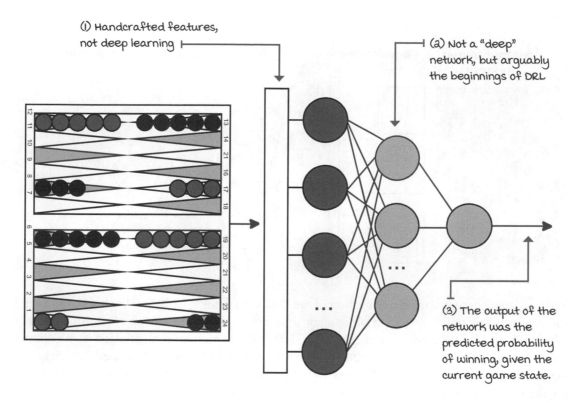

In 2004, Andrew Ng et al. developed an autonomous helicopter that taught itself to fly stunts by observing hours of human-experts flights. They used a technique known as *inverse reinforcement learning,* in which an agent learns from expert demonstrations. The same year, Nate Kohl and Peter Stone used a class of DRL methods known as *policy-gradient methods* to develop a soccer-playing robot for the RoboCup tournament. They used RL to teach the agent forward motion. After only three hours of training, the robot achieved the fastest forward-moving speed of any robot with the same hardware.

There were other successes in the 2000s, but the field of DRL really only started growing after the DL field took off around 2010. In 2013 and 2015, Mnih et al. published a couple of papers presenting the DQN algorithm. DQN learned to play Atari games from raw pixels. Using a convolutional neural network (CNN) and a single set of hyperparameters, DQN performed better than a professional human player in 22 out of 49 games.

Atari DQN network architecture

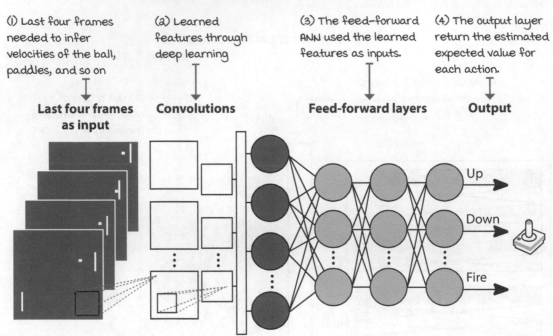

(1) Last four frames needed to infer velocities of the ball, paddles, and so on

(2) Learned features through deep learning

(3) The feed-forward ANN used the learned features as inputs.

(4) The output layer return the estimated expected value for each action.

Last four frames as input   **Convolutions**   **Feed-forward layers**   **Output**

Up

Down

Fire

This accomplishment started a revolution in the DRL community: In 2014, Silver et al. released the deterministic policy gradient (DPG) algorithm, and a year later Lillicrap et al. improved it with deep deterministic policy gradient (DDPG). In 2016, Schulman et al. released trust region policy optimization (TRPO) and generalized advantage estimation (GAE) methods, Sergey Levine et al. published Guided Policy Search (GPS), and Silver et al. demoed AlphaGo. The following year, Silver et al. demonstrated AlphaZero. Many other algorithms were released during these years: double deep Q-networks (DDQN), prioritized experience replay (PER), proximal policy optimization (PPO), actor-critic with experience replay (ACER), asynchronous advantage actor-critic (A3C), advantage actor-critic (A2C), actor-critic using Kronecker-factored trust region (ACKTR), Rainbow, Unicorn (these are actual names, BTW), and so on. In 2019, Oriol Vinyals et al. showed the AlphaStar agent beat professional players at the game of StarCraft II. And a few months later, Jakub Pachocki et al. saw their team of Dota-2-playing bots, called Five, become the first AI to beat the world champions in an e-sports game.

Thanks to the progress in DRL, we've gone in two decades from solving backgammon, with its 10^{20} perfect-information states, to solving the game of Go, with its 10^{170} perfect-information states, or better yet, to solving StarCraft II, with its 10^{270} imperfect-information states. It's hard to conceive a better time to enter the field. Can you imagine what the next two decades will bring us? Will you be part of it? DRL is a booming field, and I expect its rate of progress to continue.

Game of Go: enormous branching factor

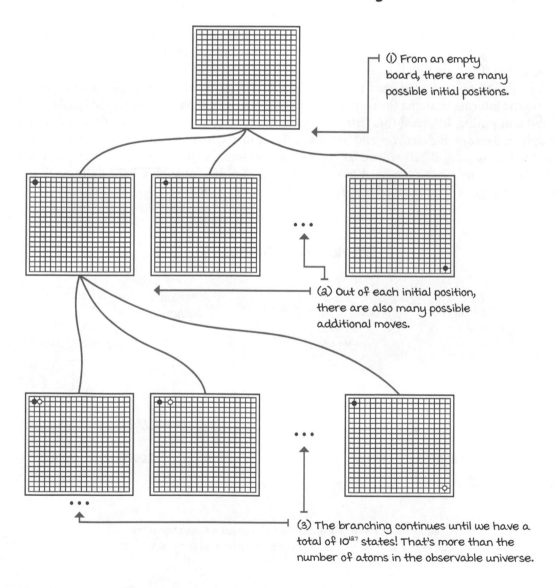

(1) From an empty board, there are many possible initial positions.

(2) Out of each initial position, there are also many possible additional moves.

(3) The branching continues until we have a total of 10^{127} states! That's more than the number of atoms in the observable universe.

Opportunities ahead

I believe AI is a field with unlimited potential for positive change, regardless of what fear-mongers say. Back in the 1750s, there was chaos due to the start of the industrial revolution. Powerful machines were replacing repetitive manual labor and mercilessly displacing humans. Everybody was concerned: machines that can work faster, more effectively, and more cheaply than humans? These machines will take all our jobs! What are we going to do for a living now? And it happened. But the fact is that many of these jobs were not only unfulfilling, but also dangerous.

One hundred years after the industrial revolution, the long-term effects of these changes were benefiting communities. People who usually owned only a couple of shirts and a pair of pants could get much more for a fraction of the cost. Indeed, change was difficult, but the long-term effects benefited the entire world.

The digital revolution started in the 1970s with the introduction of personal computers. Then, the internet changed the way we do things. Because of the internet, we got big data and cloud computing. ML used this fertile ground for sprouting into what it is today. In the next couple of decades, the changes and impact of AI on society may be difficult to accept at first, but the long-lasting effects will be far superior to any setback along the way. I expect in a few decades humans won't even need to work for food, clothing, or shelter because these things will be automatically produced by AI. We'll thrive with abundance.

Workforce revolutions

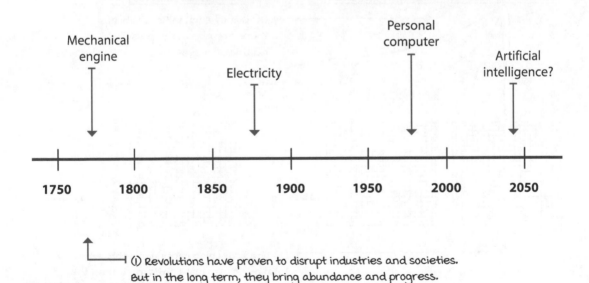

(i) Revolutions have proven to disrupt industries and societies. But in the long term, they bring abundance and progress.

As we continue to push the intelligence of machines to higher levels, certain AI researchers think we might find an AI with intelligence superior to our own. At this point, we unlock a phenomenon known as the *singularity*; an AI more intelligent than humans allows for the improvement of AI at a much faster pace, given that the self-improvement cycle no longer has the bottleneck, namely, humans. But we must be prudent, because this is more of an ideal than a practical aspect to worry about.

Singularity could be a few decades away

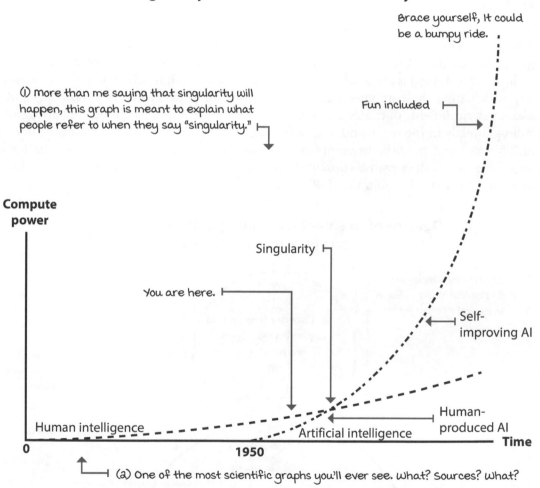

(a) One of the most scientific graphs you'll ever see. What? Sources? What?

While one must be always aware of the implications of AI and strive for AI safety, the singularity isn't an issue today. On the other hand, many issues exist with the current state of DRL, as you'll see in this book. These issues make better use of our time.

The suitability of deep reinforcement learning

You could formulate any ML problem as a DRL problem, but this isn't always a good idea for multiple reasons. You should know the pros and cons of using DRL in general, and you should be able to identify what kinds of problems and settings DRL is good and not so good for.

What are the pros and cons?

Beyond a technological comparison, I'd like you to think about the inherent advantages and disadvantages of using DRL for your next project. You'll see that each of the points highlighted can be either a pro or a con depending on what kind of problem you're trying to solve. For instance, this field is about letting the machine take control. Is this good or bad? Are you okay with letting the computer make the decisions for you? There's a reason why DRL research environments of choice are games: it could be costly and dangerous to have agents training directly in the real world. Can you imagine a self-driving car agent learning not to crash by crashing? In DRL, the agents will have to make mistakes. Can you afford that? Are you willing to risk the negative consequences—actual harm—to humans? Considered these questions before starting your next DRL project.

Deep reinforcement learning agents will explore!
Can you afford mistakes?

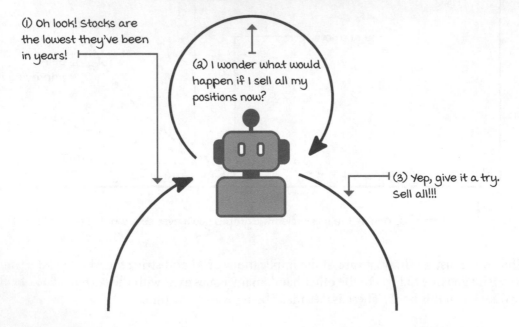

You'll also need to consider how your agent will explore its environment. For instance, most value-based methods explore by randomly selecting an action. But other methods can have more strategic exploration strategies. Now, there are pros and cons to each, and this is a trade-off you'll have to become familiar with.

Finally, training from scratch every time can be daunting, time consuming, and resource intensive. However, there are a couple of areas that study how to bootstrap previously acquired knowledge. First, there's *transfer learning*, which is about transferring knowledge gained in tasks to new ones. For example, if you want to teach a robot to use a hammer and a screwdriver, you could reuse low-level actions learned on the "pick up the hammer" task and apply this knowledge to start learning the "pick up the screwdriver" task. This should make intuitive sense to you, because humans don't have to relearn low-level motions each time they learn a new task. Humans seem to form hierarchies of actions as we learn. The field of *hierarchical reinforcement learning* tries to replicate this in DRL agents.

Deep reinforcement learning's strengths

DRL is about mastering specific tasks. Unlike SL, in which generalization is the goal, RL is good at concrete, well-specified tasks. For instance, each Atari game has a particular task. DRL agents aren't good at generalizing behavior across different tasks; it's not true that because you train an agent to play Pong, this agent can also play Breakout. And if you naively try to teach your agent Pong and Breakout simultaneously, you'll likely end up with an agent that isn't good at either. SL, on the other hand, is pretty good a classifying multiple objects at once. The point is the strength of DRL is well-defined single tasks.

In DRL, we use generalization techniques to learn simple skills directly from raw sensory input. The performance of generalization techniques, new tips, and tricks on training deeper networks, and so on, are some of the main improvements we've seen in recent years. Lucky for us, most DL advancements directly enable new research paths in DRL.

Deep reinforcement learning's weaknesses

Of course, DRL isn't perfect. One of the most significant issues you'll find is that in most problems, agents need millions of samples to learn well-performing policies. Humans, on the other hand, can learn from a few interactions. Sample efficiency is probably one of the top areas of DRL that could use improvements. We'll touch on this topic in several chapters because it's a crucial one.

**Deep reinforcement learning agents need
lots of interaction samples!**

Episode 2,324,532

ⓘ I almost drove inside the lanes that last time, boss.
Let me drive just one more car!

Another issue with DRL is with reward functions and understanding the meaning of rewards. If a human expert will define the rewards the agent is trying to maximize, does that mean that we're somewhat "supervising" this agent? And is this something good? Should the reward be as dense as possible, which makes learning faster, or as sparse as possible, which makes the solutions more exciting and unique?

We, as humans, don't seem to have explicitly defined rewards. Often, the same person can see an event as positive or negative by simply changing their perspective. Additionally, a reward function for a task such as walking isn't straightforward to design. Is it the forward motion that we should target, or is it not falling? What is the "perfect" reward function for a human walk?!

There's ongoing interesting research on reward signals. One I'm particularly interested in is called *intrinsic motivation*. Intrinsic motivation allows the agent to explore new actions just for the sake of it, out of curiosity. Agents that use intrinsic motivation show improved learning performance in environments with sparse rewards, which means we get to keep exciting and unique solutions. The point is if you're trying to solve a task that hasn't been modeled or doesn't have a distinct reward function, you'll face challenges.

Setting clear two-way expectations

Let's now touch on another important point going forward. What to expect? Honestly, to me, this is very important. First, I want you to know what to expect from the book so there are no surprises later on. I don't want people to think that from this book, they'll be able to come up with a trading agent that will make them rich. Sorry, I wouldn't be writing this book if it was that simple. I also expect that people who are looking to learn put in the necessary work. The fact is that learning will come from the combination of me putting in the effort to make concepts understandable and you putting in the effort to understand them. I did put in the effort. But, if you decide to skip a box you didn't think was necessary, we both lose.

What to expect from the book?

My goal for this book is to take you, an ML enthusiast, from no prior DRL experience to capable of developing state-of-the-art DRL algorithms. For this, the book is organized into roughly two parts. In chapters 3 through 7, you learn about agents that can learn from sequential and evaluative feedback, first in isolation, and then in interplay. In chapters 8 through 12, you dive into core DRL algorithms, methods, and techniques. Chapters 1 and 2 are about introductory concepts applicable to DRL in general, and chapter 13 has concluding remarks.

My goal for the first part (chapters 3 through 7) is for you to understand "tabular" RL. That is, RL problems that can be exhaustively sampled, problems in which there's no need for neural networks or function approximation of any kind. Chapter 3 is about the sequential aspect of RL and the temporal credit assignment problem. Then, we'll study, also in isolation, the challenge of learning from evaluative feedback and the exploration versus exploitation trade-off in chapter 4. Last, you learn about methods that can deal with these two challenges simultaneously. In chapter 5, you study agents that learn to estimate the results of fixed behavior. Chapter 6 deals with learning to improve behavior, and chapter 7 shows you techniques that make RL more effective and efficient.

My goal for the second part (chapters 8 through 12) is for you to grasp the details of core DRL algorithms. We dive deep into the details; you can be sure of that. You learn about the many different types of agents from value- and policy-based to actor-critic methods. In chapters 8 through 10, we go deep into value-based DRL. In chapter 11, you learn about policy-based DRL and actor-critic, and chapter 12 is about deterministic policy gradient (DPG) methods, soft actor-critic (SAC) and proximal policy optimization (PPO) methods.

The examples in these chapters are repeated throughout agents of the same type to make comparing and contrasting agents more accessible. You still explore fundamentally different kinds of problems, from small, continuous to image-based state spaces, and from discrete to continuous action spaces. But, the book's focus isn't about modeling problems, which is a skill of its own; instead, the focus is about solving already modeled environments.

Comparison of different algorithmic approaches to deep reinforcement learning

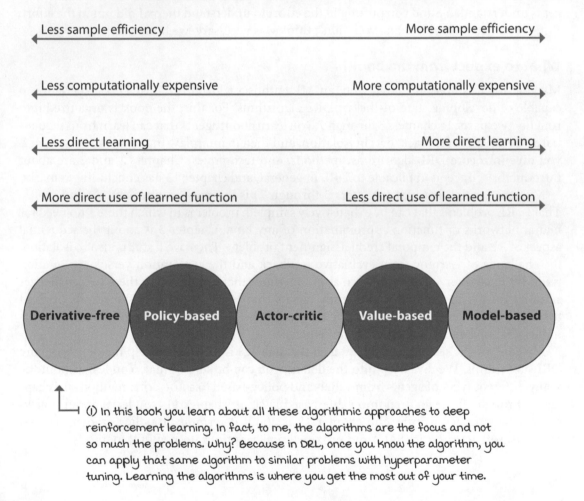

Less sample efficiency ← → More sample efficiency

Less computationally expensive ← → More computationally expensive

Less direct learning ← → More direct learning

More direct use of learned function ← → Less direct use of learned function

Derivative-free **Policy-based** **Actor-critic** **Value-based** **Model-based**

(1) In this book you learn about all these algorithmic approaches to deep reinforcement learning. In fact, to me, the algorithms are the focus and not so much the problems. Why? Because in DRL, once you know the algorithm, you can apply that same algorithm to similar problems with hyperparameter tuning. Learning the algorithms is where you get the most out of your time.

How to get the most out of this book

There are a few things you need to bring to the table to come out grokking deep reinforcement learning. You need to bring a little prior basic knowledge of ML and DL. You need to be comfortable with Python code and simple math. And most importantly, you must be willing to put in the work.

I assume that the reader has a solid basic understanding of ML. You should know what ML is beyond what's covered in this chapter; you should know how to train simple SL models, perhaps the Iris or Titanic datasets; you should be familiar with DL concepts such as tensors and matrices; and you should have trained at least one DL model, say a convolutional neural network (CNN) on the MNIST dataset.

This book is focused on DRL topics, and there's no DL in isolation. There are many useful resources out there that you can leverage. But, again, you need a basic understanding; If you've trained a CNN before, then you're fine. Otherwise, I highly recommend you follow a couple of DL tutorials before starting the second part of the book.

Another assumption I'm making is that the reader is comfortable with Python code. Python is a somewhat clear programming language that can be straightforward to understand, and people not familiar with it often get something out of merely reading it. Now, my point is that you should be comfortable with it, willing and looking forward to reading the code. If you don't read the code, then you'll miss out on a lot.

Likewise, there are many math equations in this book, and that's a good thing. Math is the perfect language, and there's nothing that can replace it. However, I'm asking people to be comfortable with math, willing to read, and nothing else. The equations I show are heavily annotated so that people "not into math" can still take advantage of the resources.

Finally, I'm assuming you're willing to put in the work. By that I mean you really want to learn DRL. If you decide to skip the math boxes, or the Python snippets, or a section, or one page, or chapter, or whatever, you'll miss out on a lot of relevant information. To get the most out of this book, I recommend you read the entire book front to back. Because of the different format, figures and sidebars are part of the main narrative in this book.

Also, make sure you run the book source code (the next section provides more details on how to do this), and play around and extend the code you find most interesting.

Deep reinforcement learning development environment

Along with this book, you're provided with a fully tested environment and code to reproduce my results. I created a Docker image and several Jupyter Notebooks so that you don't have to mess around with installing packages and configuring software, or copying and pasting code. The only prerequisite is Docker. Please, go ahead and follow the directions at https://github.com/mimoralea/gdrl on running the code. It's pretty straightforward.

The code is written in Python, and I make heavy use of NumPy and PyTorch. I chose PyTorch, instead of Keras, or TensorFlow, because I found PyTorch to be a "Pythonic" library. Using PyTorch feels natural if you have used NumPy, unlike TensorFlow, for instance, which feels like a whole new programming paradigm. Now, my intention is not to start a "PyTorch versus TensorFlow" debate. But, in my experience from using both libraries, PyTorch is a library much better suited for research and teaching.

DRL is about algorithms, methods, techniques, tricks, and so on, so it's pointless for us to rewrite a NumPy or a PyTorch library. But, also, in this book, we write DRL algorithms from scratch; I'm not teaching you how to use a DRL library, such as Keras-RL, or Baselines, or RLlib. I want you to learn DRL, and therefore we write DRL code. In the years that I've been teaching RL, I've noticed those who write RL code are more likely to understand RL. Now, this isn't a book on PyTorch either; there's no separate PyTorch review or anything like that, just PyTorch code that I explain as we move along. If you're somewhat familiar with DL concepts, you'll be able to follow along with the PyTorch code I use in this book. Don't worry, you don't need a separate PyTorch resource before you get to this book. I explain everything in detail as we move along.

As for the environments we use for training the agents, we use the popular OpenAI Gym package and a few other libraries that I developed for this book. But we're also not going into the ins and outs of Gym. Just know that Gym is a library that provides environments for training RL agents. Beyond that, remember our focus is the RL algorithms, the solutions, not the environments, or modeling problems, which, needless to say, are also critical.

Since you should be familiar with DL, I presume you know what a graphics processing unit (GPU) is. DRL architectures don't need the level of computation commonly seen on DL models. For this reason, the use of a GPU, while a good thing, is not required. Conversely, unlike DL models, some DRL agents make heavy use of a central processing unit (CPU) and thread count. If you're planning on investing in a machine, make sure to account for CPU power (well, technically, number of cores, not speed) as well. As you'll see later, certain algorithms massively parallelize processing, and in those cases, it's the CPU that becomes the bottleneck, not the GPU. However, the code runs fine in the container regardless of your CPU or GPU. But, if your hardware is severely limited, I recommend checking out cloud platforms. I've seen services, such as Google Colab, that offer DL hardware for free.

Summary

Deep reinforcement learning is challenging because agents must learn from feedback that is simultaneously sequential, evaluative, and sampled. Learning from sequential feedback forces the agent to learn how to balance immediate and long-term goals. Learning from evaluative feedback makes the agent learn to balance the gathering and utilization of information. Learning from sampled feedback forces the agent to generalize from old to new experiences.

Artificial intelligence, the main field of computer science into which reinforcement learning falls, is a discipline concerned with creating computer programs that display human-like intelligence. This goal is shared across many other disciplines, such as control theory and operations research. Machine learning is one of the most popular and successful approaches to artificial intelligence. Reinforcement learning is one of the three branches of machine learning, along with supervised learning, and unsupervised learning. Deep learning, an approach to machine learning, isn't tied to any specific branch, but its power helps advance the entire machine learning community.

Deep reinforcement learning is the use of multiple layers of powerful function approximators known as neural networks (deep learning) to solve complex sequential decision-making problems under uncertainty. Deep reinforcement learning has performed well in many control problems, but, nevertheless, it's essential to have in mind that releasing human control for critical decision making shouldn't be taken lightly. Several of the core needs in deep reinforcement learning are algorithms with better sample complexity, better-performing exploration strategies, and safe algorithms.

Still, the future of deep reinforcement learning is bright, and there are perhaps dangers ahead as the technology matures, but more importantly, there's potential in this field, and you should feel excited and compelled to bring your best and embark on this journey. The opportunity to be part of a potential change this big happens only every few generations. You should be glad you're living during these times. Now, let's be part of it.

By now, you

- Understand what deep reinforcement learning is and how it compares with other machine learning approaches

- Are aware of the recent progress in the field of deep reinforcement learning, and intuitively understand that it has the potential to be applied to a wide variety of problems

- Have a sense as to what to expect from this book, and how to get the most out of it

TWEETABLE FEAT

Work on your own and share your findings

At the end of every chapter, I'll give several ideas on how to take what you've learned to the next level. If you'd like, share your results with the rest of the world, and make sure to check out what others have done, too. It's a win-win situation, and hopefully, you'll take advantage of it.

- **#gdrl_ch01_tf01:** Supervised, unsupervised, and reinforcement learning are essential machine learning branches. And while it's crucial to know the differences, it's equally important to know the similarities. Write a post analyzing how these different approaches compare and how they could be used together to solve an AI problem. All branches are going after the same goal: to create artificial general intelligence, it's vital for all of us to better understand how to use the tools available.

- **#gdrl_ch01_tf02:** I wouldn't be surprised if you don't have a machine learning or computer science background, yet are still interested in what this book has to offer. One essential contribution is to post resources from other fields that study decision-making. Do you have an operations research background? Psychology, philosophy, or neuroscience background? Control theory? Economics? How about you create a list of resources, blog posts, YouTube videos, books, or any other medium and share it with the rest of us also studying decision-making?

- **#gdrl_ch01_tf03:** Part of the text in this chapter has information that could be better explained through graphics, tables, and other forms. For instance, I talked about the different types of reinforcement learning agents (value-based, policy-based, actor-critic, model-based, gradient-free). Why don't you grab text that's dense, distill the knowledge, and share your summary with the world?

- **#gdrl_ch01_tf04:** In every chapter, I'm using the final hashtag as a catchall hashtag. Feel free to use this one to discuss anything else that you worked on relevant to this chapter. There's no more exciting homework than that which you create for yourself. Make sure to share what you set yourself to investigate and your results.

Write a tweet with your findings, tag me @mimoralea (I'll retweet), and use the particular hashtag from this list to help interested folks find your results. There are no right or wrong results; you share your findings and check others' findings. Take advantage of this to socialize, contribute, and get yourself out there! We're waiting for you!

Here is a tweet example:

"Hey, @mimoralea. I created a blog post with a list of resources to study deep reinforcement learning. Check it out at <link>. #gdrl_ch01_tf01"

I'll make sure to retweet and help others find your work.

Mathematical foundations of reinforcement learning | 2

In this chapter

- You will learn about the core components of reinforcement learning.

- You will learn to represent sequential decision-making problems as reinforcement learning environments using a mathematical framework known as Markov decision processes.

- You will build from scratch environments that reinforcement learning agents learn to solve in later chapters.

You pick up this book and decide to read one more chapter despite having limited free time. A coach benches their best player for tonight's match ignoring the press criticism. A parent invests long hours of hard work and unlimited patience in teaching their child good manners. These are all examples of complex sequential decision-making under uncertainty.

I want to bring to your attention three of the words in play in this phrase: complex sequential decision-making under uncertainty. The first word, *complex*, refers to the fact that agents may be learning in environments with vast state and action spaces. In the coaching example, even if you discover that your best player needs to rest every so often, perhaps resting them in a match with a specific opponent is better than with other opponents. Learning to generalize accurately is challenging because we learn from sampled feedback.

The second word I used is *sequential*, and this one refers to the fact that in many problems, there are delayed consequences. In the coaching example, again, let's say the coach benched their best player for a seemingly unimportant match midway through the season. But, what if the action of resting players lowers their morale and performance that only manifests in finals? In other words, what if the actual consequences are delayed? The fact is that assigning credit to your past decisions is challenging because we learn from sequential feedback.

Finally, the word *uncertainty* refers to the fact that we don't know the actual inner workings of the world to understand how our actions affect it; everything is left to our interpretation. Let's say the coach did bench their best player, but they got injured in the next match. Was the benching decision the reason the player got injured because the player got out of shape? What if the injury becomes a team motivation throughout the season, and the team ends up winning the final? Again, was benching the right decision? This uncertainty gives rise to the need for exploration. Finding the appropriate balance between exploration and exploitation is challenging because we learn from evaluative feedback.

In this chapter, you'll learn to represent these kinds of problems using a mathematical framework known as *Markov decision processes* (MDPs). The general framework of MDPs allows us to model virtually any complex sequential decision-making problem under uncertainty in a way that RL agents can interact with and learn to solve solely through experience.

We'll dive deep into the challenges of learning from sequential feedback in chapter 3, then into the challenges of learning from evaluative feedback in chapter 4, then into the challenges of learning from feedback that's simultaneously sequential and evaluative in chapters 5 through 7, and then chapters 8 through 12 will add complex into the mix.

Components of reinforcement learning

The two core components in RL are the *agent* and the *environment*. The agent is the decision maker, and is the solution to a problem. The environment is the representation of a problem. One of the fundamental distinctions of RL from other ML approaches is that the agent and the environment interact; the agent attempts to influence the environment through actions, and the environment reacts to the agent's actions.

The reinforcement learning-interaction cycle

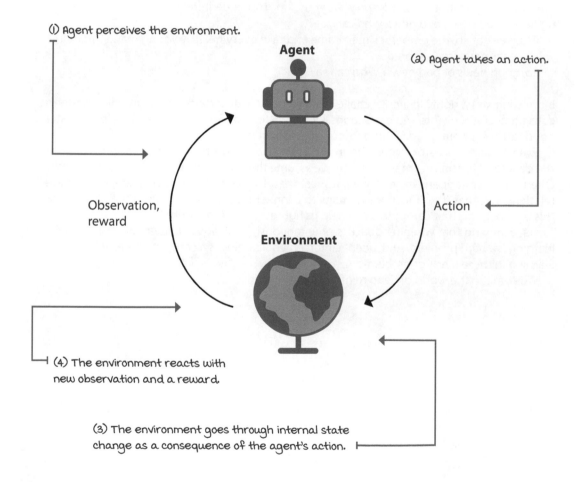

(1) Agent perceives the environment.

Agent

(2) Agent takes an action.

Observation, reward

Action

Environment

(4) The environment reacts with new observation and a reward.

(3) The environment goes through internal state change as a consequence of the agent's action.

MIGUEL'S ANALOGY
The parable of a Chinese farmer

There's an excellent parable that shows how difficult it is to interpret feedback that's simultaneously sequential, evaluative, and sampled. The parable goes like this:

A Chinese farmer gets a horse, which soon runs away. A neighbor says, "So, sad. That's bad news." The farmer replies, "Good news, bad news, who can say?"

The horse comes back and brings another horse with him. The neighbor says, "How lucky. That's good news." The farmer replies, "Good news, bad news, who can say?"

The farmer gives the second horse to his son, who rides it, then is thrown and badly breaks his leg. The neighbor says, "So sorry for your son. This is definitely bad news." The farmer replies, "Good news, bad news, who can say?"

In a week or so, the emperor's men come and take every healthy young man to fight in a war. The farmer's son is spared.

So, good news or bad news? Who can say?

Interesting story, right? In life, it's challenging to know with certainty what are the long-term consequences of events and our actions. Often, we find misfortune responsible for our later good fortune, or our good fortune responsible for our later misfortune.

Even though this story could be interpreted as a lesson that "beauty is in the eye of the beholder," in reinforcement learning, we assume there's a correlation between actions we take and what happens in the world. It's just that it's so complicated to understand these relationships, that it's difficult for humans to connect the dots with certainty. But, perhaps this is something that computers can help us figure out. Exciting, right?

Have in mind that when feedback is simultaneously evaluative, sequential, and sampled, learning is a hard problem. And, deep reinforcement learning is a computational approach to learning in these kinds of problems.

Welcome to the world of deep reinforcement learning!

Examples of problems, agents, and environments

The following are abbreviated examples of RL problems, agents, environments, possible actions, and observations:

- **Problem**: You're training your dog to sit. **Agent**: The part of your brain that makes decisions. **Environment**: Your dog, the treats, your dog's paws, the loud neighbor, and so on. **Actions**: Talk to your dog. Wait for dog's reaction. Move your hand. Show treat. Give treat. Pet. **Observations**: Your dog is paying attention to you. Your dog is getting tired. Your dog is going away. Your dog sat on command.

- **Problem**: Your dog wants the treats you have. **Agent**: The part of your dog's brain that makes decisions. **Environment**: You, the treats, your dog's paws, the loud neighbor, and so on. **Actions**: Stare at owner. Bark. Jump at owner. Try to steal the treat. Run. Sit. **Observations**: Owner keeps talking loud at dog. Owner is showing the treat. Owner is hiding the treat. Owner gave the dog the treat.

- **Problem**: A trading agent investing in the stock market. **Agent**: The executing DRL code in memory and in the CPU. **Environment**: Your internet connection, the machine the code is running on, the stock prices, the geopolitical uncertainty, other investors, day traders, and so on. **Actions**: Sell n stocks of y company. Buy n stocks of y company. Hold. **Observations**: Market is going up. Market is going down. There are economic tensions between two powerful nations. There's danger of war in the continent. A global pandemic is wreaking havoc in the entire world.

- **Problem**: You're driving your car. **Agent**: The part of your brain that makes decisions. **Environment**: The make and model of your car, other cars, other drivers, the weather, the roads, the tires, and so on. **Actions**: Steer by x, accelerate by y. Break by z. Turn the headlights on. Defog windows. Play music. **Observations**: You're approaching your destination. There's a traffic jam on Main Street. The car next to you is driving recklessly. It's starting to rain. There's a police officer driving in front of you.

As you can see, problems can take many forms: from high-level decision-making problems that require long-term thinking and broad general knowledge, such as investing in the stock market, to low-level control problems, in which geopolitical tensions don't seem to play a direct role, such as driving a car.

Also, you can represent a problem from multiple agents' perspectives. In the dog training example, in reality, there are two agents each interested in a different goal and trying to solve a different problem.

Let's zoom into each of these components independently.

The agent: The decision maker

As I mentioned in chapter 1, this whole book is about agents, except for this chapter, which is about the environment. Starting with chapter 3, you dig deep into the inner workings of agents, their components, their processes, and techniques to create agents that are effective and efficient.

For now, the only important thing for you to know about agents is that they are the decision-makers in the RL big picture. They have internal components and processes of their own, and that's what makes each of them unique and good at solving specific problems.

If we were to zoom in, we would see that most agents have a three-step process: all agents have an interaction component, a way to gather data for learning; all agents evaluate their current behavior; and all agents improve something in their inner components that allows them to improve (or at least attempt to improve) their overall performance.

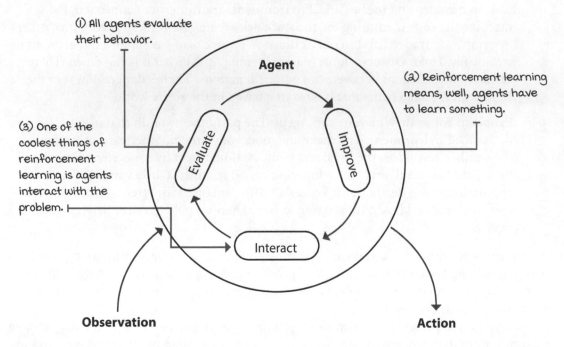

**The three internal steps that every
reinforcement learning agent goes through**

(1) All agents evaluate their behavior.

(2) Reinforcement learning means, well, agents have to learn something.

(3) One of the coolest things of reinforcement learning is agents interact with the problem.

Agent

Evaluate

Improve

Interact

Observation   **Action**

We'll continue discussing the inner workings of agents starting with the next chapter. For now, let's discuss a way to represent environments, how they look, and how we should model them, which is the goal of this chapter.

The environment: Everything else

Most real-world decision-making problems can be expressed as RL environments. A common way to represent decision-making processes in RL is by modeling the problem using a mathematical framework known as Markov decision processes (MDPs). In RL, we assume all environments have an MDP working under the hood. Whether an Atari game, the stock market, a self-driving car, your significant other, you name it, every problem has an MDP running under the hood (at least in the RL world, whether right or wrong).

The environment is represented by a set of variables related to the problem. The combination of all the possible values this set of variables can take is referred to as the *state space*. A state is a specific set of values the variables take at any given time.

Agents may or may not have access to the actual environment's state; however, one way or another, agents can observe something from the environment. The set of variables the agent perceives at any given time is called an *observation*.

The combination of all possible values these variables can take is the *observation space*. Know that state and observation are terms used interchangeably in the RL community. This is because often agents are allowed to see the internal state of the environment, but this isn't always the case. In this book, I use state and observation interchangeably as well. But you need to know that there might be a difference between states and observations, even though the RL community often uses the terms interchangeably.

At every state, the environment makes available a set of actions the agent can choose from. Often the set of actions is the same for all states, but this isn't required. The set of all actions in all states is referred to as the *action space*.

The agent attempts to influence the environment through these actions. The environment may change states as a response to the agent's action. The function that is responsible for this transition is called the *transition function*.

After a transition, the environment emits a new observation. The environment may also provide a reward signal as a response. The function responsible for this mapping is called the *reward function*. The set of transition and reward function is referred to as the *model* of the environment.

A CONCRETE EXAMPLE
The bandit walk environment

Let's make these concepts concrete with our first RL environment. I created this very simple environment for this book; I call it the bandit walk (BW).

BW is a simple *grid-world* (GW) environment. GWs are a common type of environment for studying RL algorithms that are grids of any size. GWs can have any model (transition and reward functions) you can think of and can make any kind of actions available.

But, they all commonly make move actions available to the agent: Left, Down, Right, Up (or West, South, East, North, which is more precise because the agent has no heading and usually has no visibility of the full grid, but cardinal directions can also be more confusing). And, of course, each action corresponds with its logical transition: Left goes left, and Right goes right. Also, they all tend to have a fully observable discrete state and observation spaces (that is, state equals observation) with integers representing the cell id location of the agent. A "walk" is a special case of grid-world environments with a single row. In reality, what I call a "walk" is more commonly referred to as a "Corridor." But, in this book, I use the term "walk" for all the grid-world environments with a single row.

The bandit walk (BW) is a walk with three states, but only one non-terminal state. Environments that have a single non-terminal state are called "bandit" environments. "Bandit" here is an analogy to slot machines, which are also known as "one-armed bandits"; they have one arm and, if you like gambling, can empty your pockets, the same way a bandit would.

The BW environment has just two actions available: a Left (action 0) and an Right (action 1) action. BW has a deterministic transition function: a Left action always moves the agent to the Left, and a Right action always moves the agent to the right. The reward signal is a +1 when landing on the rightmost cell, 0 otherwise. The agent starts in the middle cell.

The bandit walk (BW) environment

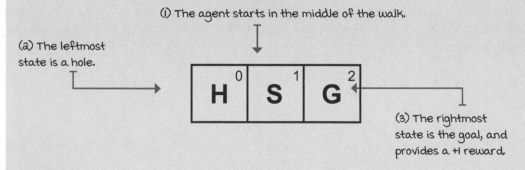

(1) The agent starts in the middle of the walk.

(2) The leftmost state is a hole.

| H 0 | S 1 | G 2 |

(3) The rightmost state is the goal, and provides a +1 reward.

A graphical representation of the BW environment would look like the following.

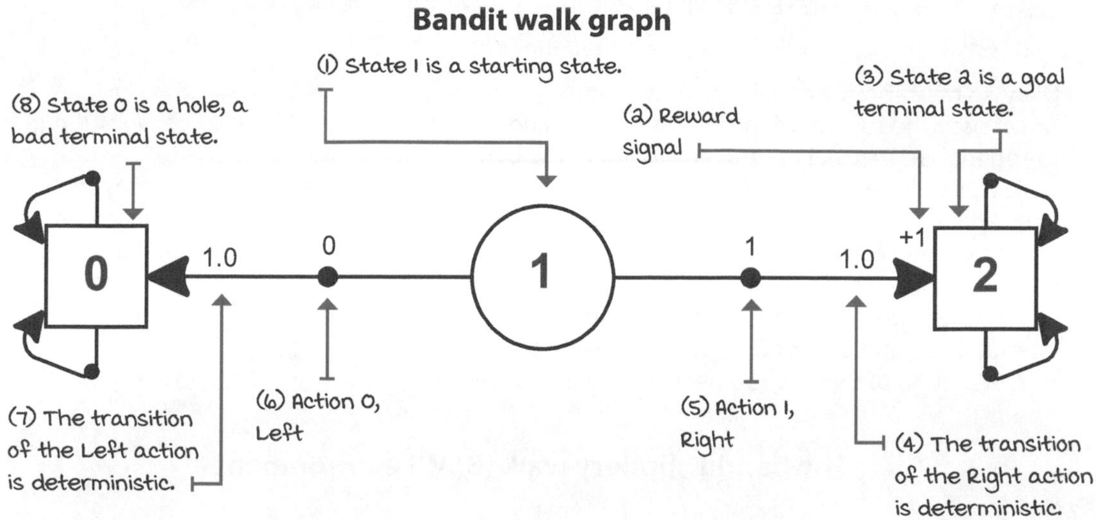

Bandit walk graph

(1) State 1 is a starting state.

(8) State 0 is a hole, a bad terminal state.

(2) Reward signal

(3) State 2 is a goal terminal state.

(7) The transition of the Left action is deterministic.

(6) Action 0, Left

(5) Action 1, Right

(4) The transition of the Right action is deterministic.

I hope this raises several questions, but you'll find the answers throughout this chapter. For instance, why do the terminal states have actions that transition to themselves: seems wasteful, doesn't? Any other questions? Like, what if the environment is stochastic? What exactly is an environments that is "stochastic"?! Keep reading.

We can also represent this environment in a table form.

State	Action	Next state	Transition probability	Reward signal
0 (Hole)	0 (Left)	0 (Hole)	1.0	0
0 (Hole)	1 (Right)	0 (Hole)	1.0	0
1 (Start)	0 (Left)	0 (Hole)	1.0	0
1 (Start)	1 (Right)	2 (Goal)	1.0	+1
2 (Goal)	0 (Left)	2 (Goal)	1.0	0
2 (Goal)	1 (Right)	2 (Goal)	1.0	0

Interesting, right? Let's look at another simple example.

A CONCRETE EXAMPLE

The bandit slippery walk environment

Okay, so how about we make this environment stochastic?

Let's say the surface of the walk is slippery and each action has a 20% chance of sending the agent backwards. I call this environment the bandit slippery walk (BSW).

BSW is still a one-row-grid world, a walk, a corridor, with only Left and Right actions available. Again, three states and two actions. The reward is the same as before, +1 when landing at the rightmost state (except when coming from the rightmost state—from itself), and zero otherwise.

However, the transition function is different: 80% of the time the agent moves to the intended cell, and 20% of time in the opposite direction.

A depiction of this environment would look as follows.

The bandit slippery walk (BSW) environment

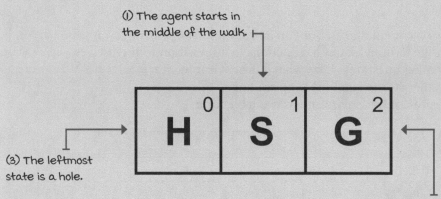

(1) The agent starts in the middle of the walk.

(3) The leftmost state is a hole.

(2) The rightmost state is the goal, and provides a +1 reward.

Identical to the BW environment! Interesting . . .

How do we know that the action effects are stochastic? How do we represent the "slippery" part of this problem? The graphical and table representations can help us with that.

A graphical representation of the BSW environment would look like the following.

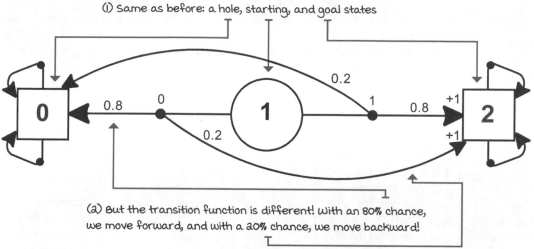

Bandit slippery walk graph

(1) Same as before: a hole, starting, and goal states

(2) But the transition function is different! With an 80% chance, we move forward, and with a 20% chance, we move backward!

See how the transition function is different now? The BSW environment has a stochastic transition function. Let's now represent this environment in a table form as well.

State	Action	Next state	Transition probability	Reward signal
0 (Hole)	0 (Left)	0 (Hole)	1.0	0
0 (Hole)	1 (Right)	0 (Hole)	1.0	0
1 (Start)	0 (Left)	0 (Hole)	0.8	0
1 (Start)	0 (Left)	2 (Goal)	0.2	+1
1 (Start)	1 (Right)	2 (Goal)	0.8	+1
1 (Start)	1 (Right)	0 (Hole)	0.2	0
2 (Goal)	0 (Left)	2 (Goal)	1.0	0
2 (Goal)	1 (Right)	2 (Goal)	1.0	0

And, we don't have to limit ourselves to thinking about environments with discrete state and action spaces or even walks (corridors) or bandits (which we discuss in-depth in the next chapter) or grid worlds. Representing environments as MDPs is a surprisingly powerful and straightforward approach to modeling complex sequential decision-making problems under uncertainty.

Here are a few more examples of environments that are powered by underlying MDPs.

Description	Observation space	Sample observation	Action space	Sample action	Reward function
Hotter, colder: Guess a randomly selected number using hints.	Int range 0–3. 0 means no guess yet submitted, 1 means guess is lower than the target, 2 means guess is equal to the target, and 3 means guess is higher than the target.	2	Float from −2000.0–2000.0. The float number the agent is guessing.	−909.37	The reward is the squared percentage of the way the agent has guessed toward the target.
Cart pole: Balance a pole in a cart.	A four-element vector with ranges: from [−4.8, −Inf, −4.2, −Inf] to [4.8, Inf, 4.2, Inf]. First element is the cart position, second is the cart velocity, third is pole angle in radians, fourth is the pole velocity at tip.	[−0.16, −1.61, 0.17, 2.44]	Int range 0–1. 0 means push cart left, 1 means push cart right.	0	The reward is 1 for every step taken, including the termination step.
Lunar lander: Navigate a lander to its landing pad.	An eight-element vector with ranges: from [−Inf, −Inf, −Inf, −Inf, −Inf, −Inf, 0, 0] to [Inf, Inf, Inf, Inf, Inf, Inf, 1, 1]. First element is the x position, the second the y position, the third is the x velocity, the fourth is the y velocity, fifth is the vehicle's angle, sixth is the angular velocity, and the last two values are Booleans indicating legs contact with the ground.	[0.36 , 0.23, −0.63, −0.10, −0.97, −1.73, 1.0, 0.0]	Int range 0–3. No-op (do nothing), fire left engine, fire main engine, fire right engine.	2	Reward for landing is 200. There's a reward for moving from the top to the landing pad, for crashing or coming to rest, for each leg touching the ground, and for firing the engines.

Pong: Bounce the ball past the opponent, and avoid letting the ball pass you.	A tensor of shape 210, 160, 3. Values ranging 0–255. Represents a game screen image.	[[[246, 217, 64], [55, 184, 230], [46, 231, 179], . . ., [28, 104, 249], [25, 5, 22], [173, 186, 1]], . . .]]	Int range 0–5. Action 0 is No-op, 1 is Fire, 2 is up, 3 is right, 4 is Left, 5 is Down. Notice how some actions don't affect the game in any way. In reality the paddle can only move up or down, or not move.	3	The reward is a 1 when the ball goes beyond the opponent, and a –1 when your agent's paddle misses the ball.
Humanoid: Make robot run as fast as possible and not fall.	A 44-element (or more, depending on the implementation) vector. Values ranging from –Inf to Inf. Represents the positions and velocities of the robot's joints.	[0.6, 0.08, 0.9, 0. 0, 0.0, 0.0, 0.0, 0.0, 0.045, 0.0, 0.47, . . ., 0.32, 0.0, –0.22, . . ., 0.]	A 17-element vector. Values ranging from –Inf to Inf. Represents the forces to apply to the robot's joints.	[–0.9, –0.06, 0.6, 0.6, 0.6, –0.06, –0.4, –0.9, 0.5, –0.2, 0.7, –0.9, 0.4, –0.8, –0.1, 0.8, –0.03]	The reward is calculated based on forward motion with a small penalty to encourage a natural gait.

Notice I didn't add the transition function to this table. That's because, while you can look at the code implementing the dynamics for certain environments, other implementations are not easily accessible. For instance, the transition function of the cart pole environment is a small Python file defining the mass of the cart and the pole and implementing basic physics equations, while the dynamics of Atari games, such as Pong, are hidden inside an Atari emulator and the corresponding game-specific ROM file.

Notice that what we're trying to represent here is the fact that the environment "reacts" to the agent's actions in some way, perhaps even by ignoring the agent's actions. But at the end of the day, there's an internal process that's uncertain (except in this and the next chapter). To represent the ability to interact with an environment in an MDP, we need states, observations, actions, a transition, and a reward function.

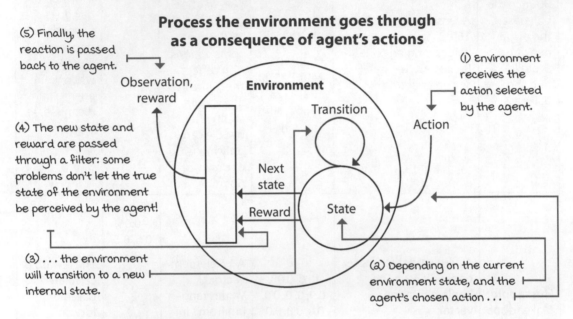

Process the environment goes through as a consequence of agent's actions

(5) Finally, the reaction is passed back to the agent.

Observation, reward

(4) The new state and reward are passed through a filter: some problems don't let the true state of the environment be perceived by the agent!

(3) . . . the environment will transition to a new internal state.

Environment

Transition

Next state

Reward

State

Action

(1) Environment receives the action selected by the agent.

(2) Depending on the current environment state, and the agent's chosen action . . .

Agent-environment interaction cycle

The environment commonly has a well-defined task. The goal of this task is defined through the reward signal. The reward signal can be dense, sparse, or anything in between. When you design environments, reward signals are the way to train your agent the way you want. The more dense, the more supervision the agent will have, and the faster the agent will learn, but the more bias you'll inject into your agent, and the less likely the agent will come up with unexpected behaviors. The more sparse, the less supervision, and therefore, the higher the chance of new, emerging behaviors, but the longer it'll take the agent to learn.

The interactions between the agent and the environment go on for several cycles. Each cycle is called a *time step*. A time step is a unit of time, which can be a millisecond, a second, 1.2563 seconds, a minute, a day, or any other period of time.

At each time step, the agent observes the environment, takes action, and receives a new observation and reward. Notice that, even though rewards can be negative values, they are still called rewards in the RL world. The set of the observation (or state), the action, the reward, and the new observation (or new state) is called an *experience tuple*.

The task the agent is trying to solve may or may not have a natural ending. Tasks that have a natural ending, such as a game, are called *episodic tasks*. Tasks that don't, such as learning forward motion, are called *continuing tasks*. The sequence of time steps from the beginning to the end of an episodic task is called an *episode*. Agents may take several time steps and episodes to learn to solve a task. The sum of rewards collected in a single episode is called a *return*. Agents are often designed to maximize the return. A time step limit is often added to continuing tasks, so they become episodic tasks, and agents can maximize the return.

Every experience tuple has an opportunity for learning and improving performance. The agent may have one or more components to aid learning. The agent may be designed to learn mappings from observations to actions called policies. The agent may be designed to learn mappings from observations to new observations and/or rewards called models. The agent may be designed to learn mappings from observations (and possibly actions) to reward-to-go estimates (a slice of the return) called value functions.

For the rest of this chapter, we'll put aside the agent and the interactions, and we'll examine the environment and inner MDP in depth. In chapter 3, we'll pick back up the agent, but there will be no interactions because the agent won't need them as it'll have access to the MDPs. In chapter 4, we'll remove the agent's access to MDPs and add interactions back into the equation, but it'll be in single-state environments (bandits). Chapter 5 is about learning to estimate returns in multi-state environments when agents have no access to MDPs. Chapters 6 and 7 are about optimizing behavior, which is the full reinforcement learning problem. Chapters 5, 6, and 7 are about agents learning in environments where there's no need for function approximation. After that, the rest of the book is all about agents that use neural networks for learning.

MDPs: The engine of the environment

Let's build MDPs for a few environments as we learn about the components that make them up. We'll create Python dictionaries representing MDPs from descriptions of the problems. In the next chapter, we'll study algorithms for planning on MDPs. These methods can devise solutions to MDPs and will allow us to find optimal solutions to all problems in this chapter.

The ability to build environments yourself is an important skill to have. However, often you find environments for which somebody else has already created the MDP. Also, the dynamics of the environments are often hidden behind a simulation engine and are too complex to examine in detail; certain dynamics are even inaccessible and hidden behind the real world. In reality, RL agents don't need to know the precise MDP of a problem to learn robust behaviors, but knowing about MDPs, in general, is crucial for you because agents are commonly designed with the assumption that an MDP, even if inaccessible, is running under the hood.

A CONCRETE EXAMPLE
The frozen lake environment

This is another, more challenging problem for which we will build an MDP in this chapter. This environment is called the frozen lake (FL).

FL is a simple grid-world (GW) environment. It also has discrete state and action spaces. However, this time, four actions are available: move Left, Down, Right, or Up.

The task in the FL environment is similar to the task in the BW and BSW environments: to go from a start location to a goal location while avoiding falling into holes. The challenge is similar to the BSW, in that the surface of the FL environment is slippery, it's a frozen lake after all. But the environment itself is larger. Let's look at a depiction of the FL.

The frozen lake (FL) environment

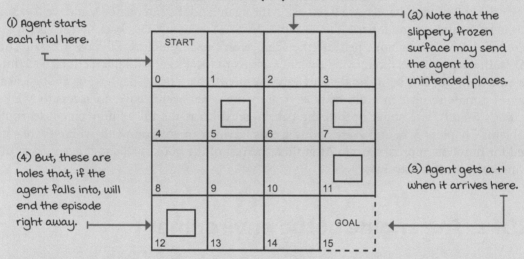

(1) Agent starts each trial here.

(2) Note that the slippery, frozen surface may send the agent to unintended places.

(4) But, these are holes that, if the agent falls into, will end the episode right away.

(3) Agent gets a +1 when it arrives here.

The FL is a 4 × 4 grid (it has 16 cells, ids 0–15). The agent shows up in the START cell every new episode. Reaching the GOAL cell gives a +1 reward; anything else is a 0. Because the surface are slippery, the agent moves only a third of the time as intended. The other two-thirds are split evenly in orthogonal directions. For example, if the agent chooses to move down, there's a 33.3% chance it moves down, 33.3% chance it moves left, and 33.3% chance it moves right. There's a fence around the lake, so if the agent tries to move out of the grid world, it will bounce back to the cell from which it tried to move. There are four holes in the lake. If the agent falls into one of these holes, it's game over.

Are you ready to start building a representation of these dynamics? We need a Python dictionary representing the MDP as described here. Let's start building the MDP.

States: Specific configurations of the environment

A *state* is a unique and self-contained configuration of the problem. The set of all possible states, the *state space*, is defined as the set S. The state space can be finite or infinite. But notice that the state space is different than the set of variables that compose a single state. This other set must always be finite and of constant size from state to state. In the end, the state space is a set of sets. The inner set must be of equal size and finite, as it contains the number of variables representing the states, but the outer set can be infinite depending on the types of elements of the inner sets.

State space: A set of sets

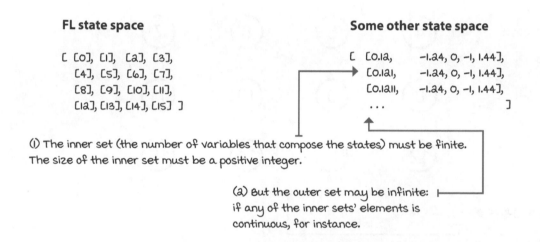

FL state space

[[0], [1], [2], [3],
  [4], [5], [6], [7],
  [8], [9], [10], [11],
  [12], [13], [14], [15]]

Some other state space

[[0.12,   −1.24, 0, −1, 1.44],
  [0.121,   −1.24, 0, −1, 1.44],
  [0.1211, −1.24, 0, −1, 1.44],
  . . .   ]

(1) The inner set (the number of variables that compose the states) must be finite. The size of the inner set must be a positive integer.

(2) But the outer set may be infinite: if any of the inner sets' elements is continuous, for instance.

For the BW, BSW, and FL environments, the state is composed of a single variable containing the id of the cell where the agent is at any given time. The agent's location cell id is a discrete variable. But state variables can be of any kind, and the set of variables can be larger than one. We could have the Euclidean distance that would be a continuous variable and an infinite state space; for example, 2.124, 2.12456, 5.1, 5.1239458, and so on. We could also have multiple variables defining the state, for instance, the number of cells away from the goal in the x- and y-axis. That would be two variables representing a single state. Both variables would be discrete, therefore, the state space finite. However, we could also have variables of mixed types; for instance, one could be discrete, another continuous, another Boolean.

With this state representation for the BW, BSW, and FL environments, the size of the state space is 3, 3, and 16, respectively. Given we have 3, 3, or 16 cells, the agent can be at any given time, then we have 3, 3, and 16 possible states in the state space. We can set the ids of each cell starting from zero, going left to right, top to bottom.

In the FL, we set the ids from zero to 15, left to right, top to bottom. You could set the ids in any other way: in a random order, or group cells by proximity, or whatever. It's up to you; as long as you keep them consistent throughout training, it will work. However, this representation is adequate, and it works well, so it's what we'll use.

States in the FL contain a single variable indicating the id of the cell in which the agent is at any given time step

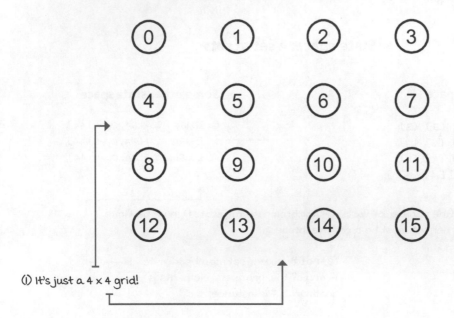

(i) It's just a 4 x 4 grid!

In the case of MDPs, the states are fully observable: we can see the internal state of the environment at each time step, that is, the observations and the states are the same. *Partially observable Markov decision processes* (POMDPs) is a more general framework for modeling environments in which observations, which still depend on the internal state of the environment, are the only things the agent can see instead of the state. Notice that for the BW, BSW, and FL environments, we're creating an MDP, so the agent will be able to observe the internal state of the environment.

States must contain all the variables necessary to make them independent of all other states. In the FL environment, you only need to know the current state of the agent to tell its next possible states. That is, you don't need the history of states visited by the agent for anything. You know that from state 2 the agent can only transition to states 1, 3, 6, or 2, and this is true regardless of whether the agent's previous state was 1, 3, 6, or 2.

The probability of the next state, given the current state and action, is independent of the history of interactions. This memoryless property of MDPs is known as the *Markov property*: the probability of moving from one state *s* to another state *s* on two separate occasions, given the same action *a*, is the same regardless of all previous states or actions encountered before that point.

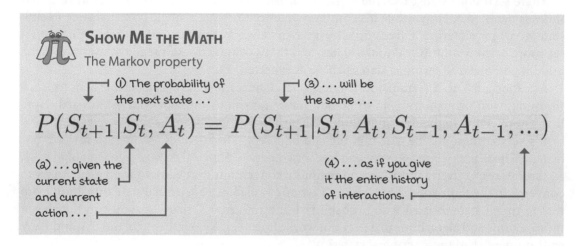

SHOW ME THE MATH

The Markov property

(1) The probability of the next state . . .

(3) . . . will be the same . . .

$$P(S_{t+1}|S_t, A_t) = P(S_{t+1}|S_t, A_t, S_{t-1}, A_{t-1}, \dots)$$

(2) . . . given the current state and current action . . .

(4) . . . as if you give it the entire history of interactions.

But why do you care about this? Well, in the environments we've explored so far it's not that obvious, and it's not that important. But because most RL (and DRL) agents are designed to take advantage of the Markov assumption, you must make sure you feed your agent the necessary variables to make it hold as tightly as possible (completely keeping the Markov assumption is impractical, perhaps impossible).

For example, if you're designing an agent to learn to land a spacecraft, the agent must receive all variables that indicate velocities along with its locations. Locations alone are not sufficient to land a spacecraft safely, and because you must assume the agent is memoryless, you need to feed the agent more information than just its x, y, z coordinates away from the landing pad.

But, you probably know that acceleration is to velocity what velocity is to position: the derivative. You probably also know that you can keep taking derivatives beyond acceleration. To make the MDP completely Markovian, how deep do you have to go? This is more of an art than a science: the more variables you add, the longer it takes to train an agent, but the fewer variables, the higher the chance the information fed to the agent is not sufficient, and the harder it is to learn anything useful. For the spacecraft example, often locations and velocities are adequate, and for grid-world environments, only the state id location of the agent is sufficient.

The set of all states in the MDP is denoted S^+. There is a subset of S^+ called the set of *starting* or *initial states*, denoted S^i. To begin interacting with an MDP, we draw a state from S^i from a probability distribution. This distribution can be anything, but it must be fixed throughout training: that is, the probabilities must be the same from the first to the last episode of training and for agent evaluation.

There's a unique state called the *absorbing* or *terminal state*, and the set of all non-terminal states is denoted S. Now, while it's common practice to create a single terminal state (a sink state) to which all terminal transitions go, this isn't always implemented this way. What you'll see more often is multiple terminal states, and that's okay. It doesn't really matter under the hood if you make all terminal states behave as expected.

As expected? Yes. A terminal state is a special state: it must have all available actions transitioning, with probability 1, to itself, and these transitions must provide no reward. Note that I'm referring to the transitions from the terminal state, not to the terminal state.

It's very commonly the case that the end of an episode provides a non-zero reward. For instance, in a chess game you win, you lose, or you draw. A logical reward signal would be +1, −1, and 0, respectively. But it's a compatibility convention that allows for all algorithms to converge to the same solution to make all actions available in a terminal state transition from that terminal state to itself with probability 1 and reward 0. Otherwise, you run the risk of infinite sums and algorithms that may not work altogether. Remember how the BW and BSW environments had these terminal states?

In the FL environment, for instance, there's only one starting state (which is state 0) and five terminal states (or five states that transition to a single terminal state, whichever you prefer). For clarity, I use the convention of multiple terminal states (5, 7, 11, 12, and 15) for the illustrations and code; again, each terminal state is a separate terminal state.

States in the frozen lake environment

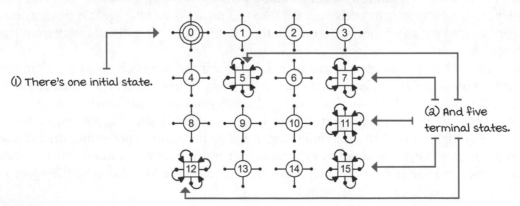

(1) There's one initial state.

(2) And five terminal states.

Actions: A mechanism to influence the environment

MDPs make available a set of actions A that depends on the state. That is, there might be actions that aren't allowed in a state—in fact, A is a function that takes a state as an argument; that is, A(s). This function returns the set of available actions for state s. If needed, you can define this set to be constant across the state space; that is, all actions are available at every state. You can also set all transitions from a state-action pair to zero if you want to deny an action in a given state. You could also set all transitions from state s and action a to the same state s to denote action a as a no-intervene or no-op action.

Just as with the state, the action space may be finite or infinite, and the set of variables of a single action may contain more than one element and must be finite. However, unlike the number of state variables, the number of variables that compose an action may not be constant. The actions available in a state may change depending on that state. For simplicity, most environments are designed with the same number of actions in all states.

The environment makes the set of all available actions known in advance. Agents can select actions either deterministically or stochastically. This is different than saying the environment reacts deterministically or stochastically to agents' actions. Both are true statements, but I'm referring here to the fact that agents can either select actions from a lookup table or from per-state probability distributions.

In the BW, BSW, and FL environments, actions are singletons representing the direction the agent will attempt to move. In FL, there are four available actions in all states: Up, Down, Right, or Left. There's one variable per action, and the size of the action space is four.

The frozen lake environment has four simple move actions

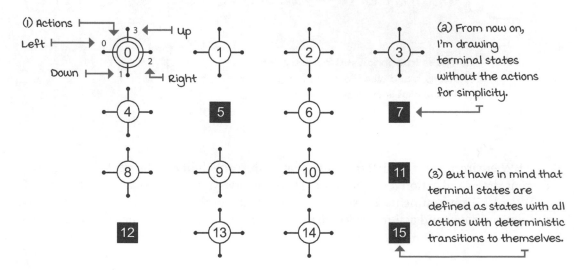

Transition function: Consequences of agent actions

The way the environment changes as a response to actions is referred to as the *state-transition probabilities*, or more simply, the *transition function*, and is denoted by $T(s, a, s')$. The transition function T maps a transition tuple s, a, s' to a probability; that is, you pass in a state s, an action a, and a next state s', and it'll return the corresponding probability of transition from state s to state s' when taking action a. You could also represent it as $T(s, a)$ and return a dictionary with the next states for its keys and probabilities for its values.

Notice that T also describes a probability distribution $p(\cdot \mid s, a)$ determining how the system will evolve in an interaction cycle from selecting action a in state s. When integrating over the next states s', as any probability distribution, the sum of these probabilities must equal one.

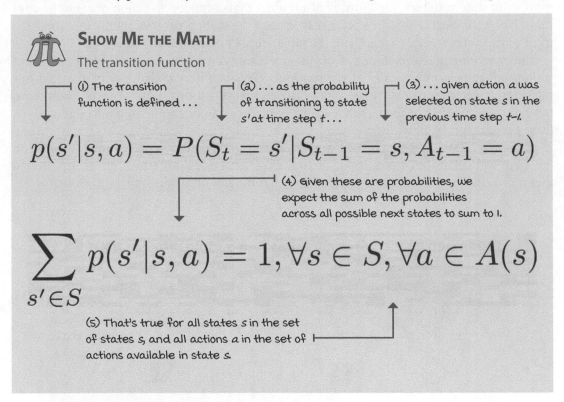

SHOW ME THE MATH

The transition function

(1) The transition function is defined . . .

(2) . . . as the probability of transitioning to state s' at time step t . . .

(3) . . . given action a was selected on state s in the previous time step t–1.

$$p(s' \mid s, a) = P(S_t = s' \mid S_{t-1} = s, A_{t-1} = a)$$

(4) Given these are probabilities, we expect the sum of the probabilities across all possible next states to sum to 1.

$$\sum_{s' \in S} p(s' \mid s, a) = 1, \forall s \in S, \forall a \in A(s)$$

(5) That's true for all states s in the set of states s, and all actions a in the set of actions available in state s.

The BW environment was deterministic; that is, the probability of the next state s' given the current state s and action a was always 1. There was always a single possible next state s'. The BSW and FL environments are stochastic; that is, the probability of the next state s' given the current state s and action a is less than 1. There are more than one possible next state s's.

One key assumption of many RL (and DRL) algorithms is that this distribution is stationary. That is, while there may be highly stochastic transitions, the probability distribution may not change during training or evaluation. Just as with the Markov assumption, the stationarity assumption is often relaxed to an extent. However, it's important for most agents to interact with environments that at least appear to be stationary.

In the FL environment, we know that there's a 33.3% chance we'll transition to the intended cell (state) and a 66.6% chance we'll transition to orthogonal directions. There's also a chance we'll bounce back to the state we're coming from if it's next to the wall.

For simplicity and clarity, I've added to the following image only the transition function for all actions of states 0, 2, 5, 7, 11, 12, 13, and 15 of the FL environment. This subset of states allows for the illustration of all possible transitions without too much clutter.

The transition function of the frozen lake environment

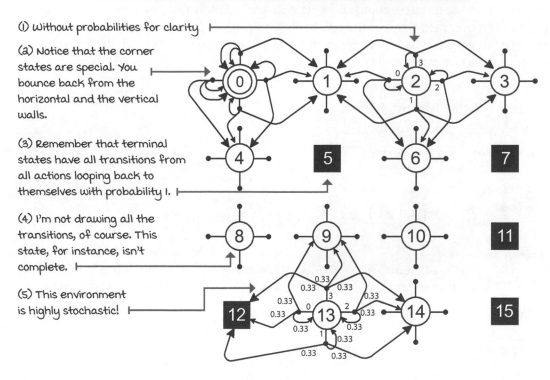

It might still be a bit confusing, but look at it this way: for consistency, each action in non-terminal states has three separate transitions (certain actions in corner states could be represented with only two, but again, let me be consistent): one to the intended cell and two to the cells in orthogonal directions.

Reward signal: Carrots and sticks

The reward function *R* maps a transition tuple *s, a, s'* to a scalar. The reward function gives a numeric signal of goodness to transitions. When the signal is positive, we can think of the reward as an income or a reward. Most problems have at least one positive signal—winning a chess match or reaching the desired destination, for example. But, rewards can also be negative, and we can see these as cost, punishment, or penalty. In robotics, adding a time step cost is a common practice because we usually want to reach a goal, but within a number of time steps. One thing to clarify is that whether positive or negative, the scalar coming out of the reward function is always referred to as the *reward*. RL folks are happy folks.

It's also important to highlight that while the reward function can be represented as *R(s,a,s')*, which is explicit, we could also use *R(s,a)*, or even *R(s)*, depending on our needs. Sometimes rewarding the agent based on state is what we need; sometimes it makes more sense to use the action and the state. However, the most explicit way to represent the reward function is to use a state, action, and next state triplet. With that, we can compute the marginalization over next states in *R(s,a,s')* to obtain *R(s,a)*, and the marginalization over actions in *R(s,a)* to get *R(s)*. But, once we're in *R(s)* we can't recover *R(s,a)* or *R(s,a,s')*, and once we're in *R(s,a)* we can't recover *R(s,a,s')*.

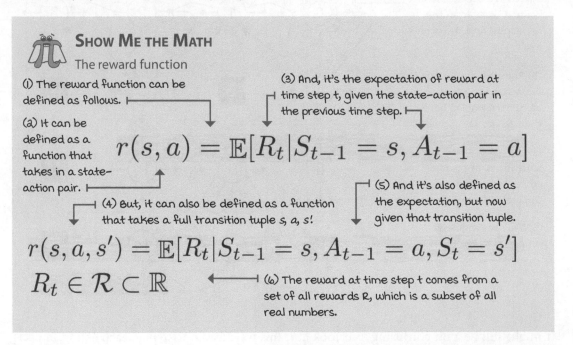

SHOW ME THE MATH
The reward function

(1) The reward function can be defined as follows.

(2) It can be defined as a function that takes in a state-action pair.

(3) And, it's the expectation of reward at time step t, given the state-action pair in the previous time step.

$$r(s, a) = \mathbb{E}[R_t | S_{t-1} = s, A_{t-1} = a]$$

(4) But, it can also be defined as a function that takes a full transition tuple s, a, s!

(5) And it's also defined as the expectation, but now given that transition tuple.

$$r(s, a, s') = \mathbb{E}[R_t | S_{t-1} = s, A_{t-1} = a, S_t = s']$$

$$R_t \in \mathcal{R} \subset \mathbb{R}$$

(6) The reward at time step t comes from a set of all rewards R, which is a subset of all real numbers.

In the FL environment, the reward function is +1 for landing in state 15, 0 otherwise. Again, for clarity to the following image, I've only added the reward signal to transitions that give a non-zero reward, landing on the final state (state 15.)

There are only three ways to land on 15. (1) Selecting the Right action in state 14 will transition the agent with 33.3% chance there (33.3% to state 10 and 33.3% back to 14). But, (2) selecting the Up and (3) the Down action from state 14 will unintentionally also transition the agent there with 33.3% probability for each action. See the difference between actions and transitions? It's interesting to see how stochasticity complicates things, right?

Reward signal for states with non-zero reward transitions

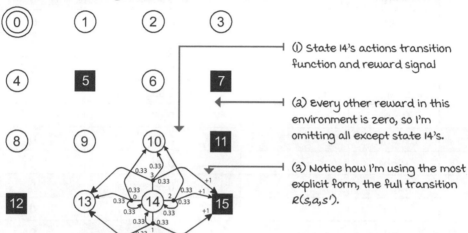

① State 14's actions transition function and reward signal

② Every other reward in this environment is zero, so I'm omitting all except state 14's.

③ Notice how I'm using the most explicit form, the full transition R(s,a,s').

Expanding the transition and reward functions into a table form is also useful. The following is the format I recommend for most problems. Notice that I've only added a subset of the transitions (rows) to the table to illustrate the exercise. Also notice that I'm being explicit, and several of these transitions could be grouped and refactored (for example, corner cells).

State	Action	Next state	Transition probability	Reward signal
0	Left	0	0.33	0
0	Left	0	0.33	0
0	Left	4	0.33	0
0	Down	0	0.33	0
0	Down	4	0.33	0
0	Down	1	0.33	0
0	Right	4	0.33	0
0	Right	1	0.33	0
0	Right	0	0.33	0

State	Action	Next state	Transition probability	Reward signal
0	Up	1	0.33	0
0	Up	0	0.33	0
0	Up	0	0.33	0
1	Left	1	0.33	0
1	Left	0	0.33	0
1	Left	5	0.33	0
1	Down	0	0.33	0
1	Down	5	0.33	0
1	Down	2	0.33	0
1	Right	5	0.33	0
1	Right	2	0.33	0
1	Right	1	0.33	0
2	Left	1	0.33	0
2	Left	2	0.33	0
2	Left	6	0.33	0
2	Down	1	0.33	0
...	...	...	...	...
14	Down	14	0.33	0
14	Down	15	0.33	1
14	Right	14	0.33	0
14	Right	15	0.33	1
14	Right	10	0.33	0
14	Up	15	0.33	1
14	Up	10	0.33	0
...	...	...	...	...
15	Left	15	1.0	0
15	Down	15	1.0	0
15	Right	15	1.0	0
15	Up	15	1.0	0

Horizon: Time changes what's optimal

We can represent time in MDPs as well. A *time step*, also referred to as epoch, cycle, iteration, or even interaction, is a global clock syncing all parties and discretizing time. Having a clock gives rise to a couple of possible types of tasks. An *episodic* task is a task in which there's a finite number of time steps, either because the clock stops or because the agent reaches a terminal state. There are also continuing tasks, which are tasks that go on forever; there are no terminal states, so there's an infinite number of time steps. In this type of task, the agent must be stopped manually.

Episodic and continuing tasks can also be defined from the agent's perspective. We call it the *planning horizon*. On the one hand, a *finite horizon* is a planning horizon in which the agent knows the task will terminate in a finite number of time steps: if we forced the agent to complete the frozen lake environment in 15 steps, for example. A special case of this kind of planning horizon is called a *greedy horizon*, of which the planning horizon is one. The BW and BSW have both a greedy planning horizon: the episode terminates immediately after one interaction. In fact, all bandit environments have greedy horizons.

On the other hand, an *infinite horizon* is when the agent doesn't have a predetermined time step limit, so the agent plans for an infinite number of time steps. Such a task may still be episodic and therefore terminate, but from the perspective of the agent, its planning horizon is infinite. We refer to this type of infinite planning horizon task as an *indefinite horizon* task. The agent plans for infinite, but interactions may be stopped at any time by the environment.

For tasks in which there's a high chance the agent gets stuck in a loop and never terminates, it's common practice to add an artificial terminal state based on the time step: a hard time step limit using the transition function. These cases require special handling of the time step limit terminal state. The environment for chapters 8, 9, and 10, the cart pole environment, has this kind of artificial terminal step, and you'll learn to handle these special cases in those chapters.

The BW, BSW, and FL environment are episodic tasks, because there are terminal states; there are a clear goal and failure states. FL is an indefinite planning horizon; the agent plans for infinite number of steps, but interactions may stop at any time. We won't add a time step limit to the FL environment because there's a high chance the agent will terminate naturally; the environment is highly stochastic. This kind of task is the most common in RL.

We refer to the sequence of consecutive time steps from the beginning to the end of an episodic task as an *episode, trial, period,* or *stage*. In indefinite planning horizons, an episode is a collection containing all interactions between an initial and a terminal state.

Discount: The future is uncertain, value it less

Because of the possibility of infinite sequences of time steps in infinite horizon tasks, we need a way to discount the value of rewards over time; that is, we need a way to tell the agent that getting +1's is better sooner than later. We commonly use a positive real value less than one to exponentially discount the value of future rewards. The further into the future we receive the reward, the less valuable it is in the present.

This number is called the *discount factor,* or *gamma.* The discount factor adjusts the importance of rewards over time. The later we receive rewards, the less attractive they are to present calculations. Another important reason why the discount factor is commonly used is to reduce the variance of return estimates. Given that the future is uncertain, and that the further we look into the future, the more stochasticity we accumulate and the more variance our value estimates will have, the discount factor helps reduce the degree to which future rewards affect our value function estimates, which stabilizes learning for most agents.

Effect of discount factor and time on the value of rewards

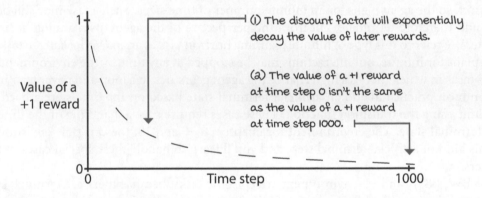

Interestingly, gamma is part of the MDP definition: the problem, and not the agent. However, often you'll find no guidance for the proper value of gamma to use for a given environment. Again, this is because gamma is also used as a hyperparameter for reducing variance, and therefore left for the agent to tune.

You can also use gamma as a way to give a sense of "urgency" to the agent. To wrap your head around that, imagine that I tell you I'll give you $1,000 once you finish reading this book, but I'll discount (gamma) that reward by 0.5 daily. This means that every day I cut the value that I pay in half. You'll probably finish reading this book today. If I say gamma is 1, then it doesn't matter when you finish it, you still get the full amount.

For the BW and BSW environments, a gamma of 1 is appropriate; for the FL environment, however, we'll use a gamma of 0.99, a commonly used value.

SHOW ME THE MATH
The discount factor (gamma)

(1) The sum of all rewards obtained during the course of an episode is referred to as the return.

$$G_t = R_{t+1} + R_{t+2} + R_{t+3} + ... + R_T$$

(2) But we can also use the discount factor this way and obtain the discounted return. The discounted return will downweight rewards that occur later during the episode.

$$G_t = R_{t+1} + \gamma R_{t+2} + \gamma^2 R_{t+3} + ... + \gamma^{T-1} R_T$$

(3) We can simplify the equation and have a more general equation, such as this one.

$$G_t = \sum_{k=0}^{\infty} \gamma^k R_{t+k+1}$$

(4) Finally, take a look a this interesting recursive definition. In the next chapter, we spend time exploiting this form.

$$G_t = R_{t+1} + \gamma G_{t+1}$$

Extensions to MDPs

There are many extensions to the MDP framework, as we've discussed. They allow us to target slightly different types of RL problems. The following list isn't comprehensive, but it should give you an idea of how large the field is. Know that the acronym MDPs is often used to refer to all types of MDPs. We're currently looking only at the tip of the iceberg:

- Partially observable Markov decision process (POMDP): When the agent cannot fully observe the environment state

- Factored Markov decision process (FMDP): Allows the representation of the transition and reward function more compactly so that we can represent large MDPs

- Continuous [Time|Action|State] Markov decision process: When either time, action, state or any combination of them are continuous

- Relational Markov decision process (RMDP): Allows the combination of probabilistic and relational knowledge

- Semi-Markov decision process (SMDP): Allows the inclusion of abstract actions that can take multiple time steps to complete

- Multi-agent Markov decision process (MMDP): Allows the inclusion of multiple agents in the same environment

- Decentralized Markov decision process (Dec-MDP): Allows for multiple agents to collaborate and maximize a common reward

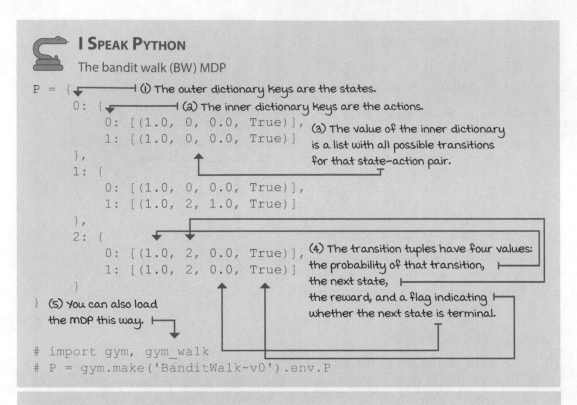

I Speak Python

The bandit walk (BW) MDP

```
P = {                    (1) The outer dictionary keys are the states.
    0: {                 (2) The inner dictionary keys are the actions.
        0: [(1.0, 0, 0.0, True)],
        1: [(1.0, 0, 0.0, True)]     (3) The value of the inner dictionary
    },                                   is a list with all possible transitions
    1: {                                 for that state-action pair.
        0: [(1.0, 0, 0.0, True)],
        1: [(1.0, 2, 1.0, True)]
    },
    2: {
        0: [(1.0, 2, 0.0, True)],    (4) The transition tuples have four values:
        1: [(1.0, 2, 0.0, True)]         the probability of that transition,
    }                                    the next state,
}                                        the reward, and a flag indicating
  (5) You can also load                  whether the next state is terminal.
  the MDP this way.
# import gym, gym_walk
# P = gym.make('BanditWalk-v0').env.P
```

I Speak Python

The bandit slippery walk (BSW) MDP

```
P = {                    (1) Look at the terminal states. States 0 and 2 are terminal.
    0: {
        0: [(1.0, 0, 0.0, True)],
        1: [(1.0, 0, 0.0, True)]
    },
    1: {         (2) This is how you build stochastic transitions. This is state 1, action 0.
        0: [(0.8, 0, 0.0, True), (0.2, 2, 1.0, True)],
        1: [(0.8, 2, 1.0, True), (0.2, 0, 0.0, True)]
    },           (3) These are the transitions after taking action 1 in state 1.
    2: {
        0: [(1.0, 2, 0.0, True)],    (4) This is how you can load
        1: [(1.0, 2, 0.0, True)]         the Bandit Slippery Walk in
    }                                    the Notebook; make sure
}                                        to check them out!
# import gym, gym_walk
# P = gym.make('BanditSlipperyWalk-v0').env.P
```

I SPEAK PYTHON

The frozen lake (FL) MDP

```
P = {
    0: {
        0: [(0.6666666666666666, 0, 0.0, False),
            (0.3333333333333333, 4, 0.0, False)
        ],
        <...>
        3: [(0.3333333333333333, 1, 0.0, False),
            (0.3333333333333333, 0, 0.0, False),
            (0.3333333333333333, 0, 0.0, False)
        ]
    },
    <...>
    14: {
        <...>
        1: [(0.3333333333333333, 13, 0.0, False),
            (0.3333333333333333, 14, 0.0, False),
            (0.3333333333333333, 15, 1.0, True)
        ],
        2: [(0.3333333333333333, 14, 0.0, False),
            (0.3333333333333333, 15, 1.0, True),
            (0.3333333333333333, 10, 0.0, False)
        ],
        3: [(0.3333333333333333, 15, 1.0, True),
            (0.3333333333333333, 10, 0.0, False),
            (0.3333333333333333, 13, 0.0, False)
        ]
    },
    15: {
        0: [(1.0, 15, 0, True)],
        1: [(1.0, 15, 0, True)],
        2: [(1.0, 15, 0, True)],
        3: [(1.0, 15, 0, True)]
    }
}

# import gym
# P = gym.make('FrozenLake-v0').env.P
```

(1) Probability of landing in state 0 when selecting action 0 in state 0

(2) Probability of landing in state 4 when selecting action 0 in state 0

(3) You can group the probabilities, such as in this line.

(4) Or be explicit, such as in these two lines. It works fine either way.

(5) Lots removed from this example for clarity.

(6) Go to the Notebook for the complete FL MDP.

(7) State 14 is the only state that provides a non-zero reward. Three out of four actions have a single transition that leads to state 15. Landing on state 15 provides a +1 reward.

(8) State 15 is a terminal state.

(9) Again, you can load the MDP like so.

Putting it all together

Unfortunately, when you go out to the real world, you'll find many different ways that MDPs are defined. Moreover, certain sources describe POMDPs and refer to them as MDPs without full disclosure. All of this creates confusion to newcomers, so I have a few points to clarify for you going forward. First, what you saw previously as Python code isn't a complete MDP, but instead only the transition functions and reward signals. From these, we can easily infer the state and action spaces. These code snippets come from a few packages containing several environments I developed for this book, and the FL environment is part of the OpenAI Gym package mentioned in the first chapter. Several of the additional components of an MDP that are missing from the dictionaries above, such as the initial state distribution S_θ that comes from the set of initial state S^i, are handled internally by the Gym framework and not shown here. Further, other components, such as the discount factor γ and the horizon H, are not shown in the previous dictionary, and the OpenAI Gym framework doesn't provide them to you. Like I said before, discount factors are commonly considered hyperparameters, for better or worse. And the horizon is often assumed to be infinity.

But don't worry about this. First, to calculate optimal policies for the MDPs presented in this chapter (which we'll do in the next chapter), we only need the dictionary shown previously containing the transition function and reward signal; from these, we can infer the state and action spaces, and I'll provide you with the discount factors. We'll assume horizons of infinity, and won't need the initial state distribution. Additionally, the most crucial part of this chapter is to give you an awareness of the components of MDPs and POMDPs. Remember, you won't have to do much more building of MDPs than what you've done in this chapter. Nevertheless, let me define MDPs and POMDPs so we're in sync.

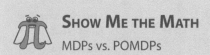

SHOW ME THE MATH
MDPs vs. POMDPs

$$\rightarrow MDP(\mathcal{S}, \mathcal{A}, \mathcal{T}, \mathcal{R}, \mathcal{S}_\theta, \gamma, \mathcal{H})$$

(1) MDPs have state space S, action space A, transition function T, reward signal R. They also has a set of initial states distribution S_θ, the discount factor γ, and the horizon H.

$$\rightarrow POMDP(\mathcal{S}, \mathcal{A}, \mathcal{T}, \mathcal{R}, \mathcal{S}_\theta, \gamma, \mathcal{H}, \mathcal{O}, \mathcal{E})$$

(2) To define a POMDP, you add the observation space O and an emission probability ε that defines the probability of showing an observation o_t given a state s_t. Very simple.

Summary

Okay. I know this chapter is heavy on new terms, but that's its intent. The best summary for this chapter is on the previous page, more specifically, the definition of an MDP. Take another look at the last two equations and try to remember what each letter means. Once you do so, you can be assured that you got what's necessary out of this chapter to proceed.

At the highest level, a reinforcement learning problem is about the interactions between an agent and the environment in which the agent exists. A large variety of issues can be modeled under this setting. The Markov decision process is a mathematical framework for representing complex decision-making problems under uncertainty.

Markov decision processes (MDPs) are composed of a set of system states, a set of per-state actions, a transition function, a reward signal, a horizon, a discount factor, and an initial state distribution. States describe the configuration of the environment. Actions allow agents to interact with the environment. The transition function tells how the environment evolves and reacts to the agent's actions. The reward signal encodes the goal to be achieved by the agent. The horizon and discount factor add a notion of time to the interactions.

The state space, the set of all possible states, can be infinite or finite. The number of variables that make up a single state, however, must be finite. States can be fully observable, but in a more general case of MDPs, a POMDP, the states are partially observable. This means the agent can't observe the full state of the system, but can observe a noisy state instead, called an observation.

The action space is a set of actions that can vary from state to state. However, the convention is to use the same set for all states. Actions can be composed with more than one variable, just like states. Action variables may be discrete or continuous.

The transition function links a state (a next state) to a state-action pair, and it defines the probability of reaching that future state given the state-action pair. The reward signal, in its more general form, maps a transition tuple s, a, s' to scalar, and it indicates the goodness of the transition. Both the transition function and reward signal define the model of the environment and are assumed to be stationary, meaning probabilities stay the same throughout.

By now, you

- Understand the components of a reinforcement learning problem and how they interact with each other

- Recognize Markov decision processes and know what they are composed from and how they work

- Can represent sequential decision-making problems as MDPs

TWEETABLE FEAT

Work on your own and share your findings

Here are several ideas on how to take what you have learned to the next level. If you'd like, share your results with the rest of the world, and make sure to check out what others have done, too. It's a win-win situation, and hopefully, you'll take advantage of it.

- **#gdrl_ch02_tf01:** Creating environments is a crucial skill that deserves a book of its own. How about you create a grid-world environment of your own? Here, look at the code for the walk environments in this chapter (https://github.com/mimoralea /gym-walk) and some other grid-world environments (https://github.com/mimoralea /gym-aima, https://github.com/mimoralea/gym-bandits, https://github.com/openai /gym/tree/master/gym/envs/toy_text). Now, create a Python package with a new grid-world environment! Don't limit yourself to simple move actions; you can create a 'teleport' action, or anything else. Also, maybe add creatures to the environment other than your agent. Maybe add little monsters that your agent needs to avoid. Get creative here. There's so much you could do.

- **#gdrl_ch02_tf02:** Another thing to try is to create what is called a "Gym environment" for a simulation engine of your choosing. First, investigate what exactly is a "Gym environment." Next, explore the following Python packages (https://github .com/openai/mujoco-py, https://github.com/openai/atari-py, https://github.com /google-research/football, and many of the packages at https://github.com/openai /gym/blob/master/docs/environments.md). Then, try to understand how others have exposed simulation engines as Gym environments. Finally, create a Gym environment for a simulation engine of your choosing. This is a challenging one!

- **#gdrl_ch02_tf03:** In every chapter, I'm using the final hashtag as a catchall hashtag. Feel free to use this one to discuss anything else that you worked on relevant to this chapter. There's no more exciting homework than that which you create for yourself. Make sure to share what you set yourself to investigate and your results.

Write a tweet with your findings, tag me @mimoralea (I'll retweet), and use the particular hashtag from this list to help interested folks find your results. There are no right or wrong results; you share your findings and check others' findings. Take advantage of this to socialize, contribute, and get yourself out there! We're waiting for you!

Here's a tweet example:

"Hey, @mimoralea. I created a blog post with a list of resources to study deep reinforcement learning. Check it out at <link>. #gdrl_ch01_tf01"

I'll make sure to retweet and help others find your work.

Balancing immediate and long-term goals | 3

In this chapter

- You will learn about the challenges of learning from sequential feedback and how to properly balance immediate and long-term goals.

- You will develop algorithms that can find the best policies of behavior in sequential decision-making problems modeled with MDPs.

- You will find the optimal policies for all environments for which you built MDPs in the previous chapter.

> 66 *In preparing for battle I have always found that* 99
> *plans are useless, but planning is indispensable.*
>
> — Dwight D. Eisenhower
> United States Army five-star general and
> 34th President of the United States

In the last chapter, you built an MDP for the BW, BSW, and FL environments. MDPs are the motors moving RL environments. They define the problem: they describe how the agent interacts with the environment through state and action spaces, the agent's goal through the reward function, how the environment reacts from the agent's actions through the transition function, and how time should impact behavior through the discount factor.

In this chapter, you'll learn about algorithms for solving MDPs. We first discuss the objective of an agent and why simple plans are not sufficient to solve MDPs. We then talk about the two fundamental algorithms for solving MDPs under a technique called *dynamic programming*: *value iteration* (VI) and *policy iteration* (PI).

You'll soon notice that these methods in a way "cheat": they require full access to the MDP, and they depend on knowing the dynamics of the environment, which is something we can't always obtain. However, the fundamentals you'll learn are still useful for learning about more advanced algorithms. In the end, VI and PI are the foundations from which virtually every other RL (and DRL) algorithm originates.

You'll also notice that when an agent has full access to an MDP, there's no uncertainty because you can look at the dynamics and rewards and calculate expectations directly. Calculating expectations directly means that there's no need for exploration; that is, there's no need to balance exploration and exploitation. There's no need for interaction, so there's no need for trial-and-error learning. All of this is because the feedback we're using for learning in this chapter isn't evaluative but supervised instead.

Remember, in DRL, agents learn from feedback that's simultaneously sequential (as opposed to one shot), evaluative (as opposed to supervised), and sampled (as opposed to exhaustive). What I'm doing in this chapter is eliminating the complexity that comes with learning from evaluative and sampled feedback, and studying sequential feedback in isolation. In this chapter, we learn from feedback that's sequential, supervised, and exhaustive.

The objective of a decision-making agent

At first, it seems the agent's goal is to find a sequence of actions that will maximize the return: the sum of rewards (discounted or undiscounted—depending on the value of gamma) during an episode or the entire life of the agent, depending on the task.

Let me introduce a new environment to explain these concepts more concretely.

CONCRETE EXAMPLE
The Slippery Walk Five (SWF) environment

The Slippery Walk Five (SWF) is a one-row grid-world environment (a walk), that's stochastic, similar to the Frozen Lake, and it has only five non-terminal states (seven total if we count the two terminal).

The Slippery Walk Five environment

(1) This environment is stochastic, and even if the agent selects the Right action, there's a chance it goes left!

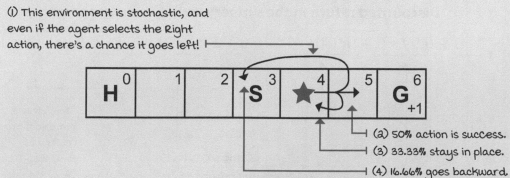

(2) 50% action is success.

(3) 33.33% stays in place.

(4) 16.66% goes backward.

The agent starts in *S*, *H* is a hole, *G* is the goal and provides a +1 reward.

 ## SHOW ME THE MATH
The return G

(1) The return is the sum of rewards encounter from step *t*, until the final step *T*.

$$G_t = R_{t+1} + R_{t+2} + R_{t+3} + ... + R_T$$

(2) As I mentioned in the previous chapter, we can combine the return and time using the discount factor, gamma. This is then the discounted return, which prioritizes early rewards.

$$G_t = R_{t+1} + \gamma R_{t+2} + \gamma^2 R_{t+3} + ... + \gamma^{T-1} R_T$$

(3) We can simplify the equation and have a more general equation, such as this one.

$$G_t = \sum_{k=0}^{\infty} \gamma^k R_{t+k+1}$$

$$G_t = R_{t+1} + \gamma G_{t+1}$$

(4) And stare at this recursive definition of G for a while.

You can think of returns as backward looking—"how much you got" from a past time step; but another way to look at it is as a "reward-to-go"—basically, forward looking. For example, imagine an episode in the SWF environment went this way: State 3 (0 reward), state 4 (0 reward), state 5 (0 reward), state 4 (0 reward), state 5 (0 reward), state 6 (+1 reward). We can shorten it: 3/0, 4/0, 5/0, 4/0, 5/0, 6/1. What's the return of this trajectory/episode?

Well, if we use discounting the math would work out this way.

Discounted return in the slippery walk five environment

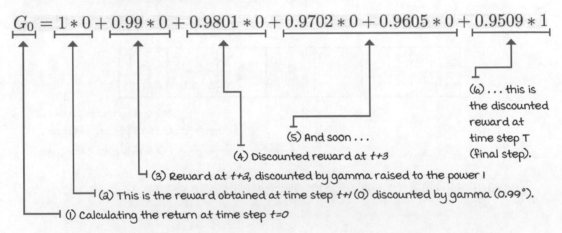

$$G_0 = 1 * 0 + 0.99 * 0 + 0.9801 * 0 + 0.9702 * 0 + 0.9605 * 0 + 0.9509 * 1$$

(6) . . . this is the discounted reward at time step T (final step).

(5) And soon . . .

(4) Discounted reward at *t+3*

(3) Reward at *t+2*, discounted by gamma raised to the power 1

(2) This is the reward obtained at time step *t+1* (0) discounted by gamma (0.99°).

(1) Calculating the return at time step *t=0*

If we don't use discounting, well, the return would be 1 for this trajectory and all trajectories that end in the right-most cell, state 6, and 0 for all trajectories that terminate in the left-most cell, state 0.

In the SWF environment, it's evident that going right is the best thing to do. It may seem, therefore, that all the agent must find is something called a *plan*—that is, a sequence of actions from the START state to the GOAL state. But this doesn't always work.

A solid plan in the SWF environment

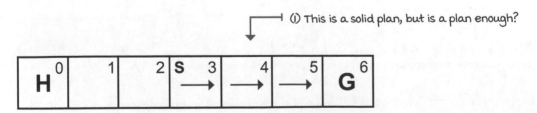

(1) This is a solid plan, but is a plan enough?

| H⁰ | 1 | 2 | S 3 → | 4 → | 5 → | G⁶ |

In the FL environment, a plan would look like the following.

A solid plan in the FL environment

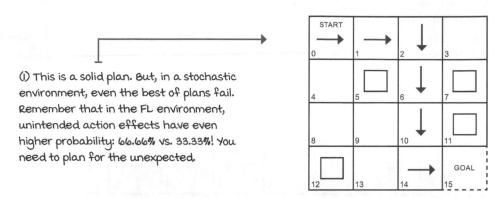

(1) This is a solid plan. But, in a stochastic environment, even the best of plans fail. Remember that in the FL environment, unintended action effects have even higher probability: 66.66% vs. 33.33%! You need to plan for the unexpected.

But this isn't enough! The problem with plans is they don't account for stochasticity in environments, and both the SWF and FL are stochastic; actions taken won't always work the way we intend. What would happen if, due to the environment's stochasticity, our agent lands on a cell not covered by our plan?

A possible hole in our plan

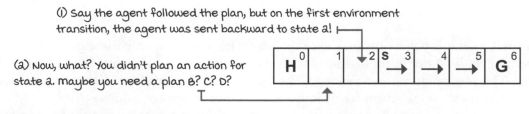

(1) Say the agent followed the plan, but on the first environment transition, the agent was sent backward to state 2!

(2) Now, what? You didn't plan an action for state 2. Maybe you need a plan B? C? D?

Same happens in the FL environment.

Plans aren't enough in stochastic environments

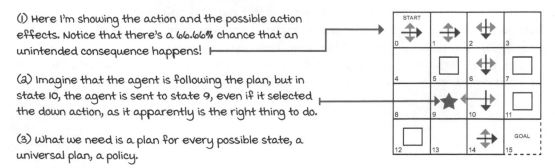

(1) Here I'm showing the action and the possible action effects. Notice that there's a 66.66% chance that an unintended consequence happens!

(2) Imagine that the agent is following the plan, but in state 10, the agent is sent to state 9, even if it selected the down action, as it apparently is the right thing to do.

(3) What we need is a plan for every possible state, a universal plan, a policy.

What the agent needs to come up with is called a *policy*. Policies are universal plans; policies cover all possible states. We need to plan for every possible state. Policies can be stochastic or deterministic: the policy can return action-probability distributions or single actions for a given state (or observation). For now, we're working with deterministic policies, which is a lookup table that maps actions to states.

In the SWF environment, the optimal policy is always going right, for every single state. Great, but there are still many unanswered questions. For instance, how much reward should

Optimal policy in the SWF environment

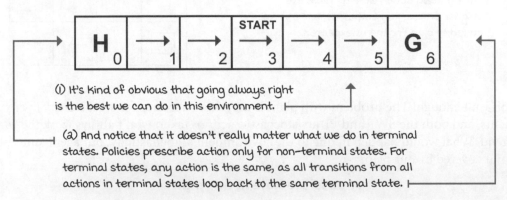

① It's kind of obvious that going always right is the best we can do in this environment.

② And notice that it doesn't really matter what we do in terminal states. Policies prescribe action only for non-terminal states. For terminal states, any action is the same, as all transitions from all actions in terminal states loop back to the same terminal state.

I expect from this policy? Because, even though we know how to act optimally, the environment might send our agent backward to the hole even if we always select to go toward the goal. This is why returns aren't enough. The agent is really looking to maximize the expected return; that means the return taking into account the environment's stochasticity.

Also, we need a method to automatically find optimal policies, because in the FL example, for instance, it isn't obvious at all what the optimal policy looks like!

There are a few components that are kept internal to the agent that can help it find optimal behavior: there are policies, there can be multiple policies for a given environment, and in fact, in certain environments, there may be multiple optimal policies. Also, there are value functions to help us keep track of return estimates. There's a single optimal value function for a given MDP, but there may be multiple value functions in general.

Let's look at all the components internal to a reinforcement learning agent that allow them to learn and find optimal policies, with examples to make all of this more concrete.

Policies: Per-state action prescriptions

Given the stochasticity in the Frozen Lake environment (and most reinforcement learning problems,) the agent needs to find a policy, denoted as π. A policy is a function that prescribes actions to take for a given nonterminal state. (Remember, policies can be stochastic: either directly over an action or a probability distribution over actions. We'll expand on stochastic policies in later chapters.)

Here's a sample policy.

A randomly generated policy

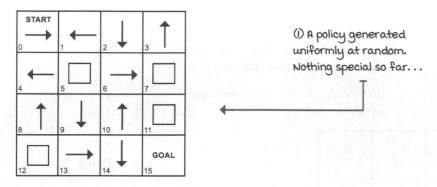

(1) A policy generated uniformly at random. Nothing special so far...

One immediate question that arises when looking at a policy is this: how good is this policy? If we find a way to put a number to policies, we could also ask the question, how much better is this policy compared to another policy?

How can we compare policies?

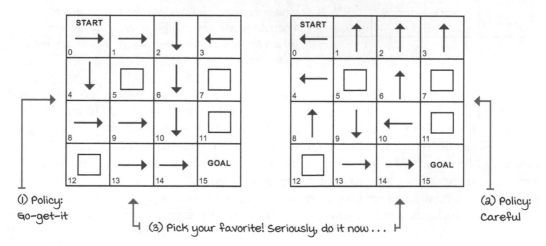

(1) Policy: Go-get-it

(2) Policy: Careful

(3) Pick your favorite! Seriously, do it now...

State-value function: What to expect from here?

Something that'd help us compare policies is to put numbers to states for a given policy. That is, if we're given a policy and the MDP, we should be able to calculate the expected return starting from every single state (we care mostly about the START state). How can we calculate how valuable being in a state is? For instance, if our agent is in state 14 (to the left of the GOAL), how is that better than being in state 13 (to the left of 14)? And precisely how much better is it? More importantly, under which policy would we have better results, the Go-get-it or the Careful policy?

Let's give it a quick try with the Go-get-it policy. What is the value of being in state 14 under the Go-get-it policy?

What's the value of being in state 14 when running the Go-get-it policy?

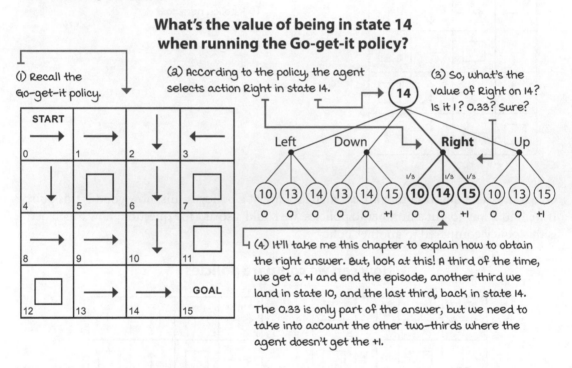

(1) Recall the Go-get-it policy.

(2) According to the policy, the agent selects action Right in state 14.

(3) So, what's the value of Right on 14? Is it 1? 0.33? Sure?

(4) It'll take me this chapter to explain how to obtain the right answer. But, look at this! A third of the time, we get a +1 and end the episode, another third we land in state 10, and the last third, back in state 14. The 0.33 is only part of the answer, but we need to take into account the other two–thirds where the agent doesn't get the +1.

Okay, so it isn't that straightforward to calculate the value of state 14 when following the Go-get-it policy because of the dependence on the values of other states (10 and 14, in this case), which we don't have either. It's like the chicken-or-the-egg problem. Let's keep going.

We defined the return as the sum of rewards the agent obtains from a trajectory. Now, this return can be calculated without paying attention to the policy the agent is following: you sum all of the rewards obtained, and you're good to go. But, the number we're looking for now is the expectation of returns (from state 14) if we follow a given policy π. Remember, we're under stochastic environments, so we must account for all the possible ways the environment can react to our policy! That's what an expectation gives us.

We now define the value of a state *s* when following a policy π: the value of a state *s* under policy π is the expectation of returns if the agent follows policy π starting from state *s*. Calculate this for every state, and you get the state-value function, or V-function or value function. It represents the expected return when following policy π from state *s*.

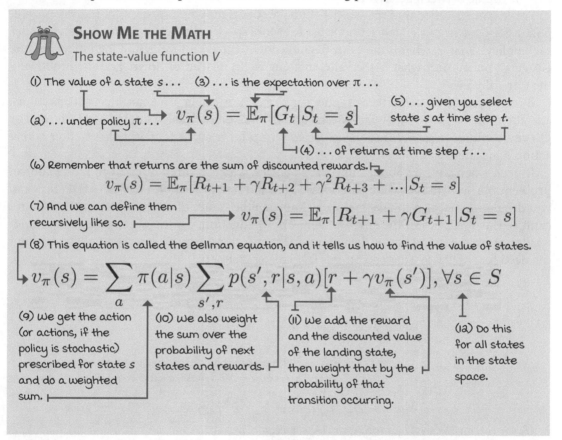

SHOW ME THE MATH

The state-value function *V*

(1) The value of a state *s* ... (3) ... is the expectation over π ...

(2) ... under policy π ... $v_\pi(s) = \mathbb{E}_\pi[G_t|S_t = s]$ (5) ... given you select state *s* at time step *t*.

(4) ... of returns at time step *t* ...

(6) Remember that returns are the sum of discounted rewards.

$$v_\pi(s) = \mathbb{E}_\pi[R_{t+1} + \gamma R_{t+2} + \gamma^2 R_{t+3} + ...|S_t = s]$$

(7) And we can define them recursively like so. $v_\pi(s) = \mathbb{E}_\pi[R_{t+1} + \gamma G_{t+1}|S_t = s]$

(8) This equation is called the Bellman equation, and it tells us how to find the value of states.

$$v_\pi(s) = \sum_a \pi(a|s) \sum_{s',r} p(s',r|s,a)[r + \gamma v_\pi(s')], \forall s \in S$$

(9) We get the action (or actions, if the policy is stochastic) prescribed for state *s* and do a weighted sum.

(10) We also weight the sum over the probability of next states and rewards.

(11) We add the reward and the discounted value of the landing state, then weight that by the probability of that transition occurring.

(12) Do this for all states in the state space.

These equations are fascinating. A bit of a mess given the recursive dependencies, but still interesting. Notice how the value of a state depends recursively on the value of possibly many other states, which values may also depend on others, including the original state!

The recursive relationship between states and successive states will come back in the next section when we look at algorithms that can iteratively solve these equations and obtain the state-value function of any policy in the FL environment (or any other environment, really).

For now, let's continue exploring other components commonly found in RL agents. We'll learn how to calculate these values later in this chapter. Note that the state-value function is often referred to as the value function, or even the V-function, or more simply $V^\pi(s)$. It may be confusing, but you'll get used to it.

Action-value function: What should I expect from here if I do this?

Another critical question that we often need to ask isn't merely about the value of a state but the value of taking action *a* in a state *s*. Differentiating answers to this kind of question will help us decide between actions.

For instance, notice that the Go-get-it policy goes right when in state 14, but the Careful policy goes down. But which action is better? More specifically, which action is better under each policy? That is, what is the value of going down, instead of right, and then following the Go-get-it policy, and what is the value of going right, instead of down, and then following the Careful policy?

By comparing between different actions under the same policy, we can select better actions, and therefore improve our policies. The *action-value function*, also known as *Q-function* or *Q*π*(s,a)*, captures precisely this: the expected return if the agent follows policy π after taking action *a* in state *s*.

In fact, when we care about improving policies, which is often referred to as the control problem, we need action-value functions. Think about it: if you don't have an MDP, how can you decide what action to take merely by knowing the values of all states? V-functions don't capture the dynamics of the environment. The Q-function, on the other hand, does somewhat capture the dynamics of the environment and allows you to improve policies without the need for MDPs. We expand on this fact in later chapters.

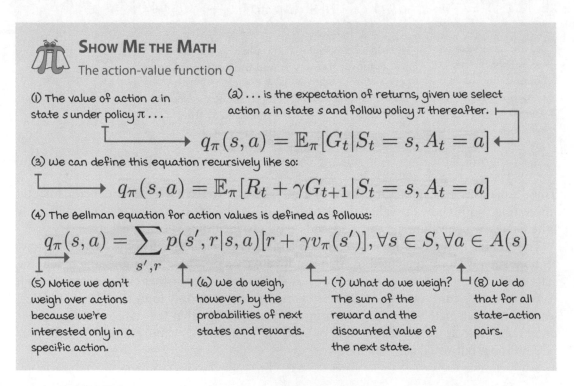

SHOW ME THE MATH
The action-value function Q

(1) The value of action *a* in state *s* under policy π . . .

(2) . . . is the expectation of returns, given we select action *a* in state *s* and follow policy π thereafter.

$$q_\pi(s, a) = \mathbb{E}_\pi[G_t | S_t = s, A_t = a]$$

(3) We can define this equation recursively like so:

$$q_\pi(s, a) = \mathbb{E}_\pi[R_t + \gamma G_{t+1} | S_t = s, A_t = a]$$

(4) The Bellman equation for action values is defined as follows:

$$q_\pi(s, a) = \sum_{s',r} p(s', r | s, a)[r + \gamma v_\pi(s')], \forall s \in S, \forall a \in A(s)$$

(5) Notice we don't weigh over actions because we're interested only in a specific action.

(6) We do weigh, however, by the probabilities of next states and rewards.

(7) What do we weigh? The sum of the reward and the discounted value of the next state.

(8) We do that for all state-action pairs.

Action-advantage function: How much better if I do that?

Another type of value function is derived from the previous two. The *action-advantage function*, also known as *advantage function, A-function*, or $A^{\pi}(s, a)$, is the difference between the action-value function of action a in state s and the state-value function of state s under policy π.

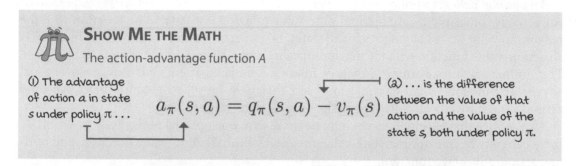

SHOW ME THE MATH

The action-advantage function A

(1) The advantage of action a in state s under policy π . . .

$$a_{\pi}(s, a) = q_{\pi}(s, a) - v_{\pi}(s)$$

(2) . . . is the difference between the value of that action and the value of the state s, both under policy π.

The advantage function describes how much better it is to take action a instead of following policy π: the advantage of choosing action a over the default action.

Look at the different value functions for a (dumb) policy in the SWF environment. Remember, these values depend on the policy. In other words, the $Q_{\pi}(s, a)$ assumes you'll follow policy π (always left in the following example) and right after taking action a in state s.

State-value, action-value, and action-advantage functions

(1) Notice how $Q_{\pi}(s,a)$ allows us to improve policy π, by showing the highest valued action under the policy.

(2) Also notice there's no advantage for taking the same action as policy π recommends.

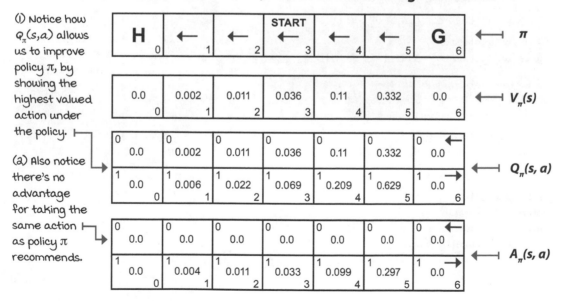

Optimality

Policies, state-value functions, action-value functions, and action-advantage functions are the components we use to describe, evaluate, and improve behaviors. We call it *optimality* when these components are the best they can be.

An *optimal policy* is a policy that for every state can obtain expected returns greater than or equal to any other policy. An optimal state-value function is a state-value function with the maximum value across all policies for all states. Likewise, an optimal action-value function is an action-value function with the maximum value across all policies for all state-action pairs. The optimal action-advantage function follows a similar pattern, but notice an optimal advantage function would be equal to or less than zero for all state-action pairs, since no action could have any advantage from the optimal state-value function.

Also, notice that although there could be more than one optimal policy for a given MDP, there can only be one optimal state-value function, optimal action-value function, and optimal action-advantage function.

You may also notice that if you had the optimal V-function, you could use the MDP to do a one-step search for the optimal Q-function and then use this to build the optimal policy. On the other hand, if you had the optimal Q-function, you don't need the MDP at all. You could use the optimal Q-function to find the optimal V-function by merely taking the maximum over the actions. And you could obtain the optimal policy using the optimal Q-function by taking the argmax over the actions.

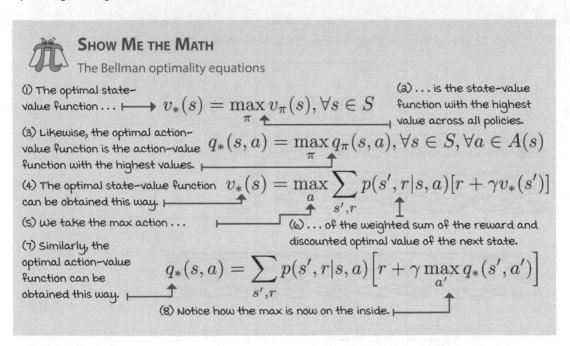

SHOW ME THE MATH
The Bellman optimality equations

(1) The optimal state-value function . . . $\longmapsto$ $v_*(s) = \max_{\pi} v_\pi(s), \forall s \in S$ (2) . . . is the state-value function with the highest value across all policies.

(3) Likewise, the optimal action-value function is the action-value function with the highest values. $\quad$ $q_*(s, a) = \max_{\pi} q_\pi(s, a), \forall s \in S, \forall a \in A(s)$

(4) The optimal state-value function can be obtained this way. $\quad$ $v_*(s) = \max_{a} \sum_{s', r} p(s', r | s, a)[r + \gamma v_*(s')]$

(5) We take the max action . . . $\quad$ (6) . . . of the weighted sum of the reward and discounted optimal value of the next state.

(7) Similarly, the optimal action-value function can be obtained this way. $\quad$ $q_*(s, a) = \sum_{s', r} p(s', r | s, a)\left[r + \gamma \max_{a'} q_*(s', a')\right]$

(8) Notice how the max is now on the inside.

Planning optimal sequences of actions

We have state-value functions to keep track of the values of states, action-value functions to keep track of the values of state-action pairs, and action-advantage functions to show the "advantage" of taking specific actions. We have equations for all of these to evaluate current policies, that is, to go from policies to value functions, and to calculate and find optimal value functions and, therefore, optimal policies.

Now that we've discussed the reinforcement learning problem formulation, and we've defined the objective we are after, we can start exploring methods for finding this objective. Iteratively computing the equations presented in the previous section is one of the most common ways to solve a reinforcement learning problem and obtain optimal policies when the dynamics of the environment, the MDPs, are known. Let's look at the methods.

Policy evaluation: Rating policies

We talked about comparing policies in the previous section. We established that policy π is better than or equal to policy π' if the expected return is better than or equal to π' for all states. Before we can use this definition, however, we must devise an algorithm for evaluating an arbitrary policy. Such an algorithm is known as an *iterative policy evaluation* or just *policy evaluation*.

The policy-evaluation algorithm consists of calculating the V-function for a given policy by sweeping through the state space and iteratively improving estimates. We refer to the type of algorithm that takes in a policy and outputs a value function as an algorithm that solves the **prediction problem**, which is calculating the values of a predetermined policy.

 ### SHOW ME THE MATH
The policy-evaluation equation

(1) The policy-evaluation algorithm consist of the iterative approximation of the state-value function of the policy under evaluation. The algorithm converges as k approaches infinity. ⌐

(2) Initialize $v_0(s)$ for all s in s arbitrarily, and to 0 if s is terminal. Then, increase k and iteratively improve the estimates by following the equation below.

$$v_{k+1}(s) = \sum_{a} \pi(a|s) \sum_{s',r} p(s',r|s,a)\Big[r + \gamma v_k(s')\Big]$$

(3) Calculate the value of a state s as the weighted sum of the reward and the discounted estimated value of the next state s'. ⌐

Using this equation, we can iteratively approximate the true V-function of an arbitrary policy. The iterative policy-evaluation algorithm is guaranteed to converge to the value function of the policy if given enough iterations, more concretely as we approach infinity. In practice, however, we use a small threshold to check for changes in the value function we're approximating. Once the changes in the value function are less than this threshold, we stop.

Let's see how this algorithm works in the SWF environment, for the always-left policy.

Initial calculations of policy evaluation

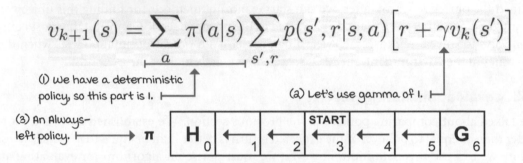

$$v_{k+1}(s) = \sum_a \pi(a|s) \sum_{s',r} p(s',r|s,a)\Big[r + \gamma v_k(s')\Big]$$

(1) We have a deterministic policy, so this part is 1.

(2) Let's use gamma of 1.

(3) An Always-left policy. ⟶ π

H	←	←	START ←	←	←	G
0	1	2	3	4	5	6

State 5, Iteration 1 (initialized to 0 in iteration 0):

$v_1^\pi(5)= p(s'=4 \mid s=5, a=\text{Left}) * [\, R(5, \text{Left}, 4) + v_0^\pi(4)\,] +$

$\qquad p(s'=5 \mid s=5, a=\text{Left}) * [\, R(5, \text{Left}, 5) + v_0^\pi(5)\,] +$

$\qquad p(s'=6 \mid s=5, a=\text{Left}) * [\, R(5, \text{Left}, 6) + v_0^\pi(6)\,]$

$v_1^\pi(5)= 0.50 * (0+0) \ + \ 0.33 * (0+0) \ + \ 0.166 * (1+0) = 0.166$ ⟵ (4) Yep, this is the value of state 5 after 1 iteration of policy evaluation ($v_1^\pi(5)$).

You then calculate the values for all states 0–6, and when done, move to the next iteration. Notice that to calculate $V_2^\pi(s)$ you'd have to use the estimates obtained in the previous iteration, $V_1^\pi(s)$. This technique of calculating an estimate from an estimate is referred to as *bootstrapping*, and it's a widely used technique in RL (including DRL).

Also, it's important to notice that the k's here are iterations across estimates, but they're not interactions with the environment. These aren't episodes that the agent is out and about selecting actions and observing the environment. These aren't time steps either. Instead, these are the iterations of the iterative policy-evaluation algorithm. Do a couple more of these estimates. The following table shows you the results you should get.

k	$V^\pi(0)$	$V^\pi(1)$	$V^\pi(2)$	$V^\pi(3)$	$V^\pi(4)$	$V^\pi(5)$	$V^\pi(6)$
0	0	0	0	0	0	0	0
1	0	0	0	0	0	0.1667	0
2	0	0	0	0	0.0278	0.2222	0
3	0	0	0	0.0046	0.0463	0.2546	0
4	0	0	0.0008	0.0093	0.0602	0.2747	0
5	0	0.0001	0.0018	0.0135	0.0705	0.2883	0
6	0	0.0003	0.0029	0.0171	0.0783	0.2980	0
7	0	0.0006	0.0040	0.0202	0.0843	0.3052	0
8	0	0.0009	0.0050	0.0228	0.0891	0.3106	0
9	0	0.0011	0.0059	0.0249	0.0929	0.3147	0
10	0	0.0014	0.0067	0.0267	0.0959	0.318	0
...	...	...	...	...	...	...	...
104	0	0.0027	0.011	0.0357	0.1099	0.3324	0

What are several of the things the resulting state-value function tells us?

Well, to begin with, we can say we get a return of 0.0357 in expectation when starting an episode in this environment and following the always-left policy. Pretty low.

We can also say, that even when we find ourselves in state 1 (the leftmost non-terminal state), we still have a chance, albeit less than one percent, to end up in the GOAL cell (state 6). To be exact, we have a 0.27% chance of ending up in the GOAL state when we're in state 1. And we select left all the time! Pretty interesting.

Interestingly also, due to the stochasticity of this environment, we have a 3.57% chance of reaching the GOAL cell (remember this environment has 50% action success, 33.33% no effects, and 16.66% backward). Again, this is when under an always-left policy. Still, the Left action could send us right, then right and right again, or left, right, right, right, right, and so on.

Think about how the probabilities of trajectories combine. Also, pay attention to the iterations and how the values propagate backward from the reward (transition from state 5 to state 6) one step at a time. This backward propagation of the values is a common characteristic among RL algorithms and comes up again several times.

I SPEAK PYTHON
The policy-evaluation algorithm

```python
def policy_evaluation(pi, P, gamma=1.0, theta=1e-10):
```
(1) This is a full implementation of the policy-evaluation algorithm. All we need is the policy we're trying to evaluate and the MDP the policy runs on. The discount factor, gamma, defaults to 1, and theta is a small number that we use to check for convergence.

```python
    prev_V = np.zeros(len(P))
```
(2) Here we initialize the first-iteration estimates of the state-value function to zero.

```python
    while True:
```
(3) We begin by looping "forever" . . .

```python
        V = np.zeros(len(P))
```
(4) We initialize the current-iteration estimates to zero as well.

```python
        for s in range(len(P)):
```
(5) And then loop through all states to estimate the state-value function.

(6) See here how we use the policy pi to get the possible transitions.

```python
            for prob, next_state, reward, done in P[s][pi(s)]:
```
(7) Each transition tuple has a probability, next state, reward, and a done flag indicating whether the 'next_state' is terminal or not.

(8) We calculate the value of that state by summing up the weighted value of that transition.

```python
                V[s] += prob * (reward + gamma * \
                            prev_V[next_state] * (not done))
```
(9) Notice how we use the 'done' flag to ensure the value of the next state when landing on a terminal state is zero. We don't want infinite sums.

```python
        if np.max(np.abs(prev_V - V)) < theta:
            break
```
(10) At the end of each iteration (a state sweep), we make sure that the state-value functions are changing; otherwise, we call it converged.

```python
        prev_V = V.copy()
    return V
```
(11) Finally, "copy" to get ready for the next iteration or return the latest state-value function.

Let's now run policy evaluation in the randomly generated policy presented earlier for the FL environment.

Recall the randomly generated policy

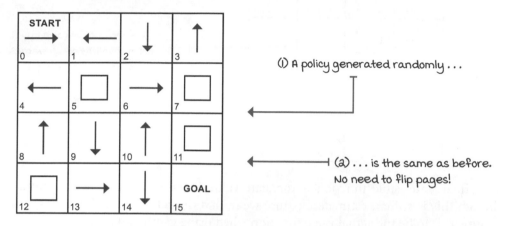

(1) A policy generated randomly . . .

(2) . . . is the same as before. No need to flip pages!

The following shows the progress policy evaluation makes on accurately estimating the state-value function of the randomly generated policy after only eight iterations.

Policy evaluation on the randomly generated policy for the FL environment

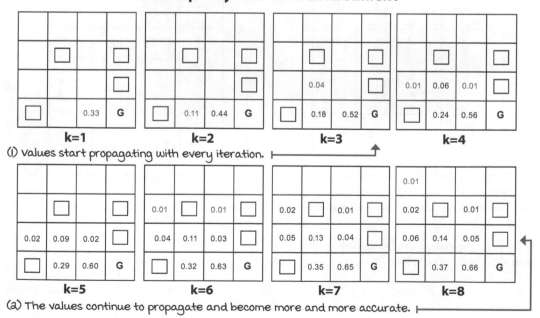

(1) Values start propagating with every iteration.

(2) The values continue to propagate and become more and more accurate.

State-value function of the randomly generated policy

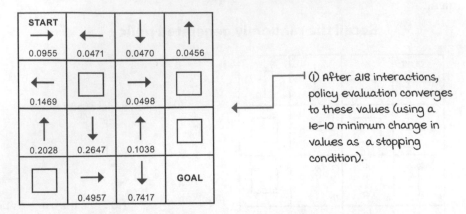

① After 218 interactions, policy evaluation converges to these values (using a 1e-10 minimum change in values as a stopping condition).

This final state-value function is the state-value function for this policy. Note that even though this is still an estimate, because we're in a discrete state and action spaces, we can assume this to be the actual value function when using gamma of 0.99.

In case you're wondering about the state-value functions of the two policies presented earlier, here are the results.

Results of policy evolution

The Go-get-it policy:

START → 0.0342	→ 0.0231	↓ 0.0468	← 0.0231
↓ 0.0463	☐	↓ 0.0957	☐
→ 0.0940	→ 0.2386	↓ 0.2901	☐
☐	→ 0.4329	→ 0.6404	GOAL

The Careful policy:

START ↑ 0.4079	↑ 0.3754	↑ 0.3543	↑ 0.3438
← 0.4263	☐	↑ 0.1169	☐
↑ 0.4454	↓ 0.4840	← 0.4328	☐
☐	→ 0.5884	→ 0.7107	GOAL

① The state-value function of this policy converges after 66 iterations. The policy reaches the goal state a mere 3.4% of the time.

② For this policy, the state-value function converges after 546 iterations. The policy reaches the goal 53.70% of the time!

③ By the way, I calculated these values empirically by running the policies 100 times. Therefore, these values are noisy, but you get the idea.

It seems being a Go-get-it policy doesn't pay well in the FL environment! Fascinating results, right? But a question arises: Are there any better policies for this environment?

Policy improvement: Using ratings to get better

The motivation is clear now. You have a way of evaluating any policy. This already gives you some freedom: you can evaluate many policies and rank them by the state-value function of the START state. After all, that number tells you the expected cumulative reward the policy in question will obtain if you run many episodes. Cool, right?

No! Makes no sense. Why would you randomly generate a bunch of policies and evaluate them all? First, that's a total waste of computing resources, but more importantly, it gives you no guarantee that you're finding better and better policies. There has to be a better way.

The key to unlocking this problem is the action-value function, the Q-function. Using the V-function and the MDP, you get an estimate of the Q-function. The Q-function will give you a glimpse of the values of all actions for all states, and these values, in turn, can hint at how to improve policies. Take a look at the Q-function of the Careful policy and ways we can improve this policy:

How can the Q-function help us improve policies ?

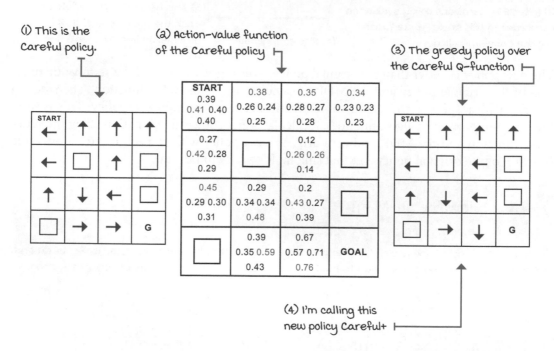

(1) This is the Careful policy.

(2) Action-value function of the Careful policy

(3) The greedy policy over the Careful Q-function

(4) I'm calling this new policy Careful+

Notice how if we act greedily with respect to the Q-function of the policy, we obtain a new policy: Careful+. Is this policy any better? Well, policy evaluation can tell us! Let's find out!

State-value function of the Careful policy

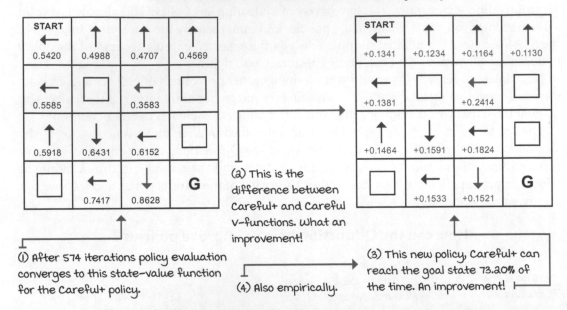

(2) This is the difference between Careful+ and Careful v-functions. What an improvement!

(1) After 574 iterations policy evaluation converges to this state-value function for the Careful+ policy.

(4) Also empirically.

(3) This new policy, Careful+ can reach the goal state 73.20% of the time. An improvement!

The new policy is better than the original policy. This is great! We used the state-value function of the original policy and the MDP to calculate its action-value function. Then, acting greedily with respect to the action-value function gave us an improved policy. This is what the *policy-improvement* algorithm does: it calculates an action-value function using the state-value function and the MDP, and it returns a *greedy* policy with respect to the action-value function of the original policy. Let that sink in, it's pretty important.

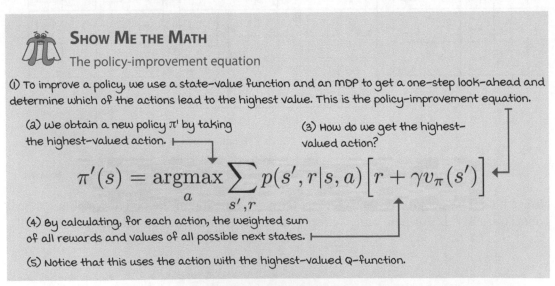

SHOW ME THE MATH
The policy-improvement equation

(1) To improve a policy, we use a state-value function and an MDP to get a one-step look-ahead and determine which of the actions lead to the highest value. This is the policy-improvement equation.

(2) We obtain a new policy π' by taking the highest-valued action.

(3) How do we get the highest-valued action?

$$\pi'(s) = \operatorname*{argmax}_{a} \sum_{s',r} p(s',r|s,a)\Big[r + \gamma v_\pi(s')\Big]$$

(4) By calculating, for each action, the weighted sum of all rewards and values of all possible next states.

(5) Notice that this uses the action with the highest-valued Q-function.

This is how the policy-improvement algorithm looks in Python.

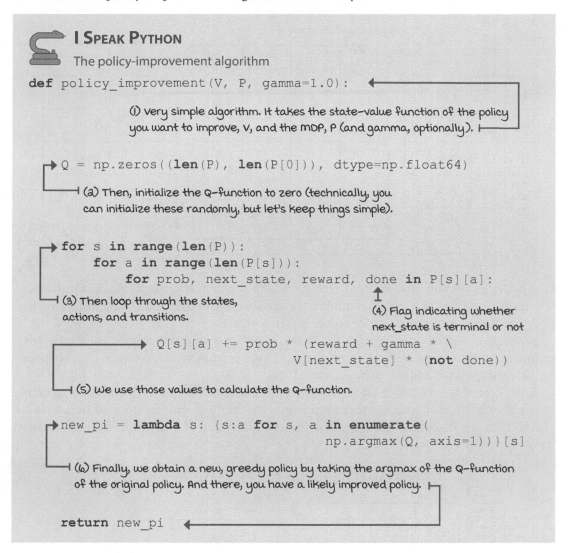

I SPEAK PYTHON
The policy-improvement algorithm

```python
def policy_improvement(V, P, gamma=1.0):
```

(1) Very simple algorithm. It takes the state-value function of the policy you want to improve, V, and the MDP, P (and gamma, optionally).

```python
    Q = np.zeros((len(P), len(P[0])), dtype=np.float64)
```

(2) Then, initialize the Q-function to zero (technically, you can initialize these randomly, but let's keep things simple).

```python
    for s in range(len(P)):
        for a in range(len(P[s])):
            for prob, next_state, reward, done in P[s][a]:
```

(3) Then loop through the states, actions, and transitions.

(4) Flag indicating whether next_state is terminal or not

```python
                Q[s][a] += prob * (reward + gamma * \
                              V[next_state] * (not done))
```

(5) We use those values to calculate the Q-function.

```python
    new_pi = lambda s: {s:a for s, a in enumerate(
                          np.argmax(Q, axis=1))}[s]
```

(6) Finally, we obtain a new, greedy policy by taking the argmax of the Q-function of the original policy. And there, you have a likely improved policy.

```python
    return new_pi
```

The natural next questions are these: Is there a better policy than this one? Can we do any better than Careful+? Can we evaluate the Careful+ policy, and then improve it again? Maybe! But, there's only one way to find out. Let's give it a try!

Can we improve over the Careful+ policy ?

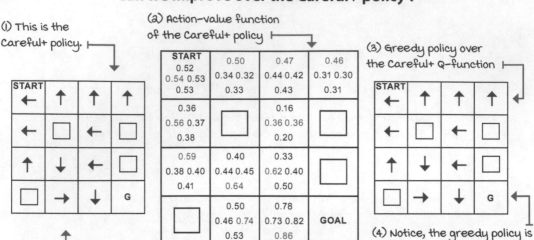

(1) This is the Careful+ policy.

(2) Action-value function of the Careful+ policy

(3) Greedy policy over the Careful+ Q-function

(4) Notice, the greedy policy is the same as the original policy. There's no improvement now.

I ran policy evaluation on the Careful+ policy, and then policy improvement. The Q-functions of Careful and Careful+ are different, but the greedy policies over the Q-functions are identical. In other words, there's no improvement this time.

No improvement occurs because the Careful+ policy is an optimal policy of the FL environment (with gamma 0.99). We only needed one improvement over the Careful policy because this policy was good to begin with.

Now, even if we start with an adversarial policy designed to perform poorly, alternating over policy evaluation and improvement would still end up with an optimal policy. Want proof? Let's do it! Let's make up an adversarial policy for FL environment and see what happens.

Adversarial policy for the FL environment

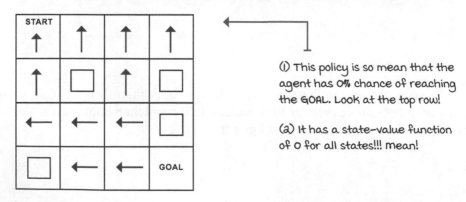

(1) This policy is so mean that the agent has 0% chance of reaching the GOAL. Look at the top row!

(2) It has a state-value function of 0 for all states!!! mean!

Policy iteration: Improving upon improved behaviors

The plan with this adversarial policy is to alternate between policy evaluation and policy improvement until the policy coming out of the policy-improvement phase no longer yields a different policy. The fact is that, if instead of starting with an adversarial policy, we start with a randomly generated policy, this is what an algorithm called *policy iteration* does.

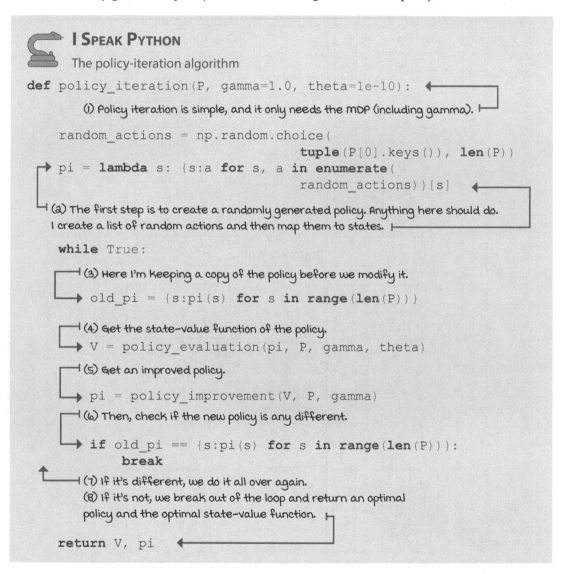

I SPEAK PYTHON
The policy-iteration algorithm

```python
def policy_iteration(P, gamma=1.0, theta=1e-10):
```
(1) Policy iteration is simple, and it only needs the MDP (including gamma).

```python
    random_actions = np.random.choice(
                            tuple(P[0].keys()), len(P))
    pi = lambda s: {s:a for s, a in enumerate(
                            random_actions)}[s]
```
(2) The first step is to create a randomly generated policy. Anything here should do. I create a list of random actions and then map them to states.

```python
    while True:
```
(3) Here I'm keeping a copy of the policy before we modify it.
```python
        old_pi = {s:pi(s) for s in range(len(P))}
```
(4) Get the state-value function of the policy.
```python
        V = policy_evaluation(pi, P, gamma, theta)
```
(5) Get an improved policy.
```python
        pi = policy_improvement(V, P, gamma)
```
(6) Then, check if the new policy is any different.
```python
        if old_pi == {s:pi(s) for s in range(len(P))}:
            break
```
(7) If it's different, we do it all over again.
(8) If it's not, we break out of the loop and return an optimal policy and the optimal state-value function.

```python
    return V, pi
```

Great! But, let's first try it starting with the adversarial policy and see what happens.

Improving upon the adversarial policy 1/2

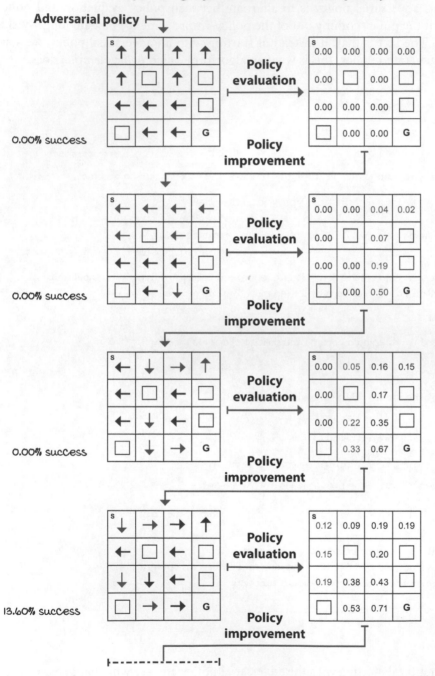

Improving upon the adversarial policy 2/2

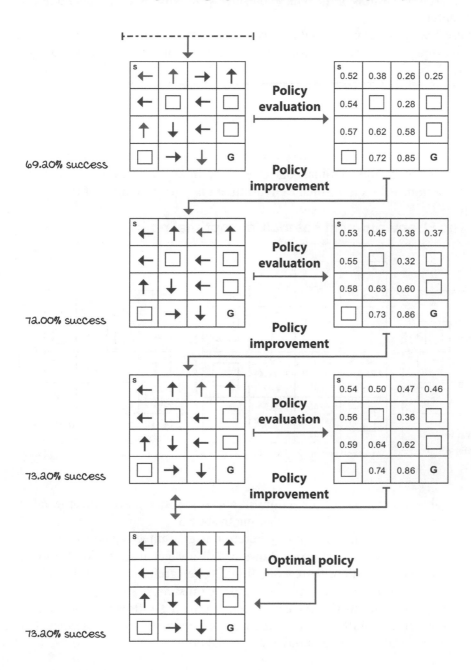

As mentioned, alternating policy evaluating and policy improvement yields an optimal policy and state-value function regardless of the policy you start with. Now, a few points I'd like to make about this sentence.

Notice how I use "*an* optimal policy," but also use "*the* optimal state-value function." This is not a coincidence or a poor choice of words; this is, in fact, a property that I'd like to highlight again. An MDP can have more than one optimal policy, but it can only have a single optimal state-value function. It's not too hard to wrap your head around that.

State-value functions are collections of numbers. Numbers can have infinitesimal accuracy, because they're numbers. There will be only one optimal state-value function (the collection with the highest numbers for all states). However, a state-value function may have actions that are equally valued for a given state; this includes the optimal state-value function. In this case, there could be multiple optimal policies, each optimal policy selecting a different, but equally valued, action. Take a look: the FL environment is a great example of this.

The FL environment has multiple optimal policies

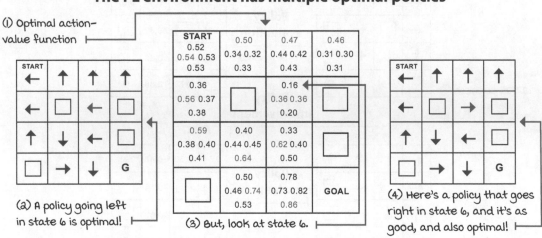

(1) Optimal action-value function

(2) A policy going left in state 6 is optimal!

(3) But, look at state 6.

(4) Here's a policy that goes right in state 6, and it's as good, and also optimal!

By the way, it's not shown here, but all the actions in a terminal state have the same value, zero, and therefore a similar issue that I'm highlighting in state 6.

As a final note, I want to highlight that policy iteration is guaranteed to converge to the exact optimal policy: the mathematical proof shows it will not get stuck in local optima. However, as a practical consideration, there's one thing to be careful about. If the action-value function has a tie (for example, right/left in state 6), we must make sure not to break ties randomly. Otherwise, policy improvement could keep returning different policies, even without any real improvement. With that out of the way, let's look at another essential algorithm for finding optimal state-value functions and optimal policies.

Value iteration: Improving behaviors early

You probably notice the way policy evaluation works: values propagate consistently on each iteration, but slowly. Take a look.

Policy evaluation on the always-left policy on the SWF environment

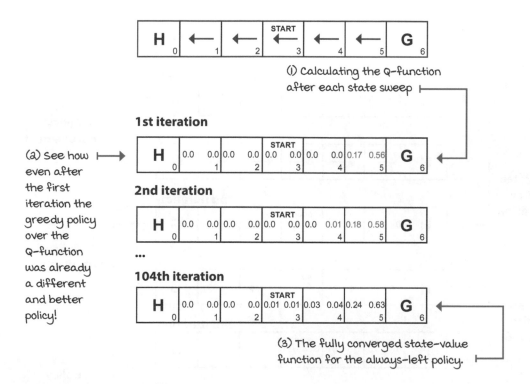

(1) Calculating the Q-function after each state sweep

1st iteration

(2) See how even after the first iteration the greedy policy over the Q-function was already a different and better policy!

2nd iteration

...

104th iteration

(3) The fully converged state-value function for the always-left policy.

The image shows a single state-space sweep of policy evaluation followed by an estimation of the Q-function. We do this by using the truncated estimate of the V-function and the MDP, on each iteration. By doing so, we can more easily see that even after the first iteration, a greedy policy over the early Q-function estimates would be an improvement. Look at the Q-values for state 5 in the first iteration; changing the action to point towards the GOAL state is obviously already better.

In other words, even if we truncated policy evaluation after a single iteration, we could still improve upon the initial policy by taking the greedy policy of the Q-function estimation after a single state-space sweep of policy evaluation. This algorithm is another fundamental algorithm in RL: it's called *value iteration* (VI).

VI can be thought of "greedily greedifying policies," because we calculate the greedy policy as soon as we can, greedily. VI doesn't wait until we have an accurate estimate of the policy before it improves it, but instead, VI truncates the policy-evaluation phase after a single state sweep. Take a look at what I mean by "greedily greedifying policies."

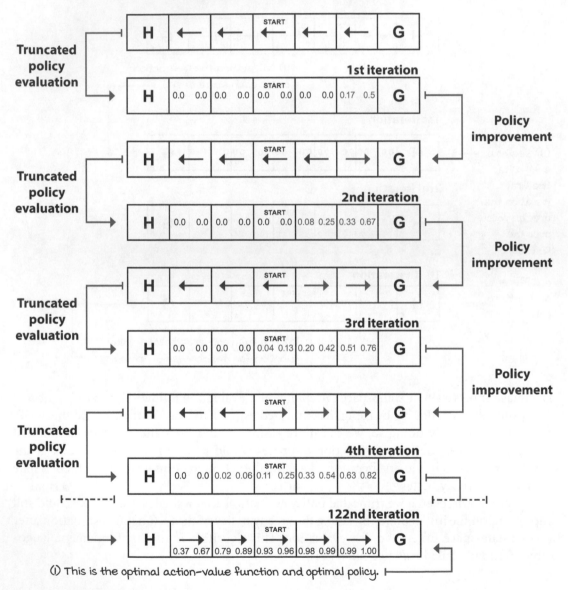

Greedily greedifying the always-left policy of the SFW environment

If we start with a randomly generated policy, instead of this adversarial policy always-left for the SWF environment, VI would still converge to the optimal state-value function. VI is a straightforward algorithm that can be expressed in a single equation.

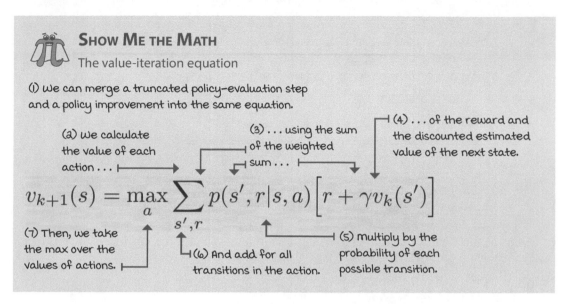

SHOW ME THE MATH

The value-iteration equation

(1) We can merge a truncated policy-evaluation step and a policy improvement into the same equation.

(2) We calculate the value of each action . . .

(3) . . . using the sum of the weighted sum . . .

(4) . . . of the reward and the discounted estimated value of the next state.

$$v_{k+1}(s) = \max_a \sum_{s',r} p(s',r|s,a)\Big[r + \gamma v_k(s')\Big]$$

(7) Then, we take the max over the values of actions.

(6) And add for all transitions in the action.

(5) Multiply by the probability of each possible transition.

Notice that in practice, in VI, we don't have to deal with policies at all. VI doesn't have any separate evaluation phase that runs to convergence. While the goal of VI is the same as the goal of PI—to find the optimal policy for a given MDP—VI happens to do this through the value functions; thus the name value iteration.

Again, we only have to keep track of a V-function and a Q-function (depending on implementation). Remember that to get the greedy policy over a Q-function, we take the arguments of the maxima (argmax) over the actions of that Q-function. Instead of improving the policy by taking the argmax to get a better policy and then evaluating this improved policy to obtain a value function again, we directly calculate the maximum (max, instead of argmax) value across the actions to be used for the next sweep over the states.

Only at the end of the VI algorithm, after the Q-function converges to the optimal values, do we extract the optimal policy by taking the argmax over the actions of the Q-function, as before. You'll see it more clearly in the code snippet on the next page.

One important thing to highlight is that whereas VI and PI are two different algorithms, in a more general view, they are two instances of *generalized policy iteration* (GPI). GPI is a general idea in RL in which policies are improved using their value function estimates, and value function estimates are improved toward the actual value function for the current policy. Whether you wait for the perfect estimates or not is just a detail.

I SPEAK PYTHON

The value-iteration algorithm

```python
def value_iteration(P, gamma=1.0, theta=1e-10):
```

(1) Like policy iteration, value iteration is a method for obtaining optimal policies. For this, we need an MDP (including gamma). Theta is the convergence criteria. 1e-10 is sufficiently accurate.

```python
    V = np.zeros(len(P), dtype=np.float64)
```

(2) First thing is to initialize a state-value function. Know that a V-function with random numbers should work fine.

```python
    while True:
```

(3) We get in this loop and initialize a Q-function to zero.

(4) Notice this one over here has to be zero. Otherwise, the estimate would be incorrect.

```python
        Q = np.zeros((len(P), len(P[0])), dtype=np.float64)
```

(5) Then, for every transition of every action in every state, we ...

```python
        for s in range(len(P)):
            for a in range(len(P[s])):
                for prob, next_state, reward, done in P[s][a]:
```

(6) ... calculate the action-value function ...

```python
                    Q[s][a] += prob * (reward + gamma * \
                               V[next_state] * (not done))
```

(7) ... notice, using V, which is the old "truncated" estimate.

```python
        if np.max(np.abs(V - np.max(Q, axis=1))) < theta:
            break
```

(8) After each sweep over the state space, we make sure the state-value function keeps changing. Otherwise, we found the optimal V-function and should break out.

```python
        V = np.max(Q, axis=1)
```

(9) Thanks to this short line, we don't need a separate policy-improvement phase. It's not a direct replacement, but instead a combination of improvement and evaluation.

```python
    pi = lambda s: {s:a for s, a in enumerate(
                    np.argmax(Q, axis=1))}[s]
    return V, pi
```

(10) Only at the end do we extract the optimal policy and return it along with the optimal state-value function.

Summary

The objective of a reinforcement learning agent is to maximize the expected return, which is the total reward over multiple episodes. For this, agents must use policies, which can be thought of as universal plans. Policies prescribe actions for states. They can be deterministic, meaning they return single actions, or stochastic, meaning they return probability distributions. To obtain policies, agents usually keep track of several summary values. The main ones are state-value, action-value, and action-advantage functions.

State-value functions summarize the expected return from a state. They indicate how much reward the agent will obtain from a state until the end of an episode in expectation. Action-value functions summarize the expected return from a state-action pair. This type of value function tells the expected reward-to-go after an agent selects a specific action in a given state. Action-value functions allow the agent to compare across actions and therefore solve the control problem. Action-advantage functions show the agent how much better than the default it can do if it were to opt for a specific state-action pair. All of these value functions are mapped to specific policies, perhaps an optimal policy. They depend on following what the policies prescribe until the end of the episode.

Policy evaluation is a method for estimating a value function from a policy and an MDP. Policy improvement is a method for extracting a greedy policy from a value function and an MDP. Policy iteration consists of alternating between policy-evaluation and policy improvement to obtain an optimal policy from an MDP. The policy evaluation phase may run for several iterations before it accurately estimates the value function for the given policy. In policy iteration, we wait until policy evaluation finds this accurate estimate. An alternative method, called value iteration, truncates the policy-evaluation phase and exits it, entering the policy-improvement phase early.

The more general view of these methods is generalized policy iteration, which describes the interaction of two processes to optimize policies: one moves value function estimates closer to the real value function of the current policy, another improves the current policy using its value function estimates, getting progressively better and better policies as this cycle continues.

By now, you

- Know the objective of a reinforcement learning agent and the different statistics it may hold at any given time

- Understand methods for estimating value functions from policies and methods for improving policies from value functions

- Can find optimal policies in sequential decision-making problems modeled by MDPs

TWEETABLE FEAT
Work on your own and share your findings

Here are several ideas on how to take what you have learned to the next level. If you'd like, share your results with the rest of the world and check out what others have done, too. It's a win-win situation, and hopefully, you'll take advantage of it.

- **#gdrl_ch03_tf01:** Many of the grid-world environments out there have MDPs available that can be solved with the policy iteration and value iteration functions presented in this chapter. Surprised? Use "env.unwrapped.P" and pass that variable to the functions in this chapter. More explicitly, do that for a few environments that we did not used in this chapter, environments created by others, or perhaps the environment you created yourself in the last chapter.

- **#gdrl_ch03_tf02:** The discount factor, gamma, was introduced in the previous chapter as part of the MDP definition. However, we didn't go into the details of this crucial variable. How about you run policy iteration and value iteration with several different values of gamma, capture the sum of rewards agents obtain with each, as well as the optimal policies. How do these compare? Can you find anything interesting that can help others better understand the role of the discount factor?

- **#gdrl_ch03_tf03:** Policy iteration and value iteration both do the same thing: they take an MDP definition and solve for the optimal value function and optimal policies. However, an interesting question is, how do these compare? Can you think of an MDP that's challenging for policy iteration and easy for value iteration to solve or the other way around? Create such an environment as a Python package, and share it with the world. What did you find that others may want to know? How do VI and PI compare?

- **#gdrl_ch03_tf04:** In every chapter, I'm using the final hashtag as a catchall hashtag. Feel free to use this one to discuss anything else that you worked on relevant to this chapter. There's no more exciting homework than that which you create for yourself. Make sure to share what you set yourself to investigate and your results.

Write a tweet with your findings, tag me @mimoralea (I'll retweet), and use the particular hashtag from this list to help interested folks find your results. There are no right or wrong results; you share your findings and check others' findings. Take advantage of this to socialize, contribute, and get yourself out there! We're waiting for you!

Here's a tweet example:

"Hey, @mimoralea. I created a blog post with a list of resources to study deep reinforcement learning. Check it out at <link>. #gdrl_ch01_tf01"

I'll make sure to retweet and help others find your work.

Balancing the gathering and use of information | 4

In this chapter

- You will learn about the challenges of learning from evaluative feedback and how to properly balance the gathering and utilization of information.

- You will develop exploration strategies that accumulate low levels of regret in problems with unknown transition function and reward signals.

- You will write code with trial-and-error learning agents that learn to optimize their behavior through their own experiences in many-options, one-choice environments known as multi-armed bandits.

> 66 *Uncertainty and expectation are the joys of life.* 99
> *Security is an insipid thing.*
>
> — WILLIAM CONGREVE
> ENGLISH PLAYWRIGHT AND POET OF THE RESTORATION PERIOD
> AND POLITICAL FIGURE IN THE BRITISH WHIG PARTY

No matter how small and unimportant a decision may seem, every decision you make is a trade-off between information gathering and information exploitation. For example, when you go to your favorite restaurant, should you order your favorite dish, yet again, or should you request that dish you've been meaning to try? If a Silicon Valley startup offers you a job, should you make a career move, or should you stay put in your current role?

These kinds of questions illustrate the exploration-exploitation dilemma and are at the core of the reinforcement learning problem. It boils down to deciding when to acquire knowledge and when to capitalize on knowledge previously learned. It's a challenge to know whether the good we already have is good enough. When do we settle? When do we go for more? What are your thoughts: is a bird in the hand worth two in the bush or not?

The main issue is that rewarding moments in life are relative; you have to compare events to see a clear picture of their value. For example, I'll bet you felt amazed when you were offered your first job. You perhaps even thought that was the best thing that ever happened to you. But, then life continues, and you experience things that appear even more rewarding—maybe, when you get a promotion, a raise, or get married, who knows!

And that's the core issue: even if you rank moments you have experienced so far by "how amazing" they felt, you can't know what's the most amazing moment you could experience in your life—life is uncertain; you don't have life's transition function and reward signal, so you must keep on exploring. In this chapter, you learn about how important it is for your agent to explore when interacting with uncertain environments, problems in which the MDP isn't available for planning.

In the previous chapter, you learned about the challenges of learning from sequential feedback and how to properly balance immediate and long-term goals. In this chapter, we examine the challenges of learning from evaluative feedback, and we do so in environments that aren't sequential, but one-shot instead: *multi-armed bandits* (MABs).

MABs isolate and expose the challenges of learning from evaluative feedback. We'll dive into many different techniques for balancing exploration and exploitation in these particular type of environments: single-state environments with multiple options, but a single choice. Agents will operate under uncertainty, that is, they won't have access to the MDP. However, they will interact with one-shot environments without the sequential component.

Remember, in DRL, agents learn from feedback that's simultaneously sequential (as opposed to one shot), evaluative (as opposed to supervised), and sampled (as opposed to exhaustive). In this chapter, I eliminate the complexity that comes along with learning from sequential and sampled feedback, and we study the intricacies of evaluative feedback in isolation. Let's get to it.

The challenge of interpreting evaluative feedback

In the last chapter, when we solved the FL environment, we knew beforehand how the environment would react to any of our actions. Knowing the exact transition function and reward signal of an environment allows us to compute an optimal policy using planning algorithms, such as PI and VI, without having to interact with the environment at all.

But, knowing an MDP in advance oversimplifies things, perhaps unrealistically. We cannot always assume we'll know with precision how an environment will react to our actions—that's not how the world works. We could opt for learning such things, as you'll learn in later chapters, but the bottom line is that we need to let our agents interact and experience the environment by themselves, learning this way to behave optimally, solely from their own experience. This is what's called trial-and-error learning.

In RL, when the agent learns to behave from interaction with the environment, the environment asks the agent the same question over and over: what do you want to do now? This question presents a fundamental challenge to a decision-making agent. What action should it do now? Should the agent exploit its current knowledge and select the action with the highest current estimate? Or should it explore actions that it hasn't tried enough? But many additional questions follow: when do you know your estimates are good enough? How do you know you have tried an apparently bad action enough? And so on.

You will learn more effective ways for dealing with the exploration-exploitation trade-off

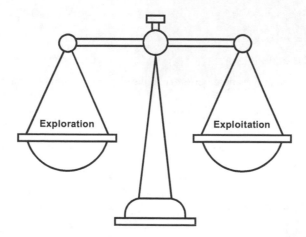

This is the key intuition: exploration builds the knowledge that allows for effective exploitation, and maximum exploitation is the ultimate goal of any decision maker.

Bandits: Single-state decision problems

Multi-armed bandits (MAB) are a special case of an RL problem in which the size of the state space and horizon equal one. A MAB has multiple actions, a single state, and a greedy horizon; you can also think of it as a "many-options, single-choice" environment. The name comes from slot machines (bandits) with multiple arms to choose from (more realistically, multiple slot machines to choose from).

There are many commercial applications for the methods coming out of MAB research. Advertising companies need to find the right way to balance showing you an ad they predict you're likely to click on and showing you a new ad with the potential of it being an even better fit for you. Websites that raise money, such as charities or political campaigns, need to balance between showing the layout that has led to the most contributions and new designs that haven't been sufficiently utilized but still have potential

Multi-armed bandit problem

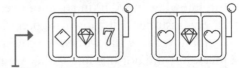

(i) A two-armed bandit is a decision-making problem with two choices. You need to try them both sufficient to correctly assess each option. How do you best handle the exploration-exploitation trade-off?

for even better outcomes. Likewise, e-commerce websites need to balance recommending you best-seller products as well as promising new products. In medical trials, there's a need to learn the effects of medicines in patients as quickly as possible. Many other problems benefit from the study of the exploration-exploitation trade-off: oil drilling, game playing, and search engines, to name a few. Our reason for studying MABs isn't so much a direct application to the real world, but instead how to integrate a suitable method for balancing exploration and exploitation in RL agents.

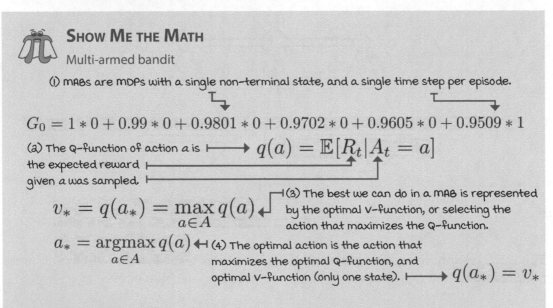

SHOW ME THE MATH

Multi-armed bandit

(i) MABs are MDPs with a single non-terminal state, and a single time step per episode.

$$G_0 = 1*0 + 0.99*0 + 0.9801*0 + 0.9702*0 + 0.9605*0 + 0.9509*1$$

(2) The Q-function of action a is $\longmapsto q(a) = \mathbb{E}[R_t | A_t = a]$
the expected reward given a was sampled.

$$v_* = q(a_*) = \max_{a \in A} q(a)$$

(3) The best we can do in a MAB is represented by the optimal V-function, or selecting the action that maximizes the Q-function.

$$a_* = \operatorname*{argmax}_{a \in A} q(a)$$

(4) The optimal action is the action that maximizes the optimal Q-function, and optimal V-function (only one state). $\longmapsto q(a_*) = v_*$

Regret: The cost of exploration

The goal of MABs is very similar to that of RL. In RL, the agent needs to maximize the expected cumulative discounted reward (maximize the expected return). This means to get as much reward (maximize) through the course of an episode (cumulative) as soon as possible (if discounted—later rewards are discounted more) despite the environment's stochasticity (expected). This makes sense when the environment has multiple states and the agent interacts with it for multiple time steps per episode. But in MABs, while there are multiple episodes, we only have a single chance of selecting an action in each episode.

Therefore, we can exclude the words that don't apply to the MAB case from the RL goal: we remove "cumulative" because there's only a single time step per episode, and "discounted" because there are no next states to account for. This means, in MABs, the goal is for the agent to maximize the expected reward. Notice that the word "expected" stays there because there's stochasticity in the environment. In fact, that's what MAB agents need to learn: the underlying probability distribution of the reward signal.

However, if we leave the goal to "maximize the expected reward," it wouldn't be straightforward to compare agents. For instance, let's say an agent learns to maximize the expected reward by selecting random actions in all but the final episode, while a much more sample-efficient agent uses a clever strategy to determine the optimal action quickly. If we only compare the final-episode performance of these agents, which isn't uncommon to see in RL, these two agents would have equally good performance, which is obviously not what we want.

A robust way to capture a more complete goal is for the agent to maximize the per-episode expected reward while still minimizing the total expected reward loss of rewards across all episodes. To calculate this value, called *total regret*, we sum the per-episode difference of the true expected reward of the optimal action and the true expected reward of the selected action. Obviously, the lower the total regret, the better. Notice I use the word true here; to calculate the regret, you must have access to the MDP. That doesn't mean your agent needs the MDP, only that you need it to compare agents' exploration strategy efficiency.

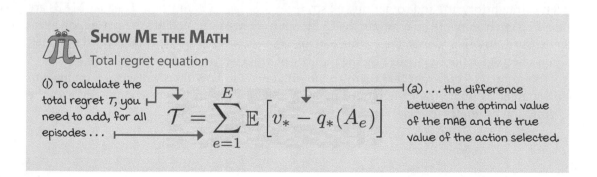

Show Me the Math
Total regret equation

(1) To calculate the total regret T, you need to add, for all episodes . . .

$$T = \sum_{e=1}^{E} \mathbb{E}\left[v_* - q_*(A_e)\right]$$

(2) . . . the difference between the optimal value of the MAB and the true value of the action selected.

Approaches to solving MAB environments

There are three major kinds of approaches to tackling MABs. The most popular and straightforward approach involves exploring by injecting randomness in our action-selection process; that is, our agent will exploit most of the time, and sometimes it'll explore using randomness. This family of approaches is called *random exploration strategies*. A basic example of this family would be a strategy that selects the greedy action most of the time, and with an epsilon threshold, it chooses uniformly at random. Now, multiple questions arise from this strategy; for instance, should we keep this epsilon value constant throughout the episodes? Should we maximize exploration early on? Should we periodically increase the epsilon value to ensure the agent always explores?

Another approach to dealing with the exploration-exploitation dilemma is to be optimistic. Yep, your mom was right. The family of *optimistic exploration strategies* is a more systematic approach that quantifies the uncertainty in the decision-making problem and increases the preference for states with the highest uncertainty. The bottom line is that being optimistic will naturally drive you toward uncertain states because you'll assume that states you haven't experienced yet are the best they can be. This assumption will help you explore, and as you explore and come face to face with reality, your estimates will get lower and lower as they approach their true values.

The third approach to dealing with the exploration-exploitation dilemma is the family of *information state-space exploration strategies*. These strategies will model the information state of the agent as part of the environment. Encoding the uncertainty as part of the state space means that an environment state will be seen differently when unexplored or explored. Encoding the uncertainty as part of the environment is a sound approach but can also considerably increase the size of the state space and, therefore, its complexity.

In this chapter, we'll explore a few instances of the first two approaches. We'll do this in a handful of different MAB environments with different properties, pros and cons, and this will allow us to compare the strategies in depth.

It's important to notice that the estimation of the Q-function in MAB environments is pretty straightforward and something all strategies will have in common. Because MABs are one-step environments, to estimate the Q-function we need to calculate the per-action average reward. In other words, the estimate of an action a is equal to the total reward obtained when selecting action a, divided by the number of times action a has been selected.

It's essential to highlight that there are no differences in how the strategies we evaluate in this chapter estimate the Q-function; the only difference is in how each strategy uses the Q-function estimates to select actions.

CONCRETE EXAMPLE
The slippery bandit walk (SBW) environment is back!

The first MAB environment that we'll consider is one we have played with before: the bandit slippery walk (BSW).

The bandit slippery walk environment

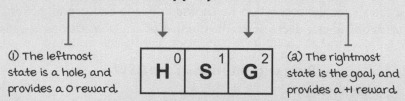

(1) The leftmost state is a hole, and provides a 0 reward.

(2) The rightmost state is the goal, and provides a +1 reward.

Remember, BSW is a grid world with a single row, thus, a walk. But a special feature of this walk is that the agent starts at the middle, and any action sends the agent to a terminal state immediately. Because it is a one-time-step, it's a bandit environment.

BSW is a two-armed bandit, and it can appear to the agent as a two-armed Bernoulli bandit. Bernoulli bandits pay a reward of +1 with a probability p and a reward of 0 with probability $q = 1 - p$. In other words, the reward signal is a Bernoulli distribution.

In the BSW, the two terminal states pay either 0 or +1. If you do the math, you'll notice that the probability of a +1 reward when selecting action 0 is 0.2, and when selecting action 1 is 0.8. But your agent doesn't know this, and we won't share that info. The question we're trying to ask is this: how quickly can your agent figure out the optimal action? How much total regret will agents accumulate while learning to maximize expected rewards? Let's find out.

Bandit slippery walk graph

(1) Remember: a hole, starting, and goal state

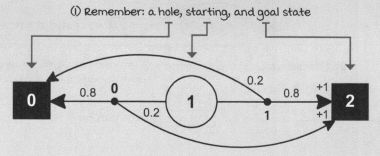

Greedy: Always exploit

The first strategy I want you to consider isn't really a strategy but a baseline, instead. I already mentioned we need to have some exploration in our algorithms; otherwise, we risk convergence to a suboptimal action. But, for the sake of comparison, let's consider an algorithm with no exploration at all.

This baseline is called a *greedy strategy*, or *pure exploitation strategy*. The greedy action-selection approach consists of always selecting the action with the highest estimated value. While there's a chance for the first action we choose to be the best overall action, the likelihood of this lucky coincidence decreases as the number of available actions increases.

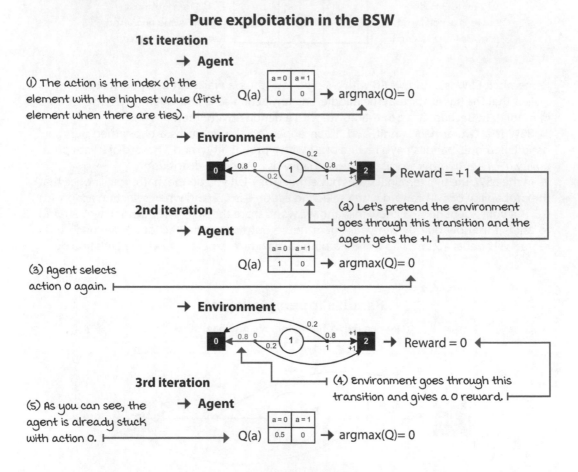

Pure exploitation in the BSW

As you might have expected, the greedy strategy gets stuck with the first action immediately. If the Q-table is initialized to zero, and there are no negative rewards in the environment, the greedy strategy will always get stuck with the first action.

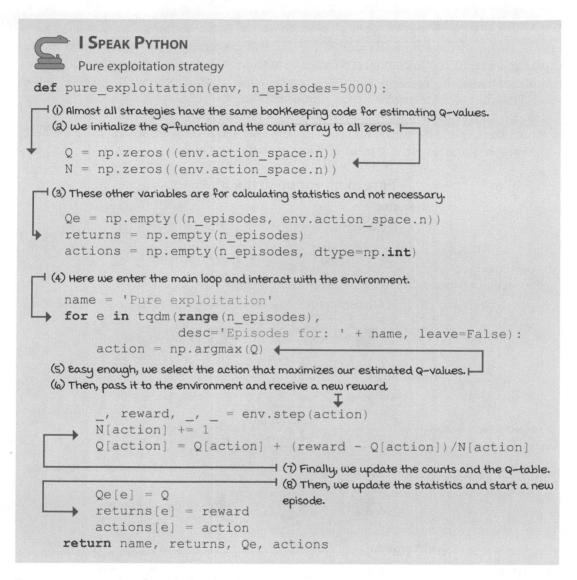

I Speak Python

Pure exploitation strategy

```python
def pure_exploitation(env, n_episodes=5000):
```

(1) Almost all strategies have the same bookkeeping code for estimating Q-values.
(2) We initialize the Q-function and the count array to all zeros.

```python
    Q = np.zeros((env.action_space.n))
    N = np.zeros((env.action_space.n))
```

(3) These other variables are for calculating statistics and not necessary.

```python
    Qe = np.empty((n_episodes, env.action_space.n))
    returns = np.empty(n_episodes)
    actions = np.empty(n_episodes, dtype=np.int)
```

(4) Here we enter the main loop and interact with the environment.

```python
    name = 'Pure exploitation'
    for e in tqdm(range(n_episodes),
                    desc='Episodes for: ' + name, leave=False):
        action = np.argmax(Q)
```

(5) Easy enough, we select the action that maximizes our estimated Q-values.
(6) Then, pass it to the environment and receive a new reward.

```python
        _, reward, _, _ = env.step(action)
        N[action] += 1
        Q[action] = Q[action] + (reward - Q[action])/N[action]
```

(7) Finally, we update the counts and the Q-table.
(8) Then, we update the statistics and start a new episode.

```python
        Qe[e] = Q
        returns[e] = reward
        actions[e] = action
    return name, returns, Qe, actions
```

I want you to notice the relationship between a greedy strategy and time. If your agent only has one episode left, the best thing is to act greedily. If you know you only have one day to live, you'll do things you enjoy the most. To some extent, this is what a greedy strategy does: it does the best it can do with your current view of life assuming limited time left.

And this is a reasonable thing to do when you have limited time left; however, if you don't, then you appear to be shortsighted because you can't trade-off immediate satisfaction or reward for gaining of information that would allow you better long-term results.

Random: Always explore

Let's also consider the opposite side of the spectrum: a strategy with exploration but no exploitation at all. This is another fundamental baseline that we can call a *random strategy* or a *pure exploration strategy*. This is simply an approach to action selection with no exploitation at all. The sole goal of the agent is to gain information.

Do you know people who, when starting a new project, spend a lot of time "researching" without jumping into the water? Me too! They can take weeks just reading papers. Remember, while exploration is essential, it must be balanced well to get maximum gains.

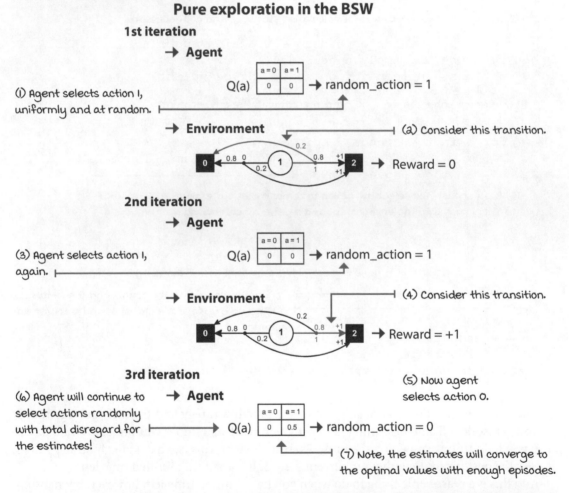

Pure exploration in the BSW

A random strategy is obviously not a good strategy either and will also give you suboptimal results. Similar to exploiting all the time, you don't want to explore all the time, either. We need algorithms that can do both exploration and exploitation: gaining and using information.

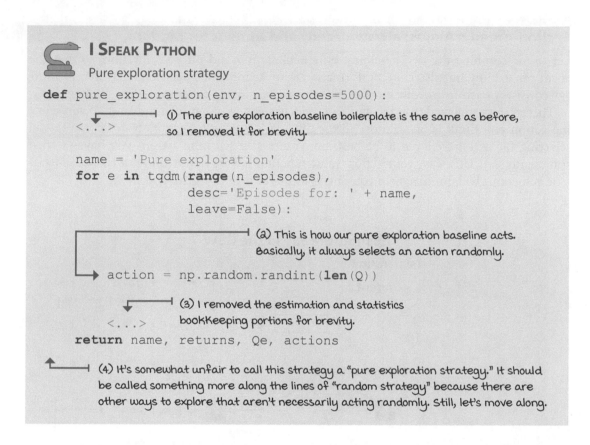

I SPEAK PYTHON

Pure exploration strategy

```python
def pure_exploration(env, n_episodes=5000):
```

< . . . > (1) The pure exploration baseline boilerplate is the same as before, so I removed it for brevity.

```python
    name = 'Pure exploration'
    for e in tqdm(range(n_episodes),
                  desc='Episodes for: ' + name,
                  leave=False):
```

(2) This is how our pure exploration baseline acts. Basically, it always selects an action randomly.

```python
        action = np.random.randint(len(Q))
```

< . . . > (3) I removed the estimation and statistics bookkeeping portions for brevity.

```python
    return name, returns, Qe, actions
```

(4) It's somewhat unfair to call this strategy a "pure exploration strategy." It should be called something more along the lines of "random strategy" because there are other ways to explore that aren't necessarily acting randomly. Still, let's move along.

I left a note in the code snippet, and I want to restate and expand on it. The pure exploration strategy I presented is one way to explore, that is, random exploration. But you can think of many other ways. Perhaps based on counts, that is, how many times you try one action versus the others, or maybe based on the variance of the reward obtained.

Let that sink in for a second: while there's only a single way to exploit, there are multiple ways to explore. Exploiting is nothing but doing what you think is best; it's pretty straight‑forward. You think A is best, and you do A. Exploring, on the other hand, is much more complex. It's obvious you need to collect information, but how is a different question. You could try gathering information to support your current beliefs. You could gather informa‑tion to attempt proving yourself wrong. You could explore based on confidence, or based on uncertainty. The list goes on.

The bottom line is intuitive: exploitation is your goal, and exploration gives you informa‑tion about obtaining your goal. You must gather information to reach your goals, that is clear. But, in addition to that, there are several ways to collect information, and that's where the challenge lies.

Epsilon-greedy: Almost always greedy and sometimes random

Let's now combine the two baselines, pure exploitation and pure exploration, so that the agent can exploit, but also collect information to make informed decisions. The hybrid strategy consists of acting greedily most of the time and exploring randomly every so often.

This strategy, referred to as the *epsilon-greedy strategy*, works surprisingly well. If you select the action you think is best almost all the time, you'll get solid results because you're still selecting the action believed to be best, but you're also selecting actions you haven't tried sufficiently yet. This way, your action-value function has an opportunity to converge to its true value; this will, in turn, help you obtain more rewards in the long term.

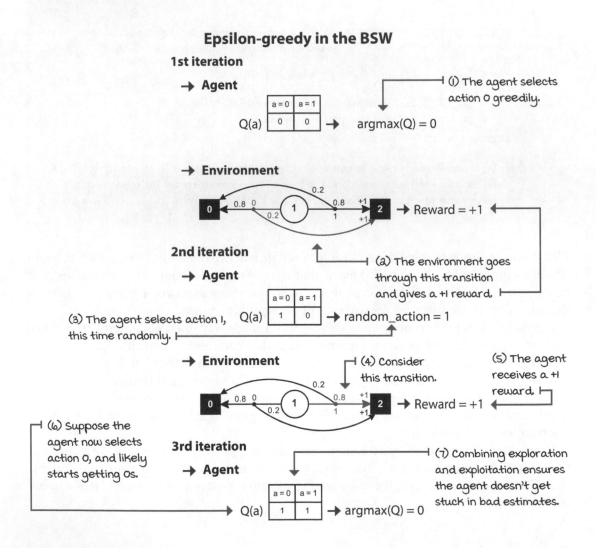

Epsilon-greedy in the BSW

1st iteration

→ **Agent**

(1) The agent selects action 0 greedily.

Q(a) | argmax(Q) = 0

→ **Environment**

(2) The environment goes through this transition and gives a +1 reward.

→ Reward = +1

2nd iteration

→ **Agent**

(3) The agent selects action 1, this time randomly.

Q(a) → random_action = 1

→ **Environment**

(4) Consider this transition.

(5) The agent receives a +1 reward.

→ Reward = +1

(6) Suppose the agent now selects action 0, and likely starts getting 0s.

3rd iteration

→ **Agent**

(7) Combining exploration and exploitation ensures the agent doesn't get stuck in bad estimates.

Q(a) → argmax(Q) = 0

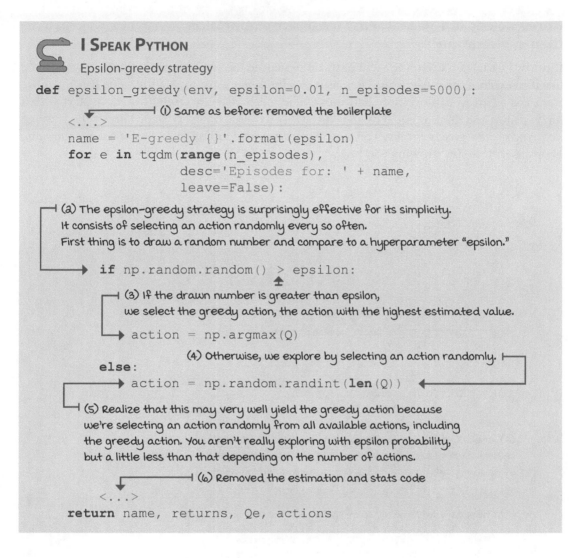

I Speak Python

Epsilon-greedy strategy

```python
def epsilon_greedy(env, epsilon=0.01, n_episodes=5000):
```

(1) Same as before: removed the boilerplate

```python
    <...>
    name = 'E-greedy {}'.format(epsilon)
    for e in tqdm(range(n_episodes),
                  desc='Episodes for: ' + name,
                  leave=False):
```

(2) The epsilon-greedy strategy is surprisingly effective for its simplicity. It consists of selecting an action randomly every so often. First thing is to draw a random number and compare to a hyperparameter "epsilon."

```python
        if np.random.random() > epsilon:
```

(3) If the drawn number is greater than epsilon, we select the greedy action, the action with the highest estimated value.

```python
            action = np.argmax(Q)
```

(4) Otherwise, we explore by selecting an action randomly.

```python
        else:
            action = np.random.randint(len(Q))
```

(5) Realize that this may very well yield the greedy action because we're selecting an action randomly from all available actions, including the greedy action. You aren't really exploring with epsilon probability, but a little less than that depending on the number of actions.

(6) Removed the estimation and stats code

```python
    <...>
    return name, returns, Qe, actions
```

The epsilon-greedy strategy is a random exploration strategy because we use randomness to select the action. First, we use randomness to choose whether to exploit or explore, but also we use randomness to select an exploratory action. There are other random-exploration strategies, such as softmax (discussed later in this chapter), that don't have that first random decision point.

I want you to notice that if epsilon is 0.5 and you have two actions, you can't say your agent will explore 50% of the time, if by "explore" you mean selecting the non-greedy action. Notice that the "exploration step" in epsilon-greedy includes the greedy action. In reality, your agent will explore a bit less than the epsilon value depending on the number of actions.

Decaying epsilon-greedy: First maximize exploration, then exploitation

Intuitively, early on when the agent hasn't experienced the environment enough is when we'd like it to explore the most; while later, as it obtains better estimates of the value functions, we want the agent to exploit more and more. The mechanics are straightforward: start with a high epsilon less than or equal to one, and decay its value on every step. This strategy, called *decaying epsilon-greedy strategy*, can take many forms depending on how you change the value of epsilon. Here I'm showing you two ways.

I Speak Python
Linearly decaying epsilon-greedy strategy

```python
def lin_dec_epsilon_greedy(env,
                           init_epsilon=1.0,
                           min_epsilon=0.01,
                           decay_ratio=0.05,
                           n_episodes=5000):
```
(1) Again, boilerplate is gone!
```python
<...>
name = 'Lin e-greedy {} {} {}'.format(
            init_epsilon, min_epsilon, decay_ratio)
for e in tqdm(range(n_episodes),
            desc='Episodes for: ' + name,
            leave=False):
```
(2) Linearly decaying epsilon-greedy consists of making epsilon decay linearly with the number of steps. We start by calculating the number of episodes we'd like to decay epsilon to the minimum value.
```python
    decay_episodes = n_episodes * decay_ratio
```
(3) Then, calculate the value of epsilon for the current episode.
```python
    epsilon = 1 - e / decay_episodes
    epsilon *= init_epsilon - min_epsilon
    epsilon += min_epsilon
    epsilon = np.clip(epsilon, min_epsilon, init_epsilon)
```
(4) After that, every thing is the same as the epsilon-greedy strategy.
```python
    if np.random.random() > epsilon:
        action = np.argmax(Q)
    else:
        action = np.random.randint(len(Q))
    <...>
return name, returns, Qe, actions
```
(5) Stats are removed here.

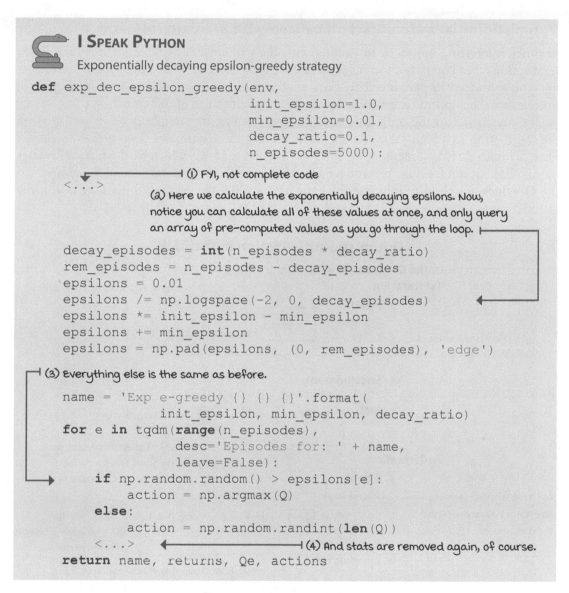

I SPEAK PYTHON
Exponentially decaying epsilon-greedy strategy

```python
def exp_dec_epsilon_greedy(env,
                           init_epsilon=1.0,
                           min_epsilon=0.01,
                           decay_ratio=0.1,
                           n_episodes=5000):
```

(1) FYI, not complete code

`<...>`

(2) Here we calculate the exponentially decaying epsilons. Now, notice you can calculate all of these values at once, and only query an array of pre-computed values as you go through the loop.

```python
    decay_episodes = int(n_episodes * decay_ratio)
    rem_episodes = n_episodes - decay_episodes
    epsilons = 0.01
    epsilons /= np.logspace(-2, 0, decay_episodes)
    epsilons *= init_epsilon - min_epsilon
    epsilons += min_epsilon
    epsilons = np.pad(epsilons, (0, rem_episodes), 'edge')
```

(3) Everything else is the same as before.

```python
    name = 'Exp e-greedy {} {} {}'.format(
            init_epsilon, min_epsilon, decay_ratio)
    for e in tqdm(range(n_episodes),
                desc='Episodes for: ' + name,
                leave=False):
        if np.random.random() > epsilons[e]:
            action = np.argmax(Q)
        else:
            action = np.random.randint(len(Q))
    <...>
    return name, returns, Qe, actions
```

(4) And stats are removed again, of course.

There are many other ways you can handle the decaying of epsilon: from a simple 1/episode to dampened sine waves. There are even different implementations of the same linear and exponential techniques presented. The bottom line is that the agent should explore with a higher chance early and exploit with a higher chance later. Early on, there's a high likelihood that value estimates are wrong. Still, as time passes and you acquire knowledge, the likelihood that your value estimates are close to the actual values increases, which is when you should explore less frequently so that you can exploit the knowledge acquired.

Optimistic initialization: Start off believing it's a wonderful world

Another interesting approach to dealing with the exploration-exploitation dilemma is to treat actions that you haven't sufficiently explored as if they were the best possible actions—like you're indeed in paradise. This class of strategies is known as *optimism in the face of uncertainty*. The optimistic initialization strategy is an instance of this class.

The mechanics of the optimistic initialization strategy are straightforward: we initialize the Q-function to a high value and act greedily using these estimates. Two points to clarify: First "a high value" is something we don't have access to in RL, which we'll address this later in this chapter; but for now, pretend we have that number in advance. Second, in addition to the Q-values, we need to initialize the counts to a value higher than one. If we don't, the Q-function will change too quickly, and the effect of the strategy will be reduced.

Optimistic initialization in the BSW

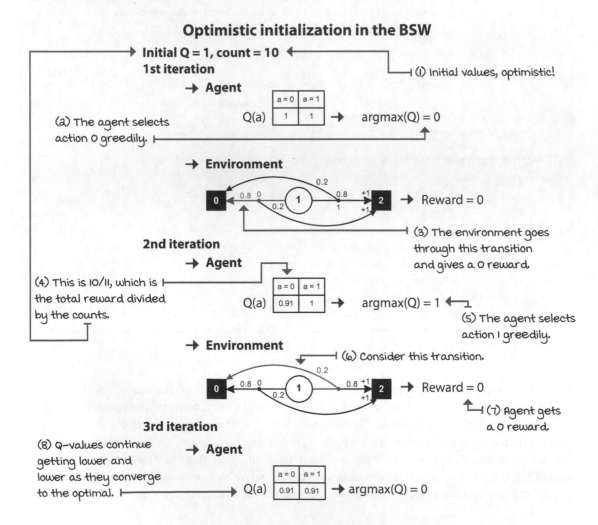

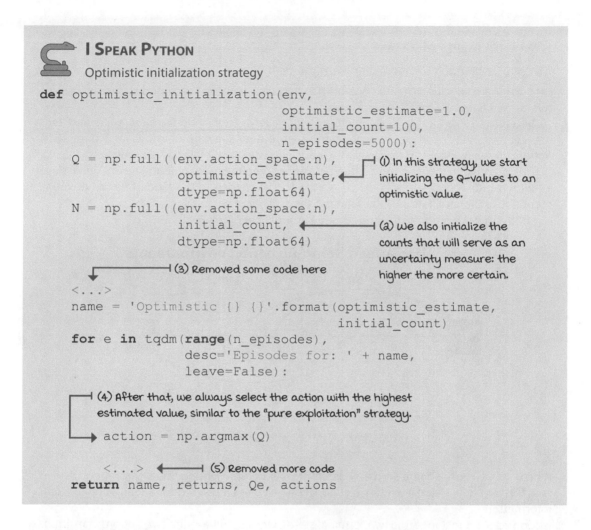

Optimistic initialization strategy

```python
def optimistic_initialization(env,
                              optimistic_estimate=1.0,
                              initial_count=100,
                              n_episodes=5000):
    Q = np.full((env.action_space.n),
                optimistic_estimate,
                dtype=np.float64)
    N = np.full((env.action_space.n),
                initial_count,
                dtype=np.float64)
    <...>
    name = 'Optimistic {} {}'.format(optimistic_estimate,
                                     initial_count)
    for e in tqdm(range(n_episodes),
                  desc='Episodes for: ' + name,
                  leave=False):

        action = np.argmax(Q)

    <...>
    return name, returns, Qe, actions
```

(1) In this strategy, we start initializing the Q-values to an optimistic value.

(2) We also initialize the counts that will serve as an uncertainty measure: the higher the more certain.

(3) Removed some code here

(4) After that, we always select the action with the highest estimated value, similar to the "pure exploitation" strategy.

(5) Removed more code

Interesting, right? Momma was right! Because the agent initially expects to obtain more reward than it actually can, it goes around exploring until it finds sources of reward. As it gains experience, the "naiveness" of the agent goes away, that is, the Q-values get lower and lower until they converge to their actual values.

Again, by initializing the Q-function to a high value, we encourage the exploration of unexplored actions. As the agent interacts with the environment, our estimates will start converging to lower, but more accurate, estimates, allowing the agent to find and converge to the action with the actual highest payoff.

The bottom line is if you're going to act greedily, at least be optimistic.

CONCRETE EXAMPLE
Two-armed Bernoulli bandit environment

Let's compare specific instantiations of the strategies we have presented so far on a set of two-armed Bernoulli bandit environments.

Two-armed Bernoulli bandit environments have a single non-terminal state and two actions. Action 0 has an α chance of paying a +1 reward, and with $1-\alpha$, it will pay 0 rewards. Action 1 has a β chance of paying a +1 reward, and with $1-\beta$, it will pay 0 rewards.

This is similar to the BSW to an extent. BSW has complimentary probabilities: action 0 pays +1 with α probability, and action 1 pays +1 with $1-\alpha$ chance. In this kind of bandit environment, these probabilities are independent; they can even be equal.

Look at my depiction of the two-armed Bernoulli bandit MDP.

Two-armed Bernoulli bandit environments

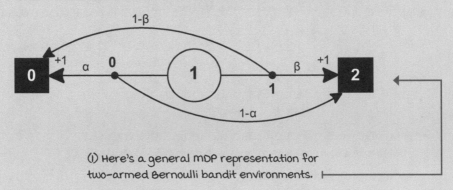

(1) Here's a general MDP representation for two-armed Bernoulli bandit environments.

It's crucial you notice there are many different ways of representing this environment. And in fact, this isn't how I have it written in code, because there's much redundant and unnecessary information.

Consider, for instance, the two terminal states. One could have the two actions transitioning to the same terminal state. But, you know, drawing that would make the graph too convoluted.

The important lesson here is you're free to build and represent environments your own way; there isn't a single correct answer. There are definitely multiple incorrect ways, but there are also multiple correct ways. Make sure to *explore*!

Yeah, I went there.

TALLY IT UP

Simple exploration strategies in two-armed Bernoulli bandit environments

I ran two hyperparameter instantiations of all strategies presented so far: the epsilon-greedy, the two decaying, and the optimistic approach, along with the pure exploitation and exploration baselines on five two-armed Bernoulli bandit environments with probabilities α and β initialized uniformly at random, and five seeds. Results are means across 25 runs.

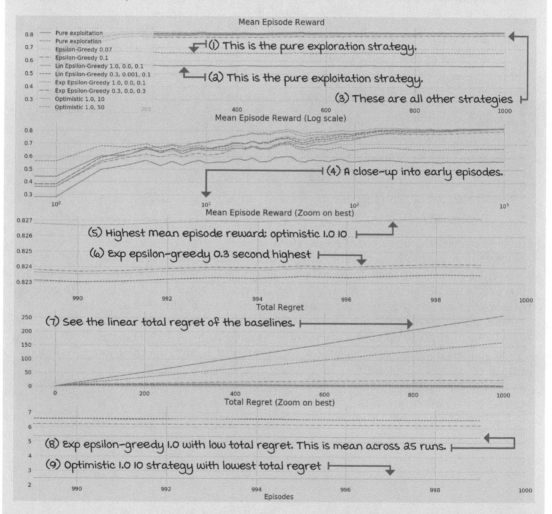

The best performing strategy in this experiment is the optimistic with 1.0 initial Q-values and 10 initial counts. All strategies perform pretty well, and these weren't highly tuned, so it's just for the fun of it and nothing else. Head to chapter 4's Notebook and play, have fun.

IT'S IN THE DETAILS

Simple strategies in the two-armed Bernoulli bandit environments

Let's talk about several of the details in this experiment.

First, I ran five different seeds (12, 34, 56, 78, 90) to generate five different two-armed Bernoulli bandit environments. Remember, all Bernoulli bandits pay a +1 reward with certain probability for each arm.

The resulting environments and their probability of payoff look as follows:

Two-armed bandit with seed 12:

- Probability of reward: [0.41630234, 0.5545003]

Two-armed bandit with seed 34:

- Probability of reward: [0.88039337, 0.56881791]

Two-armed bandit with seed 56:

- Probability of reward: [0.44859284, 0.9499771]

Two-armed bandit with seed 78:

- Probability of reward: [0.53235706, 0.84511988]

Two -armed bandit with seed 90:

- Probability of reward: [0.56461729, 0.91744039]

The mean optimal value across all seeds is 0.83.

All of the strategies were run against each of the environments above with five different seeds (12, 34, 56, 78, 90) to smooth and factor out the randomness of the results. For instance, I first used seed 12 to create a Bernoulli bandit, then I used seeds 12, 34, and so on, to get the performance of each strategy under the environment created with seed 12.

Then, I used seed 34 to create another Bernoulli bandit and used 12, 34, and so on, to evaluate each strategy under the environment created with seed 34. I did this for all strategies in all five environments. Overall, the results are the means over the five environments and five seeds, so 25 different runs per strategy.

I tuned each strategy independently but also manually. I used approximately 10 hyperparameter combinations and picked the top two from those.

Strategic exploration

Alright, imagine you're tasked with writing a reinforcement learning agent to learn driving a car. You decide to implement an epsilon-greedy exploration strategy. You flash your agent into the car's computer, start the car, push that beautiful bright green button, and then your car starts exploring. It will flip a coin and decide to explore with a random action, say to drive on the other side of the road. Like it? Right, me neither. I hope this example helps to illustrate the need for different exploration strategies.

Let me be clear that this example is, of course, an exaggeration. You wouldn't put an untrained agent directly into the real world to learn. In reality, if you're trying to use RL in a real car, drone, or in the real world in general, you'd first pre-train your agent in simulation, and/or use more sample-efficient methods.

But, my point holds. If you think about it, while humans explore, we don't explore randomly. Maybe infants do. But not adults. Maybe imprecision is the source of our randomness, but we don't randomly marry someone just because (unless you go to Vegas.) Instead, I'd argue that adults have a more strategic way of exploring. We know that we're sacrificing short- for long-term satisfaction. We know we want to acquire information. We explore by trying things we haven't sufficiently tried but have the potential to better our lives. Perhaps, our exploration strategies are a combination of estimates and their uncertainty. For instance, we might prefer a dish that we're likely to enjoy, and we haven't tried, over a dish that we like okay, but we get every weekend. Perhaps we explore based on our "curiosity" or our prediction error. For instance, we might be more inclined to try new dishes at a restaurant that we thought would be okay-tasting food, but it resulted in the best food you ever had. That "prediction error" and that "surprise" could be our metric for exploration at times.

In the rest of this chapter, we'll look at slightly more advanced exploration strategies. Several are still random exploration strategies, but they apply this randomness in proportion to the current estimates of the actions. Other exploration strategies take into account the confidence and uncertainty levels of the estimates.

All this being said, I want to reiterate that the epsilon-greedy strategy (and its decaying versions) is still the most popular exploration strategy in use today, perhaps because it performs well, perhaps because of its simplicity. Maybe it's because most reinforcement learning environments today live inside a computer, and there are very few safety concerns with the virtual world. It's important for you to think hard about this problem. Balancing the exploration versus exploitation trade-off, the gathering and utilization of information is central to human intelligence, artificial intelligence, and reinforcement learning. I'm certain the advancements in this area will have a big impact in the fields of artificial intelligence, reinforcement learning, and all other fields interested in this fundamental trade-off.

Softmax: Select actions randomly in proportion to their estimates

Random exploration strategies make more sense if they take into account Q-value estimates. By doing so, if there is an action that has a really low estimate, we're less likely to try it. There's a strategy, called *softmax strategy*, that does this: it samples an action from a probability distribution over the action-value function such that the probability of selecting an action is proportional to its current action-value estimate. This strategy, which is also part of the family of random exploration strategies, is related to the epsilon-greedy strategy because of the injection of randomness in the exploration phase. Epsilon-greedy samples uniformly at random from the full set of actions available at a given state, while softmax samples based on preferences of higher valued actions.

By using the softmax strategy, we're effectively making the action-value estimates an indicator of preference. It doesn't matter how high or low the values are; if you add a constant to all of them, the probability distribution will stay the same. You put preferences over the Q-function and sample an action from a probability distribution based on this preference. The difference between Q-value estimates will create a tendency to select actions with the highest estimates more often, and actions with the lowest estimates less frequently.

We can also add a hyperparameter to control the algorithm's sensitivity to the differences in Q-value estimates. That hyperparameter, called the temperature (a reference to statistical mechanics), works in such a way that as it approaches infinity, the preferences over the Q-values are equal. Basically, we sample an action uniformly. But, as the temperature value approaches zero, the action with the highest estimated value will be sampled with probability of one. Also, we can decay this hyperparameter either linearly, exponentially, or another way. But, in practice, for numerical stability reasons, we can't use infinity or zero as the temperature; instead, we use a very high or very low positive real number, and normalize these values.

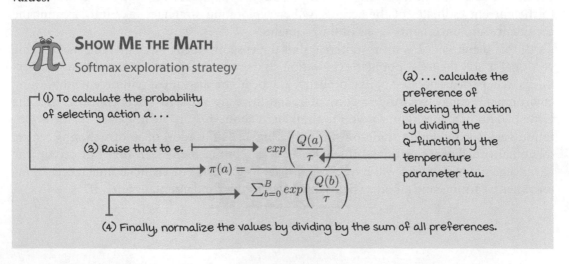

SHOW ME THE MATH

Softmax exploration strategy

(1) To calculate the probability of selecting action a . . .

(3) Raise that to e.

(2) . . . calculate the preference of selecting that action by dividing the Q-function by the temperature parameter tau.

$$\pi(a) = \frac{exp\left(\dfrac{Q(a)}{\tau}\right)}{\sum_{b=0}^{B} exp\left(\dfrac{Q(b)}{\tau}\right)}$$

(4) Finally, normalize the values by dividing by the sum of all preferences.

I SPEAK PYTHON
Softmax strategy

```python
def softmax(env,
            init_temp=1000.0,
            min_temp=0.01,
            decay_ratio=0.04,
            n_episodes=5000):
```

(1) Code was removed here for simplicity.

```python
    <...>
    name = 'SoftMax {} {} {}'.format(init_temp,
                                     min_temp,
                                     decay_ratio)
    for e in tqdm(range(n_episodes),
                  desc='Episodes for: ' + name,
                  leave=False):
```

(2) First, we calculate the linearly decaying temperature the same way we did with the linearly decaying epsilon.

```python
        decay_episodes = n_episodes * decay_ratio
        temp = 1 - e / decay_episodes
        temp *= init_temp - min_temp
        temp += min_temp
        temp = np.clip(temp, min_temp, init_temp)
```

(3) I make sure min_temp isn't 0, to avoid div by zero. Check the Notebook for details.

(4) Next we calculate the probabilities by applying the softmax function to the Q-values.

```python
        scaled_Q = Q / temp
        norm_Q = scaled_Q - np.max(scaled_Q)
        exp_Q = np.exp(norm_Q)
        probs = exp_Q / np.sum(exp_Q)
```

(5) Normalize for numeric stability.

(6) Finally, we make sure we got good probabilities and select the action based on them.

```python
        assert np.isclose(probs.sum(), 1.0)
        action = np.random.choice(np.arange(len(probs)),
                                  size=1,
                                  p=probs)[0]

        _, reward, _, _ = env.step(action)
        <...>
```

(7) Code was removed here too.

```python
    return name, returns, Qe, actions
```

UCB: It's not about optimism, it's about realistic optimism

In the last section, I introduced the optimistic initialization strategy. This is a clever (and perhaps philosophical) approach to dealing with the exploration versus exploitation trade-off, and it's the simplest method in the optimism in the face of uncertainty family of strategies. But, there are two significant inconveniences with the specific algorithm we looked at. First, we don't always know the maximum reward the agent can obtain from an environment. If you set the initial Q-value estimates of an optimistic strategy to a value much higher than its actual maximum value, unfortunately, the algorithm will perform sub-optimally because the agent will take many episodes (depending on the "counts" hyperparameter) to bring the estimates near the actual values. But even worse, if you set the initial Q-values to a value lower than the environment's maximum, the algorithm will no longer be optimistic, and it will no longer work.

The second issue with this strategy as we presented it is that the "counts" variable is a hyperparameter and it needs tuning, but in reality, what we're trying to represent with this variable is the uncertainty of the estimate, which shouldn't be a hyperparameter. A better strategy, instead of believing everything is roses from the beginning and arbitrarily setting certainty measure values, follows the same principles as optimistic initialization while using statistical techniques to calculate the value estimates uncertainty and uses that as a bonus for exploration. This is what the *upper confidence bound* (UCB) strategy does.

In UCB, we're still optimistic, but it's a more a realistic optimism; instead of blindly hoping for the best, we look at the uncertainty of value estimates. The more uncertain a Q-value estimate, the more critical it is to explore it. Note that it's no longer about believing the value will be the "maximum possible," though it might be! The new metric that we care about here is uncertainty; we want to give uncertainty the benefit of the doubt.

SHOW ME THE MATH
Upper confidence bound (UCB) equation

(1) To select the action at episode e...

(2) ... add the Q-value estimates ...

(3) ... and an uncertainty bonus.

$$A_e = \underset{a}{\operatorname{argmax}} \left[Q_e(a) + c\sqrt{\frac{\ln e}{N_e(a)}} \right]$$

(4) Then select the action with the maximum total value.

To implement this strategy, we select the action with the highest sum of its Q-value estimate and an action-uncertainty bonus U. That is, we're going to add a bonus, upper confidence bound $U_t(a)$, to the Q-value estimate of action a, such that if we attempt action a only a few times, the U bonus is large, thus encouraging exploring this action. If the number of attempts is significant, we add only a small U bonus value to the Q-value estimates, because we are more confident of the Q-value estimates; they're not as critical to explore.

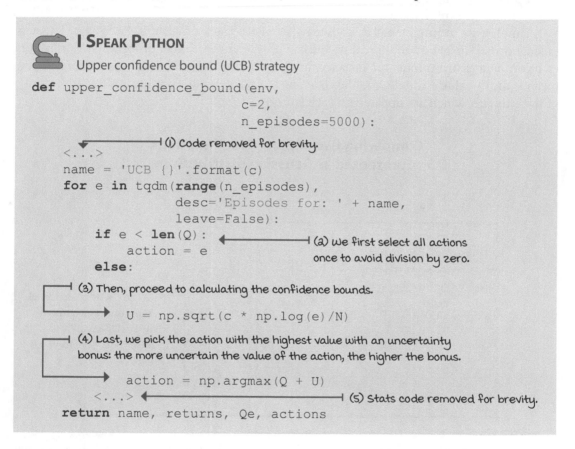

I SPEAK PYTHON
Upper confidence bound (UCB) strategy

```
def upper_confidence_bound(env,
                           c=2,
                           n_episodes=5000):
    <...>                               (1) Code removed for brevity.
    name = 'UCB {}'.format(c)
    for e in tqdm(range(n_episodes),
                  desc='Episodes for: ' + name,
                  leave=False):
        if e < len(Q):                  (2) We first select all actions
            action = e                  once to avoid division by zero.
        else:
                                        (3) Then, proceed to calculating the confidence bounds.
            U = np.sqrt(c * np.log(e)/N)
                                        (4) Last, we pick the action with the highest value with an uncertainty
                                        bonus: the more uncertain the value of the action, the higher the bonus.
            action = np.argmax(Q + U)
    <...>                               (5) Stats code removed for brevity.
    return name, returns, Qe, actions
```

On a practical level, if you plot U as a function of the episodes and counts, you'll notice it's much like an exponentially decaying function with a few differences. Instead of the smooth decay exponential functions show, there's a sharp decay early on and a long tail. This makes it so that early on when the episodes are low, there's a higher bonus for smaller differences between actions, but as more episode pass, and counts increase, the difference in bonuses for uncertainty become smaller. In other words, a 0 versus 100 attempts should give a higher bonus to 0 than to a 100 in a 100 versus 200 attempts. Finally, the c hyperparameter controls the scale of the bonus: a higher c means higher bonuses, lower c lower bonuses.

Thompson sampling: Balancing reward and risk

The UCB algorithm is a frequentist approach to dealing with the exploration versus exploitation trade-off because it makes minimal assumptions about the distributions underlying the Q-function. But other techniques, such as Bayesian strategies, can use priors to make reasonable assumptions and exploit this knowledge. The *Thompson sampling* strategy is a sample-based probability matching strategy that allows us to use Bayesian techniques to balance the exploration and exploitation trade-off.

A simple way to implement this strategy is to keep track of each Q-value as a Gaussian (a.k.a. normal) distribution. In reality, you can use any other kind of probability distribution as prior; beta distributions, for instance, are a common choice. In our case, the Gaussian mean is the Q-value estimate, and the Gaussian standard deviation measures the uncertainty of the estimate, which are updated on each episode.

Comparing two action-value functions represented as Gaussian distributions

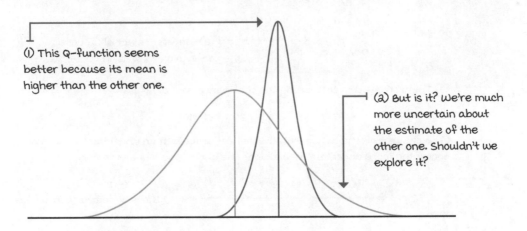

(1) This Q-function seems better because its mean is higher than the other one.

(2) But is it? We're much more uncertain about the estimate of the other one. Shouldn't we explore it?

As the name suggests, in Thompson sampling, we sample from these normal distributions and pick the action that returns the highest sample. Then, to update the Gaussian distributions' standard deviation, we use a formula similar to the UCB strategy in which, early on when the uncertainty is higher, the standard deviation is more significant; therefore, the Gaussian is broad. But as the episodes progress, and the means shift toward better and better estimates, the standard deviations gets lower, and the Gaussian distribution shrinks, and so its samples are more and more likely to be near the estimated mean.

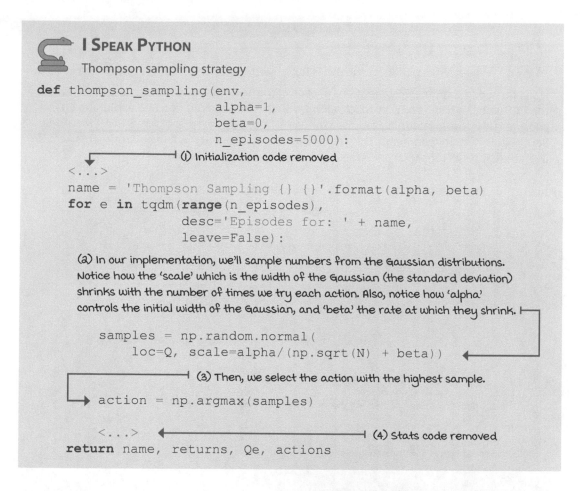

I Speak Python

Thompson sampling strategy

```python
def thompson_sampling(env,
                      alpha=1,
                      beta=0,
                      n_episodes=5000):
```
(1) Initialization code removed
```python
<...>
name = 'Thompson Sampling {} {}'.format(alpha, beta)
for e in tqdm(range(n_episodes),
              desc='Episodes for: ' + name,
              leave=False):
```
(2) In our implementation, we'll sample numbers from the Gaussian distributions. Notice how the 'scale' which is the width of the Gaussian (the standard deviation) shrinks with the number of times we try each action. Also, notice how 'alpha' controls the initial width of the Gaussian, and 'beta' the rate at which they shrink.
```python
    samples = np.random.normal(
        loc=Q, scale=alpha/(np.sqrt(N) + beta))
```
(3) Then, we select the action with the highest sample.
```python
    action = np.argmax(samples)

    <...>
return name, returns, Qe, actions
```
(4) Stats code removed

In this particular implementation, I use two hyperparameters: alpha, to control the scale of the Gaussian, or how large the initial standard deviation will be, and beta, to shift the decay such that the standard deviation shrinks more slowly. In practice, these hyperparameters need little tuning for the examples in this chapter because, as you probably already know, a standard deviation of just five, for instance, is almost a flat-looking Gaussian representing over a ten-unit spread. Given our problems have rewards (and Q-values) between 0 and 1, and approximately between –3 and 3 (the example coming up next), we wouldn't need any Gaussian with standard deviations too much greater than 1.

Finally, I want to reemphasize that using Gaussian distributions is perhaps not the most common approach to Thompson sampling. Beta distributions seem to be the favorites here. I prefer Gaussian for these problems because of their symmetry around the mean, and because their simplicity makes them suitable for teaching purposes. However, I encourage you to dig more into this topic and share what you find.

![Tally marks icon] **TALLY IT UP**

Advanced exploration strategies in two-armed Bernoulli bandit environments

I ran two hyperparameter instantiations of each of the new strategies introduced: the softmax, the UCB, and the Thompson approach, along with the pure exploitation and exploration baselines, and the top-performing simple strategies from earlier on the same five two-armed Bernoulli bandit environments. This is again a total of 10 agents in five environments across five seeds. It's a 25 runs total per strategy. The results are averages across these runs.

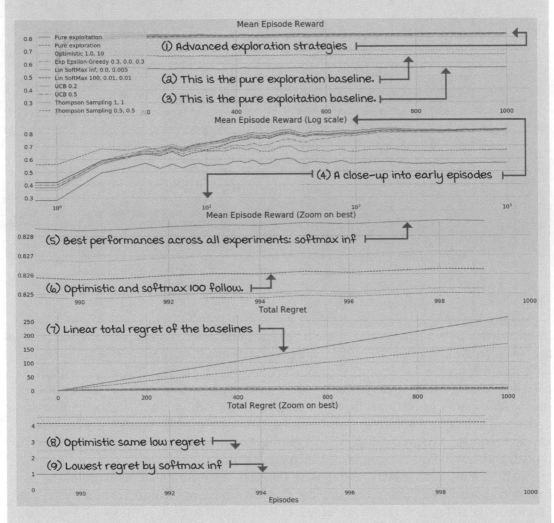

Besides the fact that the optimistic strategy uses domain knowledge that we cannot assume we'll have, the results indicate that the more advanced approaches do better.

CONCRETE EXAMPLE
10-armed Gaussian bandit environments

10-armed Gaussian bandit environments still have a single non-terminal state; they're bandit environments. As you probably can tell, they have ten arms or actions instead of two like their Bernoulli counterparts. But, the probability distributions and reward signals are different from the Bernoulli bandits. First, Bernoulli bandits have a probability of payoff of p, and with 1–p, the arm won't pay anything. Gaussian bandits, on the other hand, will always pay something (unless they sample a 0—more on this next). Second, Bernoulli bandits have a binary reward signal: you either get a +1 or a 0. Instead, Gaussian bandits pay every time by sampling a reward from a Gaussian distribution.

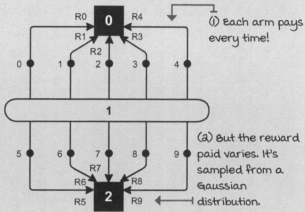

10-armed Gaussian bandit

(I) Each arm pays every time!

(2) But the reward paid varies. It's sampled from a Gaussian distribution.

To create a 10-armed Gaussian bandit environment, you first sample from a standard normal (Gaussian with mean 0 and variance 1) distribution 10 times to get the optimal action-value function $q*(a_k)$ for all k (10) arms. These values will become the mean of the reward signal for each action. To get the reward for action k at episode e, we sample from another Gaussian with mean $q*(a_k)$, and variance 1.

 ## SHOW ME THE MATH
10-armed Gaussian bandit reward function

(I) Prior to interacting with the environment, we create it by calculating the optimal action-value for each arm/action k.

(2) We do this by sampling from a standard Gaussian distribution: that's a Gaussian with mean 0 and variance I.

$$a_\pi(s, a) = q_\pi(s, a) - v_\pi(s)$$

(3) Once our agent is interacting with the environment, to sample the reward R for arm/action k in episode e...

(4) ... we sample from a Gaussian distribution centered on the optimal Q-value, and variance I.

$$R_{k,e} \sim \mathcal{N}(\mu = q^*(a_k), \sigma^2 = 1)$$

TALLY IT UP
Advanced exploration strategies in 10-armed Gaussian bandit environments

I ran the same hyperparameter instantiations of the simple strategies introduced earlier, now on five 10-armed Gaussian bandit environments. This is obviously an "unfair" experiment because these techniques can perform well in this environment if properly tuned, but my goal is to show that the most advanced strategies still do well with the old hyperparameters, despite the change of the environment. You'll see that in the next example.

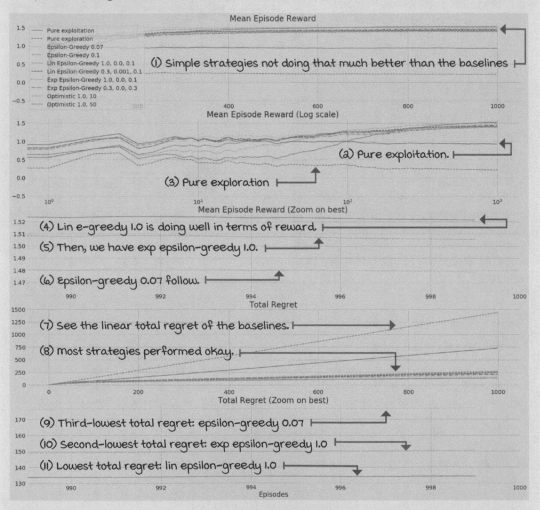

Look at that, several of the most straightforward strategies have the lowest total regret and the highest expected reward across the five different scenarios. Think about that for a sec!

![Tally marks icon] **T**ALLY **I**T **U**P

Advanced exploration strategies in 10-armed Gaussian bandit environments

I then ran the advanced strategies with the same hyperparameters as before. I also added the two baselines and the top two performing simple strategies in the 10-armed Gaussian bandit. As with all other experiments, this is a total of 25 five runs.

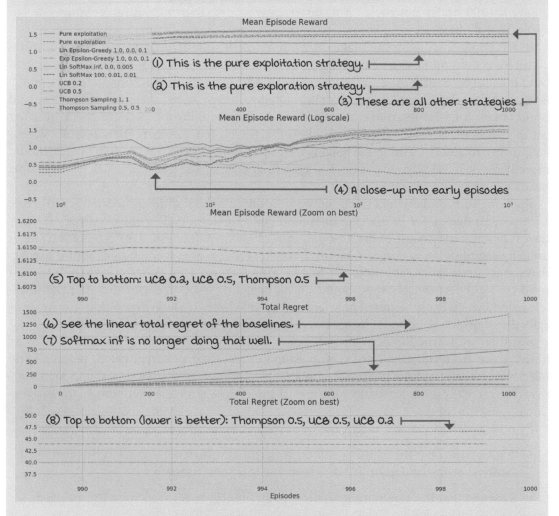

This time only the advanced strategies make it on top, with apretty decent total regret. What you should do now is head to the Notebook and have fun! Please, also share with the community your results, if you run additional experiments. I can't wait to see how you extend these experiments. Enjoy!

Summary

Learning from evaluative feedback is a fundamental challenge that makes reinforcement learning unique. When learning from evaluative feedback, that is, +1, +1.345, +1.5, −100, −4, your agent doesn't know the underlying MDP and therefore cannot determine what the maximum reward it can obtain is. Your agent "thinks": "Well, I got a +1, but I don't know, maybe there's a +100 under this rock?" This uncertainty in the environment forces you to design agents that explore.

But as you learned, you can't take exploration lightly. Fundamentally, exploration wastes cycles that could otherwise be used for maximizing reward, for exploitation, yet, your agent can't maximize reward, or at least pretend it can, without gathering information first, which is what exploration does. All of a sudden, your agent has to learn to balance exploration and exploitation; it has to learn to compromise, to find an equilibrium between two crucial yet competing sides. We've all faced this fundamental trade-off in our lives, so these issues should be intuitive to you: "A bird in the hand is worth two in the bush," yet "A man's reach should exceed his grasp." Pick your poison, and have fun doing it, just don't get stuck to either one. Balance them!

Knowing this fundamental trade-off, we introduced several different techniques to create agents, or strategies, for balancing exploration and exploitation. The epsilon-greedy strategy does it by exploiting most of the time and exploring only a fraction. This exploration step is done by sampling an action at random. Decaying epsilon-greedy strategies capture the fact that agents need more exploration at first because they need to gather information to start making a right decision, but they should quickly begin to exploit to ensure they don't accumulate regret, which is a measure of how far from optimal we act. Decaying epsilon-greedy strategies decay epsilon as episodes increase and, hopefully, as our agent gathers information.

But then we learned about other strategies that try to ensure that "hopefully" is more likely. These strategies take into account estimates and their uncertainty and potential and select accordingly: optimistic initialization, UCB, Thompson sampling, and although softmax doesn't really use uncertainty measures, it explores by selecting randomly in the proportion of the estimates.

By now, you

- Understand that the challenge of learning from evaluative feedback is because agents cannot see the underlying MDP governing their environments

- Learned that the exploration versus exploitation trade-off rises from this problem

- Know about many strategies that are commonly used for dealing with this issue

TWEETABLE FEAT
Work on your own and share your findings

Here are several ideas on how to take what you've learned to the next level. If you'd like, share your results with the rest of the world and make sure to check out what others have done, too. It's a win-win situation, and hopefully, you'll take advantage of it.

- **#gdrl_ch04_tf01:** There are many more techniques for solving bandit environments. Try exploring other resources out there and tell us techniques that are important. Research Bayesian approaches to action selection, and also, action-selection strategies that are based on information gain. What is information gain, again? Why is this important in the context of RL? Can you develop other interesting action-selection strategies, including decaying strategies that use information to decay the exploration rate of agents? For instance, imagine an agent the decays epsilon based on state visits—perhaps on another metric.

- **#gdrl_ch04_tf02:** Can you think of a few other bandit environments that are interesting to examine? Clone my bandit repository (https://github.com/mimoralea/gym-bandits—which is forked, too,) and add a few other bandit environments to it.

- **#gdrl_ch04_tf03:** After bandit environments, but before reinforcement learning algorithms, there's another kind of environment called contextual bandit problems. What are these kinds of problems? Can you help us understand what these are? But, don't just create a blog post about them. Also create a Gym environment with contextual bandits. Is that even possible? Create those environments in a Python package, and another Python package with algorithms that can solve contextual bandit environments.

- **#gdrl_ch04_tf04:** In every chapter, I'm using the final hashtag as a catchall hashtag. Feel free to use this one to discuss anything else that you worked on relevant to this chapter. There's no more exciting homework than that which you create for yourself. Make sure to share what you set yourself to investigate and your results.

Write a tweet with your findings, tag me @mimoralea (I'll retweet), and use the particular hashtag from this list to help interested folks find your results. There are no right or wrong results; you share your findings and check others' findings. Take advantage of this to socialize, contribute, and get yourself out there! We're waiting for you!

Here's a tweet example:

"Hey, @mimoralea. I created a blog post with a list of resources to study deep reinforcement learning. Check it out at <link>. #gdrl_ch01_tf01"

I'll make sure to retweet and help others find your work.

In this chapter

- You will learn about estimating policies when learning from feedback that is simultaneously sequential and evaluative.

- You will develop algorithms for evaluating policies in reinforcement learning environments when the transition and reward functions are unknown.

- You will write code for estimating the value of policies in environments in which the full reinforcement learning problem is on display.

> *I conceive that the great part of the miseries of mankind are brought upon them by false estimates they have made of the value of things.*
>
> — Benjamin Franklin
> Founding Father of the United States
> an author, politician, inventor, and a civic activist

You know how challenging it is to balance immediate and long-term goals. You probably experience this multiple times a day: should you watch movies tonight or keep reading this book? One has an immediate satisfaction to it; you watch the movie, and you go from poverty to riches, from loneliness to love, from overweight to fit, and so on, in about two hours and while eating popcorn. Reading this book, on the other hand, won't really give you much tonight, but maybe, and only maybe, will provide much higher satisfaction in the long term.

And that's a perfect lead-in to precisely the other issue we discussed. How much more satisfaction in the long term, exactly, you may ask. Can we tell? Is there a way to find out? Well, that's the beauty of life: I don't know, you don't know, and we won't know unless we try it out, unless we explore it. Life doesn't give you its MDP; life is uncertain. This is what we studied in the last chapter: balancing information gathering and information utilization.

However, in the previous chapter, we studied this challenge in isolation from the sequential aspect of RL. Basically, you assume your actions have no long-term effect, and your only concern is to find the best thing to do for the current situation. For instance, your concern may be selecting a good movie, or a good book, but without thinking how the movie or the book will impact the rest of your life. Here, your actions don't have a "compounding effect."

Now, in this chapter, we look at agents that learn from feedback that's simultaneously sequential and evaluative; agents need to simultaneously balance immediate and long-term goals, and balance information gathering and utilization. Back to our "movie or book" example, where you need to decide what to do today knowing each decision you make builds up, accumulates, and compounds in the long term. Since you are a near-optimal decision maker under uncertainty, just as most humans, will you watch a movie or keep on reading? Hint!

You're smart. . . . In this chapter, we'll study agents that can learn to estimate the value of policies, similar to the policy-evaluation method, but this time without the MDP. This is often called the prediction problem because we're estimating value functions, and these are defined as the expectation of future discounted rewards, that is, they contain values that depend on the future, so we're learning to predict the future in a sense. Next chapter, we'll look at optimizing policies without MDPs, which is called the control problem because we attempt to improve agents' behaviors. As you'll see in this book, these two are equally essential aspects of RL. In machine learning, the saying goes, "The model is only as good as the data." In RL, I say, "The policy is only as good as the estimates," or, detailed, "The improvement of a policy is only as good as the accuracy and precision of its estimates."

Once again, in DRL, agents learn from feedback that's simultaneously sequential (as opposed to one-shot), evaluative (as opposed to supervised) and sampled (as opposed to exhaustive). In this chapter, we're looking at agents that learn from feedback that's simultaneously sequential and evaluative. We're temporarily shelving the "sampled" part, but we'll open those gates in chapter 8, and there will be fun galore. I promise.

Learning to estimate the value of policies

As I mentioned before, this chapter is about learning to estimate the value of existing policies. When I was first introduced to this prediction problem, I didn't get the motivation. To me, if you want to estimate the value of a policy, the straightforward way of doing it is running the policy repeatedly and averaging what you get.

And, that's definitely a valid approach, and perhaps the most natural. What I didn't realize back then, however, is that there are many other approaches to estimating value functions. Each of these approaches has advantages and disadvantages. Many of the methods can be seen as an exact opposite alternative, but there's also a middle ground that creates a full spectrum of algorithms.

In this chapter, we'll explore a variety of these approaches and dig into their pros and cons, showing you how they relate.

 WITH AN RL ACCENT
Reward vs. return vs. value function

Reward: Refers to the one-step reward signal the agent gets: the agent observes a state, selects an action, and receives a reward signal. The reward signal is the core of RL, but it is *not* what the agent is trying to maximize! Again, the agent isn't trying to maximize the reward! Realize that while your agent maximizes the one-step reward, in the long-term, it's getting less than it could.

Return: Refers to the total discounted rewards. Returns are calculated from any state and usually go until the end of the episode. That is, when a terminal state is reached, the calculation stops. Returns are often referred to as total reward, cumulative reward, sum of rewards, and are commonly discounted: total discounted reward, cumulative discounted reward, sum of discounted reward. But, it's basically the same: a return tells you how much reward your agent *obtained* in an episode. As you can see, returns are better indicators of performance because they contain a long-term sequence, a single-episode history of rewards. But the return isn't what an agent tries to maximize, either! An agent who attempts to obtain the highest possible return may find a policy that takes it through a noisy path; sometimes, this path will provide a high return, but perhaps most of the time a low one.

Value function: Refers to the expectation of returns. Sure, we want high returns, but high in *expectation (on average)*. If the agent is in a noisy environment, or if the agent is using a stochastic policy, it's all fine. The agent is trying to maximize the expected total discounted reward, after all: value functions.

MIGUEL'S ANALOGY

Rewards, returns, value functions, and life

How do you approach life? Do you select actions that are the best for you, or are you one of those kind folks who prioritize others before themselves?

There's no shame either way! Being selfish, to me, is an excellent reward signal. It takes you places. It drives you around. Early on in life, going after the immediate reward can be a pretty solid strategy.

Many people judge others for being "too selfish," but to me, that's the way to get going. Go on and do what you want, what you dream of, what gives you satisfaction, go after the rewards! You'll look selfish and greedy. But you shouldn't care.

As you keep going, you'll realize that going after the rewards isn't the best strategy, even for your benefit. You start seeing a bigger picture. If you overeat candy, your tummy hurts; if you spend all of your money on online shopping, you can go broke.

Eventually, you start looking at the returns. You start understanding that there's more to your selfish and greedy motives. You drop the greedy side of you because it harms you in the long run, and now you can see that. But you stay selfish, you still only think in terms of rewards, just now "total" rewards, returns. No shame about that, either!

At one point, you'll realize that the world moves without you, that the world has many more moving parts than you initially thought, that the world has underlying dynamics that are difficult to comprehend. You now know that "what goes around comes around," one way or another, one day or another, but it does.

You step back once again; now instead of the going after rewards or returns, you go after value functions. You wise up! You learn that the more you help others learn, the more you learn. Not sure why, but it works. The more you love your significant other, the more they love you, crazy! The more you don't spend (save), the more you can spend. How strange! Notice, you're still selfish!

But you become aware of the complex underlying dynamics of the world and can understand that the best for yourself is to better others—a perfect win-win situation.

I'd like the differences between rewards, returns, and value functions to be ingrained in you, so hopefully this should get you thinking for a bit.

Follow the rewards!

Then, the returns!

Then, the value functions.

CONCRETE EXAMPLE
The random walk environment

The primary environment we'll use through this chapter is called the *random walk* (RW). This is a walk, single-row grid-world environment, with five non-terminal states. But it's peculiar, so I want to explain it in two ways.

On the one hand, you can think of the RW as an environment in which the probability of going left when taking the Left action is equal to the probability of going right when taking the Left action, and the probability of going right when taking the Right action is equal to the probability of going left when taking the Right action. In other words, the agent has no control of where it goes! The agent will go left with 50% and right with 50% regardless of the action it takes. It's a random walk, after all. Crazy!

Random walk environment MDP

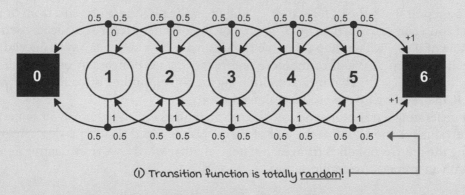

① Transition function is totally <u>random</u>!

But to me, that was an unsatisfactory explanation of the RW, maybe because I like the idea of agents controlling something. What's the point of studying RL (a framework for learning optimal control) in an environment in which there's no possible control!?

Therefore, you can think of the RW as an environment with a deterministic transition function (meaning that if the agent chooses left, the agent moves left, and it moves right if it picks right—as expected). But pretend the agent wants to evaluate a stochastic policy that selects actions uniformly at random. That's half the time it chooses left, and the other half, right.

Either way, the concept is the same: we have a five non-terminal state walk in which the agent moves left and right uniformly at random. The goal is to estimate the expected total discounted reward the agent can obtain given these circumstances.

First-visit Monte Carlo: Improving estimates after each episode

Alright! The goal is to estimate the value of a policy, that is, to learn how much total reward to expect from a policy. More properly, the goal is to estimate the state-value function $v_\pi(s)$ of a policy π. The most straightforward approach that comes to mind is one I already mentioned: it's to run several episodes with this policy collecting hundreds of trajectories, and then calculate averages for every state, just as we did in the bandit environments. This method of estimating value functions is called *Monte Carlo prediction* (MC).

MC is easy to implement. The agent will first interact with the environment using policy π until the agent hits a terminal state S_T. The collection of state S_t, action A_t, reward R_{t+1}, and next state S_{t+1} is called an *experience tuple*. A sequence of experiences is called a *trajectory*. The first thing you need to do is have your agent generate a trajectory.

Once you have a trajectory, you calculate the returns $G_{t:T}$ for every state S_t encountered. For instance, for state S_t, you go from time step t forward, adding up and discounting the rewards received along the way: R_{t+1}, R_{t+2}, R_{t+3}, . . . , R_T, until the end of the trajectory at time step T. Then, you repeat that process for state S_{t+1}, adding up the discounted reward from time step $t+1$ until you again reach T; then for S_{t+2} and so on for all states except S_T, which by definition has a value of 0. $G_{t:T}$ will end up using the rewards from time step $t+1$, up to the end of the episode at time step T. We discount those rewards with an exponentially decaying discount factor: γ^0, γ^1, γ^2, . . . , γ^{T-1}. That means multiplying the corresponding discount factor γ by the reward R, then adding up the products along the way.

After generating a trajectory and calculating the returns for all states S_t, you can estimate the state-value function $v_\pi(s)$ at the end of every episode e and final time step T by merely averaging the returns obtained from each state s. In other words, we're estimating an expectation with an average. As simple as that.

Monte Carlo prediction

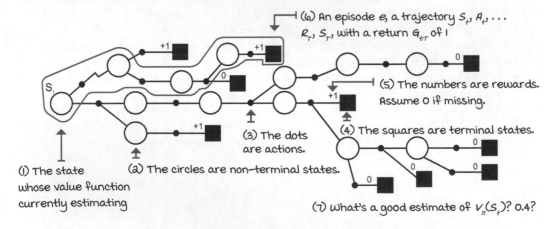

(6) An episode e, a trajectory S_t, A_t, . . . R_T, S_T, with a return $G_{t:T}$ of 1

(5) The numbers are rewards. Assume 0 if missing.

(4) The squares are terminal states.

(3) The dots are actions.

(2) The circles are non-terminal states.

(1) The state whose value function currently estimating

(7) What's a good estimate of $v_\pi(S_t)$? 0.4?

SHOW ME THE MATH

Monte Carlo learning

(1) WARNING: I'm heavily abusing notation to make sure you get the whole picture. In specific, you need to notice when each thing is calculated. For instance, when you see a subscript $t:T$, that means it's derived from time step t until the final time step T. When you see T, that means it's computed at the end of the episode at the final time step T.

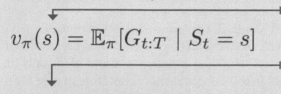

$$v_\pi(s) = \mathbb{E}_\pi[G_{t:T} \mid S_t = s]$$

(2) As a reminder, the action-value function is the expectation of returns. This is a definition good to remember.

(3) And the returns are the total discounted reward.

$$G_{t:T} = R_{t+1} + \gamma R_{t+2} + ... + \gamma^{T-1} R_T$$

(4) In MC, the first thing we do is sample the policy for a trajectory.

(5) Given that trajectory, we can calculate the return for all states encountered.

$$S_t, A_t, R_{t+1}, S_{t+1}, ..., R_T, S_T \sim \pi_{t:T}$$

$$T_T(S_t) = T_T(S_t) + G_{t:T}$$

(6) Then, add up the per-state returns.

(7) And, increment a count (more on this later).

$$N_T(S_t) = N_T(S_t) + 1$$

(8) We can estimate the expectation using the empirical mean, so, the estimated state-value function for a state is the mean return for that state.

$$V_T(S_t) = \frac{T_T(S_t)}{N_T(S_t)}$$

(9) As the counts approach infinity, the estimate will approach the true value.

$$N(s) \to \infty \quad V(s) \to v_\pi(s)$$

(10) But, notice that means can be calculated incrementally. There's no need to keep track of the sum of returns for all states. This equation is equivalent and more efficient.

$$V_T(S_t) = V_{T-1}(S_t) + \frac{1}{N_t(S_t)}\left[G_{t:T} - V_{T-1}(S_t)\right]$$

(11) On this one, we replace the mean for a learning value that can be time dependent or constant.

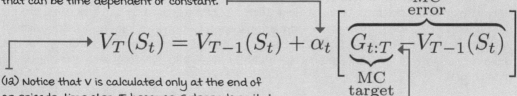

$$V_T(S_t) = V_{T-1}(S_t) + \alpha_t\left[\overbrace{G_{t:T} - V_{T-1}(S_t)}^{\text{MC error}}\right]$$

MC target

(12) Notice that V is calculated only at the end of an episode, time step T, because G depends on it.

Every-visit Monte Carlo: A different way of handling state visits

You probably notice that in practice, there are two different ways of implementing an averaging-of-returns algorithm. This is because a single trajectory may contain multiple visits to the same state. In this case, should we calculate the returns following each of those visits independently and then include all of those targets in the averages, or should we only use the first visit to each state?

Both are valid approaches, and they have similar theoretical properties. The more "standard" version is *first-visit MC* (FVMC), and its convergence properties are easy to justify because each trajectory is an independent and identically distributed (IID) sample of $v_\pi(s)$, so as we collect infinite samples, the estimates will converge to their true values. *Every-visit MC* (EVMC) is slightly different because returns are no longer independent and identically distributed when states are visited multiple times in the same trajectory. But, fortunately for us, EVMC has also been proven to converge given infinite samples.

BOIL IT DOWN
First- vs. every-visit MC

MC prediction estimates $v_\pi(s)$ as the average of returns of π. FVMC uses only one return per state per episode: the return following a first visit. EVMC averages the returns following all visits to a state, even if in the same episode.

0001 A BIT OF HISTORY
First-visit Monte Carlo prediction

You've probably heard the term "Monte Carlo simulations" or "runs" before. Monte Carlo methods, in general, have been around since the 1940s and are a broad class of algorithms that use random sampling for estimation. They are ancient and widespread. However, it was in 1996 that first- and every-visit MC methods were identified in the paper "Reinforcement Learning with Replacing Eligibility Traces," by Satinder Singh and Richard Sutton.

Satinder Singh and Richard Sutton each obtained their PhD in Computer Science from the University of Massachusetts Amherst, were advised by Professor Andy Barto, became prominent figures in RL due to their many foundational contributions, and are now Distinguished Research Scientists at Google DeepMind. Rich got his PhD in 1984 and is a professor at the University of Alberta, whereas Satinder got his PhD in 1994 and is a professor at the University of Michigan.

I SPEAK PYTHON

Exponentially decaying schedule

```python
def decay_schedule(init_value, min_value,
                   decay_ratio, max_steps,
                   log_start=-2, log_base=10):
    decay_steps = int(max_steps * decay_ratio)
    rem_steps = max_steps - decay_steps
```

(1) This function allows you to calculate all the values for alpha for the full training process.

(2) First, calculate the number of steps to decay the values using the decay_ratio variable.

(3) Then, calculate the actual values as an inverse log curve. Notice we then normalize between 0 and 1, and finally transform the points to lay between init_value and min_value.

```python
    values = np.logspace(log_start, 0, decay_steps,
                         base=log_base, endpoint=True)[::-1]
    values = (values - values.min()) / \
                            (values.max() - values.min())
    values = (init_value - min_value) * values + min_value
    values = np.pad(values, (0, rem_steps), 'edge')
    return values
```

I SPEAK PYTHON

Generate full trajectories

```python
def generate_trajectory(pi, env, max_steps=20):
    done, trajectory = False, []
    while not done:
        state = env.reset()
        for t in count():
            action = pi(state)
            next_state, reward, done, _ = env.step(action)
            experience = (state, action, reward,
                          next_state, done)
            trajectory.append(experience)
            if done:
                break
            if t >= max_steps - 1:
                trajectory = []
                break
            state = next_state
    return np.array(trajectory, np.object)
```

(1) This is a straightforward function. It's running a policy and extracting the collection of experience tuples (the trajectories) for off-line processing.

(2) This allows you to pass a maximum number of steps so that you can truncate long trajectories if desired.

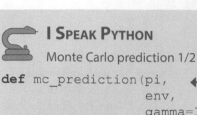

I SPEAK PYTHON

Monte Carlo prediction 1/2

```python
def mc_prediction(pi,
                  env,
                  gamma=1.0,
                  init_alpha=0.5,
                  min_alpha=0.01,
                  alpha_decay_ratio=0.3,
                  n_episodes=500,
                  max_steps=100,
                  first_visit=True):
```

(1) The mc_prediction function works for both first- and every-visit MC. The hyperparameters you see here are standard. Remember, the discount factor, gamma, depends on the environment.

(2) For the learning rate, alpha, I'm using a decaying value from init_alpha of 0.5 down to min_alpha of 0.01, decaying within the first 30% (alpha_decay_ratio of 0.3) of the 500 total max_episodes. We already discussed max_steps on the previous function, so I'm passing the argument around. And first_visit toggles between FVMC and EVMC.

```python
nS = env.observation_space.n
discounts = np.logspace(
       0, max_steps, num=max_steps,
       base=gamma, endpoint=False)
alphas = decay_schedule(
       init_alpha, min_alpha,
       alpha_decay_ratio, n_episodes)
```

(3) This is cool. I'm calculating all possible discounts at once. This logspace function for a gamma of 0.99 and a max_step of 100 returns a 100 number vector: [1, 0.99, 0.9801, . . ., 0.3697].

(4) Here I'm calculating all of the alphas!

(5) Here we're initializing variables we'll use inside the main loop: the current estimate of the state-value function V, and a per-episode copy of V for offline analysis.

```python
V = np.zeros(nS)
V_track = np.zeros((n_episodes, nS))
```

(6) We loop for every episode. Note that we're using 'tqdm' here. This package prints a progress bar, and it's useful for impatient people like me. You may not need it (unless you're also impatient).

```python
    for e in tqdm(range(n_episodes), leave=False):

        trajectory = generate_trajectory(
                pi, env, max_steps)

        visited = np.zeros(nS, dtype=np.bool)
        for t, (state, _, reward, _, _) in enumerate(
                trajectory):
```

(7) Generate a full trajectory.

(8) Initialize a visits check bool vector.

(9) This last line is repeated on the next page for your reading convenience.

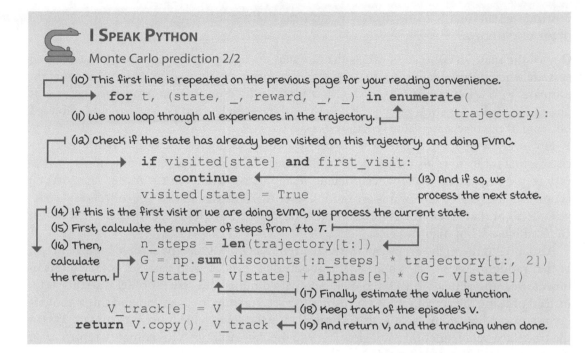

I SPEAK PYTHON

Monte Carlo prediction 2/2

(10) This first line is repeated on the previous page for your reading convenience.

```
for t, (state, _, reward, _, _) in enumerate(
                                        trajectory):
```

(11) We now loop through all experiences in the trajectory.

(12) Check if the state has already been visited on this trajectory, and doing FVMC.

```
        if visited[state] and first_visit:
            continue
        visited[state] = True
```

(13) And if so, we process the next state.

(14) If this is the first visit or we are doing EVMC, we process the current state.

(15) First, calculate the number of steps from *t* to *T*.

(16) Then, calculate the return.

```
        n_steps = len(trajectory[t:])
        G = np.sum(discounts[:n_steps] * trajectory[t:, 2])
        V[state] = V[state] + alphas[e] * (G - V[state])
```

(17) Finally, estimate the value function.

```
    V_track[e] = V
```

(18) Keep track of the episode's V.

```
    return V.copy(), V_track
```

(19) And return V, and the tracking when done.

ŘŁ WITH AN RL ACCENT

Incremental vs. sequential vs. trial-and-error

Incremental methods: Refers to the iterative improvement of the estimates. Dynamic programming is an incremental method: these algorithms iteratively compute the answers. They don't "interact" with an environment, but they reach the answers through successive iterations, incrementally. Bandits are also incremental: they reach good approximations through successive episodes or trials. Reinforcement learning is incremental, as well. Depending on the specific algorithm, estimates are improved on an either per-episode or per-time-step basis, incrementally.

Sequential methods: Refers to learning in an environment with more than one non-terminal (and reachable) state. Dynamic programming is a sequential method. Bandits are not sequential, they are one-state one-step MDPs. There's no long-term consequence for the agent's actions. Reinforcement learning is certainly sequential.

Trial-and-error methods: Refers to learning from interaction with the environment. Dynamic programming is not trial-and-error learning. Bandits are trial-and-error learning. Reinforcement learning is trial-and-error learning, too.

Temporal-difference learning: Improving estimates after each step

One of the main drawbacks of MC is the fact that the agent has to wait until the end of an episode when it can obtain the actual return $G_{t:T}$ before it can update the state-value function estimate $V_T(S_t)$. On the one hand, MC has pretty solid convergence properties because it updates the value function estimate $V_T(S_t)$ toward the actual return $G_{t:T}$, which is an unbiased estimate of the true state-value function $v_\pi(s)$.

However, while the actual returns are pretty accurate estimates, they are also not very precise. Actual returns are also high-variance estimates of the true state-value function $v_\pi(s)$. It's easy to see why: actual returns accumulate many random events in the same trajectory; all actions, all next states, all rewards are random events. The actual return $G_{t:T}$ collects and compounds all of that randomness for multiple time steps, from t to T. Again, the actual return $G_{t:T}$ is unbiased, but high variance.

Also, due to the high variance of the actual returns $G_{t:T}$, MC can be sample inefficient. All of that randomness becomes noise that can only be alleviated with data, lots of data, lots of trajectories, and actual return samples. One way to diminish the issues of high variance is to, instead of using the actual return $G_{t:T}$, estimate a return. Stop for a second and think about it before proceeding: your agent is already calculating the state-value function estimate $V(s)$ of the true state-value function $v_\pi(s)$. How can you use those estimates to estimate a return, even if just partially estimated? Think!

Yes! You can use a single-step reward R_{t+1}, and once you observe the next state S_{t+1}, you can use the state-value function estimates $V(S_{t+1})$ as an estimate of the return at the next step $G_{t+1:T}$. This is the relationship in the equations that *temporal-difference* (TD) methods exploit. These methods, unlike MC, can learn from incomplete episodes by using the one-step actual return, which is the immediate reward R_{t+1}, but then an estimate of the return from the next state onwards, which is the state-value function estimate of the next state $V(S_{t+1})$: that is, $R_{t+1} + \gamma V(S_{t+1})$, which is called the **TD target**.

 BOIL IT DOWN

Temporal-difference learning and bootstrapping

TD methods estimate $v_\pi(s)$ using an estimate of $v_\pi(s)$. It bootstraps and makes a guess from a guess; it uses an estimated return instead of the actual return. More concretely, it uses $R_{t+1} + \gamma V_t(S_{t+1})$ to calculate and estimate $V_{t+1}(S_t)$.

Because it also uses one step of the actual return R_{t+1}, things work out fine. That reward signal R_{t+1} progressively "injects reality" into the estimates.

Show Me the Math
Temporal-difference learning equations

(1) We again start from the definition of the state-value function . . .

$$v_\pi(s) = \mathbb{E}_\pi[G_{t:T} \mid S_t = s]$$

(2) . . . and the definition of the return.

$$G_{t:T} = R_{t+1} + \gamma R_{t+2} + \dots + \gamma^{T-1} R_T$$

(3) From the return, we can rewrite the equation by grouping up some terms. Check it out.

$$
\begin{aligned}
G_{t:T} &= R_{t+1} + \gamma R_{t+2} + \gamma^2 R_{t+3} + \dots + \gamma^{T-1} R_T \\
&= R_{t+1} + \gamma(R_{t+2} + \gamma R_{t+3} + \dots + \gamma^{T-2} R_T) \\
&= R_{t+1} + \gamma G_{t+1:T}
\end{aligned}
$$

(4) Now, the same return has a recursive style.

(5) We can use this new definition to also rewrite the state-value function definition equation.

$$
\begin{aligned}
v_\pi(s) &= \mathbb{E}_\pi[G_{t:T} \mid S_t = s] \\
&= \mathbb{E}_\pi[R_{t+1} + \gamma G_{t+1:T} \mid S_t = s] \\
&= \mathbb{E}_\pi[R_{t+1} + \gamma v_\pi(S_{t+1}) \mid S_t = s]
\end{aligned}
$$

(6) And because the expectation of the returns from the next state is the state-value function of the next state, we get this.

(7) This means we could estimate the state-value function on every time step.

(8) We roll out a single interaction step . . .

$$S_t, A_t, R_{t+1}, S_{t+1} \sim \pi_{t:t+1}$$

(9) . . . and can obtain an estimate $v(s)$ of the true state-value function $v_\pi(s)$ a different way than with MC.

(10) The key difference to realize is we're now estimating $v_\pi(s_t)$ with an estimate of $v_\pi(s_{t+1})$. We're using an estimated, not actual, return.

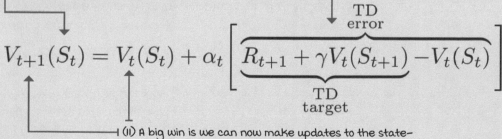

$$V_{t+1}(S_t) = V_t(S_t) + \alpha_t \left[\underbrace{R_{t+1} + \gamma V_t(S_{t+1})}_{\text{TD target}} - V_t(S_t) \right]$$

(11) A big win is we can now make updates to the state-value function estimates $v(s)$ every time step.

I SPEAK PYTHON

The temporal-difference learning algorithm

```python
def td(pi,
       env,
       gamma=1.0,
       init_alpha=0.5,
       min_alpha=0.01,
       alpha_decay_ratio=0.3,
       n_episodes=500):
```

(1) td is a prediction method. It takes in a policy pi, an environment env to interact with, and the discount factor gamma.

(2) The learning method has a configurable hyperparameter alpha, which is the learning rate.

(3) One of the many ways of handling the learning rate is to exponentially decay it. The initial value is init_alpha, min_alpha, the minimum value, and alpha_decay_ratio is the fraction of episodes that it will take to decay alpha from init_alpha to min_alpha.

```python
    nS = env.observation_space.n
    V = np.zeros(nS)
    V_track = np.zeros((n_episodes, nS))
    alphas = decay_schedule(
        init_alpha, min_alpha,
        alpha_decay_ratio, n_episodes)
```

(4) We initialize the variables needed.

(5) And we calculate the learning rate schedule for all episodes . . .

(6) . . . and loop for n_episodes.

```python
    for e in tqdm(range(n_episodes), leave=False):
```

(7) We get the initial state and then enter the interaction loop.

```python
        state, done = env.reset(), False
        while not done:
```

(8) First thing is to sample the policy pi for the action to take in state.

```python
            action = pi(state)
```

(9) We then use the action to interact with the environment... We roll out the policy one step.

```python
            next_state, reward, done, _ = env.step(action)
```

(10) We can immediately calculate a target to update the state-value function estimates . . .

```python
            td_target = reward + gamma * V[next_state] * \
                                                (not done)
```

(11) . . . and with the target, an error.

```python
            td_error = td_target - V[state]
            V[state] = V[state] + alphas[e] * td_error
```

(12) Finally update v(s)

```python
            state = next_state
```

(13) Don't forget to update the state variable for the next iteration. Bugs like this can be hard to find!

```python
        V_track[e] = V
    return V, V_track
```

(14) And return the v function and the tracking variable.

ŘŁ WITH AN RL ACCENT
True vs. actual vs. estimated

True value function: Refers to the exact and perfectly accurate value function, as if given by an oracle. The true value function is the value function agents estimate through samples. If we had the true value function, we could easily estimate returns.

Actual return: Refers to the experienced return, as opposed to an estimated return. Agents can only experience actual returns, but they can use estimated value functions to estimate returns. *Actual return* refers to the full experienced return.

Estimated value function or estimated return: Refers to the rough calculation of the true value function or actual return. "Estimated" means an approximation, a guess. True value functions let you estimate returns, and estimated value functions add bias to those estimates.

Now, to be clear, the TD target is a biased estimate of the true state-value function $v_\pi(s)$, because we use an estimate of the state-value function to calculate an estimate of the state-value function. Yeah, weird, I know. This way of updating an estimate with an estimate is referred to as bootstrapping, and it's much like what the dynamic programming methods we learned about in chapter 3 do. The thing is, though, DP methods bootstrap on the one-step expectation while TD methods bootstrap on a sample of the one-step expectation. That word *sample* makes a whole lot of a difference.

On the good side, while the new estimated return, the TD target, is a biased estimate of the true state-value function $v_\pi(s)$, it also has a much lower variance than the actual return $G_{t:T}$ we use in Monte Carlo updates. This is because the TD target depends only on a single action, a single transition, and a single reward, so there's much less randomness being accumulated. As a consequence, TD methods usually learn much faster than MC methods.

0001 A BIT OF HISTORY
Temporal-difference learning

In 1988, Richard Sutton released a paper titled "Learning to Predict by the Methods of Temporal Differences" in which he introduced the TD learning method. The RW environment we're using in this chapter was also first presented in this paper. The critical contribution of this paper was the realization that while methods such as MC calculate errors using the differences between predicted and actual returns, TD was able to use the difference between temporally successive predictions, thus, the name temporal-difference learning.

TD learning is the precursor of methods such as SARSA, Q-learning, double Q-learning, deep Q-networks (DQN), double deep Q-networks (DDQN), and more. We'll learn about these methods in this book.

TD prediction

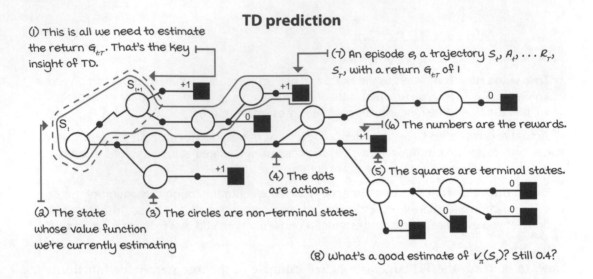

(1) This is all we need to estimate the return $G_{t:T}$. That's the key insight of TD.

(7) An episode e, a trajectory S_t, A_t, ... R_T, S_T, with a return $G_{t:T}$ of 1

(6) The numbers are the rewards.

(2) The state whose value function we're currently estimating

(3) The circles are non-terminal states.

(4) The dots are actions.

(5) The squares are terminal states.

(8) What's a good estimate of $v_\pi(S_t)$? Still 0.4?

 ### IT'S IN THE DETAILS

FVMC, EVMC, and TD on the RW environment

I ran these three policy evaluation algorithms on the RW environment. All methods evaluated an all-left policy. Now, remember, the dynamics of the environment make it such that any action, Left or Right, has a uniform probability of transition (50% Left and 50% Right). In this case, the policy being evaluated is irrelevant.

I used the same schedule for the learning rate, alpha, in all algorithms: alpha starts at 0.5, and it decreases exponentially to 0.01 in 250 episodes out of the 500 total episodes. That's 50% of the total number of episodes. This hyperparameter is essential. Often, alpha is a positive constant less than 1. Having a constant alpha helps with learning in non-stationary environments.

However, I chose to decay alpha to show convergence. The way I'm decaying alpha helps the algorithms get close to converging, but because I'm not decreasing alpha all the way to zero, they don't fully converge. Other than that, these results should help you gain some intuition about the differences between these methods.

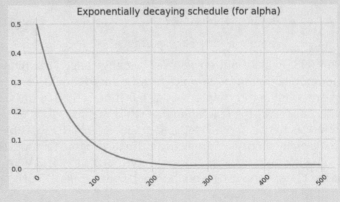

Exponentially decaying schedule (for alpha)

Tally it Up

MC and TD both nearly converge to the true state-value function

(1) Here I'll show only first-visit Monte Carlo prediction (FVMC) and temporal-difference learning (TD). If you head to the Notebook for this chapter, you'll also see the results for every-visit Monte Carlo prediction, and several additional plots that may be of interest to you!

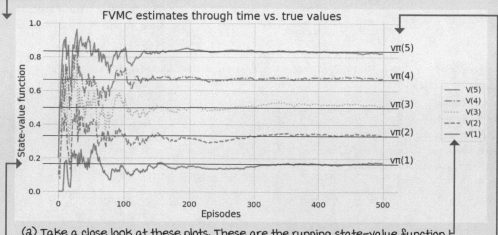

(2) Take a close look at these plots. These are the running state-value function estimates $V(s)$ of an all-left policy in the random-walk environment. As you can see in these plots, both algorithms show near-convergence to the true values.

(3) Now, see the difference trends of these algorithms. FVMC running estimates are very noisy; they jump back and forth around the true values.

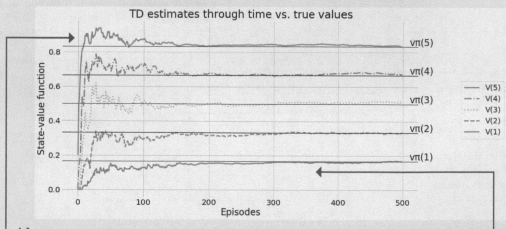

(4) TD running estimates don't jump as much, but they are off-center for most of the episodes. For instance $V(5)$ is usually higher than $V_\pi(5)$, while $V(1)$ is usually lower than $V_\pi(1)$. But if you compare those values with FVMC estimates, you notice a different trend.

Tally it Up

MC estimates are noisy; TD estimates are off-target

$$V_T(S_t) = V_{T-1}(S_t) + \alpha_t \left[\overbrace{\underbrace{G_{t:T}}_{\substack{\text{MC} \\ \text{target}}} - V_{T-1}(S_t)}^{\substack{\text{MC} \\ \text{error}}} \right]$$

(1) If we get a close-up (log-scale plot) of these trends, you'll see what's happening. mc estimates jump around the true values. This is because of the high variance of the mc targets.

(2) A couple of pros though; first, you can see all estimates get close to their true values *very early* on. Also, the estimates jump around the *true* values.

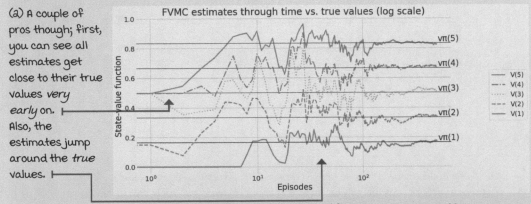

$$V_{t+1}(S_t) = V_t(S_t) + \alpha_t \left[\overbrace{\underbrace{G_{t:t+1}}_{\substack{\text{TD} \\ \text{target}}} - V_t(S_t)}^{\substack{\text{TD} \\ \text{error}}} \right]$$

(3) TD estimates are off-target most of the time, but they're less jumpy. This is because TD targets are low variance, though biased. They use an estimated return for target.

(4) The bias shows, too. In the end, TD targets give up accuracy in order to become more precise. Also, they take a bit long before estimates ramp up, at least in this environment.

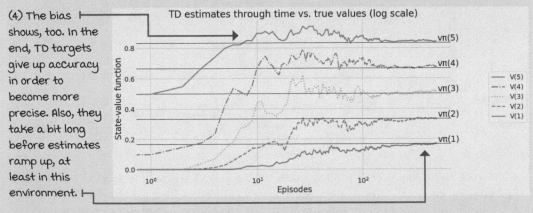

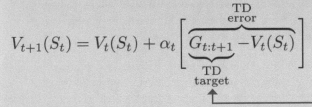

Learning to estimate from multiple steps   149

MC targets high variance; TD targets bias

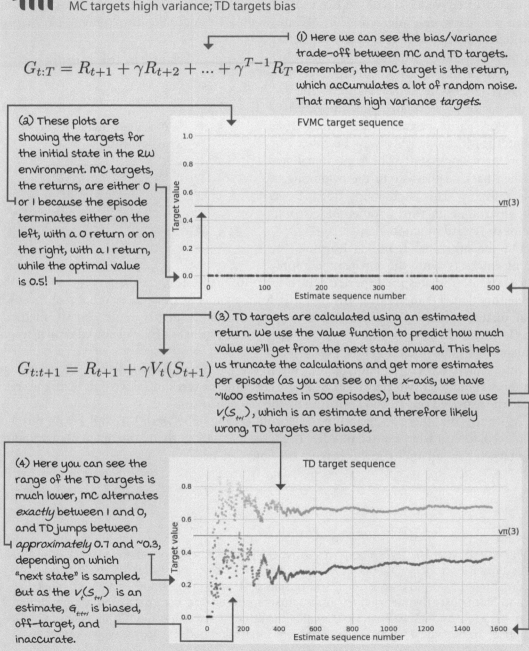

$$G_{t:T} = R_{t+1} + \gamma R_{t+2} + ... + \gamma^{T-1} R_T$$

(1) Here we can see the bias/variance trade-off between MC and TD targets. Remember, the MC target is the return, which accumulates a lot of random noise. That means high variance *targets*.

(2) These plots are showing the targets for the initial state in the RW environment. MC targets, the returns, are either 0 or 1 because the episode terminates either on the left, with a 0 return or on the right, with a 1 return, while the optimal value is 0.5!

(3) TD targets are calculated using an estimated return. We use the value function to predict how much value we'll get from the next state onward. This helps us truncate the calculations and get more estimates per episode (as you can see on the x-axis, we have ~1600 estimates in 500 episodes), but because we use $V_t(S_{t+1})$, which is an estimate and therefore likely wrong, TD targets are biased.

$$G_{t:t+1} = R_{t+1} + \gamma V_t(S_{t+1})$$

(4) Here you can see the range of the TD targets is much lower, MC alternates *exactly* between 1 and 0, and TD jumps between *approximately* 0.7 and ~0.3, depending on which "next state" is sampled. But as the $V_t(S_{t+1})$ is an estimate, $G_{t:t+1}$ is biased, off-target, and inaccurate.

Learning to estimate from multiple steps

In this chapter, we looked at the two central algorithms for estimating value functions of a given policy through interaction. In MC methods, we sample the environment all the way through the end of the episode before we estimate the value function. These methods spread the actual return, the discounted total reward, on all states. For instance, if the discount factor is less than 1 and the return is only 0 or 1, as is the case in the RW environment, the MC target will always be either 0 or 1 for every single state. The same signal gets pushed back all the way to the beginning of the trajectory. This is obviously not the case for environments with a different discount factor or reward function.

What's in the middle?

On the other hand, in TD learning, the agent interacts with the environment only once, and it estimates the expected return to go to, then estimates the target, and then the value function. TD methods bootstrap: they form a guess from a guess. What that means is that, instead of waiting until the end of an episode to get the actual return like MC methods do, TD methods use a single-step reward but then an estimate of the expected return-to-go, which is the value function of the next state.

But, is there something in between? I mean, that's fine that TD bootstraps after one step, but how about after two steps? Three? Four? How many steps should we wait before we estimate the expected return and bootstrap on the value function?

As it turns out, there's a spectrum of algorithms lying in between MC and TD. In this section, we'll look at what's in the middle. You'll see that we can tune how much bootstrapping our targets depend on, letting us balance bias and variance.

☺! Miguel's Analogy

MC and TD have distinct personalities

I like to think of MC-style algorithms as type-A personality agents and TD-style algorithms as type-B personality agents. If you look it up you'll see what I mean. Type-A people are outcome-driven, time-conscious, and businesslike, while type-B are easygoing, reflective, and hippie-like. The fact that MC uses actual returns and TD uses predicted returns should make you wonder if there is a personality to each of these target types. Think about it for a while; I'm sure you'll be able to notice several interesting patterns to help you remember.

N-step TD learning: Improving estimates after a couple of steps

The motivation should be clear; we have two extremes, Monte Carlo methods and temporal-difference methods. One can perform better than the other, depending on the circumstances. MC is an infinite-step method because it goes all the way until the end of the episode.

I know, "infinite" may sound confusing, but recall in chapter 2, we defined a terminal state as a state with all actions and all transitions coming from those actions looping back to that same state with no reward. This way, you can think of an agent "getting stuck" in this loop forever and therefore doing an infinite number of steps without accumulating a reward or updating the state-value function.

TD, on the other hand, is a one-step method because it interacts with the environment for a single step before bootstrapping and updating the state-value function. You can generalize these two methods into an *n*-step method. Instead of doing a single step, like TD, or the full episode like MC, why not use *n*-steps to calculate value functions and abstract *n* out? This method is called *n-step TD*, which does an *n*-step bootstrapping. Interestingly, an intermediate *n* value often performs the better than either extreme. You see, you shouldn't become an extremist!

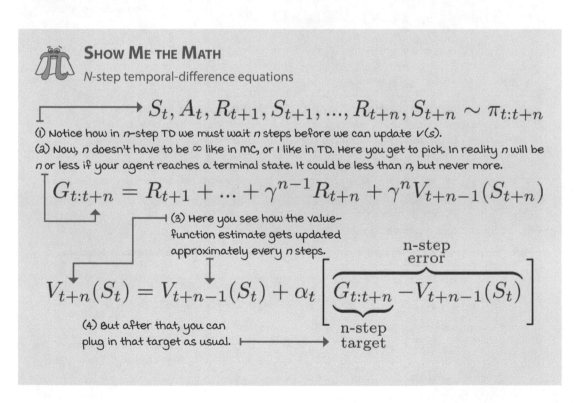

SHOW ME THE MATH

N-step temporal-difference equations

$$S_t, A_t, R_{t+1}, S_{t+1}, ..., R_{t+n}, S_{t+n} \sim \pi_{t:t+n}$$

(1) Notice how in *n*-step TD we must wait *n* steps before we can update $v(s)$.

(2) Now, *n* doesn't have to be ∞ like in MC, or 1 like in TD. Here you get to pick. In reality *n* will be *n* or less if your agent reaches a terminal state. It could be less than *n*, but never more.

$$G_{t:t+n} = R_{t+1} + ... + \gamma^{n-1} R_{t+n} + \gamma^n V_{t+n-1}(S_{t+n})$$

(3) Here you see how the value-function estimate gets updated approximately every *n* steps.

n-step error

$$V_{t+n}(S_t) = V_{t+n-1}(S_t) + \alpha_t \left[\underbrace{G_{t:t+n}}_{\text{n-step target}} - V_{t+n-1}(S_t) \right]$$

(4) But after that, you can plug in that target as usual.

I Speak Python

N-step TD 1/2

```python
def ntd(pi,
        env,
        gamma=1.0,
        init_alpha=0.5,
        min_alpha=0.01,
        alpha_decay_ratio=0.5,
        n_step=3,
        n_episodes=500):
```

(1) Here's my implementation of the *n*-step TD algorithm. There are many ways you can code this up; this is one of them for your reference.

(2) Here we're using the same hyperparameters as before. Notice n_step is a default of 3. That is three steps and then bootstrap, or less if we hit a terminal state, in which case we don't bootstrap (again, the value of a terminal state is zero by definition.)

```python
nS = env.observation_space.n
V = np.zeros(nS)
V_track = np.zeros((n_episodes, nS))
```

(3) Here we have the usual suspects.

```python
alphas = decay_schedule(
        init_alpha, min_alpha,
        alpha_decay_ratio, n_episodes)
```

(4) Calculate all alphas in advance.

(5) Now, here's a hybrid between MC and TD. Notice we calculate the discount factors, but instead of going to max_steps like in my MC implementation, we go to n_step + 1 to include *n* steps and the bootstrapping estimate.

```python
discounts = np.logspace(
        0, n_step+1, num=n_step+1, base=gamma, endpoint=False)
```

(6) We get into the episodes loop.

```python
    for e in tqdm(range(n_episodes), leave=False):
```

(7) This path variable will hold the n_step-most-recent experiences. A partial trajectory.

```python
        state, done, path = env.reset(), False, []
```

(8) We're going until we hit done and the path is set to none. You'll see soon.

```python
        while not done or path is not None:
            path = path[1:]
```

(9) Here, we're "popping" the first element of the path.

```python
            while not done and len(path) < n_step:
```

(10) This line repeats on the next page.

I SPEAK PYTHON

N-step TD 2/2

(11) Same. Just for you to follow the indentation.

```
while not done and len(path) < n_step:
```

(12) This is the interaction block. We're basically collecting experiences until we hit done or the length of the path is equal to n_step.

```
    action = pi(state)
    next_state, reward, done, _ = env.step(action)
    experience = (state, reward, next_state, done)
    path.append(experience)
    state = next_state
    if done:
        break
```

(13) *n* here could be 'n_step' but it could also be a smaller number if a terminal state is in the 'path.'

```
n = len(path)
est_state = path[0][0]
```

(14) Here we're extracting the state we're estimating, which isn't state.

(15) rewards is a vector of all rewards encountered from the est_state until *n*.

```
rewards = np.array(path)[:,1]
```

(16) partial_return is a vector of *discounted* rewards from est_state to *n*.

```
partial_return = discounts[:n] * rewards
```

(17) bs_val is the bootstrapping value. Notice that in this case next state is correct.

```
bs_val = discounts[-1] * V[next_state] * (not done)
```

(18) ntd_target is the sum of the partial return and bootstrapping value.

```
ntd_target = np.sum(np.append(partial_return,
                              bs_val))
```

(19) This is the error, like we've been calculating all along.

```
ntd_error = ntd_target - V[est_state]
```

(20) The update to the state-value function

```
V[est_state] = V[est_state] + alphas[e] * ntd_error
```

(21) Here we set path to None to break out of the episode loop, if path has only one experience and the done flag of that experience is True (only a terminal state in path.)

```
    if len(path) == 1 and path[0][3]:
        path = None
V_track[e] = V
return V, V_track
```

(22) We return V and V_track as usual.

Forward-view TD(λ): Improving estimates of all visited states

But, a question emerges: what is a good *n* value, then? When should you use a one-step, two-step, three-step, or anything else? I already gave practical advice that values of *n* higher than one are usually better, but we shouldn't go all the way out to actual returns either. Bootstrapping helps, but its bias is a challenge.

How about using a weighted combination of all *n*-step targets as a single target? I mean, our agent could go out and calculate the *n*-step targets corresponding to the one-, two-, three-, . . ., infinite-step target, then mix all of these targets with an exponentially decaying factor. Gotta have it!

This is what a method called *forward-view TD(λ)* does. Forward-view TD(λ) is a prediction method that combines multiple *n*-steps into a single update. In this particular version, the agent will have to wait until the end of an episode before it can update the state-value function estimates. However, another method, called, *backward-view TD(λ)*, can split the corresponding updates into partial updates and apply those partial updates to the state-value function estimates on every step, like leaving a trail of TD updates along a trajectory. Pretty cool, right? Let's take a deeper look.

Generalized bootstrapping

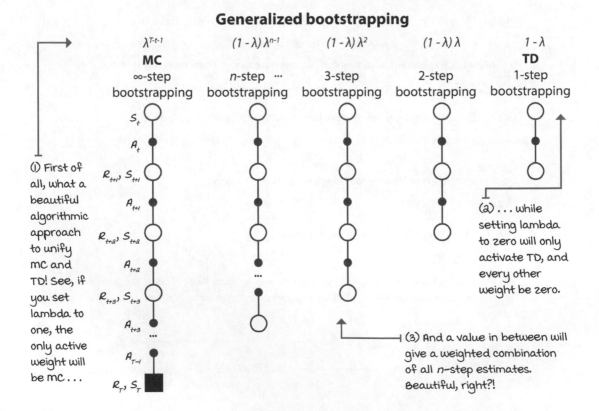

SHOW ME THE MATH
Forward-view TD(λ)

(1) Sure, this is a loaded equation; we'll unpack it here. The bottom line is that we're using all n-step returns until the final step T, and weighting it with an exponentially decaying value.

$$G_{t:T}^{\lambda} = (1 - \lambda) \sum_{n=1}^{T-t-1} \lambda^{n-1} G_{t:t+n} + \lambda^{T-t-1} G_{t:T}$$

Sum of weighted returns from 1-step to T-1 steps

Weighted final return (T)

(2) The thing is, because T is variable, we need to weight the actual return with a normalizing value so that all weights add up to 1.

(3) All this equation is saying is that we'll calculate the one-step return and weight it with the following factor . . .

$$G_{t:t+1} = R_{t+1} + \gamma V_t(S_{t+1})$$

$\longmapsto 1 - \lambda$

(4) . . . and also the two-step return and weight it with this factor.

$$G_{t:t+2} = R_{t+1} + \gamma R_{t+2} + \gamma^2 V_{t+1}(S_{t+2})$$

$(1 - \lambda)\lambda$

(5) Then the same for the three-step return and this factor.

$$G_{t:t+3} = R_{t+1} + \gamma R_{t+2} + \gamma^2 R_{t+3} + \gamma^3 V_{t+2}(S_{t+3})$$

$(1 - \lambda)\lambda^2$

(6) You do this for all n-steps . . .

$$G_{t:t+n} = R_{t+1} + ... + \gamma^{n-1} R_{t+n} + \gamma^n V_{t+n-1}(S_{t+n})$$

$(1 - \lambda)\lambda^{n-1}$

(7) . . . until your agent reaches a terminal state. Then you weight by this normalizing factor.

$$G_{t:T} = R_{t+1} + \gamma R_{t+2} + ... + \gamma^{T-1} R_T$$

$\longrightarrow \lambda^{T-t-1}$

(8) Notice the issue with this approach is that you must sample an entire trajectory before you can calculate these values.

(9) Here you have it, V will become available at time T . . .

$$S_t, A_t, R_{t+1}, S_{t+1}, ..., R_T, S_T \sim \pi_{t:T}$$

$\lambda-\text{error}$

$$V_T(S_t) = V_{T-1}(S_t) + \alpha_t \left[\overbrace{G_{t:T}^{\lambda} - V_{T-1}(S_t)} \right]$$

λ-return

(10) . . . because of this.

TD(λ): Improving estimates of all visited states after each step

MC methods are under "the curse of the time step" because they can only apply updates to the state-value function estimates after reaching a terminal state. With *n*-step bootstrapping, you're still under "the curse of the time step" because you still have to wait until *n* interactions with the environment have passed before you can make an update to the state-value function estimates. You're basically playing catch-up with an *n*-step delay. For instance, in a five-step bootstrapping method, you'll have to wait until you've seen five (or fewer when reaching a terminal state) states, and five rewards before you can make any calculations, a little bit like MC methods.

With forward-view TD(λ), we're back at MC in terms of the time step; the forward-view TD(λ) must also wait until the end of an episode before it can apply the corresponding update to the state-value function estimates. But at least we gain something: we can get lower-variance targets if we're willing to accept bias.

In addition to generalizing and unifying MC and TD methods, backward-view TD(λ), or **TD(λ)** for short, can still tune the bias/variance trade-off in addition to the ability to apply updates on every time step, just like TD.

The mechanism that provides TD(λ) this advantage is known as *eligibility traces*. An eligibility trace is a memory vector that keeps track of recently visited states. The basic idea is to track the states that are eligible for an update on every step. We keep track, not only of whether a state is eligible or not, but also by how much, so that the corresponding update is applied correctly to eligible states.

Eligibility traces for a four-state environment during an eight-step episode

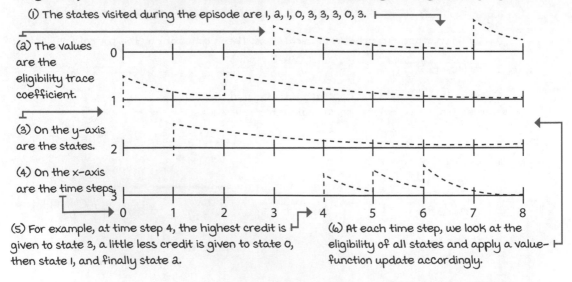

(1) The states visited during the episode are 1, 2, 1, 0, 3, 3, 3, 0, 3.

(2) The values are the eligibility trace coefficient.

(3) On the y-axis are the states.

(4) On the x-axis are the time steps.

(5) For example, at time step 4, the highest credit is given to state 3, a little less credit is given to state 0, then state 1, and finally state 2.

(6) At each time step, we look at the eligibility of all states and apply a value-function update accordingly.

For example, all eligibility traces are initialized to zero, and when you encounter a state, you add a one to its trace. Each time step, you calculate an update to the value function for all states and multiply it by the eligibility trace vector. This way, only eligible states will get updated. After the update, the eligibility trace vector is decayed by the λ (weight mix-in factor) and γ (discount factor), so that future reinforcing events have less impact on earlier states. By doing this, the most recent states get more significant credit for a reward encountered in a recent transition than those states visited earlier in the episode, given that λ isn't set to one; otherwise, this is similar to an MC update, which gives equal credit (assuming no discounting) to all states visited during the episode.

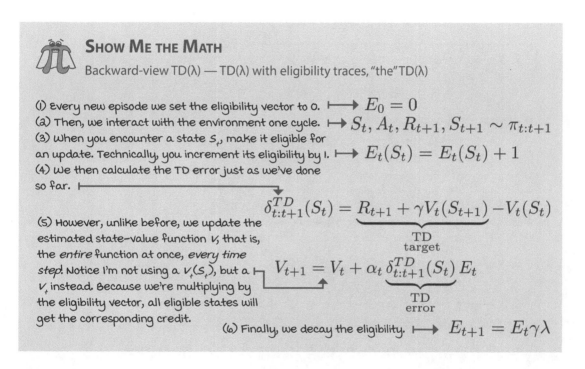

Show Me the Math

Backward-view TD(λ) — TD(λ) with eligibility traces, "the" TD(λ)

(1) Every new episode we set the eligibility vector to 0. $\longmapsto E_0 = 0$

(2) Then, we interact with the environment one cycle. $\longmapsto S_t, A_t, R_{t+1}, S_{t+1} \sim \pi_{t:t+1}$

(3) When you encounter a state s_t, make it eligible for an update. Technically, you increment its eligibility by 1. $\longmapsto E_t(S_t) = E_t(S_t) + 1$

(4) We then calculate the TD error just as we've done so far.

$$\delta_{t:t+1}^{TD}(S_t) = \underbrace{R_{t+1} + \gamma V_t(S_{t+1})}_{\substack{\text{TD} \\ \text{target}}} - V_t(S_t)$$

(5) However, unlike before, we update the estimated state-value function V, that is, the *entire* function at once, *every time step*! Notice I'm not using a $V_t(S_t)$, but a V_t instead. Because we're multiplying by the eligibility vector, all eligible states will get the corresponding credit.

$$V_{t+1} = V_t + \alpha_t \underbrace{\delta_{t:t+1}^{TD}(S_t)}_{\substack{\text{TD} \\ \text{error}}} E_t$$

(6) Finally, we decay the eligibility. $\longmapsto E_{t+1} = E_t \gamma \lambda$

A final thing I wanted to reiterate is that TD(λ) when $\lambda=0$ is equivalent to the TD method we learned about before. For this reason, TD is often referred to as **TD(0)**; on the other hand, TD(λ), when $\lambda=1$ is equivalent to MC, well kind of. In reality, it's equal to MC assuming offline updates, assuming the updates are accumulated and applied at the end of the episode. With online updates, the estimated state-value function changes likely every step, and therefore the bootstrapping estimates vary, changing, in turn, the progression of estimates. Still, **TD(1)** is commonly assumed equal to MC. Moreover, a recent method, called *true online TD(λ)*, is a different implementation of TD(λ) that achieves perfect equivalence of TD(0) with TD and TD(1) with MC.

⌇ | SPEAK PYTHON

The TD(λ) algorithm, a.k.a. backward-view TD(λ)

```
def td_lambda(pi,
              env,
              gamma=1.0,
              init_alpha=0.5,
              min_alpha=0.01,
              alpha_decay_ratio=0.3,
              lambda_=0.3,
              n_episodes=500):
```

(1) The method td_lambda has a signature very similar to all other methods. The only new hyperparameter is lambda_ (the underscore is because lambda is a restricted keyword in Python).

(2) Set the usual suspects.

```
    nS = env.observation_space.n
    V = np.zeros(nS)
    V_track = np.zeros((n_episodes, nS))
    E = np.zeros(nS)
    alphas = decay_schedule(
        init_alpha, min_alpha,
        alpha_decay_ratio, n_episodes)
```

(3) Add a new guy: the eligibility trace vector.

(4) Calculate alpha for all episodes.

(5) Here we enter the episode loop.

```
    for e in tqdm(range(n_episodes), leave=False):
        E.fill(0)
```

(6) Set E to zero every new episode.

```
        state, done = env.reset(), False
```

(7) Set initial variables.

```
        while not done:
            action = pi(state)
            next_state, reward, done, _ = env.step(action)
```

(8) Get into the time step loop.

(9) We first interact with the environment for one step and get the experience tuple.

(10) Then, we use that experience to calculate the TD error as usual.

```
            td_target = reward + gamma * V[next_state] * \
                                                    (not done)
            td_error = td_target - V[state]
```

(11) We increment the eligibility of state by 1.

```
            E[state] = E[state] + 1
            V = V + alphas[e] * td_error * E
            E = gamma * lambda_ * E
```

(12) And apply the error update to all eligible states as indicated by E.

```
            state = next_state
        V_track[e] = V
    return V, V_track
```

(13) We decay E . . .

(14) . . . and continue our lives as usual.

Tally it Up
Running estimates that *n*-step TD and TD(λ) produce in the RW environment

(1) I think the most interesting part of the differences and similarities of MC, TD, *n*-step TD, and TD(lambda) can be visualized side by side. For this, I highly recommend you head to the book repository and check out the corresponding Notebook for this chapter. You'll find much more than what I've shown you in the text.

(2) But for now I can highlight that *n*-step TD curves are a bit more like MC: noisy and centered, while TD(lambda) is a bit more like TD: smooth and off-target.

(3) When we look at the log-scale plots, we can see how the high variance estimates of *n*-step TD (at least higher than TD(lambda) in this experiment), and how the running estimates move above and below the true values, though they're centered.

(4) TD(lambda) values aren't centered, but are also much smoother than MC. These two are interesting properties. Go compare them with the rest of the methods you've learned about so far!

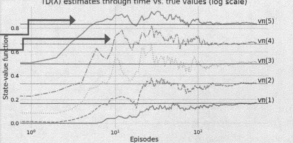

CONCRETE EXAMPLE

Evaluating the optimal policy of the Russell and Norvig's Gridworld environment

Let's run all algorithms in a slightly different environment. The environment is one you've probably come across multiple times in the past. It is from Russell and Norvig's book on AI.

Russell and Norvig's Gridworld

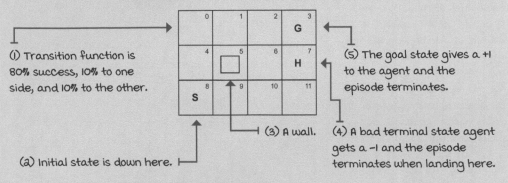

(1) Transition function is 80% success, 10% to one side, and 10% to the other.

(2) Initial state is down here.

(3) A wall.

(4) A bad terminal state agent gets a –1 and the episode terminates when landing here.

(5) The goal state gives a +1 to the agent and the episode terminates.

This environment, which I will call Russell and Norvig's Gridworld (RNG), is a 3 x 4 grid world in which the agent starts at the bottom-left corner, and it has to reach the top-right corner. There is a hole, similar to the frozen lake environment, south of the goal, and a wall near the start. The transition function has a 20% noise; that is, 80% the action succeeds, and 20% it fails uniformly at random in orthogonal directions. The reward function is a –0.04 living penalty, a +1 for landing on the goal, and a –1 for landing on the hole.

Now, what we're doing is evaluating a policy. I happen to include the optimal policy in chapter 3's Notebook: I didn't have space in that chapter to talk about it. In fact, make sure you check all the Notebooks provided with the book.

Optimal policy in the RNG environment

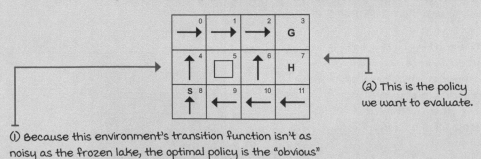

(2) This is the policy we want to evaluate.

(1) Because this environment's transition function isn't as noisy as the frozen lake, the optimal policy is the "obvious" optimal policy. Assume a gamma of 1.

Ⅲ TALLY IT UP
FVMC, TD, *n*-step TD, and TD(λ) in the RNG environment

(1) I ran the same exact hyperparameter as before except for 1000 episodes instead of the 500 for the RW. The results shown on the right are the running estimates of the state-value function for five randomly selected states out of the total 12 states. (Randomly, but with the same seed for each plot for easy comparison—also not really 100% random. I first filter estimated values lower than a threshold, 0.1.) I did this so that you can better appreciate meaningful trends from a handful of states.

(2) As you can see, all four algorithms (five if you head to the Notebook!) find a pretty good estimate of the true state-value function. If you look closely, you can see that TD and TD(lambda) show the two smoothest curves. MC, on the other hand, followed by *n*-step TD show the most centered trends.

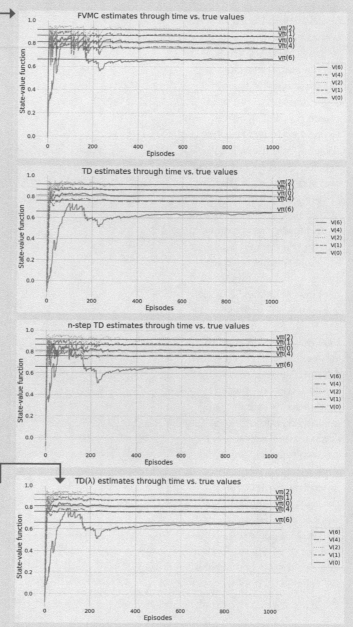

TALLY IT UP
RNG shows a bit better the bias and variance effects on estimates

(1) Alright, so I figure I probably need to "zoom in" and show you the front of the curves. These plots are not log scale like the other ones I showed in the past. These are a slice on the first 50 episodes. Also, I'm showing only the values greater than 0.1, but as you can see, that includes most states. Value functions of states 3, 5, and 7 are 0, and 10 and 11 are far from being ran by the optimal policy because the action in the state 9 and 6 points left and up, respectively, which is away from state 10 and 11.

(2) Look at the trends this time around. They're easier to spot. For instance, MC is jagged, showing those up-and-down trends. TD is smooth but slow. *n*-step TD is somewhat in between, and TD(lambda), interestingly, shows the smoothness of TD, which you can probably easily appreciate, but also it isn't as slow. For instance, look at the curve of V(6): it first crosses the 0.4 line around 25 episodes, TD all the way at 45.

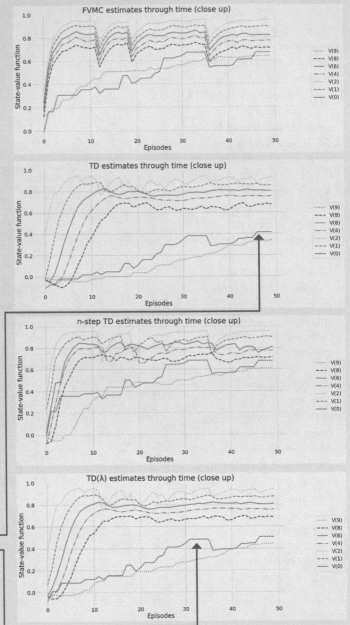

Tally it Up

FVMC and TD targets of the RNG's initial state

(1) These final plots are the sequence of target values of the initial state. As you might expect, the MC targets are independent of the sequence number, because they're actual returns and don't bootstrap on the state-value function.

(2) You can probably also notice they're high variance. These are mostly concentrated on top, but there's a handful down here.

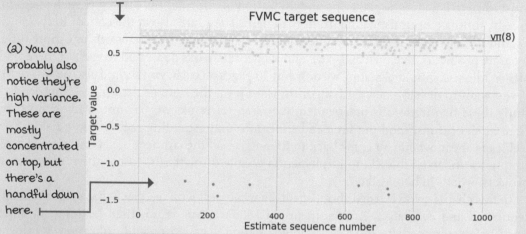

(3) TD targets are a bit more dependent on the sequence. Notice that early on, the targets are way off and somewhat noisy. However, as the targets add up, they become much more stable.

(4) You may notice three lines start to form. Remember, these are targets for the initial state, state 8. If you look at the policy, you'll notice that going up in state 8 can only have three transitions . . .

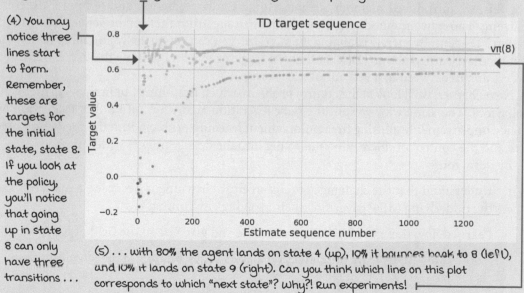

(5) . . . with 80% the agent lands on state 4 (up), 10% it bounces back to 8 (left), and 10% it lands on state 9 (right). Can you think which line on this plot corresponds to which "next state"? Why?! Run experiments!

Summary

Learning from sequential feedback is challenging; you learned quite a lot about it in chapter 3. You created agents that balance immediate and long-term goals. Methods such as value iteration (VI) and policy iteration (PI) are central to RL. Learning from evaluative feedback is also very difficult. Chapter 4 was all about a particular type of environment in which agents must learn to balance the gathering and utilization of information. Strategies such as epsilon-greedy, softmax, optimistic initialization, to name a few, are also at the core of RL.

And I want you to stop for a second and think about these two trade-offs one more time as separate problems. I've seen 500-page and longer textbooks dedicated to each of these trade-offs. While you should be happy we only put 30 pages on each, you should also be wondering. If you want to develop new DRL algorithms, to push the state of the art, I recommend you study these two trade-offs independently. Search for books on "planning algorithms" and "bandit algorithms," and put time and effort into understanding each of those fields. You'll feel leaps ahead when you come back to RL and see all the connections. Now, if your goal is simply to understand DRL, to implement a couple of methods, to use them on your own projects, what's in here will do.

In this chapter, you learned about agents that can deal with feedback that's simultaneously sequential and evaluative. And as mentioned before, this is no small feat! To simultaneously balance immediate and long-term goals and the gathering and utilization of information is something even most humans have problems with! Sure, in this chapter, we restricted ourselves to the prediction problem, which consists of estimating values of agents' behaviors. For this, we introduced methods such as Monte Carlo prediction and temporal-difference learning. Those two methods are the extremes in a spectrum that can be generalized with the n-step TD agent. By merely changing the step size, you can get virtually any agent in between. But then we learned about TD(λ) and how a single agent can combine the two extremes and everything in between in a very innovative way.

Next chapter, we'll look at the control problem, which is nothing but improving the agents' behaviors. The same way we split the policy-iteration algorithm into policy evaluation and policy improvement, splitting the reinforcement learning problem into the prediction problem and the control problem allows us to dig into the details and get better methods.

By now, you

- Understand that the challenge of reinforcement learning is because agents cannot see the underlying MDP governing their evolving environments

- Learned how these two challenges combine and give rise to the field of RL

- Know about many ways of calculating targets for estimating state-value functions

TWEETABLE FEAT

Work on your own and share your findings

Here are several ideas on how to take what you have learned to the next level. If you'd like, share your results with the rest of the world and make sure to check out what others have done, too. It's a win-win situation, and hopefully, you'll take advantage of it.

- **#gdrl_ch05_tf01:** None of the methods in this chapter handle the time step limit that's wrapped around many Gym environments. No idea what I'm talking about? No worries, I explain it in more detail in chapter 8. However, for the time being, check out this file: https://github.com/openai/gym/blob/master/gym/envs/__init__.py. See how many environments, including the frozen lake, have a variable max_episode_steps. This is a time step limit imposed over the environments. Think about this for a while: how does this time step limit affect the algorithms presented in this chapter? Go to the book's Notebook, and modify the algorithms so that they handle the time step limit correctly, and the value function estimates are more accurate. Do the value functions change? Why, why not? Note that if you don't understand what I'm referring to, you should continue and come back once you do.

- **#gdrl_ch05_tf02:** Comparing and plotting the Monte Carlo and temporal-difference targets is useful. One thing that would help you understand the difference is to do a more throughout analysis of these two types of targets, and also include the n-step and TD-lambda targets. Go ahead and start by that collecting the n-step targets for different values of time steps, and do the same for different values of lambda in TD-lambda targets. How do these compare with MC and TD? Also, find other ways to compare these prediction methods. But, do the comparison with graphs, visuals!

- **#gdrl_ch05_tf03:** In every chapter, I'm using the final hashtag as a catchall hashtag. Feel free to use this one to discuss anything else that you worked on relevant to this chapter. There's no more exciting homework than that which you create for yourself. Make sure to share what you set yourself to investigate and your results.

Write a tweet with your findings, tag me @mimoralea (I'll retweet), and use the particular hashtag from this list to help interested folks find your results. There are no right or wrong results; you share your findings and check others' findings. Take advantage of this to socialize, contribute, and get yourself out there! We're waiting for you!

Here's a tweet example:

"Hey, @mimoralea. I created a blog post with a list of resources to study deep reinforcement learning. Check it out at <link>. #gdrl_ch01_tf01"

I'll make sure to retweet and help others find your work.

In this chapter

- You will learn about improving policies when learning from feedback that is simultaneously sequential and evaluative.

- You will develop algorithms for finding optimal policies in reinforcement learning environments when the transition and reward functions are unknown.

- You will write code for agents that can go from random to optimal behavior using only their experiences and decision making, and train the agents in a variety of environments.

Up until this chapter, you've studied in isolation and interplay learning from two of the three different types of feedback a reinforcement learning agent must deal with: sequential, evaluative, and sampled. In chapter 2, you learned to represent sequential decision-making problems using a mathematical framework known as the Markov decision processes. In chapter 3, you learned how to solve these problems with algorithms that extract policies from MDPs. In chapter 4, you learned to solve simple control problems that are multi-option, single-choice, decision-making problems, called Multi-Armed Bandits, when the MDP representation isn't available to the agent. Finally, in chapter 5, we mixed these two types of control problems, that is, we dealt with control problems that are sequential and uncertain, but we only learned to estimate value functions. We solved what's called the prediction problem, which is learning to evaluate policies, learning to predict returns.

In this chapter, we'll introduce agents that solve the control problem, which we get simply by changing two things. First, instead of estimating state-value functions, $V(s)$, we estimate action-value functions, $Q(s, a)$. The main reason for this is that Q-functions, unlike V-functions, let us see the value of actions without having to use an MDP. Second, after we obtain these Q-value estimates, we use them to improve the policies. This is similar to what we did in the policy-iteration algorithm: we evaluate, we improve, then evaluate the improved policy, then improve on this improved policy, and so on. As I mentioned in chapter 3, this pattern is called *generalized policy iteration* (GPI), and it can help us create an architecture that virtually any reinforcement learning algorithm fits under, including state-of-the-art deep reinforcement learning agents.

The outline for this chapter is as follows: First, I'll expand on the generalized policy-iteration architecture, and then you'll learn about many different types of agents that solve the control problem. You'll learn about the control version of the Monte Carlo prediction and temporal-difference learning agents. You'll also learn about slightly different kinds of agents that decouple learning from behavior. What this all means in practical terms is that in this chapter, you develop agents that learn to solve tasks by trial-and-error learning. These agents learn optimal policies solely through their interaction with the environment.

The anatomy of reinforcement learning agents

In this section, I'd like to give you a mental model that most, if not all, reinforcement learning agents fit under. First, every reinforcement learning agent gathers experience samples, either from interacting with the environment or from querying a learned model of an environment. Still, data is generated as the agents learn. Second, every reinforcement learning agent learns to estimate something, perhaps a model of the environment, or possibly a policy, a value function, or just the returns. Third, every reinforcement learning agent attempts to improve a policy; that's the whole point of RL, after all.

F5 **REFRESH MY MEMORY**

Rewards, returns, and value functions

Now is a good time to refresh your memory. You need to remember the difference between rewards, returns, and value functions, so that this chapter makes sense to you and you can develop agents that learn optimal policies through trial-and-error learning. Allow me to repeat myself.

A *reward* is a numeric signal indicating the goodness of a transition. Your agent observes state S_t, takes action A_t; then the environment changes and gives a reward R_{t+1}, and emits a new state S_{t+1}. Rewards are that single numeric signal indicating the goodness of the transition occurring on every time step of an episode.

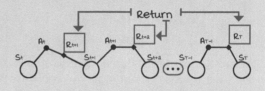

A *return* is the summation of all the rewards received during an episode. Your agent receives reward R_{t+1}, then R_{t+2}, and so on until it gets the final reward R_T right before landing in the terminal state S_T. Returns are the sum of all those rewards during an episode. Returns are often defined as the discounted sum, instead of just a sum. A discounted sum puts a priority on rewards found early in an episode (depending on the discount factor, of course.) Technically speaking, a discounted sum is a more general definition of the return, since a discount factor of one makes it a plain sum.

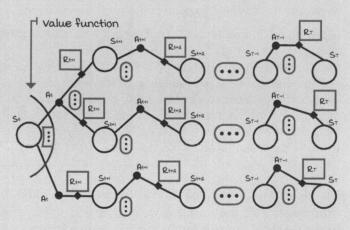

A *value* function is the expected return. Expectations are calculated as the sum of all possible values, each multiplied by the probability of its occurrence. Think of expectations as the average of an infinite number of samples; the expectation of returns is like sampling an infinite number of returns and averaging them. When you calculate a return starting after selecting an action, the expectation is the action-value function of that state-action pair, $Q(s, a)$. If you disregard the action taken and count from the state s, that becomes the state-value function $V(s)$.

Most agents gather experience samples

One of the unique characteristics of RL is that agents learn by trial and error. The agent interacts with an environment, and as it does so, it gathers data. The unusual aspect here is that gathering data is a separate challenge from learning from data. And as you'll see shortly, learning from data is also a different thing from improving from data. In RL, there is gathering, learning, and improving. For instance, an agent that's pretty good at collecting data may not be as good at learning from data; or, conversely, an agent that isn't good at collecting data may be good at learning from data, and so on. We all have that friend who didn't take good notes in school, yet they did well on tests, while others had everything written down, but didn't do as well.

In chapter 3, when we learned about dynamic programming methods, I mentioned value and policy iteration shouldn't be referred to as RL, but planning methods instead, the reason being they do not gather data. There's no need for DP methods to interact with the environment because a model of the environment, the MDP, is provided beforehand.

 WITH AN RL ACCENT

Planning vs. learning problems

Planning problems: Refers to problems in which a model of the environment is available and thus, there's no learning required. These types of problems can be solved with planning methods such as value iteration and policy iteration. The goal in these types of problems is to find, as opposed to learn, optimal policies. Suppose I give you a map and ask you to find the best route from point A to point B; there's no learning required there, just planning.

Learning problems: Refers to problems in which learning from samples is required, usually because there isn't a model of the environment available or perhaps because it's impossible to create one. The main challenge of learning problems is that we estimate using samples, and samples can have high variance, which means they'll be of poor quality and difficult to learn from. Samples can also be biased, either because of being from a different distribution than the one estimating or because of using estimates to estimate, which can make our estimates incorrect altogether. Suppose I don't give you a map of the area this time. How would you find "the best route"? By trial-and-error learning, likely.

For an algorithm to be considered a standard RL method, the aspect of interacting with the environment, with the problem we're trying to solve, should be present. Most RL agents gather experience samples by themselves, unlike supervised learning methods, for instance, which are given a dataset. RL agents have the additional challenge of selecting their datasets. Most RL agents gather experience samples because RL is often about solving interactive learning problems.

ŘŁ **WITH AN RL ACCENT**
Non-interactive vs. interactive learning problems

Non-interactive learning problems: Refers to a type of learning problem in which there's no need for or possibility of interacting with an environment. In these types of problems, there's no interaction with an environment while learning, but there is learning from data previously generated. The objective is to find something given the samples, usually a policy, but not necessarily. For instance, in inverse RL, the objective is to recover the reward function given expert-behavior samples. In apprenticeship learning, the objective is to go from this recovered reward function to a policy. In behavioral cloning, which is a form of imitation learning, the goal is to go from expert-behavior samples directly to policies using supervised learning.

Interactive learning problems: Refers to a type of learning problem in which learning and interaction are interleaved. The interesting aspect of these problems is that the learner also controls the data-gathering process. Optimal learning from samples is one challenge, and finding samples for optimal learning is another.

Most agents estimate something

After gathering data, there are multiple things an agent can do with this data. Certain agents, for instance, learn to predict expected re*turns* or value functions. In the previous chapter, you learned about many different ways of doing so, from using Monte Carlo to TD targets, from every-visit to first-visit MC targets, from n-step to λ-return targets. There are many different ways of calculating targets that can be used for estimating value functions.

But value functions aren't the only thing agents can learn with experience samples. Agents may be designed to learn models of the environment, too. As you'll see in the next chapter, model-based RL agents use the data collected for learning transition and reward functions. By learning a model of the environment, agents can predict the next state and reward. Further, with these, agents can either plan a sequence of actions similar to the way DP methods work or maybe use synthetic data generated from interacting with these learned models to learn something else. The point is that agents may be designed to learn models of the environment.

Moreover, agents can be designed to improve on policies directly using estimated returns. In later chapters, we'll see how policy gradient methods consist of approximating functions that take in a state and output a probability distribution over actions. To improve these policy functions, we can use actual returns, in the simplest case, but also estimated value functions. Finally, agents can be designed to estimate multiple things at once, and this is the typical case. The important thing is that most agents estimate something.

REFRESH MY MEMORY

Monte Carlo vs. temporal-difference targets

Other important concepts worth repeating are the different ways value functions can be estimated. In general, all methods that learn value functions progressively move estimates a fraction of the error towards the targets. The general equation that most learning methods follow is *estimate = estimate + step * error*. The error is simply the difference between a sampled target and the *current estimate: (target – estimate)*. The two main and opposite ways for calculating these targets are Monte Carlo and temporal-difference learning.

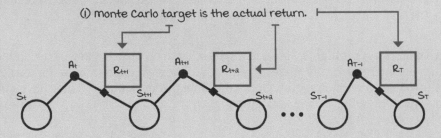

The Monte Carlo target consists of the actual return: really, nothing else. Monte Carlo estimation consists of adjusting the estimates of the value functions using the empirical (observed) mean return in place of the expected (as if you could average infinite samples) return.

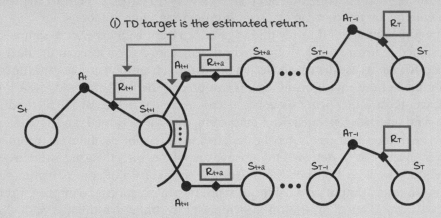

The temporal-difference target consists of an estimated return. Remember "bootstrapping"? It basically means using the estimated expected return from later states, for estimating the expected return from the current state. TD does that: learning a guess from a guess. The TD target is formed by using a single reward and the estimated expected return from the next state using the running value function estimates.

Most agents improve a policy

Lastly, most agents improve a policy. This final step heavily depends on the type of agent being trained and what the agent estimates. For instance, if the agent is estimating value functions, a common thing to improve is the target policy implicitly encoded in the value function, which is the policy being learned about. The benefit of improving the target policy is that the behavior policy, which is the data-generating policy, will consequently improve, therefore improving the quality of data the agent will subsequently gather. If the target and behavior policies are the same, then the improvement of the underlying value function explicitly increases the quality of the data generated afterward.

Now, if a policy is being represented explicitly instead of through value functions, such as in policy gradient and actor-critic methods, agents can use actual returns to improve these policies. Agents can also use value functions to estimate returns for improving policies. Finally, in model-based RL, there are multiple options for improving policies. One can use a learned model of the environment to plan a sequence of actions. In this case, there's an implicit policy being improved in the planning phase. One can use the model to learn a value function, instead, which implicitly encodes a policy. One can use the model to improve the policy directly, too. The bottom line is that all agents attempt to improve a policy.

 WITH AN RL ACCENT
Greedy vs. epsilon-greedy vs. optimal policy

Greedy policy: Refers to a policy that always selects the actions believed to yield the highest expected return from each and every state. It's essential to know that a "greedy policy" is greedy with respect to a value function. The "believed" part comes from the value function. The insight here is that when someone says, "the greedy policy," you must ask, greedy with respect to what? A greedy policy with respect to a random value function is a pretty bad policy.

Epsilon-greedy policy: Refers to a policy that often selects the actions *believed* to yield the highest expected return from each and every state. Same as before applies; an epsilon-greedy policy is epsilon-greedy with respect to a specific value function. Always make sure you understand which value function is being referenced.

Optimal policy: Refers to a policy that always selects the actions actually yielding the highest expected return from each and every state. While a greedy policy may or may not be an optimal policy, an optimal policy must undoubtedly be a greedy policy. You ask, "greedy with respect to what?" Well done! An optimal policy is a greedy policy with respect to a unique value function, the optimal value function.

Generalized policy iteration

Another simple pattern that's more commonly used to understand the architecture of rein-forcement learning algorithms is called *generalized policy iteration* (GPI). GPI is a general idea that the continuous interaction of policy evaluation and policy improvement drives policies towards optimality.

As you probably remember, in the policy iteration algorithm, we had two processes: policy evaluation and policy improvement. The policy-evaluation phase takes in any policy, and it evaluates it; it estimates the policy's value function. In policy improvement, these estimates, the value function, are used to obtain a better policy. Once policy evaluation and improvement stabilize, that is, once their interaction no longer produces any changes, then the policy and the value function are optimal.

Now, if you remember, after studying policy iteration, we learned about another algorithm, called value iteration. This one was similar to policy iteration; it had a policy-evaluation and a policy-improvement phase. The main difference, however, was that the policy-evaluation phase consisted of a single iteration. In other words, the evaluation of the policy didn't produce the actual value function. In the policy-evaluation phase of value iteration, the value function estimates move towards the actual value function, but not all the way there. Yet, even with this truncated policy-evaluation phase, the generalized policy-iteration pattern for value iteration also produces the optimal value function and policy.

The critical insight here is that policy evaluation, in general, consists of gathering and esti-mating value functions, similar to the algorithms you learned about in the previous chapter. And as you know, there are multiple ways of evaluating a policy, numerous methods of esti-mating the value function of a policy, various approaches to choose from for checking off the policy-evaluation requirement of the generalized policy-iteration pattern.

Furthermore, policy improvement consists of changing a policy to make it greedier with respect to a value function. In the policy improvement method of the policy-iteration algo-rithm, we make the policy entirely greedy with respect to the value function of the evaluated policy. But, we can completely greedify the policy only because we had the MDP of the envi-ronment. However, the policy-evaluation methods that we learned about in the previous chapter don't require an MDP of the environment, and this comes at a cost. We can no longer completely greedify policies; we need to have our agents explore. Going forward, instead of completely greedifying the policy, we make the policy greedier, leaving room for exploration. This kind of partial policy improvement was used in chapter 4 when we used different explo-rations strategies for working with estimates.

There you have it. Most RL algorithms follow this GPI pattern: they have distinct policy-evaluation and improvement phases, and all we must do is pick and choose the methods.

MIGUEL'S ANALOGY

Generalized policy iteration and why you should listen to criticism

Generalized policy iteration (GPI) is similar to the eternal dance of critics and performers. Policy evaluation gives the much-needed feedback that policy improvement uses to make policies better. In the same way, critics provide the much-needed feedback performers can use to do better.

As Benjamin Franklin said, "Critics are our friends, they show us our faults." He was a smart guy; he allowed GPI to help him improve. You let critics tell you what they think, you use that feedback to get better. It's simple! Some of the best companies out there follow this process, too. What do you think the saying "data-driven decisions" means? It's saying they make sure to use an excellent policy-evaluation process so that their policy-improvement process yields solid results; that's the same pattern as GPI! Norman Vincent Peale said, "The trouble with most of us is that we'd rather be ruined by praise than saved by criticism." Go, let critics help you.

Just beware! That they can indeed help you doesn't mean critics are always right or that you should take their advice blindly, especially if it's feedback that you hear for the first time. Critics are usually biased, and so is policy evaluation! It's your job as a great performer to listen to this feedback carefully, to get smart about gathering the best possible feedback, and to act upon it only when sure. But, in the end, the world belongs to those who do the work. Theodore Roosevelt said it best:

> "It is not the critic who counts; not the man who points out how the strong man stumbles, or where the doer of deeds could have done them better. The credit belongs to the man who is actually in the arena, whose face is marred by dust and sweat and blood; who strives valiantly; who errs, who comes short again and again, because there is no effort without error and shortcoming; but who does actually strive to do the deeds; who knows great enthusiasms, the great devotions; who spends himself in a worthy cause; who at the best knows in the end the triumph of high achievement, and who at the worst, if he fails, at least fails while daring greatly, so that his place shall never be with those cold and timid souls who neither know victory nor defeat."

In later chapters, we'll study actor-critic methods, and you'll see how this whole analogy extends, believe it or not! Actors and critics help each other. Stay tuned for more.

It's awe-inspiring that patterns in optimal decision making are valid across the board. What you learn studying DRL can help you become a better decision maker, and what you learn in your own life can help you create better agents.

Cool, right?

Learning to improve policies of behavior

In the previous chapter, you learned how to solve the prediction problem: how to make agents most accurately estimate the value function of a given policy. However, while this is a useful ability for our agents to have, it doesn't directly make them better at any task. In this section, you'll learn how to solve the control problem: how to make agents optimize policies. This new ability allows agents to learn optimal behavior by trial-and-error learning, starting from arbitrary policies and ending in optimal ones. After this chapter you can develop agents that can solve any task represented by an MDP. The task has to be a discrete state- and action-space MDP, but other than that, it's plug-and-play.

To show you a few agents, we're going to leverage the GPI pattern you learned. That is, we're going to select algorithms for the policy-evaluation phase from the ones you learned about in the last chapter, and strategies for the policy-improvement phase from the ones you learned about in the chapter before. Hopefully, this sets your imagination free on the possibilities. Just pick and choose algorithms for policy evaluation and improvement, and things will work, that's because of the interaction of these two processes.

 WITH AN RL ACCENT

Prediction vs. control problem vs. policy evaluation vs. improvement

Prediction problem: Refers to the problem of evaluating policies, of estimating value functions given a policy. Estimating value functions is nothing but learning to predict returns. State-value functions estimate expected returns from states, and action-value functions estimate expected returns from state-action pairs.

Control problem: Refers to the problem of finding optimal policies. The control problem is usually solved by following the pattern of generalized policy iteration (GPI), where the competing processes of policy evaluation and policy improvement progressively move policies towards optimality. RL methods often pair an action-value prediction method with policy improvement and action-selection strategies.

Policy evaluation: Refers to algorithms that solve the prediction problem. Note that there's a dynamic programming method called policy evaluation, but this term is also used to refer to *all algorithms* that solve the prediction problem.

Policy improvement: Refers to algorithms that make new policies that improve on an original policy by making it greedier than the original with respect to the value function of that original policy. Note that policy improvement by itself doesn't solve the control problem. Often a policy evaluation must be paired with a policy improvement to solve the control problem. Policy improvement only refers to the computation for improving a policy given its evaluation results.

CONCRETE EXAMPLE
The slippery walk seven environment

For this chapter, we use an environment called *slippery walk seven* (SWS). This environment is a walk, a single-row grid-world environment, with seven non-terminal states. The particular thing of this environment is that it's a slippery walk; action effects are stochastic. If the agent chooses to go left, there is a chance it does, but there is also a chance that it goes right, or that it stays in place.

Let me show you the MDP for this environment. Remember, though, that the agent doesn't have any access to the transition probabilities. The dynamics of this environment are unknown to the agent. I'm only giving you this information for didactic reasons.

Also, have in mind that to the agent, there are no relationships between the states in advance. The agent doesn't know that state 3 is in the middle of the entire walk, or that it's in between states 2 and 4; it doesn't even know what a "walk" is! The agent doesn't know that action zero goes left, or one goes right. Honestly, I encourage you to go to the Notebook and play with the environment yourself to gain a deeper understanding. The fact is that the agent only sees the state ids, say, 0, 1, 2, and so on, and chooses either action 0 or 1.

Slippery walk seven environment MDP

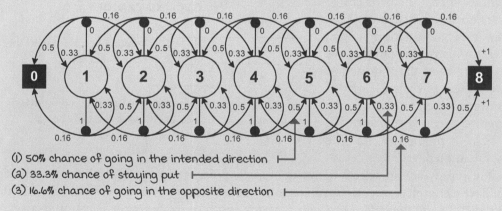

(1) 50% chance of going in the intended direction
(2) 33.3% chance of staying put
(3) 16.6% chance of going in the opposite direction

The SWS environment is similar to the random walk (RW) environment that we learned about in the previous chapter, but with the ability to do control. Remember that the random walk is an environment in which the probability of going left, when taking the Left action, is equal to the probability of going right. And the probability of going right, when taking the Right action, is equal to the probability of going left, so there's no control. This environment is noisy, but the actions the agent selects make a difference in its performance. And also, this environment has seven non-terminal states, as opposed to the five of the RW.

Monte Carlo control: Improving policies after each episode

Let's try to create a control method using Monte Carlo prediction for our policy-evaluation needs. Let's initially assume we're using the same policy-improvement step we use for the policy-iteration algorithm. That is, the policy-improvement step gets the greedy policy with respect to the value function of the policy evaluated. Would this make an algorithm that helps us find optimal policies solely through interaction? Actually, no. There are two changes we need to make before we can make this approach work.

First, we need to make sure our agent estimates the action-value function $Q(s, a)$, instead of the $V(s, a)$ that we estimated in the previous chapter. The problem with the V-function is that, without the MDP, it isn't possible to know what the best action is to take from a state. In other words, the policy-improvement step wouldn't work.

Second, we need to make sure our agent explores. The problem is that we're no longer using the MDP for our policy-evaluation needs. When we estimate from samples, we get values for all of the state-action pairs we visited, but what if part of the best states weren't visited?

Therefore, let's use first-visit Monte Carlo prediction for the policy-evaluation phase and a decay-

We need to estimate action-value functions

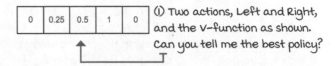

(1) Two actions, Left and Right, and the V-function as shown. Can you tell me the best policy?

(2) What if I told you Left sent you right with 70% chance?
(3) What do you think the best policy is now?
(4) See?! V-Function isn't enough.

We need to explore

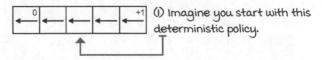

(1) Imagine you start with this deterministic policy.

(2) How can you tell whether the Right action is better than the Left if all you estimate is the Left action?
(3) See?! Your agent needs to explore.

ing epsilon-greedy action-selection strategy for the policy-improvement phase. And that's it—you have a complete, model-free RL algorithm in which we evaluate policies with Monte Carlo prediction and improve them with decaying epsilon-greedy action-selection strategy.

As with value iteration, which has a truncated policy-evaluation step, we can truncate the Monte Carlo prediction method. Instead of rolling out several episodes for estimating the value function of a single policy using Monte Carlo prediction, as we did in the previous chapter, we truncate the prediction step after a single full rollout and trajectory sample estimation, and improve the policy right after that single estimation step. We alternate a single MC-prediction step and a single decaying epsilon-greedy action-selection improvement step.

Let's look at our first RL method MC control. You'll see three functions:

- decay_schedule: Compute decaying values as specified in the function arguments.

- generate_trajectory: Roll out the policy in the environment for a full episode.

- mc_control: Complete implementation of the MC control method.

I Speak Python
Exponentially decaying schedule

```python
def decay_schedule(
        init_value, min_value,
        decay_ratio, max_steps,
        log_start=-2, log_base=10):
```

(1) The decay schedule we'll use for both alpha and epsilon is the same we used in the previous chapter for alpha. Let's go into more detail this time.

(2) What I personally like about this function is that you give it an initial value, a minimum value, and the percentage of the max_steps to decay the values from initial to minimum.

```python
    decay_steps = int(max_steps * decay_ratio)
```

(3) This decay_steps is the index where the decaying of values terminates and the min_value continues until max_steps.

(4) rem_steps is therefore the difference.

```python
    rem_steps = max_steps - decay_steps
```

(5) I'm calculating the values using the logspace starting from log_start, which I set by default to −2, and ending on 0. The number of values in that space that I ask for is decay_steps and the base is log_base, which I default to 10. Notice, I reverse those values!

```python
    values = np.logspace(
                log_start, 0, decay_steps,
                base=log_base, endpoint=True)[::-1]
```

(6) Because the values may not end exactly at 0, given it's the log, I change them to be between 0 and 1 so that the curve looks smooth and nice.

```python
    values = (values - values.min()) / \
                        (values.max() - values.min())
```

(7) Then, we can do a linear transformation and get points between init_value and min_value.

```python
    values = (init_value - min_value) * values + min_value
```

(8) This pad function just repeats the rightmost value rem_step number of times.

```python
    values = np.pad(values, (0, rem_steps), 'edge')
    return values
```

I Speak Python

Generate exploratory policy trajectories

```python
def generate_trajectory(
        select_action, Q, epsilon,
        env, max_steps=200):
```

(1) This version of the generate_ trajectory function is slightly different. We now need to take in an action-selecting strategy, instead of a greedy policy.

(2) We begin by initializing the done flag and a list of experiences named trajectory.

```python
    done, trajectory = False, []

    while not done:
        state = env.reset()
        for t in count():
```

(3) We then start looping through until the done flag is set to true.

(4) We reset the environment to interact in a new episode.

(5) Then start counting steps t.

(6) Then, use the passed 'select_action' function to pick an action.

```python
            action = select_action(state, Q, epsilon)
```

(7) We step the environment using that action and obtain the full experience tuple.

```python
            next_state, reward, done, _ = env.step(action)
            experience = (state,
                          action,
                          reward,
                          next_state,
                          done)
            trajectory.append(experience)
            if done:
                break

            if t >= max_steps - 1:
                trajectory = []
                break

            state = next_state

    return np.array(trajectory, np.object)
```

(8) We append the experience to the trajectory list.

(9) If we hit a terminal state and the 'done' flag is raised, then break and return.

(10) And if the count of steps 't' in the current trajectory hits the maximum allowed, we clear the trajectory, break, and try to obtain another trajectory.

(11) Remember to update the state.

(12) Finally, we return a NumPy version of the trajectory for easy data manipulation.

I Speak Python

Monte Carlo control 1/2

```
def mc_control(env,
               gamma=1.0,
               init_alpha=0.5,
               min_alpha=0.01,
               alpha_decay_ratio=0.5,
               init_epsilon=1.0,
               min_epsilon=0.1,
               epsilon_decay_ratio=0.9,
               n_episodes=3000,
               max_steps=200,
               first_visit=True):
```

(1) mc_control is similar to mc_prediction. The two main differences is that we now estimate the action-value function Q, and that we need to explore.

(2) Notice in the function definition we are using values for epsilon to configure a decaying schedule for random exploration.

```
    nS, nA = env.observation_space.n, env.action_space.n

    discounts = np.logspace(
        0, max_steps,
        num=max_steps, base=gamma,
        endpoint=False)
```

(3) We calculate values for the discount factors in advance. Notice we use max_steps because that's the maximum length of a trajectory.

```
    alphas = decay_schedule(
        init_alpha, min_alpha,
        alpha_decay_ratio,
        n_episodes)
```

(4) We also calculate alphas in advance using the passed values.

```
    epsilons = decay_schedule(
        init_epsilon, min_epsilon,
        epsilon_decay_ratio,
        n_episodes)
```

(5) Finally, we repeat for epsilon, and obtain an array that will work for the full training session.

(6) Here we're just setting up variables, including the Q-function.

```
    pi_track = []
    Q = np.zeros((nS, nA), dtype=np.float64)
    Q_track = np.zeros((n_episodes, nS, nA), dtype=np.float64)

    select_action = lambda state, Q, epsilon: \
        np.argmax(Q[state]) \
        if np.random.random() > epsilon \
        else np.random.randint(len(Q[state]))

    for e in tqdm(range(n_episodes), leave=False):
```

(7) This is an epsilon-greedy strategy, though we decay epsilon on each episode, not step.

(8) Continues . . .

I SPEAK PYTHON

Monte Carlo control 2/2

(9) Repeating the previous line so that you can keep up with the indentation

```
for e in tqdm(range(n_episodes), leave=False):
```

(10) Here we're entering the episode loop. We'll run for n_episodes.
Remember that tqdm shows a nice progress bar, nothing out of this world.

```
        trajectory = generate_trajectory(select_action,
                                          Q,
                                          epsilons[e],
                                          env,
                                          max_steps)
```

(11) Every new episode 'e' we generate a
new trajectory with the exploratory policy
defined by the select_action function. We
limit the trajectory length to max_steps.

(12) We now keep track of the visits to state-action pairs; this is
another important change from the mc_prediction method.

```
        visited = np.zeros((nS, nA), dtype=np.bool)
        for t, (state, action, reward, _, _) in enumerate(\
                                                 trajectory):
```

(13) Notice here we're processing trajectories *offline*, that is, after
the interactions with the environment have stopped.

```
            if visited[state][action] and first_visit:
                continue
            visited[state][action] = True
```

(14) Here we check
for state-action-
pair visits and act
accordingly.

(15) We proceed to calculating the return the same way we did with
the prediction method, except that we're using a Q-function this time.

```
            n_steps = len(trajectory[t:])
            G = np.sum(discounts[:n_steps] * trajectory[t:, 2])
            Q[state][action] = Q[state][action] + \
                    alphas[e] * (G - Q[state][action])
```

(16) Notice how we're using the alphas.
(17) After that, it's a matter of saving values for post analysis.

```
        Q_track[e] = Q
        pi_track.append(np.argmax(Q, axis=1))
    V = np.max(Q, axis=1)
    pi = lambda s: {s:a for s, a in enumerate(\
                                    np.argmax(Q, axis=1))}[s]
```

(18) At the end, we extract the state-value
function and the greedy policy.

```
    return Q, V, pi, Q_track, pi_track
```

SARSA: Improving policies after each step

As we discussed in the previous chapter, one of the disadvantages of Monte Carlo methods is that they're offline methods in an episode-to-episode sense. What that means is that we must wait until we reach a terminal state before we can make any improvements to our value function estimates. However, it's straightforward to use temporal-difference prediction for the policy-evaluation phase, instead of Monte Carlo prediction. By replacing MC with TD prediction, we now have a different algorithm, the well-known SARSA agent.

Comparison between planning and control methods

Policy iteration

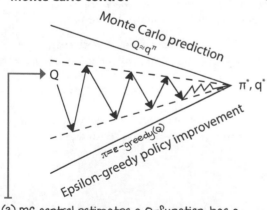

(1) Policy iteration consists of a full convergence of iterative policy evaluation alternating with greedy policy improvement.

Value iteration

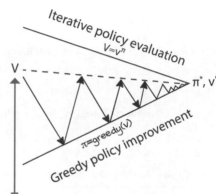

(2) Value iteration starts with an arbitrary value function and has a truncated policy evaluation step.

Monte Carlo control

(3) MC control estimates a Q-function, has a truncated MC prediction phase followed by an epsilon-greedy policy-improvement step.

SARSA

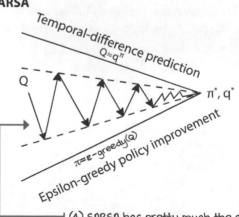

(4) SARSA has pretty much the same as MC control except a truncated TD prediction for policy evaluation.

I SPEAK PYTHON
The SARSA agent 1/2

```python
def sarsa(env,
          gamma=1.0,
          init_alpha=0.5,
          min_alpha=0.01,
          alpha_decay_ratio=0.5,
          init_epsilon=1.0,
          min_epsilon=0.1,
          epsilon_decay_ratio=0.9,
          n_episodes=3000):
```

(1) The SARSA agent is the direct conversion of TD for control problems. That is, at its core, SARSA is TD with two main changes. First, it evaluates the action-value function Q. Second, it uses an exploratory policy-improvement step.

(2) We're doing the same thing we did with mc_control using epsilon here.

(3) First, create several handy variables. Remember, pi_track will hold a greedy policy per episode.

```python
nS, nA = env.observation_space.n, env.action_space.n
pi_track = []
```

(4) Then, we create the Q-function. I'm using 'np.float64' precision . . . perhaps overkill.

```python
Q = np.zeros((nS, nA), dtype=np.float64)
Q_track = np.zeros((n_episodes, nS, nA), dtype=np.float64)
```

(5) 'Q_track' will hold the estimated Q-function per episode.

```python
select_action = lambda state, Q, epsilon: \
    np.argmax(Q[state]) \
    if np.random.random() > epsilon \
    else np.random.randint(len(Q[state]))
```

(6) The select_action function is the same as before: an epsilon-greedy strategy.

(7) In SARSA, we don't need to calculate all discount factors in advance, because we won't use full returns. Instead, we use estimated returns, so we can calculate discounts online.

```python
alphas = decay_schedule(
    init_alpha, min_alpha,
    alpha_decay_ratio,
    n_episodes)
```

(8) Notice we are, however, calculating all alphas in advance. This function call returns a vector with corresponding alphas to use.

(9) The select_action function isn't a decaying strategy on its own. We're calculating decaying epsilons in advance, so our agent will be using a decaying epsilon-greedy strategy.

```python
epsilons = decay_schedule(
    init_epsilon, min_epsilon,
    epsilon_decay_ratio,
    n_episodes)
```

(10) Let's continue on the next page.

```python
for e in tqdm(range(n_episodes), leave=False):
```

I SPEAK PYTHON

The SARSA agent 2/2

(11) Same line. You know the drill.

```
for e in tqdm(range(n_episodes), leave=False):
```

— (12) We're now inside the episode loop.

— (13) We start each episode by resetting the environment and the done flag.

```
state, done = env.reset(), False
action = select_action(state, Q, epsilons[e])
```

(14) We select the action (perhaps exploratory) for the initial state.

```
while not done:
```
← (15) We repeat until we hit a terminal state.

— (16) First, step the environment and get the experience.

```
next_state, reward, done, _ = env.step(action)
next_action = select_action(next_state,
                                           Q,
                                           epsilons[e])
```

(17) Notice that before we make any calculations, we need to obtain the action for the next step.

```
td_target = reward + gamma * \
                    Q[next_state][next_action] * (not done)
```

(18) We calculate the td_target using that next state-action pair. And we do the little trick for terminal states of multiplying by the expression (not done), which zeros out the future on terminal.
(19) Then calculate the td_error as the difference between the target and current estimate.

```
td_error = td_target - Q[state][action]
```

(20) Finally, update the Q-function by moving the estimates a bit toward the error.

```
Q[state][action] = Q[state][action] + \
                                alphas[e] * td_error
```

(21) We update the state and action for the next step.

```
state, action = next_state, next_action
```

— (22) Save the Q-function and greedy policy for analysis.

```
Q_track[e] = Q
pi_track.append(np.argmax(Q, axis=1))
V = np.max(Q, axis=1)
pi = lambda s: {s:a for s, a in enumerate(\
                              np.argmax(Q, axis=1))}[s]
```

(23) At the end, calculate the estimated optimal v-function and its greedy policy, and return all this. —

```
return Q, V, pi, Q_track, pi_track
```

ŘŁ WITH AN RL ACCENT
Batch vs. offline vs. online learning problems and methods

Batch learning problems and methods: When you hear the term "batch learning," people are referring to one of two things: they mean a type of learning problem in which experience samples are fixed and given in advance, or they mean a type of learning method which is optimized for learning synchronously from a batch of experiences, also called fitting methods. Batch learning methods are typically studied with non-interactive learning problems, more specifically, batch learning problems. But batch learning methods can also be applied to interactive learning problems. For instance, growing batch methods are batch learning methods that also collect data: they "grow" the batch. Also, batch learning problems don't have to be solved with batch learning methods, the same way that batch learning methods aren't designed exclusively to solve batch learning problems.

Offline learning problems and methods: When you hear the term "offline learning," people are usually referring to one of two things: they're either talking about a problem setting in which there's a simulation available for collecting data (as opposed to a real-world, online environment), or they could also be talking about learning methods that learn *offline*, meaning between episodes, for instance. Note that, in offline learning methods, learning and interaction can still be interleaved, but performance is only optimized after samples have been collected, similar to the growing batch described previously, but with the difference that, unlike growing batch methods, offline methods commonly discard old samples; they don't *grow* a batch. MC methods, for instance, are often considered offline because learning and interaction are interleaved on an episode-to-episode basis. There are two distinct phases, interacting and learning; MC is interactive, but also an offline learning method.

Online learning problems and methods: When you hear the term "online learning," people are referring to one of two things: either to learning while interacting with a live system, such a robot, or to methods that learn from an experience as soon as it's collected, on each and every time step.

Note that offline and online learning are often used in different contexts. I've seen offline versus online to mean non-interactive versus interactive, but I've also seen them, as I mentioned, for distinguishing between learning from a simulator versus a live system.

My definitions here are consistent with common uses of many RL researchers: Richard Sutton (2018 book), David Silver (2015 lectures), Hado van Hasselt (2018 lectures), Michael Littman (2015 paper), and Csaba Szepesvari (2009 book).

Be aware of the lingo, though. That's what's important.

Decoupling behavior from learning

I want you to think about the TD update equation for state-value functions for a second; remember, it uses $R_{t+1} + \gamma V(S_{t+1})$ as the TD target. However, if you stare at the TD update equation for action-value functions instead, which is $R_{t+1} + \gamma Q(S_{t+1}, A_{t+1})$, you may notice there are a few more possibilities there. Look at the action being used and what that means. Think about what else you can put in there. One of the most critical advancements in reinforcement learning was the development of the *Q-learning* algorithm, a model-free off-policy bootstrapping method that directly approximates the optimal policy despite the policy generating experiences. Yes, this means the agent, in theory, can act randomly and still find the optimal value function and policies. How is this possible?

Q-learning: Learning to act optimally, even if we choose not to

The SARSA algorithm is a sort of "learning on the job." The agent learns about the same policy it uses for generating experience. This type of learning is called on-policy. On-policy learning is excellent—we learn from our own mistakes. But, let me make it clear, in on-policy learning, we learn from our own current mistakes only. What if we want to learn from our own previous mistakes? What if we want to learn from the mistakes of others? In on-policy learning, you can't. Off-policy learning, on the other hand, is sort of "learning from others." The agent learns about a policy that's different from the policy-generating experiences. In off-policy learning, there are two policies: a behavior policy, used to generate experiences, to interact with the environment, and a target policy, which is the policy we're learning about. SARSA is an on-policy method; Q-learning is an off-policy one.

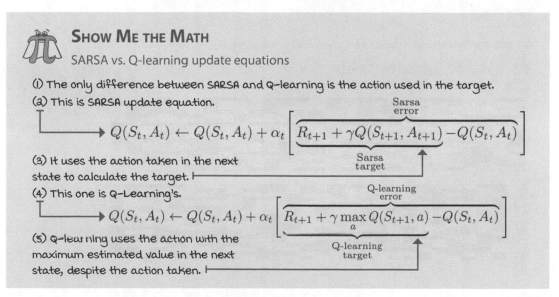

SHOW ME THE MATH

SARSA vs. Q-learning update equations

① The only difference between SARSA and Q-learning is the action used in the target.

② This is SARSA update equation.

$$Q(S_t, A_t) \leftarrow Q(S_t, A_t) + \alpha_t \left[\underbrace{R_{t+1} + \gamma Q(S_{t+1}, A_{t+1})}_{\text{Sarsa target}} - Q(S_t, A_t) \right]$$

Sarsa error

③ It uses the action taken in the next state to calculate the target.

④ This one is Q-Learning's.

$$Q(S_t, A_t) \leftarrow Q(S_t, A_t) + \alpha_t \left[\underbrace{R_{t+1} + \gamma \max_a Q(S_{t+1}, a)}_{\text{Q-learning target}} - Q(S_t, A_t) \right]$$

Q-learning error

⑤ Q-learning uses the action with the maximum estimated value in the next state, despite the action taken.

I SPEAK PYTHON

The Q-learning agent 1/2

```python
def q_learning(env,
               gamma=1.0,
               init_alpha=0.5,
               min_alpha=0.01,
               alpha_decay_ratio=0.5,
               init_epsilon=1.0,
               min_epsilon=0.1,
               epsilon_decay_ratio=0.9,
               n_episodes=3000):
```

(1) Notice that the beginning of the Q-learning agent is identical to the beginning of the SARSA agent.

(2) In fact, I'm even using the same exact hyperparameters for both algorithms.

(3) Here are several handy variables.

```python
    nS, nA = env.observation_space.n, env.action_space.n
    pi_track = []
```

(4) The Q-function and the tracking variable for offline analysis

```python
    Q = np.zeros((nS, nA), dtype=np.float64)
    Q_track = np.zeros((n_episodes, nS, nA), dtype=np.float64)
```

(5) The same epsilon-greedy action-selection strategy

```python
    select_action = lambda state, Q, epsilon: \
        np.argmax(Q[state]) \
        if np.random.random() > epsilon \
        else np.random.randint(len(Q[state]))
```

(6) The vector with all alphas to be used during learning

```python
    alphas = decay_schedule(
        init_alpha, min_alpha,
        alpha_decay_ratio,
        n_episodes)
```

(7) The vector with all epsilons to decay as desired

```python
    epsilons = decay_schedule(
        init_epsilon, min_epsilon,
        epsilon_decay_ratio,
        n_episodes)
```

(8) Let's continue on the next page.

```python
    for e in tqdm(range(n_episodes), leave=False):
```

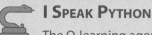

I SPEAK PYTHON

The Q-learning agent 2/2

(9) Same line as before

```python
for e in tqdm(range(n_episodes), leave=False):
```

(10) We're iterating over episodes.

```python
    state, done = env.reset(), False
```

(11) We reset the environment and get the initial state, set the done flag to false.
(12) Now enter the interaction loop for online learning (steps).

```python
    while not done:
```

(13) We repeat the loop until we hit a terminal state and a done flag is raised.
(14) First thing we do is select an action for the current state. Notice the use of epsilons.

```python
        action = select_action(state, Q, epsilons[e])
        next_state, reward, done, _ = env.step(action)
```

(15) We step the environment and get a full experience tuple (s, a, s', r, d).
(16) Next, we calculate the TD target. Q-learning is a special algorithm because it tries to learn the optimal action-value function q* even if it uses an exploratory policy such as the decaying epsilon-greedy we're running. This is called off-policy learning.

```python
        td_target = reward + gamma * \
                    Q[next_state].max() * (not done)
```

(17) Again, the "not done" ensures the max value of the next state is set to zero on terminal states. It's important that the agent doesn't expect any reward after death!!!
(18) Next, we calculate the TD error as the difference between the estimate and the target.

```python
        td_error = td_target - Q[state][action]
        Q[state][action] = Q[state][action] + \
                           alphas[e] * td_error
```

(19) We then move the Q-function for the state-action pair to be a bit closer to the error.

```python
        state = next_state
    Q_track[e] = Q
    pi_track.append(np.argmax(Q, axis=1))
```

(20) Next, we update the state.
(21) Save the Q-function and the policy.

(22) And obtain the V-function and final policy on exit.

```python
V = np.max(Q, axis=1)
pi = lambda s: {s:a for s, a in enumerate(\
                    np.argmax(Q, axis=1))}[s]
return Q, V, pi, Q_track, pi_track
```

MIGUEL'S ANALOGY
Humans also learn on-policy and off-policy

On-policy is learning about a policy that's being used to make decisions; you can think about it as "learning on the job." Off-policy learning is learning about a policy different from the policy used for making decisions. You can think about it as "learning from others' experiences," or "learning to be great, without trying to be great." Both are important ways of learning and perhaps vital for a solid decision maker. Interestingly, you can see whether a person prefers to learn on-policy or off-policy pretty quickly.

My son, for instance, tends to prefer on-policy learning. Sometimes I see him struggle playing with a toy, so I come over and try to show him how to use it, but then he complains until I leave him alone. He keeps trying and trying, and he eventually learns, but he prefers his own experience instead of others'. On-policy learning is a straightforward and stable way of learning.

My daughter, on the other hand, seems to be OK with learning off-policy. She can learn from my demonstrations before she even attempts a task. I show her how to draw a house, then she tries.

Now, beware; this is a stretch analogy. Imitation learning and off-policy learning are not the same. Off-policy learning is more about the learner using their experience at, say, running, to get better at something else, say, playing soccer. In other words, you do something while learning about something else. I'm sure you think of instances when you've done that, when you have learned about painting, while cooking. It doesn't matter where the experiences come from for doing off-policy learning; as long as the target policy and the behavior policy are different, then you can refer to that as off-policy learning.

Also, before you make conclusions about which one is "best," know that in RL, both have pros and cons. On one hand, on-policy learning is intuitive and stable. If you want to get good at playing the piano, why not practice the piano?

On the other hand, it seems useful to learn from sources other than your own hands-on experience; after all, there's only so much time in a day. Maybe meditation can teach you something about playing the piano, and help you get better at it. But, while off-policy learning helps you learn from multiple sources (and/or multiple skills), methods using off-policy learning are often of higher variance and, therefore, slower to converge.

Additionally, know that off-policy learning is one of the three elements that, when combined, have been proven to lead to divergence: off-policy learning, bootstrapping, and function approximation. These don't play nice together. You've learned about the first two, and the third one is soon to come.

ŘŁ WITH AN RL ACCENT
Greedy in the limit with infinite exploration and stochastic approx. theory

Greedy in the limit with infinite exploration (GLIE) is a set of requirements that on-policy RL algorithms, such as Monte Carlo control and SARSA, must meet to guarantee convergence to the optimal policy. The requirements are as follows:

- All state-action pairs must be explored infinitely often.
- The policy must converge on a greedy policy.

What this means in practice is that an epsilon-greedy exploration strategy, for instance, must slowly decay epsilon towards zero. If it goes down too quickly, the first condition may not be met; if it decays too slowly, well, it takes longer to converge.

Notice that for off-policy RL algorithms, such as Q-learning, the only requirement of these two that holds is the first one. The second one is no longer a requirement because in off-policy learning, the policy learned about is different than the policy we're sampling actions from. Q-learning, for instance, only requires all state-action pairs to be updated sufficiently, and that's covered by the first condition in this section.

Now, whether you can check off with certainty that requirement using simple exploration strategies such as epsilon-greedy, that's another question. In simple grid worlds and discrete action and state spaces, epsilon-greedy most likely works. But, it's easy to imagine intricate environments that would require more than random behavior.

There is another set of requirements for general convergence based on stochastic approximation theory that applies to all of these methods. Because we're learning from samples, and samples have some variance, the estimates won't converge unless we also push the learning rate, alpha, towards zero:

- The sum of learning rates must be infinite.
- The sum of squares of learning rates must be finite.

That means you must pick a learning rate that decays but never reaches zero. For instance, if you use *1/t* or *1/e*, the learning rate is initially large enough to ensure the algorithm doesn't follow only a single sample too tightly, but becomes small enough to ensure it finds the signal behind the noise.

Also, even though these convergence properties are useful to know for developing the theory of RL algorithms, in practice, learning rates are commonly set to a small-enough constant, depending on the problem. Also, know that a small constant is better for non-stationary environments, which are common in the real world.

ŘŁ **WITH AN RL ACCENT**
On-policy vs. off-policy learning

On-policy learning: Refers to methods that attempt to evaluate or improve the policy used to make decisions. It is straightforward; think about a single policy. This policy generates behavior. Your agent evaluates that behavior and select areas of improvement based on those estimates. Your agent learns to assess and improve the same policy it uses for generating the data.

Off-policy learning: Refers to methods that attempt to evaluate or improve a policy different from the one used to generate the data. This one is more complex. Think about two policies. One produces the data, the experiences, the behavior; but your agent uses that data to evaluate, improve, and overall learn about a different policy, a different behavior. Your agent learns to assess and improve a policy different than the one used for generating the data.

Double Q-learning: A max of estimates for an estimate of a max

Q-learning often overestimates the value function. Think about this. On every step, we take the maximum over the estimates of the action-value function of the next state. But what we need is the actual value of the maximum action-value function of the next state. In other words, we're using the maximum over merely estimates as an estimate of the maximum.

Doing this isn't only an inaccurate way of estimating the maximum value but also a more significant problem, given that these bootstrapping estimates, which are used to form TD targets, are often biased. The use of a maximum of biased estimates as the estimate of the maximum value is a problem known as *maximization bias*.

It's simple. Imagine an action-value function whose actual values are all zeros, but the estimates have bias: some positive, some negative: for example, 0.11, 0.65, −0.44, −0.26, and so on. We know the actual maximum of the values is zero, but the maximum over the estimates is 0.65. Now, if we sometimes pick a value with a positive bias and sometimes one with a negative bias, then perhaps the issue wouldn't be as pronounced. But because we're always taking a max, we always tend to take high values even if they have the largest bias, the biggest error. Doing this over and over again compounds the errors in a negative way.

We all know someone with a positive-bias personality who has let something go wrong in their lives: someone who's blinded by shiny things that aren't as shiny. To me, this is one of the reasons why many people advise against feeding the AI hype; because overestimation is often your enemy, and certainly something to mitigate for an improved performance.

I Speak Python

The double Q-learning agent 1/3

```python
def double_q_learning(env,
                      gamma=1.0,
                      init_alpha=0.5,
                      min_alpha=0.01,
                      alpha_decay_ratio=0.5,
                      init_epsilon=1.0,
                      min_epsilon=0.1,
                      epsilon_decay_ratio=0.9,
                      n_episodes=3000):
```

(1) As you'd expect, double Q-learning takes the same exact arguments as Q-Learning.

(2) We start with the same old handy variables.

```python
    nS, nA = env.observation_space.n, env.action_space.n
    pi_track = []
```

(3) But immediately you should see a big difference here. We're using two state-value functions Q1 and Q2. You can think of this similar to cross-validation: one Q-function estimates will help us validate the other Q-function estimates. The issue, though, is now we're splitting the experience between two separate functions. This somewhat slows down training.

```python
    Q1 = np.zeros((nS, nA), dtype=np.float64)
    Q2 = np.zeros((nS, nA), dtype=np.float64)
    Q_track1 = np.zeros((n_episodes, nS, nA), dtype=np.float64)
    Q_track2 = np.zeros((n_episodes, nS, nA), dtype=np.float64)

    select_action = lambda state, Q, epsilon: \
        np.argmax(Q[state]) \
        if np.random.random() > epsilon \
        else np.random.randint(len(Q[state]))

    alphas = decay_schedule(init_alpha,
                            min_alpha,
                            alpha_decay_ratio,
                            n_episodes)

    epsilons = decay_schedule(init_epsilon,
                              min_epsilon,
                              epsilon_decay_ratio,
                              n_episodes)

    for e in tqdm(range(n_episodes), leave=False):
```

(4) The rest on this page is pretty straightforward, and you should already know what's happening. The select_action, alphas, and epsilons are calculated the same way as before.

(5) Continues . . .

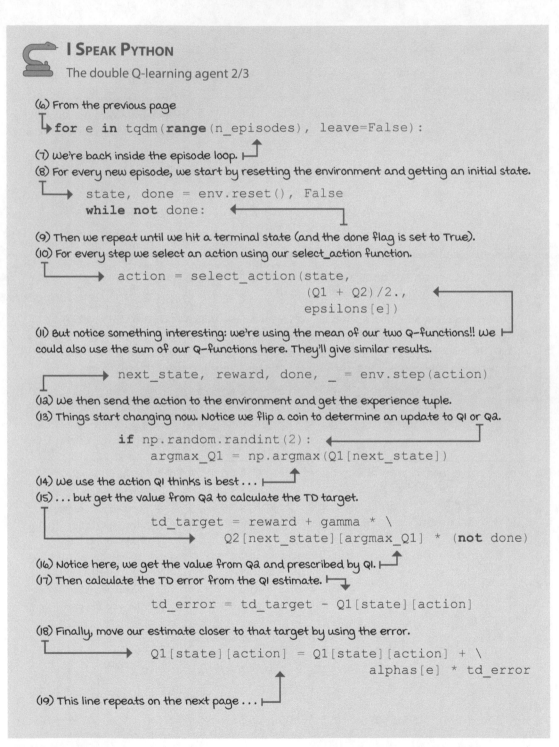

I Speak Python

The double Q-learning agent 2/3

(6) From the previous page

```
for e in tqdm(range(n_episodes), leave=False):
```

(7) We're back inside the episode loop.

(8) For every new episode, we start by resetting the environment and getting an initial state.

```
    state, done = env.reset(), False
    while not done:
```

(9) Then we repeat until we hit a terminal state (and the done flag is set to True).

(10) For every step we select an action using our select_action function.

```
        action = select_action(state,
                               (Q1 + Q2)/2.,
                               epsilons[e])
```

(11) But notice something interesting: we're using the mean of our two Q-functions!! We could also use the sum of our Q-functions here. They'll give similar results.

```
        next_state, reward, done, _ = env.step(action)
```

(12) We then send the action to the environment and get the experience tuple.

(13) Things start changing now. Notice we flip a coin to determine an update to Q1 or Q2.

```
        if np.random.randint(2):
            argmax_Q1 = np.argmax(Q1[next_state])
```

(14) We use the action Q1 thinks is best . . .

(15) . . . but get the value from Q2 to calculate the TD target.

```
            td_target = reward + gamma * \
                        Q2[next_state][argmax_Q1] * (not done)
```

(16) Notice here, we get the value from Q2 and prescribed by Q1.

(17) Then calculate the TD error from the Q1 estimate.

```
            td_error = td_target - Q1[state][action]
```

(18) Finally, move our estimate closer to that target by using the error.

```
            Q1[state][action] = Q1[state][action] + \
                                alphas[e] * td_error
```

(19) This line repeats on the next page . . .

I SPEAK PYTHON
The double Q-learning agent 3/3

(20) Okay. From the previous page, we were calculating Q1.

```
Q1[state][action] = Q1[state][action] + \
                        alphas[e] * td_error
```

(21) Now if the random int was 0 (50% of the times), we update the other Q-function, Q2.

```
else:
    argmax_Q2 = np.argmax(Q2[next_state])
```

(22) But, it's basically the mirror of the other update. We get the argmax of Q2.

(23) Then use that action, but get the estimate from the other Q-function Q1.

```
td_target = reward + gamma * \
                Q1[next_state][argmax_Q2] * (not done)
```

(24) Again, pay attention to the roles of Q1 and Q2 here reversed.

(25) We calculate the TD error from the Q2 this time.

```
td_error = td_target - Q2[state][action]
```

(26) And use it to update the Q2 estimate of the state-action pair.

```
Q2[state][action] = Q2[state][action] + \
                        alphas[e] * td_error
```

(27) Notice how we use the 'alphas' vector.

```
state = next_state
```

(28) We change the value of the state variable and keep looping, again until we land on a terminal state and the 'done' variable is set to True.

```
Q_track1[e] = Q1
Q_track2[e] = Q2
pi_track.append(np.argmax((Q1 + Q2)/2., axis=1))
```

(29) Here we store Q1 and Q2 for offline analysis.

(30) Notice the policy is the argmax of the mean of Q1 and Q2.

```
Q = (Q1 + Q2)/2.
V = np.max(Q, axis=1)
pi = lambda s: {s:a for s, a in enumerate( \
                        np.argmax(Q, axis=1))}[s]
```

(31) The final Q is the mean.

(32) The final V is the max of Q.

(33) The final policy is the argmax of the mean of Qs.

(34) We end up returning all this.

```
return Q, V, pi, (Q_track1 + Q_track2)/2., pi_track
```

One way of dealing with maximization bias is to track estimates in two Q-functions. At each time step, we choose one of them to determine the action, to determine which estimate is the highest according to that Q-function. But, then we use the other Q-function to obtain that action's estimate. By doing this, there's a lower chance of always having a positive bias error. Then, to select an action for interacting with the environment, we use the average, or the sum, across the two Q-functions for that state. That is, the maximum over $Q_1(S_{t+1})+Q_2(S_{t+1})$, for instance. The technique of using these two Q-functions is called *double learning*, and the algorithm that implements this technique is called *double Q-learning*. In a few chapters, you'll learn about a deep reinforcement learning algorithm called *double deep Q-networks* (DDQN), which uses a variant of this double learning technique.

IT'S IN THE DETAILS

FVMC, SARSA, Q-learning, and double Q-learning on the SWS environment

Let's put it all together and test all the algorithms we just learned about in the Slippery Walk Seven environment.

So you're aware, I used the same hyperparameters in all algorithms, the same gamma, alpha, epsilon, and respective decaying schedules. Remember, if you don't decay alpha toward 0, the algorithm doesn't fully converge. I'm decaying it to 0.01, which is good enough for this simple environment. Epsilon should also be decayed to zero for full convergence, but in practice this is rarely done. In fact, often state-of-the-art implementations don't even decay epsilon and use a constant value instead. Here, we're decaying to 0.1.

Another thing: note that in these runs, I set the same number of episodes for all algorithms; they all run

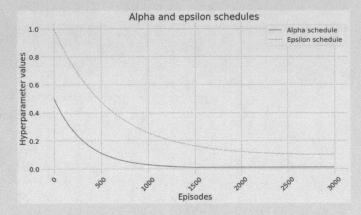

3,000 episodes in the SWS environment. You'll notice some algorithms don't converge in this many steps, but that doesn't mean they wouldn't converge at all. Also, some of the other environments in the chapter's Notebook, such as Frozen Lake, terminate on a set number of steps, that is, your agent has 100 steps to complete each episode, else it's given a done flag. This is somewhat of an issue that we'll address in later chapters. But, please, go to the Notebook and have fun! I think you'll enjoy playing around in there.

⌗ TALLY IT UP
Similar trends among bootstrapping and on-policy methods

(1) This first one is first-visit monte Carlo control. See how the estimates have high variance, as in the prediction algorithm. Also, all these algorithms are using the same action-selection strategy. The only difference is the method used in the policy-evaluation phase! Cool, right!?

(2) SARSA is an on-policy bootstrapping method; mc is on-policy, but not bootstrapping. In these experiments, you can see how SARSA has less variance than mc, yet it takes pretty much the same amount of time to get to the optimal values.

(3) Q-learning is an off-policy bootstrapping method. See how much faster the estimates track the true values. But, also, notice how the estimates are often higher and jump around somewhat aggressively.

(4) Double Q-learning, on the other hand, is slightly slower than Q-learning to get the estimates to track the optimal state-value function, but it does so in a much more stable manner. There's still a bit of over-estimation, but it's controlled.

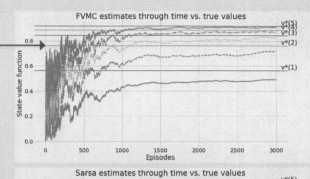

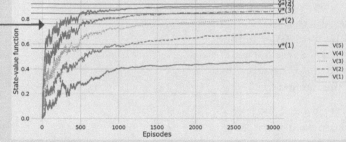

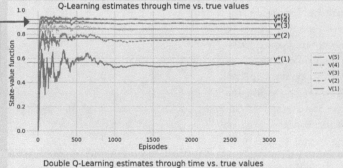

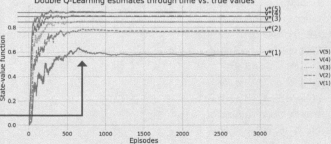

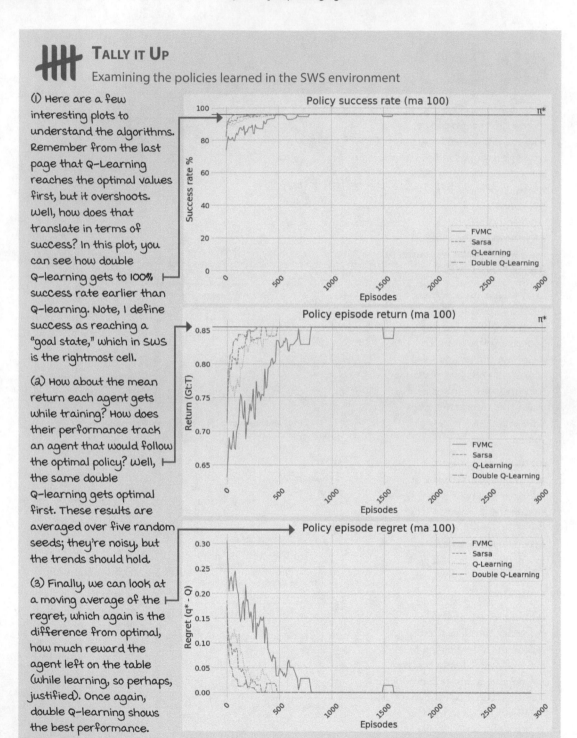

TALLY IT UP

Examining the policies learned in the SWS environment

(1) Here are a few interesting plots to understand the algorithms. Remember from the last page that Q-Learning reaches the optimal values first, but it overshoots. Well, how does that translate in terms of success? In this plot, you can see how double Q-learning gets to 100% success rate earlier than Q-learning. Note, I define success as reaching a "goal state," which in SWS is the rightmost cell.

(2) How about the mean return each agent gets while training? How does their performance track an agent that would follow the optimal policy? Well, the same double Q-learning gets optimal first. These results are averaged over five random seeds; they're noisy, but the trends should hold.

(3) Finally, we can look at a moving average of the regret, which again is the difference from optimal, how much reward the agent left on the table (while learning, so perhaps, justified). Once again, double Q-learning shows the best performance.

Examining the value functions learned in the SWS environment

(1) These are also interesting plots. I'm showing the moving average over 100 episodes of the estimated expected return: that is, how much the agent expects to get for a full episode (from an initial to a terminal state) versus how much the agent should expect to get, given the optimal v-function of the initial state. ⊢

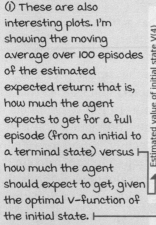

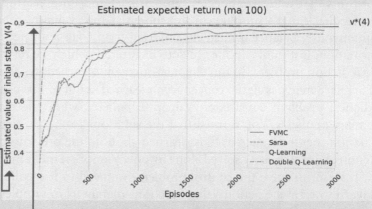

(2) In this next plot, we're looking at the state-value function, the v-function, estimation error. This is the mean absolute error across all estimates from their respective optimal. Take a look at how quickly Q-learning drops near zero, but also how ⊢ double Q-learning gets to the lowest error first. SARSA and FVMC are comparable in this simple environment.

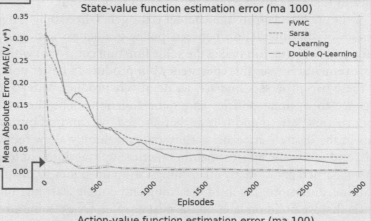

(3) Finally, we show the action-value function, the Q-function, error. These errors are different than the previous plot because for the previous, I'm using only the difference of the estimated max action and ⊣ the optimal, while here, ⊢ I'm calculating the MAE across all actions.

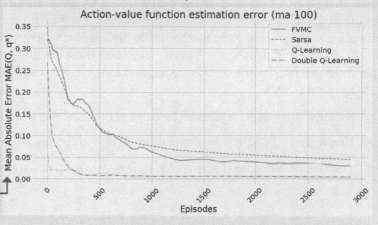

Summary

In this chapter, you put everything you've learned so far into practice. We learned about algorithms that optimize policies through trial-and-error learning. These algorithms learn from feedback that's simultaneously sequential and evaluative; that is, these agents learn to simultaneously balance immediate and long-term goals and the gathering and utilization of information. But unlike in the previous chapter, in which we restricted our agents to solving the prediction problem, in this chapter, our agents learned to solve the control problem.

There are many essential concepts you learned about in this chapter. You learned that the prediction problem consists of evaluation policies, while the control problem consists of optimizing policies. You learned that the solutions to the prediction problem are in policy evaluation methods, such as those learned about in the previous chapter. But unexpectedly, the control problem isn't solved alone by policy-improvement methods you've learned in the past. Instead, to solve the control problem, we need to use policy-evaluation methods that can learn to estimate action-value functions merely from samples and policy-improvement methods that take into account the need for exploration.

The key takeaway from this chapter is the generalized policy-iteration pattern (GPI) which consists of the interaction between policy-evaluation and policy-improvement methods. While policy evaluation makes the value function consistent with the policy evaluated, policy improvement reverses this consistency but produces a better policy. GPI tells us that by having these two processes interact, we iteratively produce better and better policies until convergence to optimal policies and value functions. The theory of reinforcement learning supports this pattern and tells us that, indeed, we can find optimal policies and value functions in the discrete state and action spaces with only a few requirements. You learned that GLIE and stochastic approximation theories apply at different levels to RL algorithms.

You learned about many other things, from on-policy to off-policy methods, from online to offline, and more. Double Q-learning and double learning, in general, are essential techniques that we build on later. In the next chapter, we examine advanced methods for solving the control problem. As environments get challenging, we use other techniques to learn optimal policies. Next, we look at methods that are more effective in solving environments, and they do so more efficiently, too. That is, they solve these environments, and do so using fewer experience samples than methods we learned about in this chapter.

By now, you

- Know that most RL agents follow a pattern known as generalized policy iteration

- Know that GPI solves the control problem with policy evaluation and improvement

- Learned about several agents that follow the GPI pattern to solve the control problem

TWEETABLE FEAT

Work on your own and share your findings

Here are several ideas on how to take what you have learned to the next level. If you'd like, share your results with the rest of the world and make sure to check out what others have done, too. It's a win-win situation, and hopefully, you'll take advantage of it.

- **#gdrl_ch06_tf01:** All the algorithms presented in this chapter use two crucial variables: the learning rate, alpha, and the discount factor, gamma. I want you to do an analysis on these two variables. For instance, how do these variables interact? How do they affect the total reward obtained by the agent, and the policy success rate?

- **#gdrl_ch06_tf02:** Another thing to think about after this chapter is that we used the same exploration strategy for all of the methods: it was an exponentially decaying epsilon-greedy strategy. But, is this the best strategy? How would you use other strategies from chapter 4? How about creating an exploration strategy of your own and testing that out? How about changing the hyperparameters related to the exploration strategy and see how results change? That shouldn't be hard at all to try. Head to the book's Notebooks and start by changing severalof the hyperparameters: then change the exploration strategy altogether, and tell us what you find.

- **#gdrl_ch06_tf03:** You're probably guessing this right. The algorithms in this chapter are also not using the time step limit correctly. Make sure to investigate what I'm alluding to, and once you find out, change the algorithms to do this right. Do the results change at all? Do agents now do better than before? Are they better in terms of estimating the optimal value function, the optimal policy, or both? How much better? Make sure to investigate, or come back after chapter 8. Share your findings.

- **#gdrl_ch06_tf04:** In every chapter, I'm using the final hashtag as a catchall hashtag. Feel free to use this one to discuss anything else that you worked on relevant to this chapter. There's no more exciting homework than that which you create for yourself. Make sure to share what you set yourself to investigate and your results.

Write a tweet with your findings, tag me @mimoralea (I'll retweet), and use the particular hashtag from the list to help interested folks find your results. There are no right or wrong results; you share your findings and check others' findings. Take advantage of this to socialize, contribute, and get yourself out there! We're waiting for you!

Here's a tweet example:

"Hey, @mimoralea. I created a blog post with a list of resources to study deep reinforcement learning. Check it out at <link>. #gdrl_ch01_tf01"

I'll make sure to retweet and help others find your work.

Achieving goals more effectively and efficiently | 7

In this chapter

- You will learn about making reinforcement learning agents more effective at reaching optimal performance when interacting with challenging environments.

- You will learn about making reinforcement learning agents more efficient at achieving goals by making the most of the experiences.

- You will improve on the agents presented in the previous chapters to have them make the most out of the data they collect and therefore optimize their performance more quickly.

Efficiency is doing things right; effectiveness is doing the right things.

— PETER DRUCKER
FOUNDER OF MODERN MANAGEMENT AND
PRESIDENTIAL MEDAL OF FREEDOM recipient

In this chapter, we improve on the agents you learned about in the previous chapter. More specifically, we take on two separate lines of improvement. First, we use the λ-return that you learned about in chapter 5 for the policy evaluation requirements of the generalized policy iteration pattern. We explore using the λ-return for both on-policy and off-policy methods. Using the λ-return with eligibility traces propagates credit to the right state-action pairs more quickly than standard methods, making the value-function estimates get near the actual values faster.

Second, we explore algorithms that use experience samples to learn a model of the environment, a Markov decision process (MDP). By doing so, these methods extract the most out of the data they collect and often arrive at optimality more quickly than methods that don't. The group of algorithms that attempt to learn a model of the environment is referred to as *model-based reinforcement learning*.

It's important to note that even though we explore these lines of improvements separately, nothing prevents you from trying to combine them, and it's perhaps something you should do after finishing this chapter. Let's get to the details right away.

ŘŁ   WITH AN RL ACCENT
Planning vs. model-free RL vs. model-based RL

Planning: Refers to algorithms that require a model of the environment to produce a policy. Planning methods can be of state-space planning type, which means they use the state space to find a policy, or they can be of plan-space planning type, meaning they search in the space of all possible plans (think about genetic algorithms.) Examples of planning algorithms that we've learned about in this book are value iteration and policy iteration.

Model-free RL: Refers to algorithms that don't use models of the environments, but are still able to produce a policy. The unique characteristic here is these methods obtain policies without the use of a map, a model, or an MDP. Instead, they use trial-and-error learning to obtain policies. Several examples of model-free RL algorithms that we have explored in this book are MC, SARSA, and Q-learning.

Model-based RL: Refers to algorithms that can learn, but don't require, a model of the environment to produce a policy. The distinction is they don't require models in advance, but can certainly make good use of them if available, and more importantly, attempt to learn the models through interaction with the environment. Several examples of model-based RL algorithms we learn about in this chapter are Dyna-Q and trajectory sampling.

Learning to improve policies using robust targets

The first line of improvement we discuss in this chapter is using more robust targets in our policy-evaluation methods. Recall that in chapter 5, we explored policy-evaluation methods that use different kinds of targets for estimating value functions. You learned about the Monte Carlo and TD approaches, but also about a target called the λ-return that uses a weighted combination of targets obtained using all visited states.

TD(λ) is the prediction method that uses the λ-return for our policy evaluation needs. However, as you remember from the previous chapter, when dealing with the control problem, we need to use a policy-evaluation method for estimating action-value functions, and a policy-improvement method that allows for exploration. In this section, we discuss control methods similar to SARSA and Q-learning, but use instead the λ-return.

CONCRETE EXAMPLE
The slippery walk seven environment

To introduce the algorithms in this chapter, we use the same environment we used in the previous chapter, called slippery walk seven (SWS). However, at the end of the chapter, we test the methods in much more challenging environments.

Recall that the SWS is a walk, a single-row grid-world environment, with seven non-terminal states. Remember that this environment is a "slippery" walk, meaning that it's noisy, that action effects are stochastic. If the agent chooses to go left, there's a chance it does, but there's also some chance that it goes right, or that it stays in place.

Slippery walk seven environment MDP

① Same environment as in the previous chapter

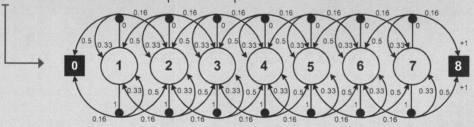

As a refresher, above is the MDP of this environments. But remember and always have in mind that the agent doesn't have any access to the transition probabilities. The dynamics of this environment are unknown to the agent. Also, to the agent, there are no relationships between the states in advance.

SARSA(λ): Improving policies after each step based on multi-step estimates

SARSA(λ) is a straightforward improvement to the original SARSA agent. The main difference between SARSA and SARSA(λ) is that instead of using the one-step bootstrapping target—the TD target, as we do in SARSA, in SARSA(λ), we use the λ-return. And that's it; you have SARSA(λ). Seriously! Did you see how learning the basics makes the more complex concepts easier?

Now, I'd like to dig a little deeper into the concept of eligibility traces that you first read about in chapter 5. The type of eligibility trace I introduced in chapter 5 is called the *accumulating trace*. However, in reality, there are multiple ways of tracing state or state-action pairs responsible for a reward.

In this section, we dig deeper into the accumulating trace and adapt it for solving the control problem, but we also explore a different kind of trace called the *replacing trace* and use them both in the SARSA(λ) agent.

0001   **A Bit of History**

Introduction of the SARSA and SARSA(λ) agents

In 1994, Gavin Rummery and Mahesan Niranjan published a paper titled "Online Q-Learning Using Connectionist Systems," in which they introduced an algorithm they called at the time "Modified Connectionist Q-Learning." In 1996, Singh and Sutton dubbed this algorithm SARSA because of the quintuple of events that the algorithm uses: $(S_t, A_t, R_{t+1}, S_{t+1}, A_{t+1})$. People often like knowing where these names come from, and as you'll soon see, RL researchers can get pretty creative with these names.

Funny enough, before this open and "unauthorized" rename of the algorithm, in 1995 in his PhD thesis titled "Problem Solving with Reinforcement Learning," Gavin issued Sutton an apology for continuing to use the name "Modified Q-Learning" despite Sutton's preference for "SARSA." Sutton also continued to use SARSA, which is ultimately the name that stuck with the algorithm in the RL community. By the way, Gavin's thesis also introduced the SARSA(λ) agent.

After obtaining his PhD in 1995, Gavin became a programmer and later a lead programmer for the company responsible for the series of the Tomb Raider games. Gavin has had a successful career as a game developer.

Mahesan, who became Gavin's PhD supervisor after the unexpected death of Gavin's original supervisor, followed a more traditional academic career holding lecturer and professor roles ever since his graduation in 1990.

For adapting the accumulating trace to solving the control problem, the only necessary change is that we must now track the visited state-action pairs, instead of visited states. Instead of using an eligibility vector for tracking visited states, we use an eligibility matrix for tracking visited state-action pairs.

The replace-trace mechanism is also straightforward. It consists of clipping eligibility traces to a maximum value of one; that is, instead of accumulating eligibility without bound, we allow traces to only grow to one. This strategy has the advantage that if your agents get stuck in a loop, the traces still don't grow out of proportion. The bottom line is that traces, in the replace-trace strategy, are set to one when a state-action pair is visited, and decay based on the λ value just like in the accumulate-trace strategy.

0001 A BIT OF HISTORY
Introduction of the eligibility trace mechanism

The general idea of an eligibility trace mechanism is probably due to A. Harry Klopf, when, in a 1972 paper titled "Brain Function and Adaptive Systems—A Heterostatic Theory," he described how synapses would become "eligible" for changes after reinforcing events. He hypothesized: "When a neuron fires, all of its excitatory and inhibitory synapses that were active during the summation of potentials leading to the response are *eligible* to undergo changes in their transmittances."

However, in the context of RL, Richard Sutton's PhD thesis (1984) introduced the mechanism of eligibility traces. More concretely, he introduced the accumulating trace that you've learned about in this book, also known as the conventional accumulating trace.

The replacing trace, on the other hand, was introduced by Satinder Singh and Richard Sutton in a 1996 paper titled "Reinforcement Learning with Replacing Eligibility Traces," which we discuss in this chapter.

They found a few interesting facts. First, they found that the replace-trace mechanism results in faster and more reliable learning than the accumulate-trace one. They also found that the accumulate-trace mechanism is biased, while the replace-trace one is unbiased. But more interestingly, they found relationships between TD(1), MC, and eligibility traces.

More concretely, they found that TD(1) with replacing traces is related to first-visit MC and that TD(1) with accumulating traces is related to every-visit MC. Moreover, they found that the offline version of the replace-trace TD(1) is identical to first-visit MC. It's a small world!

Accumulating traces in the SWS environment

Gamma=0.9, Lambda=0.5

(1) Let's calculate the eligibility trace Ɛ, and ⟼ E Q-function Q, assuming a gamma of 0.9, and a lambda of 0.5.

(2) Assume the following interactions occurred with the environment. Here the agent chose left but the environment kept the agent at the same state.

0	1	2	3	4	5	6	7	8
H				←				G

E

0	1	2	3	4	5	6	7	8
0	0	0	0	1	0	0	0	0
0	0	0	0	0	0	0	0	0

0	1	2	3	4	5	6	7	8
H				→●				G

(3) These are the eligibility traces for the actions. They're first set to 1, then decayed at a rate of 0.5 * 0.9.

E

0	1	2	3	4	5	6	7	8
0	0	0	0	0.45	0	0	0	0
0	0	0	0	1	0	0	0	0

0	1	2	3	4	5	6	7	8
H					●→			G

E

0	1	2	3	4	5	6	7	8
0	0	0	0	0.2025	0	0	0	0
0	0	0	0	0.45	1	0	0	0

...

(4) Assume there are more interactions.

0	1	2	3	4	5	6	7	8
H							●→	G

(5) Assume we reached the end of an episode and never found a reward until the end. We calculate Q with these values.

E

0	1	2	3	4	5	6	7	8
0	0	0	0	0.0410	0	0	0	0
0	0	0	0	0.09113	0.2025	0.45	1	0

TD error =1, alpha=0.1

Q

0	1	2	3	4	5	6	7	8
0	0	0	0	0.0041	0	0	0	0
0	0	0	0	0.00911	0.0203	0.045	0.1	0

(6) Can you recover additional info with what I provide?

🍲 BOIL IT DOWN
Frequency and recency heuristics in the accumulating-trace mechanism

The accumulating trace combines a frequency and a recency heuristic. When your agent tries a state-action pair, the trace for this pair is incremented by one. Now, imagine there's a loop in the environment, and the agent tries the same state-action pair several times. Should we make this state-action pair "more" responsible for rewards obtained in the future, or should we make it just responsible?

Accumulating traces allow trace values higher than one while replacing traces don't. Traces have a way for combining frequency (how often you try a state-action pair) and recency (how long ago you tried a state-action pair) heuristics implicitly encoded in the trace mechanism.

Replacing traces in the SWS environment

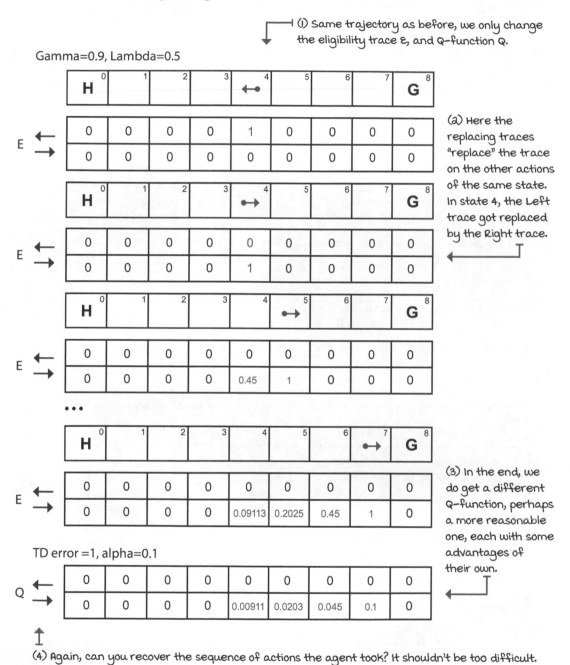

(1) Same trajectory as before, we only change the eligibility trace ε, and Q-function Q.

Gamma=0.9, Lambda=0.5

(2) Here the replacing traces "replace" the trace on the other actions of the same state. In state 4, the Left trace got replaced by the Right trace.

(3) In the end, we do get a different Q-function, perhaps a more reasonable one, each with some advantages of their own.

TD error =1, alpha=0.1

(4) Again, can you recover the sequence of actions the agent took? It shouldn't be too difficult.

I SPEAK PYTHON

The SARSA(λ) agent 1/2

```
def sarsa_lambda(env,
                 gamma=1.0,
                 init_alpha=0.5,
                 min_alpha=0.01,
                 alpha_decay_ratio=0.5,
                 init_epsilon=1.0,
                 min_epsilon=0.1,
                 epsilon_decay_ratio=0.9,
                 lambda_=0.5,
                 replacing_traces=True,
                 n_episodes=3000):
```

(1) The SARSA lambda agent is a mix of the SARSA and the TD lambda methods.

(2) Here's the lambda_ hyperparameter (ending in _ because the word lambda is reserved in Python).

(3) The replacing_traces variable sets the algorithm to use replacing or accumulating traces.

```
    nS, nA = env.observation_space.n, env.action_space.n
    pi_track = []
```

(4) We use the usual variables as we have before . . .

(5) . . . including the Q-function and the tracking matrix.

```
    Q = np.zeros((nS, nA), dtype=np.float64)
    Q_track = np.zeros((n_episodes, nS, nA),
                       dtype=np.float64)
```

(6) These are the eligibility traces that will allow us to keep track of states eligible for updates.

```
    E = np.zeros((nS, nA), dtype=np.float64)
```

```
    select_action = lambda state, Q, epsilon: \
        np.argmax(Q[state]) \
        if np.random.random() > epsilon \
        else np.random.randint(len(Q[state]))

    alphas = decay_schedule(
        init_alpha, min_alpha,
        alpha_decay_ratio, n_episodes)

    epsilons = decay_schedule(
        init_epsilon, min_epsilon,
        epsilon_decay_ratio, n_episodes)

    for e in tqdm(range(n_episodes), leave=False):
```

(7) The rest is the same as before with the select_action function, and the vectors alphas and epsilons.

(8) We continue on the next page with this line.

I SPEAK PYTHON

The SARSA(λ) agent 2/2

(9) Continues here . . .

```
for e in tqdm(range(n_episodes), leave=False):
```

(10) Every new episode, we set the eligibility of every state to zero.

```
        E.fill(0)   (11) We then reset the environment and the done flag as usual.
        state, done = env.reset(), False
        action = select_action(state, Q, epsilons[e])
```

(12) We select the action of the initial state.

```
        while not done:
```
(13) We enter the interaction loop.

(14) We send the action to the environment and receive the experience tuple.

```
            next_state, reward, done, _ = env.step(action)
            next_action = select_action(next_state,
                                        Q,
                                        epsilons[e])
```

(15) We select the action to use at the next state using the Q-table and the epsilon corresponding to this episode.

```
            td_target = reward + gamma * \
                        Q[next_state][next_action] * (not done)
            td_error = td_target - Q[state][action]
```

(16) We calculate the TD target and the TD error as in the original SARSA.

(17) Then, we increment the state-action pair trace, and clip it to 1 if it's a replacing trace.

```
            E[state][action] = E[state][action] + 1
            if replacing_traces: E.clip(0, 1, out=E)
```

(18) And notice this! We're applying the TD error to all eligible state-action pairs at once. Even though we're using the entire Q-table, E will be mostly 0, and greater than zero for eligible pairs.

```
            Q = Q + alphas[e] * td_error * E
            E = gamma * lambda_ * E
```
(19) We decay the eligibilities.

```
            state, action = next_state, next_action
```
(20) Update the variables.

```
        Q_track[e] = Q
        pi_track.append(np.argmax(Q, axis=1))
```
(21) Save Q and pi.

(22) At the end of training we extract V, pi, and return.

```
    V = np.max(Q, axis=1)
    pi = lambda s: {s:a for s, a in enumerate(\
                            np.argmax(Q, axis=1))}[s]
    return Q, V, pi, Q_track, pi_track
```

MIGUEL'S ANALOGY

Accumulating and replacing traces, and a gluten- and banana-free diet

A few months back, my daughter was having trouble sleeping at night. Every night, she would wake up multiple times, crying very loudly, but unfortunately, not telling us what the problem was.

After a few nights, my wife and I decided to do something about it and try to "trace" back the issue so that we could more effectively "assign credit" to what was causing the sleepless nights.

We put on our detective hats (if you're a parent, you know what this is like) and tried many things to diagnose the problem. After a week or so, we narrowed the issue to foods; we knew the bad nights were happening when she ate certain foods, but we couldn't determine which foods exactly were to blame. I noticed that throughout the day, she would eat lots of carbs with gluten, such as cereal, pasta, crackers, and bread. And, close to bedtime, she would snack on fruits.

An "accumulating trace" in my brain pointed to the carbs. "Of course!" I thought, "Gluten is evil; we all know that. Plus, she is eating all that gluten throughout the day." If we trace back and accumulate the number of times she ate gluten, gluten was clearly eligible, was clearly to blame, so we did remove the gluten.

But, to our surprise, the issue only subsided, it didn't entirely disappear as we hoped. After a few days, my wife remembered she had trouble eating bananas at night when she was a kid. I couldn't believe it, I mean, bananas are fruits, and fruits are only good for you, right? But funny enough, in the end, removing bananas got rid of the bad nights. Hard to believe!

But, perhaps if I would've used a "replacing trace" instead of an "accumulating trace," all of the carbs she ate multiple times throughout the day would have received a more conservative amount of blame.

Instead, because I was using an accumulating trace, it seemed to me that the many times she ate gluten were to blame. Period. I couldn't see clearly that the recency of the bananas played a role.

The bottom line is that accumulating traces can "exaggerate" when confronted with frequency while replacing traces moderate the blame assigned to frequent events. This moderation can help the more recent, but rare events surface and be taken into account.

Don't make any conclusions, yet. Like everything in life, and in RL, it's vital for you to know the tools and don't just dismiss things at first glance. I'm just showing you the available options, but it's up to you to use the right tools to achieve your goals.

Watkins's Q(λ): Decoupling behavior from learning, again

And, of course, there's an off-policy control version of the λ algorithms. **Q(λ)** is an extension of Q-learning that uses the λ-return for policy-evaluation requirements of the generalized policy-iteration pattern. Remember, the only change we're doing here is replacing the TD target for off-policy control (the one that uses the max over the action in the next state) with a λ-return for off-policy control. There are two different ways to extend Q-learning to eligibility traces, but, I'm only introducing the original version, commonly referred to as *Watkins's Q(λ)*.

0001 **A BIT OF HISTORY**
Introduction of the Q-learning and Q(λ) agents

In 1989, the Q-learning and Q(λ) methods were introduced by Chris Watkins in his PhD thesis titled "Learning from Delayed Rewards," which was foundational to the development of the current theory of reinforcement learning.

Q-learning is still one of the most popular reinforcement learning algorithms, perhaps because it's simple and it works well. Q(λ) is now referred to as Watkins's Q(λ) because there's a slightly different version of Q(λ)—due to Jing Peng and Ronald Williams—that was worked between 1993 and 1996 (that version is referred to as Peng's Q(λ).)

In 1992, Chris, along with Peter Dayan, published a paper titled "Technical Note Q-learning," in which they proved a convergence theorem for Q-learning. They showed that Q-learning converges with probability 1 to the optimum action-value function, with the assumption that all state-action pairs are repeatedly sampled and represented discretely.

Unfortunately, Chris stopped doing RL research almost right after that. He went on to work for hedge funds in London, then visited research labs, including a group led by Yann LeCun, always working AI-related problems, but not so much RL. For the past 22+ years, Chris has been a Reader in Artificial Intelligence at the University of London.

After finishing his 1991 PhD thesis titled "Reinforcing Connectionism: Learning the Statistical Way." (Yeah, connectionism is what they called neural networks back then—"deep reinforcement learning" you say? Yep!) Peter went on a couple of postdocs, including one with Geoff Hinton at the University of Toronto. Peter was a postdoc advisor to Demis Hassabis, cofounder of DeepMind. Peter has held many director positions at research labs, and the latest is the Max Planck Institute.

Since 2018 he's been a Fellow of the Royal Society, one of the highest awards given in the UK.

I SPEAK PYTHON

The Watkins's Q(λ) agent 1/3

```python
def q_lambda(env,
             gamma=1.0,
             init_alpha=0.5,
             min_alpha=0.01,
             alpha_decay_ratio=0.5,
             init_epsilon=1.0,
             min_epsilon=0.1,
             epsilon_decay_ratio=0.9,
             lambda_=0.5,
             replacing_traces=True,
             n_episodes=3000):
```

(1) The Q lambda agent is a mix between the Q-learning and the TD lambda methods.

(2) Here are the lambda_ and the replacing_traces hyperparameters.

(3) Useful variables

```python
    nS, nA = env.observation_space.n, env.action_space.n
    pi_track = []
```

(4) The Q-table

```python
    Q = np.zeros((nS, nA), dtype=np.float64)
    Q_track = np.zeros((n_episodes, nS, nA), dtype=np.float64)
```

(5) The eligibility traces matrix for all state-action pairs

```python
    E = np.zeros((nS, nA), dtype=np.float64)
```

(6) The usual suspects

```python
    select_action = lambda state, Q, epsilon: \
        np.argmax(Q[state]) \
        if np.random.random() > epsilon \
        else np.random.randint(len(Q[state]))

    alphas = decay_schedule(
        init_alpha, min_alpha,
        alpha_decay_ratio, n_episodes)

    epsilons = decay_schedule(
        init_epsilon, min_epsilon,
        epsilon_decay_ratio, n_episodes)
```

(7) To be continued . . .

```python
    for e in tqdm(range(n_episodes), leave=False):
```

I SPEAK PYTHON

The Watkins's Q(λ) agent 2/3

(8) Continues on the episodes loop ⊢────→

```python
for e in tqdm(range(n_episodes), leave=False):
```

(9) Okay. Because Q lambda is an off-policy method we must use ε with care. We're learning about the greedy policy, but following an exploratory policy. First we fill ε with zeros as before.

```python
        E.fill(0)
```
←────────────┤

(10) Reset the environment and done.

```python
        state, done = env.reset(), False
```

(11) But, notice how we are preselecting the action as in SARSA, but we didn't do that in Q-learning. This is because we need to check whether our next action is greedy!

```python
        action = select_action(state,
                               Q,
                               epsilons[e])
```

(12) Enter the interaction loop.

```python
        while not done:
```

(13) Step the environment and get the experience. ⊢──────────→

```python
            next_state, reward, done, _ = env.step(action)
```

(14) We select the next_action SARSA-style!

```python
            next_action = select_action(next_state,
                                        Q,
                                        epsilons[e])
```

(15) And use it to verify that the action on the next step will still come from the greedy policy.

```python
            next_action_is_greedy = \
                Q[next_state][next_action] == Q[next_state].max()
```

(16) On this step, we still calculate the TD target as in regular Q-learning, using the max.

```python
            td_target = reward + gamma * \
                Q[next_state].max() * (not done)
```

(17) And use the TD target to calculate the TD error.

```python
            td_error = td_target - Q[state][action]
```

(18) We continue from this line on the next page.

I Speak Python

The Watkins's Q(λ) agent 3/3

(19) Again, calculate a TD error using the target and the current estimate of the state-action pair. Notice, this isn't next_state, this is state!!!

```
td_error = td_target - Q[state][action]
```

(20) The other approach to replace-trace control methods is to zero out all action values of the current state and then increment the current action.

```
if replacing_traces: E[state].fill(0)
```

(21) We increment the eligibility of the current state-action pair by 1.

```
E[state][action] = E[state][action] + 1
Q = Q + alphas[e] * td_error * E
```

(22) And as before, we multiply the entire eligibility trace matrix by the error and the learning rate corresponding to episode e, then move the entire Q toward that error. By doing so, we're effectively dropping a signal to all visited states to a various degree.

```
if next_action_is_greedy:
    E = gamma * lambda_ * E
else:
    E.fill(0)
```

(23) Notice this too. If the action we'll take on the next state (which we already selected) is a greedy action, then we decay the eligibility matrix as usual, otherwise, we must reset the eligibility matrix to zero because we'll no longer be learning about the greedy policy.

(24) At the end of the step, we update the state and action to be the next state and action.

```
state, action = next_state, next_action
```

```
Q_track[e] = Q
pi_track.append(np.argmax(Q, axis=1))
```

(25) We save Q and pi.

(26) And at the end of training we also save V and the final pi.

```
V = np.max(Q, axis=1)
pi = lambda s: {s:a for s, a in enumerate(\
                        np.argmax(Q, axis=1))}[s]
```

(27) Finally, we return all this.

```
return Q, V, pi, Q_track, pi_track
```

Agents that interact, learn, and plan

In chapter 3, we discussed planning algorithms such as value iteration (VI) and policy iteration (PI). These are planning algorithms because they require a model of the environment, an MDP. Planning methods calculate optimal policies offline. On the other hand, in the last chapter I presented model-free reinforcement learning methods, perhaps even suggesting that they were an improvement over planning methods. But are they?

The advantage of model-free RL over planning methods is that the former doesn't require MDPs. Often MDPs are challenging to obtain in advance; sometimes MDPs are even impossible to create. Imagine representing the game of Go with 10^{170} possible states or StarCraft II with 10^{1685} states. Those are significant numbers, and that doesn't even include the action spaces or transition function, imagine! Not requiring an MDP in advance is a practical benefit.

But, let's think about this for a second: what if we don't require an MDP in advance, but perhaps learn one as we interact with the environment? Think about it: as you walk around a new area, you start building a map in your head. You walk around for a while, find a coffee shop, get coffee, and you know how to get back. The skill of learning maps should be intuitive to you. Can reinforcement learning agents do something similar to this?

In this section, we explore agents that interact with the environment, like the model-free methods, but they also learn models of the environment from these interactions, MDPs. By learning maps, agents often require fewer experience samples to learn optimal policies. These methods are called *model-based reinforcement learning*. Note that in the literature, you often see VI and PI referred to as planning methods, but you may also see them referred to as model-based methods. I prefer to draw the line and call them planning methods because they require an MDP to do anything useful at all. SARSA and Q-learning algorithms are model-free because they do not require and do not learn an MDP. The methods that you learn about in this section are model-based because they do not require, but do learn and use an MDP (or at least an approximation of an MDP).

 WITH AN RL ACCENT
Sampling models vs. distributional models

Sampling models: Refers to models of the environment that produce a single sample of how the environment will transition given some probabilities; you sample a transition from the model.

Distributional models: Refers to models of the environment that produce the probability distribution of the transition and reward functions.

Dyna-Q: Learning sample models

One of the most well-known architectures for unifying planning and model-free methods is called *Dyna-Q*. Dyna-Q consists of interleaving a model-free RL method, such as Q-learning, and a planning method, similar to value iteration, using both experiences sampled from the environment and experiences sampled from the learned model to improve the action-value function.

In Dyna-Q, we keep track of both the transition and reward function as three-dimensional tensors indexed by the state, the action, and the next state. The transition tensor keeps count of the number of times we've seen the three-tuple *(s, a, s')* indicating how many times we arrived at state *s'* from state *s* when selecting action *a*. The reward tensor holds the average reward we received on the three-tuple *(s, a, s')* indicating the expected reward when we select action *a* on state *s* and transition to state *s'*.

A model-based reinforcement learning architecture

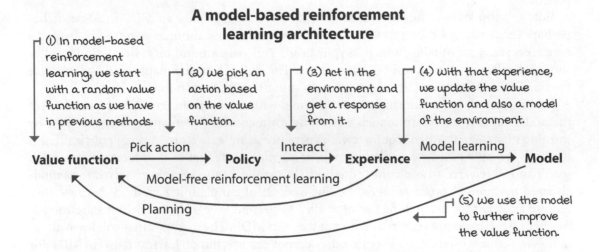

(1) In model-based reinforcement learning, we start with a random value function as we have in previous methods.

(2) We pick an action based on the value function.

(3) Act in the environment and get a response from it.

(4) With that experience, we update the value function and also a model of the environment.

(5) We use the model to further improve the value function.

Value function → Pick action → **Policy** → Interact → **Experience** → Model learning → **Model**

Model-free reinforcement learning

Planning

0001   A BIT OF HISTORY

Introduction of the Dyna-Q agent

Ideas related to model-based RL methods can be traced back many years, and are credited to several researchers, but there are three main papers that set the foundation for the Dyna architecture.

The first is a 1981 paper by Richard Sutton and Andrew Barto titled "An Adaptive Network that Constructs and Uses an Internal Model of Its World," then a 1990 paper by Richard Sutton titled "Integrated Architectures for Learning, Planning, and Reacting Based on Approximating Dynamic Programming," and, finally, a 1991 paper by Richard Sutton titled "Dyna, an Integrated Architecture for Learning, Planning, and Reacting," in which the general architecture leading to the specific Dyna-Q agent was introduced.

I SPEAK PYTHON

The Dyna-Q agent 1/3

```python
def dyna_q(env,
           gamma=1.0,
           init_alpha=0.5,
           min_alpha=0.01,
           alpha_decay_ratio=0.5,
           init_epsilon=1.0,
           min_epsilon=0.1,
           epsilon_decay_ratio=0.9,
           n_planning=3,
           n_episodes=3000):
```

(1) Dyna-Q is similar to the Q-learning agent, but it also learns a model of the environment and it uses that model to improve the estimates.

(2) This n_planning hyperparameter is the number of updates to the estimates that will run from the learned model.

(3) Most of the first part of the algorithm is the same.

```python
    nS, nA = env.observation_space.n, env.action_space.n
    pi_track = []
```

(4) We initialize the Q-function to zero, and so on.

```python
    Q = np.zeros((nS, nA), dtype=np.float64)
    Q_track = np.zeros((n_episodes, nS, nA), dtype=np.float64)
```

(5) But then, we create a function to keep track of the transition function.
(6) And another one to keep track of the reward signal.

```python
    T_count = np.zeros((nS, nA, nS), dtype=np.int)
    R_model = np.zeros((nS, nA, nS), dtype=np.float64)
```

(7) Then initialize the exploration strategy select_action, and the alphas and epsilons vectors, as usual.

```python
    select_action = lambda state, Q, epsilon: \
        np.argmax(Q[state]) \
        if np.random.random() > epsilon \
        else np.random.randint(len(Q[state]))

    alphas = decay_schedule(
        init_alpha, min_alpha,
        alpha_decay_ratio, n_episodes)

    epsilons = decay_schedule(
        init_epsilon, min_epsilon,
        epsilon_decay_ratio, n_episodes)
```

(8) To be continued . . .

```python
    for e in tqdm(range(n_episodes), leave=False):
```

I SPEAK PYTHON
The Dyna-Q agent 2/3

(9) Continues on the episode loop

```python
for e in tqdm(range(n_episodes), leave=False):
```

(10) For each new episode, we start by resetting the environment and obtaining the initial state. We also set the 'done' flag to False and enter the step-interaction loop.

```python
state, done = env.reset(), False
while not done:
```

(11) We select the action, as in original Q-learning (inside the loop only).

```python
action = select_action(state, Q, epsilons[e])
```

(12) We step the environment and get the experience tuple.

```python
next_state, reward, done, _ = env.step(action)
```

(13) Then, start learning the model! We increment the transition count for the state-action-next_state triplet indicating that full transition happened once more.

```python
T_count[state][action][next_state] += 1
```

(14) We also attempt to calculate an incremental mean of the reward signal. Get the difference.

```python
r_diff = reward - \
            R_model[state][action][next_state]
```

(15) Then use that difference and the transition count to learn the reward signal.

```python
R_model[state][action][next_state] += \
        (r_diff / T_count[state][action][next_state])
```

(16) We calculate the TD target as usual, Q-learning style (off-policy, using the max)...

```python
td_target = reward + gamma * \
                Q[next_state].max() * (not done)
```

(17) ...and the TD error, too, using the TD target and the current estimate.

```python
td_error = td_target - Q[state][action]
Q[state][action] = Q[state][action] + \
                alphas[e] * td_error
```

(18) Finally, update the Q-function.

(19) And right before we get into the planning steps, we back up the next state variable.

```python
backup_next_state = next_state
for _ in range(n_planning):
```

(20) To be continued...

I SPEAK PYTHON

The Dyna-Q agent 3/3

(21) We continue from the planning loop.

```python
for _ in range(n_planning):
```

(22) First, we want to make sure there have been updates to the Q-function before, otherwise, there's not much to plan.

```python
    if Q.sum() == 0: break
```

(23) Then we select a state from a list of states already visited by the agent in experience.

```python
    visited_states = np.where( \
                    np.sum(T_count, axis=(1, 2)) > 0)[0]
    state = np.random.choice(visited_states)
```

(24) We then select an action that has been taken on that state.

```python
    actions_taken = np.where( \
                    np.sum(T_count[state], axis=1) > 0)[0]
    action = np.random.choice(actions_taken)
```

(25) We use the count matrix to calculate probabilities of a next state and then a next state.

```python
    probs = T_count[state][action] / \
                    T_count[state][action].sum()
    next_state = np.random.choice( \
                    np.arange(nS), size=1, p=probs)[0]
```

(26) Use the reward model as the reward.

```python
    reward = R_model[state][action][next_state]
    td_target = reward + gamma * \
                    Q[next_state].max()
    td_error = td_target - Q[state][action]
    Q[state][action] = Q[state][action] + \
                    alphas[e] * td_error
```

(27) And update the Q-function using that simulated experience!

```python
    state = backup_next_state
```

(28) At the end of the planning steps, we set the state as the next state.

(29) The rest is the same.

```python
Q_track[e] = Q
pi_track.append(np.argmax(Q, axis=1))
V = np.max(Q, axis=1)
pi = lambda s: {s:a for s, a in enumerate( \
                np.argmax(Q, axis=1))}[s]
return Q, V, pi, Q_track, pi_track
```

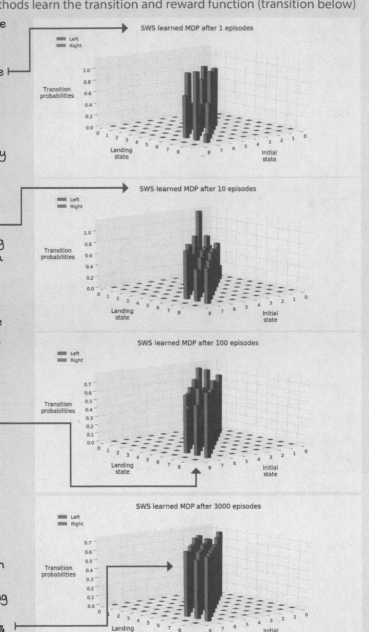

TALLY IT UP

Model-based methods learn the transition and reward function (transition below)

(1) Look at the first plot to the right. This one is the model that Dyna-Q has learned after one episode. Now, there are obvious issues with this model, but also, this is only after a single episode. This could mean trouble when using the learned model early on because there will be a bias when sampling an incorrect model.

(2) Only after 10 episodes, you can see the model taking shape. In the second plot, you should be able to see the right probabilities coming together. The axis to the right is the initial state s, the axis to the left is the landing state, the colors are the actions, and bar heights are the transition probabilities.

(3) After 100 episodes the probabilities look pretty close to the real MDP. Obviously, this is a simple environment, so the agent can gather enough experience samples for building an MDP quickly.

(4) You can see here the probabilities are good enough and describe the MDP correctly. You know that going right on state 7 should take you to state 8 with about 50% chance, to 7 with about 30% and to 6 with about 20%.

SWS learned MDP after 1 episodes

SWS learned MDP after 10 episodes

SWS learned MDP after 100 episodes

SWS learned MDP after 3000 episodes

Trajectory sampling: Making plans for the immediate future

In Dyna-Q, we learn the model as previously described, adjust action-value functions as we do in vanilla Q-learning, and then run a few planning iterations at the end of the algorithm. Notice that if we removed the model-learning and planning lines from the code, we'd be left with the same Q-learning algorithm that we had in the previous chapter.

At the planning phase, we only sample from the state-action pairs that have been visited, so that the agent doesn't waste resources with state-action pairs about which the model has no information. From those visited state-action pairs, we sample a state uniformly at random and then sample action from previously selected actions, also uniformly at random. Finally, we obtain the next state and reward sampling from the probabilities of transition given that state-action pair. But doesn't this seem intuitively incorrect? We're planning by using a state selected uniformly at random!

Couldn't this technique be more effective if we used a state that we expect to encounter during the current episode? Think about it for a second. Would you prefer prioritizing planning your day, week, month, and year, or would you instead plan a random event that "could" happen in your life? Say that you're a software engineer: would you prefer planning reading a programming book, and working on that side project, or a future possible career change to medicine? Planning for the immediate future is the smarter approach. *Trajectory sampling* is a model-based RL method that does just that.

 BOIL IT DOWN

Trajectory sampling

While Dyna-Q samples the learned MDP uniformly at random, trajectory sampling gathers trajectories, that is, transitions and rewards that can be encountered in the immediate future. You're planning your week, not a random time in your life. It makes more sense to do it this way.

The traditional trajectory-sampling approach is to sample from an initial state until reaching a terminal state using the on-policy trajectory, in other words, sampling actions from the same behavioral policy at the given time step.

However, you shouldn't limit yourself to this approach; you should experiment. For instance, my implementation samples starting from the current state, instead of an initial state, to a terminal state within a preset number of steps, sampling a policy greedy with respect to the current estimates.

But you can try something else. As long as you're sampling a trajectory, you can call that trajectory sampling.

I Speak Python

The trajectory-sampling agent 1/3

```
def trajectory_sampling(env,
                        gamma=1.0,
                        init_alpha=0.5,
                        min_alpha=0.01,
                        alpha_decay_ratio=0.5,
                        init_epsilon=1.0,
                        min_epsilon=0.1,
                        epsilon_decay_ratio=0.9,
                        max_trajectory_depth=100,
                        n_episodes=3000):
```

(1) Trajectory sampling is, for the most part, the same as Dyna-Q, with a few exceptions.

(2) Instead of n_planning we use a max_trajectory_depth to restrict the trajectory length.

(3) most of the algorithm is the same as Dyna-Q.

```
    nS, nA = env.observation_space.n, env.action_space.n
    pi_track = []
```

(4) The Q-function, and so on

```
    Q = np.zeros((nS, nA), dtype=np.float64)
    Q_track = np.zeros((n_episodes, nS, nA), dtype=np.float64)
```

(5) we create the same variables to model the transition function . . .

(6) . . . and another one for the reward signal.

```
    T_count = np.zeros((nS, nA, nS), dtype=np.int)
    R_model = np.zeros((nS, nA, nS), dtype=np.float64)
```

(7) The select_action function, the alphas vector, and epsilons vector are all the same.

```
    select_action = lambda state, Q, epsilon: \
        np.argmax(Q[state]) \
        if np.random.random() > epsilon \
        else np.random.randint(len(Q[state]))

    alphas = decay_schedule(
        init_alpha, min_alpha,
        alpha_decay_ratio, n_episodes)

    epsilons = decay_schedule(
        init_epsilon, min_epsilon,
        epsilon_decay_ratio, n_episodes)
```

(8) To be continued . . .

```
    for e in tqdm(range(n_episodes), leave=False):
```

I Speak Python

The trajectory-sampling agent 2/3

(9) Continues on the episode loop

```
for e in tqdm(range(n_episodes), leave=False):
```

(10) Again, each new episode, we start by resetting the environment and obtaining the initial state. We also set the done flag to False and enter the step interaction loop.

```
state, done = env.reset(), False
while not done:
```

(11) We select the action.

```
action = select_action(state, Q, epsilons[e])
```

(12) We step the environment and get the experience tuple.

```
next_state, reward, done, _ = env.step(action)
```

(13) We learn the model just like in Dyna-Q: increment the transition count for the state-action–next_state triplet indicating that full transition occurred.

```
T_count[state][action][next_state] += 1
```

(14) Then, again, calculate an incremental mean of the reward signal; first, get the difference.

```
r_diff = reward - \
                R_model[state][action][next_state]
```

(15) Then, use that difference and the transition count to learn the reward signal.

```
R_model[state][action][next_state] += \
        (r_diff / T_count[state][action][next_state])
```

(16) We calculate the TD target as usual.

```
td_target = reward + gamma * \
                Q[next_state].max() * (not done)
```

(17) The TD error using the TD target and the current estimate

```
td_error = td_target - Q[state][action]
Q[state][action] = Q[state][action] + \
                        alphas[e] * td_error
```

(18) Then, update the Q-function.

(19) And right before we get into the planning steps, we back up the next state variable.

```
backup_next_state = next_state
for _ in range(max_trajectory_depth):
```

(20) To be continued . . .

I Speak Python
The trajectory-sampling agent 3/3

(21) Notice we are now using a max_trajectory_depth variable, but are still planning.

```
for _ in range(max_trajectory_depth):
```

(22) We still check for the Q-function to have any difference, so it's worth our compute.

```
if Q.sum() == 0: break
```

(23) Select the action either on-policy or off-policy (using the greedy policy).

```
# action = select_action(state, Q, epsilons[e])
action = Q[state].argmax()
```

(24) If we haven't experienced the transition, planning would be a mess, so break out.

```
if not T_count[state][action].sum(): break
```

(25) Otherwise, we get the probabilities of next_state and sample the model accordingly.

```
probs = T_count[state][action] / \
                    T_count[state][action].sum()
next_state = np.random.choice( \
                np.arange(nS), size=1, p=probs)[0]
```

(26) Then, get the reward as prescribed by the reward-signal model.

```
reward = R_model[state][action][next_state]
```

(27) And continue updating the Q-function as if with real experience.

(28) Notice here we update the state variable right before we loop and continue the on-policy planning steps.

```
td_target = reward + gamma * \
                            Q[next_state].max()
td_error = td_target - Q[state][action]
Q[state][action] = Q[state][action] + \
                            alphas[e] * td_error
state = next_state
```

```
state = backup_next_state
```

(29) Outside the planning loop, we restore the state, and continue real interaction steps.

(30) Everything else as usual

```
    Q_track[e] = Q
    pi_track.append(np.argmax(Q, axis=1))
V = np.max(Q, axis=1)
pi = lambda s: {s:a for s, a in enumerate( \
                            np.argmax(Q, axis=1))}[s]
return Q, V, pi, Q_track, pi_track
```

||||| TALLY IT UP

Dyna-Q and trajectory sampling sample the learned model differently

(1) This first plot shows the states that were sampled by the planning phase of Dyna-Q and the actions selected in those states. As you can see, Dyna-Q samples uniformly at random, not only the states, but also the actions taken in those states.

(2) With trajectory sampling, you have a different sampling strategy. Remember, in the SWS environment the rightmost state, state 8, is the only non-zero reward state. Landing on state 8 provides a reward of +1. The greedy trajectory sampling strategy samples the model in an attempt to improve greedy action selection. This is the reason why the states sampled are skewed toward the goal state, state 8. The same happens with the sampling of the action. As you can see, the right action is sampled far more than the left action across the board.

(3) To understand the implications of the different sampling strategies, I plotted the landing states after sampling an action in state 7, which is the state to the left of the goal state. As we've seen, Dyna-Q does the sampling uniformly at random so probabilities reflect the MDP.

(4) Trajectory sampling, on the other hand, lands on the goal state far more often, therefore experiencing non-zero rewards from the model more frequently.

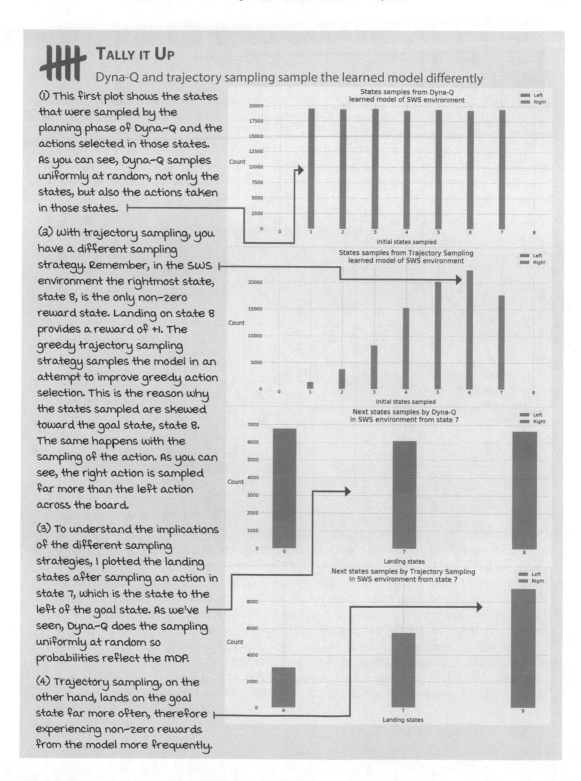

CONCRETE EXAMPLE
The frozen lake environment

In chapter 2, we developed the MDP for an environment called frozen lake (FL). As you remember, FL is a simple grid-world (GW) environment. It has discrete state and action spaces, with 16 states and four actions.

The goal of the agent is to go from a start location to a goal location while avoiding falling into holes. In this particular instantiation of the frozen lake environment, the goal is to go from state 0 to state 15. The challenge is that the surface of the lake is frozen, and therefore slippery, very slippery.

The frozen lake environment

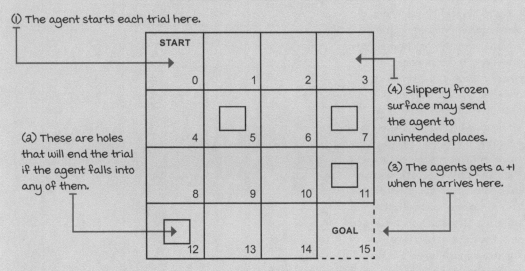

The FL environment is a 4 × 4 grid with 16 cells, states 0–15, top-left to bottom-right. State 0 is the only state in the initial state distribution, meaning that on every new episode, the agent shows up in that START state. States 5, 7, 11, 12, and 15 are terminal states: once the agent lands on any of those states, the episode terminates. States 5, 7, 11, and 12 are holes, and state 15 is the "GOAL." What makes "holes" and "GOAL" be any different is the reward function. All transitions landing on the GOAL state, state 15, provide a +1 reward, while every other transition in the entire grid world provides a 0 reward, no reward. The agent will naturally try to get to that +1 transition, and that involves avoiding the holes. The challenge of the environment is that actions have stochastic effects, so the agent moves only a third of the time as intended. The other two-thirds is split evenly in orthogonal directions. If the agent tries to move out of the grid world, it will bounce back to the cell from which it tried to move.

IT'S IN THE DETAILS
Hyperparameter values for the frozen lake environment

The frozen lake (FL) environment is a more challenging environment than, for instance, the slippery walk seven (SWS) environment. Therefore, one of the most important changes we need to make is to increase the number of episodes the agent interacts with the environment.

While in the SWS environment, we allow the agent to interact for only 3,000 episodes; in the FL environment, we let the agent gather experience for 10,000 episodes. This simple change also automatically adjusts the decay schedule for both alpha and epsilon.

Changing the value of the n_episodes parameter from 3,000 to 10,000 automatically changes the amount of exploration and learning of the agent. Alpha now decays from an initial value of 0.5 to a minimum value of 0.01 after 50% of the total episodes, which is 5,000 episodes, and epsilon decays from an initial value of 1.0 to a minimum value of 0.1 after 90% of the total episodes, which is 9,000 episodes.

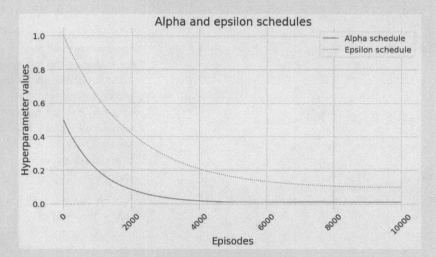

Finally, it's important to mention that I'm using a gamma of 0.99, and that the frozen lake environment, when used with OpenAI Gym, is automatically wrapped with a time limit Gym Wrapper. This "time wrapper" instance makes sure the agent terminates an episode with no more than 100 steps. Technically speaking, these two decisions (gamma and the time wrapper) change the optimal policy and value function the agent learns, and should not be taken lightly. I recommend playing with the FL environment in chapter 7's Notebook and changing gamma to different values (1, 0.5, 0) and also removing the time wrapper by getting the environment instance attribute "unwrapped," for instance, "env = env.unwrapped." Try to understand how these two things affect the policies and value functions found.

┼┼┼┼ TALLY IT UP

Model-based RL methods get estimates closer to actual in fewer episodes

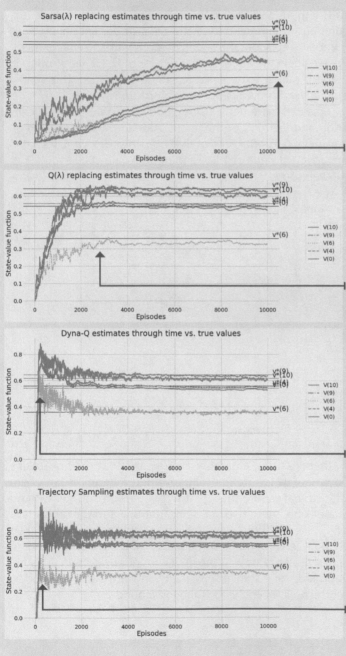

(1) One interesting experiment you should try is training vanilla SARSA and Q-learning agents on this environment and comparing the results. Look at the SARSA(λ) agent struggle to estimate the optimal state-value function. Remember in these plots the horizontal lines represent the optimal state-value function for a handful of states. In this case, I pulled states 0, 4, 6, 9, and 10.

(2) The Q(λ) agent is off-policy and you can see it moving the estimates of the optimal state-value function toward the true values, unlike SARSA(λ). Now, to be clear, this is a matter of the number of steps; I'm sure SARSA(λ) would converge to the true values if given more episodes.

(3) The Dyna-Q agent is even faster than the Q(λ) agent at tracking the true values, but notice too, how there's a large error spike at the beginning of training. This is likely because the model is incorrect early on, and Dyna-Q randomly samples states from the learned model, even states not sufficiently visited.

(4) My implementation of trajectory sampling uses the greedy trajectory, so the agent samples states likely to be encountered; perhaps, the reason why there's more stability in TS.

TALLY IT UP

Both traces and model-based methods are efficient at processing experiences

(1) Now, let's discuss how the results shown on the previous page relate to success. As you can see on the first plot to the right, all algorithms except SARSA(λ) reach the same success rate as an optimal policy. Also, model-based RL methods appear to get there first, but not by much. Recall that "success" here means the number of times the agent reached the goal state (state 15 in the FL environment).

(2) On the second plot, to the right, you can see the estimated expected return of the initial state. Notice how both model-based methods have a huge error spike at the beginning of the training run, trajectory sampling stabilizes a little bit sooner than Dyna-Q, yet the spike is still significant. Q(λ) methods get there without the spike and soon enough, while SARSA(λ) methods never make it before training is stopped.

(3) The third plot is the actual episode return averaged over 100 episodes. As you can see, both model-based methods and Q(λ) agents obtain the expected return after approximately 2,000 episodes. SARSA(λ) agents don't get there before the training process is stopped. Again, I'm pretty sure that, given enough time, SARSA(λ) agents would get there.

(4) This last plot is the action-value function mean absolute error. As you can see, the model-based methods also bring the error down close to zero, which is the fastest. However, shortly after 2,000 episodes, both model-based and Q(λ) methods are much the same. SARSA(λ) methods are also slow to optimal here.

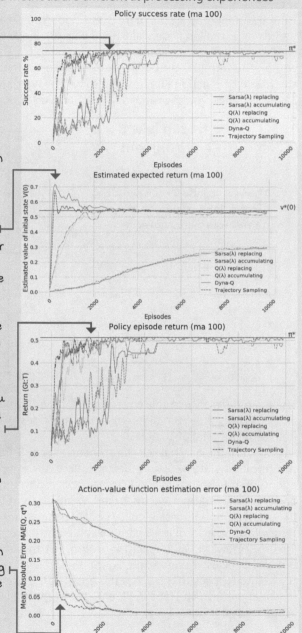

CONCRETE EXAMPLE
The frozen lake 8 x 8 environment

How about we step it up and try these algorithms in a challenging environment?

This one is called frozen lake 8 × 8 (FL8×8) and as you might expect, this is an 8-by-8 grid world with properties similar to the FL. The initial state is state 0, the state on the top-left corner; the terminal, and GOAL state is state 63, the state on the bottom-right corner. The stochasticity of action effects is the same: the agent moves to the intended cell with a mere 33.33% chance, and the rest is split evenly in orthogonal directions.

The frozen lake 8 × 8 environment

(1) The frozen lake 8 × 8 is similar to the frozen lake, only much bigger and therefore more challenging.

START							
0	1	2	3	4	5	6	7
8	9	10	11	12	13	14	15
16	17	18	19 □	20	21	22	23
24	25	26	27	28	29 □	30	31
32	33	34	35 □	36	37	38	39
40	41 □	42 □	43	44	45	46 □	47
48	49 □	50	51	52 □	53	54 □	55
56	57	58	59 □	60	61	62	GOAL 63

The main difference in this environment, as you can see, is that there are many more holes, and obviously they're in different locations. States 19, 29, 35, 41, 42, 46, 49, 52, 54, and 59 are holes; that's a total of 10 holes!

Similar to the original FL environment, in FL8×8, the right policy allows the agent to reach the terminal state 100% of the episodes. However, in the OpenAI Gym implementation, agents that learn optimal policies do not find these particular policies because of gamma and the time wrapper we discussed. Think about it for a second: given the stochasticity of these environments, a safe policy could terminate in zero rewards for the episode due to the time wrapper. Also, given a gamma value less than one, the more steps the agent takes, the lower the reward will impact the return. For these reasons, safe policies aren't necessarily optimal policies; therefore, the agent doesn't learn them. Remember that the goal isn't simply to find a policy that reaches the goal 100% of the times, but to find a policy that reaches the goal within 100 steps in FL and 200 steps in FL8×8. Agents may need to take risks to accomplish this goal.

IT'S IN THE DETAILS

Hyperparameter values for the frozen lake 8 × 8 environment

The frozen lake 8 × 8 (FL8×8) environment is the most challenging discrete state- and action-space environment that we discuss in this book. This environment is challenging for a number of reasons: first, 64 states is the largest number of states we've worked with, but more importantly having a single non-zero reward makes this environment particularly challenging.

What that really means is agents will only know they've done it right once they hit the terminal state for the first time. Remember, this is randomly! After they find the non-zero reward transition, agents such as SARSA and Q-learning (not the lambda versions, but the vanilla ones) will only update the value of the state from which the agent transitioned to the GOAL state. That's a one-step back from the reward. Then, for that value function to be propagated back one more step, guess what, the agent needs to randomly hit that second-to-final state. But, that's for the non-lambda versions. With SARSA(λ) and Q(λ), the propagation of values depends on the value of lambda. For all the experiments in this chapter, I use a lambda of 0.5, which more or less tells the agent to propagate the values half the trajectory (also depending on the type of traces being used, but as a ballpark).

Surprisingly enough, the only change we make to these agents is the number of episodes we let them interact with the environments. While in the SWS environment we allow the agent to interact for only 3,000 episodes, and in the FL environment we let the agent gather experience for 10,000 episodes; in FL8×8 we let these agents gather 30,000 episodes. This means that alpha now decays from an initial value of 0.5 to a minimum value of 0.01 after 50% of the total episodes, which is now 15,000 episodes, and epsilon decays from an initial value of 1.0 to a minimum value of 0.1 after 90% of the total episodes, which is now 27,000 episodes.

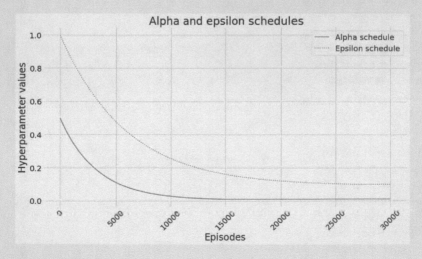

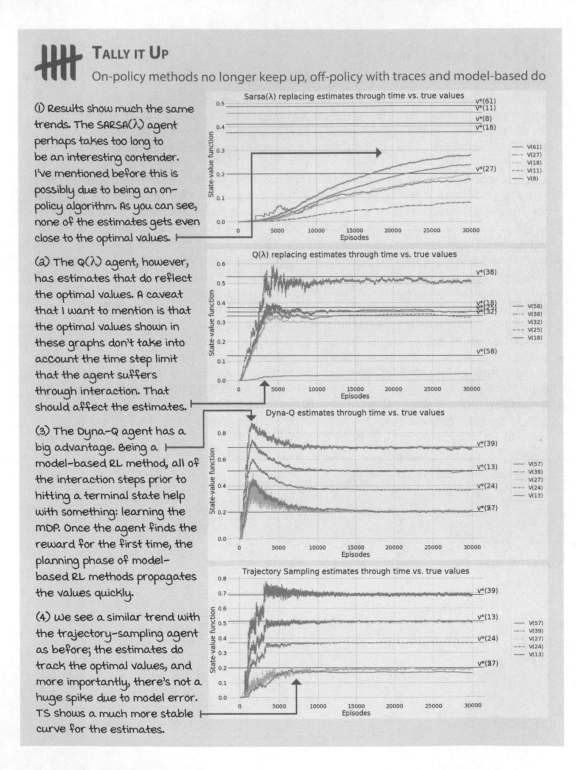

TALLY IT UP

On-policy methods no longer keep up, off-policy with traces and model-based do

(1) Results show much the same trends. The SARSA(λ) agent perhaps takes too long to be an interesting contender. I've mentioned before this is possibly due to being an on-policy algorithm. As you can see, none of the estimates gets even close to the optimal values.

Sarsa(λ) replacing estimates through time vs. true values

(2) The Q(λ) agent, however, has estimates that do reflect the optimal values. A caveat that I want to mention is that the optimal values shown in these graphs don't take into account the time step limit that the agent suffers through interaction. That should affect the estimates.

Q(λ) replacing estimates through time vs. true values

(3) The Dyna-Q agent has a big advantage. Being a model-based RL method, all of the interaction steps prior to hitting a terminal state help with something: learning the MDP. Once the agent finds the reward for the first time, the planning phase of model-based RL methods propagates the values quickly.

Dyna-Q estimates through time vs. true values

(4) We see a similar trend with the trajectory-sampling agent as before; the estimates do track the optimal values, and more importantly, there's not a huge spike due to model error. TS shows a much more stable curve for the estimates.

Trajectory Sampling estimates through time vs. true values

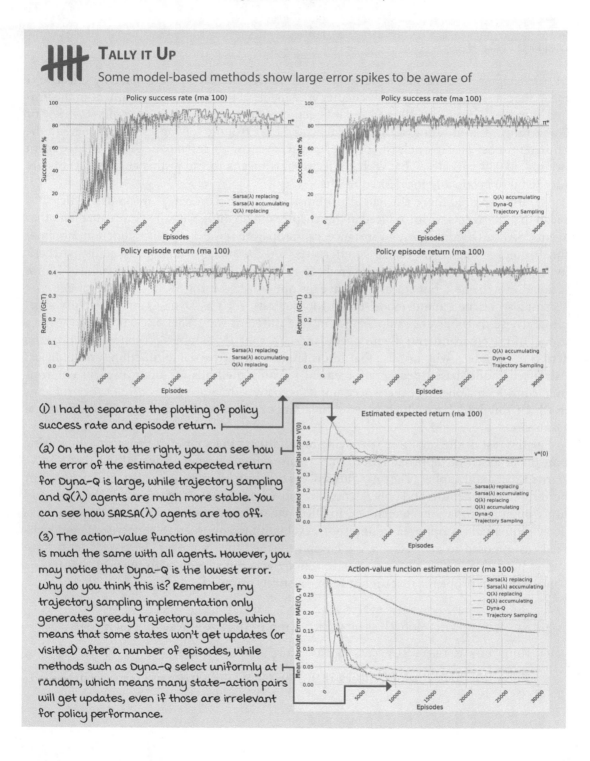

TALLY IT UP

Some model-based methods show large error spikes to be aware of

(1) I had to separate the plotting of policy success rate and episode return.

(2) On the plot to the right, you can see how the error of the estimated expected return for Dyna-Q is large, while trajectory sampling and Q(λ) agents are much more stable. You can see how SARSA(λ) agents are too off.

(3) The action-value function estimation error is much the same with all agents. However, you may notice that Dyna-Q is the lowest error. Why do you think this is? Remember, my trajectory sampling implementation only generates greedy trajectory samples, which means that some states won't get updates (or visited) after a number of episodes, while methods such as Dyna-Q select uniformly at random, which means many state-action pairs will get updates, even if those are irrelevant for policy performance.

Summary

In this chapter, you learned about making RL more effective and efficient. By effective, I mean that agents presented in this chapter are capable of solving the environment in the limited number of episodes allowed for interaction. Other agents, such as vanilla SARSA, or Q-learning, or even Monte Carlo control, would have trouble solving these challenges in the limited number of steps; at least, for sure, they'd have trouble solving the FL8x8 environment in only 30,000 episodes. That's what effectiveness means to me in this chapter; agents are successful in producing the desired results.

We also explored more efficient algorithms. And by efficient here, I mean data-efficient; I mean that the agents we introduced in this chapter can do more with the same data than other agents. SARSA(λ) and Q(λ), for instance, can propagate rewards to value-function estimates much quicker than their vanilla counterparts, SARSA and Q-learning. By adjusting the λ hyperparameter, you can even assign credit to all states visited in an episode. A value of 1 for λ is not always the best, but at least you have the option when using SARSA(λ) and Q(λ).

You also learned about model-based RL methods, such as Dyna-Q and trajectory sampling. These methods are sample efficient in a different way. They use samples to learn a model of the environment; if your agent lands 100% of 1M samples on state s' when taking action a, in state s, why not use that information to improve value functions and policies? Advanced model-based deep reinforcement learning methods are often used in environments in which gathering experience samples is costly: domains such as robotic, or problems in which you don't have a high-speed simulation, or where hardware requires large financial resources.

For the rest of the book, we're moving on to discuss the subtleties that arise when using non-linear function approximation with reinforcement learning. Everything that you've learned so far still applies. The only difference is that instead of using vectors and matrices for holding value functions and policies, now we move into the world of supervised learning and function approximation. Remember, in DRL, agents learn from feedback that's simultaneously sequential (as opposed to one-shot), evaluative (as opposed to supervised), and sampled (as opposed to exhaustive). We haven't touched the "sampled" part yet; agents have always been able to visit all states or state-action pairs, but starting with the next chapter, we concentrate on problems that cannot be exhaustively sampled.

By now, you

- Know how to develop RL agents that are more effective at reaching their goals

- Know how to make RL agents that are more sample efficient

- Know how to deal with feedback that is simultaneously sequential and evaluative

TWEETABLE FEAT

Work on your own and share your findings

Here are several ideas on how to take what you've learned to the next level. If you'd like, share your results with the rest of the world and make sure to check out what others have done, too. It's a win-win situation, and hopefully, you'll take advantage of it.

- **#gdrl_ch07_tf01:** I only test on the frozen lake 8×8 environment the algorithms presented in this chapter, but are you curious about how the algorithms in the previous chapter compare? Well, do that! Go to the book's Notebooks and copy the algorithms from the previous chapter into this chapter's Notebook, and then run, and collect information to compare all the algorithms.

- **#gdrl_ch07_tf02:** There are many more advanced algorithms for the tabular case. Compile a list of interesting algorithms and share the list with the world.

- **#gdrl_ch07_tf03:** Now, implement one algorithm from your list and implement another algorithm from someone else's list. If you're the first person posting to this hashtag, then implement two of the algorithms on your list.

- **#gdrl_ch07_tf04:** There's a fundamental algorithm called prioritized sweeping. Can you investigate this algorithm, and tell us more about it? Make sure you share your implementation, add it to this chapter's Notebook, and compare it with the other algorithms in this chapter.

- **#gdrl_ch07_tf05:** Create and environment like Frozen Lake 8×8, but much more complex, something like frozen lake 16×16, perhaps? Now test all the algorithms, and see how they perform. Are there any of the algorithms in this chapter that do considerably better than other algorithms?

- **#gdrl_ch07_tf06:** In every chapter, I'm using the final hashtag as a catchall hashtag. Feel free to use this one to discuss anything else that you worked on relevant to this chapter. There's no more exciting homework than that which you create for yourself. Make sure to share what you set yourself to investigate and your results.

Write a tweet with your findings, tag me @mimoralea (I'll retweet), and use the particular hashtag from the list to help interested folks find your results. There are no right or wrong results; you share your findings and check others' findings. Take advantage of this to socialize, contribute, and get yourself out there! We're waiting for you!

Here's a tweet example:

"Hey, @mimoralea. I created a blog post with a list of resources to study deep reinforcement learning. Check it out at <link>. #gdrl_ch01_tf01"

I'll make sure to retweet and help others find your work.

Introduction to value-based deep reinforcement learning | 8

In this chapter

- You will understand the inherent challenges of training reinforcement learning agents with non-linear function approximators.

- You will create a deep reinforcement learning agent that, when trained from scratch with minimal adjustments to hyperparameters, can solve different kinds of problems.

- You will identify the advantages and disadvantages of using value-based methods when solving reinforcement learning problems.

> 66 *Human behavior flows from three main sources:*
> *desire, emotion, and knowledge.* 99
>
> — PLATO
> A PHILOSOPHER IN CLASSICAL GREECE
> AND FOUNDER OF THE ACADEMY IN ATHENS

We've made a great deal of progress so far, and you're ready to truly grok deep reinforcement learning. In chapter 2, you learned to represent problems in a way reinforcement learning agents can solve using Markov decision processes (MDP). In chapter 3, you developed algorithms that solve these MDPs: that is, agents that find optimal behavior in sequential decision-making problems. In chapter 4, you learned about algorithms that solve one-step MDPs without having access to these MDPs. These problems are uncertain because the agents don't have access to the MDP. Agents learn to find optimal behavior through trial-and-error learning. In chapter 5, we mixed these two types of problems—sequential and uncertain—so we explore agents that learn to evaluate policies. Agents didn't find optimal policies but were able to evaluate policies and estimate value functions accurately. In chapter 6, we studied agents that find optimal policies on sequential decision-making problems under uncertainty. These agents go from random to optimal by merely interacting with their environment and deliberately gathering experiences for learning. In chapter 7, we learned about agents that are even better at finding optimal policies by getting the most out of their experiences.

Chapter 2 is a foundation for all chapters in this book. Chapter 3 is about planning algorithms that deal with sequential feedback. Chapter 4 is about bandit algorithms that deal with evaluative feedback. Chapters 5, 6, and 7 are about RL algorithms, algorithms that deal with feedback that is simultaneously sequential and evaluative. This type of problem is what people refer to as *tabular reinforcement learning*. Starting from this chapter, we dig into the details of deep reinforcement learning.

More specifically, in this chapter, we begin our incursion into the use of deep neural networks for solving reinforcement learning problems. In deep reinforcement learning, there are different ways of leveraging the power of highly non-linear function approximators, such as deep neural networks. They're value-based, policy-based, actor-critic, model-based, and gradient-free methods. This chapter goes in-depth on value-based deep reinforcement learning methods.

Types of algorithmic approaches you learn about in this book

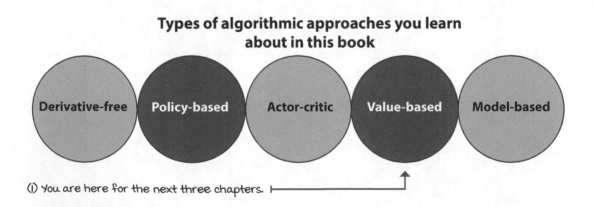

ⓘ You are here for the next three chapters.

The kind of feedback
deep reinforcement learning agents use

In deep reinforcement learning, we build agents that are capable of learning from feedback that's simultaneously evaluative, sequential, and sampled. I've emphasized this throughout the book because you need to understand what that means.

In the first chapter, I mentioned that deep reinforcement learning is about complex sequential decision-making problems under uncertainty. You probably thought, "What a bunch of words." But as I promised, all these words mean something. "Sequential decision-making problems" is what you learned about in chapter 3. "Problems under uncertainty" is what you learned about in chapter 4. In chapters 5, 6, and 7, you learned about "sequential decision-making problems under uncertainty." In this chapter, we add the "complex" part back to that whole sentence. Let's use this introductory section to review one last time the three types of feedback a deep reinforcement learning agent uses for learning.

Boil it Down
Kinds of feedback in deep reinforcement learning

	Sequential (as opposed to one-shot)	**Evaluative** (as opposed to supervised)	**Sampled** (as opposed to exhaustive)
Supervised learning	×	×	✓
Planning (Chapter 3)	✓	×	×
Bandits (Chapter 4)	×	✓	×
Tabular reinforcement learning (Chapters 5, 6, 7)	✓	✓	×
Deep reinforcement learning (Chapters 8, 9, 10, 11, 12)	✓	✓	✓

Deep reinforcement learning agents deal with sequential feedback

Deep reinforcement learning agents have to deal with sequential feedback. One of the main challenges of sequential feedback is that your agents can receive delayed information.

You can imagine a chess game in which you make a few wrong moves early on, but the consequences of those wrong moves only manifest at the end of the game when and if you materialize a loss.

Delayed feedback makes it tricky to interpret the source of the feedback. Sequential feedback gives rise to the temporal credit assignment problem, which is the challenge of determining which state, action, or state-action pair is responsible for a reward. When there's a temporal component to a problem and actions have delayed consequences, it becomes challenging to assign credit for rewards.

Sequential feedback

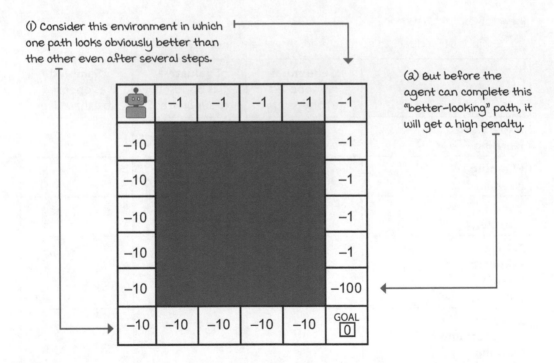

(1) Consider this environment in which one path looks obviously better than the other even after several steps.

(2) But before the agent can complete this "better-looking" path, it will get a high penalty.

(3) This is the challenge of sequential feedback, and one of the reasons we use value functions to decide on actions, and not merely rewards.

But, if it isn't sequential, what is it?

The opposite of delayed feedback is immediate feedback. In other words, the opposite of sequential feedback is one-shot feedback. In problems that deal with one-shot feedback, such as supervised learning or multi-armed bandits, decisions don't have long-term consequences. For example, in a classification problem, classifying an image, whether correctly or not, has no bearing on future performance; for instance, the images presented in the next model are not any different whether the model classified the previous batch correctly or not. In DRL, this sequential dependency exists.

Classification problem

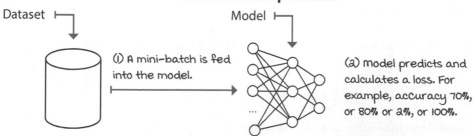

(1) A mini-batch is fed into the model.

(2) model predicts and calculates a loss. For example, accuracy 70%, or 80% or 2%, or 100%.

(3) But, the dataset doesn't really care how the model does. The model will be fed next another randomly sampled mini-batch in total disregard of model performance. In other words, there are no long-term consequences.

Moreover, in bandit problems, there's also no long-term consequence, though it's perhaps a bit harder to see why. Bandits are one-state one-step MDPs in which episodes terminate immediately after a single action selection. Therefore, actions don't have long-term consequences in the performance of the agent during that episode.

Two-armed bandit

Slot machines

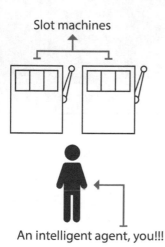

An intelligent agent, you!!!

Note: we assume slot machines have a stationary probability of payoff, meaning the probability of payoff will not change with a pull, which is likely incorrect for real slot machines.

(1) When you go to a casino and play the slot machines, your goal is to find the machine that pays the most, and then stick to that arm.

(2) In bandit problems, we assume the probability of payoff stays the same after every pull. This makes it a one-shot kind of problem.

Deep reinforcement learning agents deal with evaluative feedback

The second property we learned about is that of evaluative feedback. Deep reinforcement learning, tabular reinforcement learning, and bandits all deal with evaluative feedback. The crux of evaluative feedback is that the goodness of the feedback is only relative, because the environment is uncertain. We don't know the actual dynamics of the environment; we don't have access to the transition function and reward signal.

As a result, we must explore the environment around us to find out what's out there. The problem is that, by exploring, we miss capitalizing on our current knowledge and, therefore, likely accumulate regret. Out of all this, the exploration-exploitation trade-off arises. It's a constant by-product of uncertainty. While not having access to the model of the environment, we must explore to gather new information or improve on our current information.

Evaluative feedback

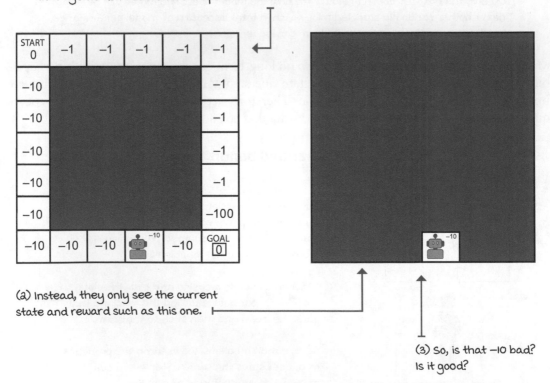

(1) To understand the challenge of evaluative feedback, you must be aware that agents don't see entire maps such as this one.

(2) Instead, they only see the current state and reward such as this one.

(3) So, is that −10 bad? Is it good?

But, if it isn't evaluative, what is it?

The opposite of evaluative feedback is supervised feedback. In a classification problem, your model receives supervision; that is, during learning, your model is given the correct labels for each of the samples provided. There's no guessing. If your model makes a mistake, the correct answer is provided immediately afterward. What a good life!

Classification is "supervised"

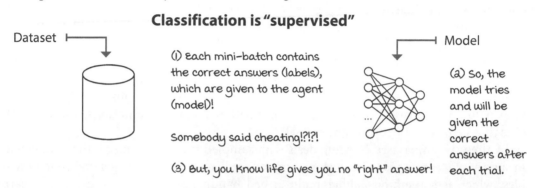

Dataset

(1) Each mini-batch contains the correct answers (labels), which are given to the agent (model)!

Somebody said cheating!?!?!

(3) But, you know life gives you no "right" answer!

Model

(2) So, the model tries and will be given the correct answers after each trial.

The fact that correct answers are given to the learning algorithm makes supervised feedback much easier to deal with than evaluative feedback. That's a clear distinction between supervised learning problems and evaluative-feedback problems, such as multi-armed bandits, tabular reinforcement learning, and deep reinforcement learning.

Bandit problems may not have to deal with sequential feedback, but they do learn from evaluative feedback. That's the core issue bandit problems solve. When under evaluative feedback, agents must balance exploration versus exploitation requirements. If the feedback is evaluative and sequential at the same time, the challenge is even more significant. Algorithms must simultaneously balance immediate- and long-term goals and the gathering and utilization of information. Both tabular reinforcement learning and DRL agents learn from feedback that's simultaneously sequential and evaluative.

Bandits deal with evaluative feedback

(1) You go pull the first arm and get $10. Is that good or bad? What if the other gives you $50? What if it gives you $1 with every pull for the next 500 pulls?!!

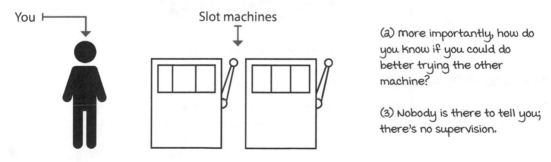

You

Slot machines

(2) More importantly, how do you know if you could do better trying the other machine?

(3) Nobody is there to tell you; there's no supervision.

Deep reinforcement learning agents deal with sampled feedback

What differentiates deep reinforcement learning from tabular reinforcement learning is the complexity of the problems. In deep reinforcement learning, agents are unlikely to sample all possible feedback exhaustively. Agents need to generalize using the gathered feedback and come up with intelligent decisions based on that generalization.

Think about it. You can't expect exhaustive feedback from life. You can't be a doctor and a lawyer and an engineer all at once, at least not if you want to be good at any of these. You must use the experience you gather early on to make more intelligent decisions for your future. It's basic. Were you good at math in high school? Great, then, pursue a math-related degree. Were you better at the arts? Then, pursue that path. Generalizing helps you narrow your path going forward by helping you find patterns, make assumptions, and connect the dots that help you reach your optimal self.

By the way, supervised learning deals with sampled feedback. Indeed, the core challenge in supervised learning is to learn from sampled feedback: to be able to generalize to new samples, which is something neither multi-armed bandit nor tabular reinforcement learning problems do.

Sampled feedback

(1) Imagine you are feeding your agent images as states.

(2) Each image is 210-by-160 pixels.

(3) They have three channels representing the amount of red, green, and blue.

(4) Each pixel in an 8-bit image can have a value from 0 to 255.

(5) How many possible states is that, you ask?

(6) That's $(255^3)^{210 \times 160} = (16,581,375)^{33,600}$ = a lot!

(7) For giggles, I ran this in Python and it returns a 242,580-digit number. To put it in perspective, the known, observable universe has between 10^{78} and 10^{82} atoms, which is an 83-digit number at most.

But, if it isn't sampled, what is it?

The opposite of sampled feedback is exhaustive feedback. To exhaustively sample environments means agents have access to all possible samples. Tabular reinforcement learning and bandits agents, for instance, only need to sample for long enough to gather all necessary information for optimal performance. To gather exhaustive feedback is also why there are optimal convergence guarantees in tabular reinforcement learning. Common assumptions, such as "infinite data" or "sampling every state-action pair infinitely often," are reasonable assumptions in small grid worlds with finite state and action spaces.

Sequential, evaluative, and exhaustive feedback

(1) Again, this is what sequential feedback looks like.

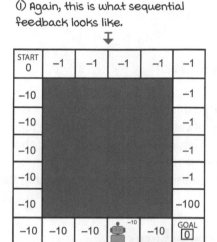

(2) And this is what evaluative feedback looks like.

(3) But, given you have a discrete number of states and actions, you can sample the environment exhaustively. In small state and action spaces, things are easy in practice, and theory is doable. As the number of state and action spaces increases, the need for function approximation becomes evident.

This dimension we haven't dealt with until now. In this book so far, we surveyed the tabular reinforcement learning problem. Tabular reinforcement learning learns from evaluative, sequential, and exhaustive feedback. But, what happens when we have more complex problems in which we cannot assume our agents will ever exhaustively sample environments? What if the state space is high dimensional, such as a Go board with 10^{170} states? How about Atari games with $(255^3)^{210 \times 160}$ at 60 Hz? What if the environment state space has continuous variables, such as a robotic arm indicating joint angles? How about problems with both high-dimensional and continuous states or even high-dimensional and continuous actions? These complex problems are the reason for the existence of the field of deep reinforcement learning.

Introduction to function approximation for reinforcement learning

It's essential to understand why we use function approximation for reinforcement learning in the first place. It's common to get lost in words and pick solutions due to the hype. You know, if you hear "deep learning," you get more excited than if you hear "non-linear function approximation," yet they're the same. That's human nature. It happens to me; it happens to many, I'm sure. But our goal is to remove the cruft and simplify our thinking.

In this section, I provide motivations for the use of function approximation to solve reinforcement learning problems in general. Perhaps a bit more specific to value functions, than RL overall, but the underlying motivation applies to all forms of DRL.

Reinforcement learning problems can have high-dimensional state and action spaces

The main drawback of tabular reinforcement learning is that the use of a table to represent value functions is no longer practical in complex problems. Environments can have high-dimensional state spaces, meaning that the number of variables that comprise a single state is vast. For example, Atari games described above are high dimensional because of the 210-by-160 pixels and the three color channels. Regardless of the values that these pixels can take when we talk about dimensionality, we're referring to the number of variables that make up a single state.

High-dimensional state spaces

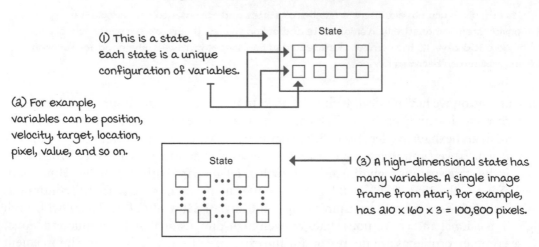

(1) This is a state. Each state is a unique configuration of variables.

(2) For example, variables can be position, velocity, target, location, pixel, value, and so on.

(3) A high-dimensional state has many variables. A single image frame from Atari, for example, has 210 x 160 x 3 = 100,800 pixels.

Reinforcement learning problems can have continuous state and action spaces

Environments can additionally have continuous variables, meaning that a variable can take on an infinite number of values. To clarify, state and action spaces can be high dimensional with discrete variables, they can be low dimensional with continuous variables, and so on.

Even if the variables aren't continuous and, therefore, not infinitely large, they can still take on a large number of values to make it impractical for learning without function approximation. This is the case with Atari, for instance, where each image-pixel can take on 256 values (0–255 integer values.) There you have a finite state-space, yet large enough to require function approximation for any learning to occur.

But, sometimes, even low-dimension state spaces can be infinitely large state spaces. For instance, imagine a problem in which only the x, y, z coordinates of a robot compose the state-space. Sure, a three-variable state-space is a pretty low-dimensional state-space environment, but what if any of the variables is provided in continuous form, that is, that variable can be of infinitesimal precision? Say, it could be a 1.56, or 1.5683, or 1.5683256, and so on. Then, how do you make a table that takes all these values into account? Yes, you could discretize the state space, but let me save you time and get right to it: you need function approximation.

Continuous state spaces

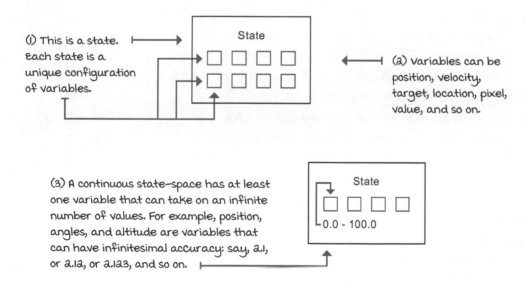

(1) This is a state. Each state is a unique configuration of variables.

State

(2) Variables can be position, velocity, target, location, pixel, value, and so on.

(3) A continuous state-space has at least one variable that can take on an infinite number of values. For example, position, angles, and altitude are variables that can have infinitesimal accuracy: say, 2.1, or 2.12, or 2.123, and so on.

State

0.0 - 100.0

CONCRETE EXAMPLE
The cart-pole environment

The cart-pole environment is a classic in reinforcement learning. The state space is low dimensional but continuous, making it an excellent environment for developing algorithms; training is fast, yet still somewhat challenging, and function approximation can help.

This is the cart-pole environment

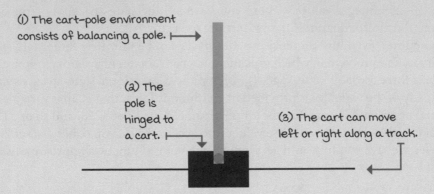

(1) The cart-pole environment consists of balancing a pole.

(2) The pole is hinged to a cart.

(3) The cart can move left or right along a track.

Its state space is comprised of four variables:

- The cart position on the track (x-axis) with a range from –2.4 to 2.4
- The cart velocity along the track (x-axis) with a range from –inf to inf
- The pole angle with a range of ~–40 degrees to ~ 40 degrees
- The pole velocity at the tip with a range of –inf to inf

There are two available actions in every state:

- Action 0 applies a –1 force to the cart (push it left)
- Action 1 applies a +1 force to the cart (push it right)

You reach a terminal state if

- The pole angle is more than 12 degrees away from the vertical position
- The cart center is more than 2.4 units from the center of the track
- The episode count reaches 500 time steps (more on this later)

The reward function is

- +1 for every time step

There are advantages when using function approximation

I'm sure you get the point that in environments with high-dimensional or continuous state spaces, there are no practical reasons for not using function approximation. In earlier chapters, we discussed planning and reinforcement learning algorithms. All of those methods represent value functions using tables.

REFRESH MY MEMORY

Algorithms such as value iteration and Q-learning use tables for value functions

Value iteration is a method that takes in an MDP and derives an optimal policy for such MDP by calculating the optimal state-value function, *v**. To do this, value iteration keeps track of the changing state-value function, *v*, over multiple iterations. In value iteration, the state-value function estimates are represented as a vector of values indexed by the states. This vector is stored with a lookup table for querying and updating estimates.

A state-value function

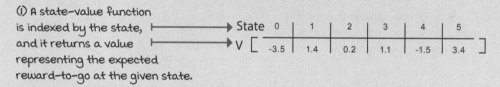

(i) A state-value function is indexed by the state, and it returns a value representing the expected reward-to-go at the given state.

The Q-learning algorithm does not need an MDP and doesn't use a state-value function. Instead, in Q-learning, we estimate the values of the optimal action-value function, *q**. Action-value functions are not vectors, but, instead, are represented by matrices. These matrices are 2D tables indexed by states and actions.

An action-value function

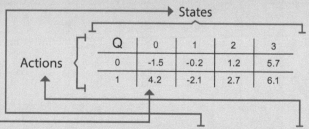

An action-value function, Q, is indexed by the state and the action, and it returns a value representing the expected reward-to-go for taking that action at that state.

BOIL IT DOWN
Function approximation can make our algorithms more efficient

In the cart-pole environment, we want to use generalization because it's a more efficient use of experiences. With function approximation, agents learn and exploit patterns with less data (and perhaps faster).

A state-value function with and without function approximation

(1) Imagine this state-value function.

$V = [-2.5, -1.1, 0.7, 3.2, 7.6]$

(2) Without function approximation, each value is independent.

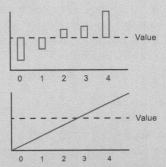

(3) With function approximation, the underlying relationship of the states can be learned and exploited.

(4) The benefit of using function approximation is particularly obvious if you imagine these plots after even a single update.

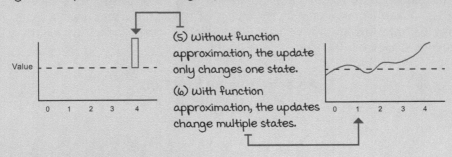

(5) Without function approximation, the update only changes one state.

(6) With function approximation, the updates change multiple states.

(7) Of course, this is a simplified example, but it helps illustrate what's happening. What would be different in "real" examples?

First, if we approximate an action-value function, Q, we'd have to add another dimension.

Also, with a non-linear function approximator, such as a neural network, more complex relationships can be discovered.

While the inability of value iteration and Q-learning to solve problems with sampled feedback make them impractical, the lack of generalization makes them inefficient. What I mean by this is that we could find ways to use tables in environments with continuous-variable states, but we'd pay a price for doing so. Discretizing values could indeed make tables possible, for instance. But, even if we could engineer a way to use tables and store value functions, by doing so, we'd miss out on the advantages of generalization.

For example, in the cart-pole environment, function approximation would help our agents learn a relationship in the x distance. Agents would likely learn that being 2.35 units away from the center is a bit more dangerous than being 2.2 away. We know that 2.4 is the x boundary. This additional reason for using generalization isn't to be understated. Value functions often have underlying relationships that agents can learn and exploit. Function approximators, such as neural networks, can discover these underlying relationships.

 BOIL IT DOWN

Reasons for using function approximation

Our motivation for using function approximation isn't only to solve problems that aren't solvable otherwise, but also to solve problems more efficiently.

NFQ: The first attempt at value-based deep reinforcement learning

The following algorithm is called *neural fitted Q* (NFQ) *iteration,* and it's probably one of the first algorithms to successfully use neural networks as a function approximation to solve reinforcement learning problems.

For the rest of this chapter, I discuss several components that most value-based deep reinforcement learning algorithms have. I want you to see it as an opportunity to decide on different parts that we could've used. For instance, when I introduce using a loss function with NFQ, I discuss a few alternatives. My choices aren't necessarily the choices that were made when the algorithm was originally introduced. Likewise, when I choose an optimization method, whether root mean square propagation (RMSprop) or adaptive moment estimation (Adam), I give a reason why I use what I use, but more importantly, I give you context so you can pick and choose as you see fit.

What I hope you notice is that my goal is not only to teach you this specific algorithm but, more importantly, to show you the different places where you could try different things. Many RL algorithms feel this "plug-and-play" way, so pay attention.

First decision point: Selecting a value function to approximate

Using neural networks to approximate value functions can be done in many different ways. To begin with, there are many different value functions we could approximate.

 REFRESH MY MEMORY

Value functions

You've learned about the following value functions:

- The state-value function *v(s)*
- The action-value function *q(s,a)*
- The action-advantage function *a(s,a)*

You probably remember that the state-value function *v(s)*, though useful for many purposes, isn't sufficient on its own to solve the control problem. Finding *v(s)* helps you know how much expected total discounted reward you can obtain from state *s* and using policy π thereafter. But, to determine which action to take with a V-function, you also need the MDP of the environment so that you can do a one-step look-ahead and take into account all possible next states after selecting each action.

You likely also remember that the action-value function *q(s,a)* allows us to solve the control problem, so it's more like what we need to solve the cart-pole environment: in the cart-pole environment, we want to learn the values of actions for all states in order to balance the pole by controlling the cart. If we had the values of state-action pairs, we could differentiate the actions that would lead us to either gain information, in the case of an exploratory action, or maximize the expected return, in the case of a greedy action.

I want you to notice, too, that what we want to estimate the optimal action-value function and not just an action-value function. However, as we learned in the generalized policy iteration pattern, we can do on-policy learning using an epsilon-greedy policy and estimate its values directly, or we can do off-policy learning and always estimate the policy greedy with respect to the current estimates, which then becomes an optimal policy.

Last, we also learned about the action-advantage function *a(s,a)*, which can help us differentiate between values of different actions, and it also lets us easily see how much better than average an action is.

We'll study how to use the *v(s)* and *a(s)* functions in a few chapters. For now, let's settle on estimating the action-value function *q(s,a)*, just like in Q-learning. We refer to the approximate action-value function estimate as $Q(s,a; \theta)$, which means the Q estimates are parameterized by θ, the weights of a neural network, a state *s* and an action *a*.

Second decision point: Selecting a neural network architecture

We settled on learning the approximate action-value function $Q(s,a; \theta)$. But although I suggested the function should be parameterized by θ, s, and a, that doesn't have to be the case. The next component we discuss is the neural network architecture.

When we implemented the Q-learning agent, you noticed how the matrix holding the action-value function was indexed by state and action pairs. A straightforward neural network architecture is to input the state (the four state variables in the cart-pole environment), and the action to evaluate. The output would then be one node representing the Q-value for that state-action pair.

This architecture would work fine for the cart-pole environment. But, a more efficient architecture consists of only inputting the state (four for the cart-pole environment) to the neural network and outputting the Q-values for all the actions in that state (two for the cart-pole environment). This is clearly advantageous

State-action-in-value-out architecture

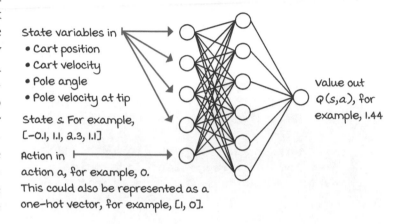

State variables in
- Cart position
- Cart velocity
- Pole angle
- Pole velocity at tip

State s. For example, [−0.1, 1.1, 2.3, 1.1]

Action in
action a, for example, 0. This could also be represented as a one-hot vector, for example, [1, 0].

Value out $Q(s,a)$, for example, 1.44

State-in-values-out architecture

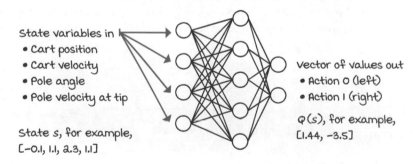

State variables in
- Cart position
- Cart velocity
- Pole angle
- Pole velocity at tip

State s, for example, [−0.1, 1.1, 2.3, 1.1]

Vector of values out
- Action 0 (left)
- Action 1 (right)

$Q(s)$, for example, [1.44, −3.5]

when using exploration strategies such as epsilon-greedy or softmax, because having to do only one pass forward to get the values of all actions for any given state yields a high-performance implementation, more so in environments with a large number of actions.

For our NFQ implementation, we use the *state-in-values-out architecture*: that is, four input nodes and two output nodes for the cart-pole environment.

I Speak Python

Fully connected Q-function (state-in-values-out)

```python
class FCQ(nn.Module):
    def __init__(self,
                 input_dim,
                 output_dim,
                 hidden_dims=(32,32),
                 activation_fc=F.relu):
        super(FCQ, self).__init__()
        self.activation_fc = activation_fc

        self.input_layer = nn.Linear(input_dim,
                                      hidden_dims[0])
        self.hidden_layers = nn.ModuleList()
        for i in range(len(hidden_dims)-1):
            hidden_layer = nn.Linear(
                hidden_dims[i], hidden_dims[i+1])
            self.hidden_layers.append(hidden_layer)
```

(1) Here you are just defining the input layer. See how we take in input_dim and output the first element of the hidden_dims vector.

(2) We then create the hidden layers. Notice how flexible this class is in that it allows you to change the number of layers and units per layer. Pass a different tuple, say (64, 32, 16), to the hidden_dims variable, and it will create a network with three hidden layers of 64, 32, and 16 units, respectively.

```python
        self.output_layer = nn.Linear(
            hidden_dims[-1], output_dim)
```

(3) We then connect the last hidden layer to the output layer.

```python
    def forward(self, state):
        x = state
        if not isinstance(x, torch.Tensor):
            x = torch.tensor(x,
                             device=self.device,
                             dtype=torch.float32)
            x = x.unsqueeze(0)

        x = self.activation_fc(self.input_layer(x))
        for hidden_layer in self.hidden_layers:
            x = self.activation_fc(hidden_layer(x))
        x = self.output_layer(x)
        return x
```

(4) In the forward function, we first take in the raw state and convert it into a tensor.

(5) We pass it through the input layer and then through the activation function.

(6) Then we do the same for all hidden layers.

(7) And finally, for the output layer, notice that we don't apply the activation function to the output but return it directly instead.

Third decision point: Selecting what to optimize

Let's pretend for a second that the cart-pole environment is a supervised learning problem. Say you have a dataset with states as inputs and a value function as labels. Which value function would you wish to have for labels?

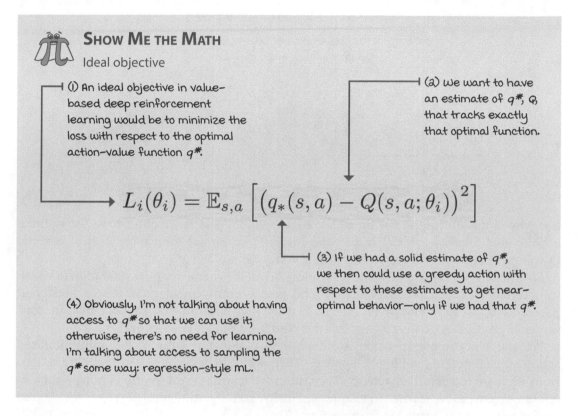

SHOW ME THE MATH

Ideal objective

(1) An ideal objective in value-based deep reinforcement learning would be to minimize the loss with respect to the optimal action-value function $q*$.

(2) We want to have an estimate of $q*$, Q, that tracks exactly that optimal function.

$$L_i(\theta_i) = \mathbb{E}_{s,a}\left[\left(q_*(s,a) - Q(s,a;\theta_i)\right)^2\right]$$

(3) If we had a solid estimate of $q*$, we then could use a greedy action with respect to these estimates to get near-optimal behavior—only if we had that $q*$.

(4) Obviously, I'm not talking about having access to $q*$ so that we can use it; otherwise, there's no need for learning. I'm talking about access to sampling the $q*$ some way: regression-style ML.

Of course, the dream labels for learning the optimal action-value function are the corresponding optimal Q-values (notice that a lowercase q refers to the true values; uppercase is commonly used to denote estimates) for the state-action input pair. That is exactly what the optimal action-value function $q*(s,a)$ represents, as you know.

If we had access to the optimal action-value function, we'd use that, but if we had access to sampling the optimal action-value function, we could then minimize the loss between the approximate and optimal action-value functions, and that would be it.

The optimal action-value function is what we're after.

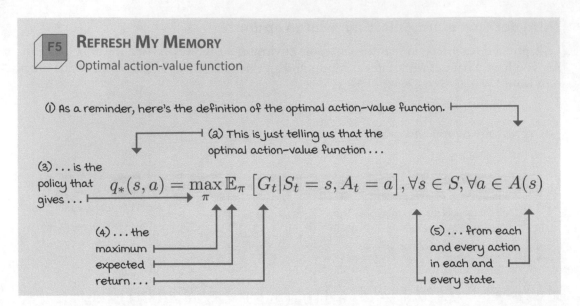

F5   REFRESH MY MEMORY

Optimal action-value function

(1) As a reminder, here's the definition of the optimal action-value function.

(2) This is just telling us that the optimal action-value function . . .

(3) . . . is the policy that gives . . .

$$q_*(s, a) = \max_{\pi} \mathbb{E}_{\pi} \left[G_t | S_t = s, A_t = a \right], \forall s \in S, \forall a \in A(s)$$

(4) . . . the maximum expected return . . .

(5) . . . from each and every action in each and every state.

But why is this an impossible dream? Well, the visible part is we don't have the optimal action-value function $q^*(s,a)$, but to top that off, we cannot even sample these optimal Q-values because we don't have the optimal policy either.

Fortunately, we can use the same principles learned in generalized policy iteration in which we alternate between policy-evaluation and policy-improvement processes to find good policies. But just so you know, because we're using non-linear function approximation, convergence guarantees no longer exist. It's the Wild West of the "deep" world.

For our NFQ implementation, we do just that. We start with a randomly initialized action-value function (and implicit policy.) Then, we evaluate the policy by sampling actions from it, as we learned in chapter 5. Then, improve it with an exploration strategy such as epsilon-greedy, as we learned in chapter 4. Finally, keep iterating until we reach the desired performance, as we learned in chapters 6 and 7.

BOIL IT DOWN

We can't use the ideal objective

We can't use the ideal objective because we don't have access to the optimal action-value function, and we don't even have an optimal policy to sample from. Instead, we must alternate between evaluating a policy (by sampling actions from it), and improving it (using an exploration strategy, such as epsilon-greedy). It's as you learned in chapter 6, in the generalized policy iteration pattern.

Fourth decision point: Selecting the targets for policy evaluation

There are multiple ways we can evaluate a policy. More specifically, there are different *targets* we can use for estimating the action-value function of a policy π. The core targets you learned about are the Monte Carlo (MC) target, the temporal-difference (TD) target, the *n*-step target, and lambda target.

MC, TD, *n*-step, and lambda targets

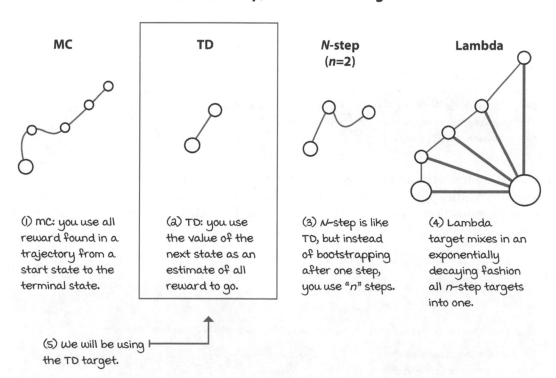

MC	TD	N-step (n=2)	Lambda

(1) MC: you use all reward found in a trajectory from a start state to the terminal state.

(2) TD: you use the value of the next state as an estimate of all reward to go.

(3) N-step is like TD, but instead of bootstrapping after one step, you use "*n*" steps.

(4) Lambda target mixes in an exponentially decaying fashion all *n*-step targets into one.

(5) We will be using the TD target.

We could use any of these targets and get solid results, but this time for our NFQ implementation, we keep it simple and use the TD target for our experiments.

You remember that the TD targets can be either on-policy or off-policy, depending on the way you bootstrap the target. The two main ways for bootstrapping the TD target are to either use the action-value function of the action the agent will take at the landing state, or alternatively, to use the value of the action with the highest estimate at the next state.

Often in the literature, the on-policy version of this target is called the SARSA target, and the off-policy version is called the Q-learning target.

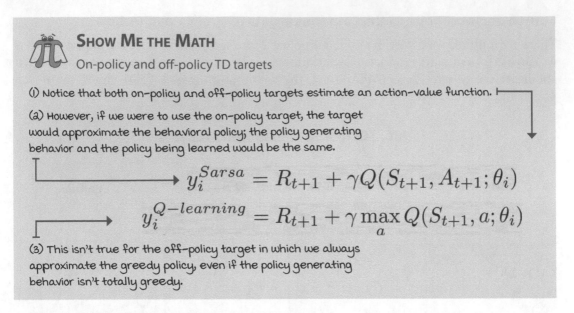

SHOW ME THE MATH

On-policy and off-policy TD targets

(1) Notice that both on-policy and off-policy targets estimate an action-value function.

(2) However, if we were to use the on-policy target, the target would approximate the behavioral policy; the policy generating behavior and the policy being learned would be the same.

$$y_i^{Sarsa} = R_{t+1} + \gamma Q(S_{t+1}, A_{t+1}; \theta_i)$$

$$y_i^{Q-learning} = R_{t+1} + \gamma \max_a Q(S_{t+1}, a; \theta_i)$$

(3) This isn't true for the off-policy target in which we always approximate the greedy policy, even if the policy generating behavior isn't totally greedy.

In our NFQ implementation, we use the same off-policy TD target we used in the Q-learning algorithm. At this point, to get an objective function, we need to substitute the optimal action-value function $q^*(s,a)$, that we had as the ideal objective equation, by the Q-learning target.

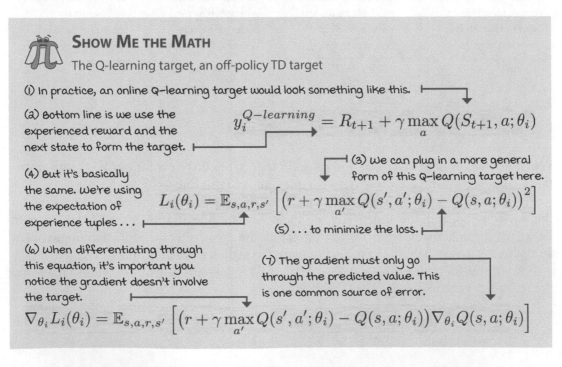

SHOW ME THE MATH

The Q-learning target, an off-policy TD target

(1) In practice, an online Q-learning target would look something like this.

(2) Bottom line is we use the experienced reward and the next state to form the target.

$$y_i^{Q-learning} = R_{t+1} + \gamma \max_a Q(S_{t+1}, a; \theta_i)$$

(3) We can plug in a more general form of this Q-learning target here.

(4) But it's basically the same. We're using the expectation of experience tuples . . .

$$L_i(\theta_i) = \mathbb{E}_{s,a,r,s'} \left[\left(r + \gamma \max_{a'} Q(s', a'; \theta_i) - Q(s, a; \theta_i) \right)^2 \right]$$

(5) . . . to minimize the loss.

(6) When differentiating through this equation, it's important you notice the gradient doesn't involve the target.

(7) The gradient must only go through the predicted value. This is one common source of error.

$$\nabla_{\theta_i} L_i(\theta_i) = \mathbb{E}_{s,a,r,s'} \left[\left(r + \gamma \max_{a'} Q(s', a'; \theta_i) - Q(s, a; \theta_i) \right) \nabla_{\theta_i} Q(s, a; \theta_i) \right]$$

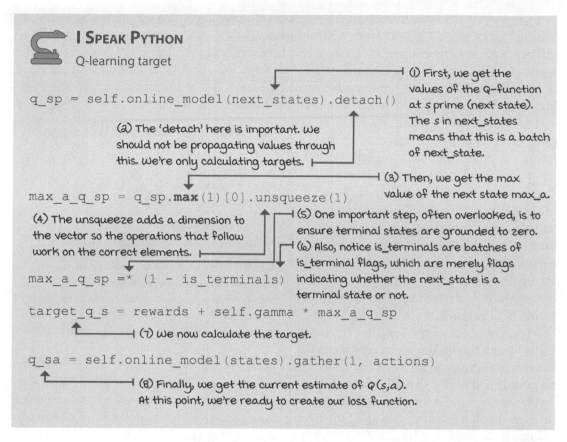

I SPEAK PYTHON

Q-learning target

```
q_sp = self.online_model(next_states).detach()
```

(1) First, we get the values of the Q-function at *s* prime (next state). The *s* in next_states means that this is a batch of next_state.

(2) The 'detach' here is important. We should not be propagating values through this. We're only calculating targets.

```
max_a_q_sp = q_sp.max(1)[0].unsqueeze(1)
```

(3) Then, we get the max value of the next state max_a.

(4) The unsqueeze adds a dimension to the vector so the operations that follow work on the correct elements.

(5) One important step, often overlooked, is to ensure terminal states are grounded to zero.

(6) Also, notice is_terminals are batches of is_terminal flags, which are merely flags indicating whether the next_state is a terminal state or not.

```
max_a_q_sp =* (1 - is_terminals)
target_q_s = rewards + self.gamma * max_a_q_sp
```

(7) We now calculate the target.

```
q_sa = self.online_model(states).gather(1, actions)
```

(8) Finally, we get the current estimate of Q(*s,a*). At this point, we're ready to create our loss function.

I want to bring to your attention two issues that I, unfortunately, see often in DRL implementations of algorithms that use TD targets.

First, you need to make sure that you only backpropagate through the predicted values. Let me explain. You know that in supervised learning, you have predicted values that come from the learning model, and true values that are commonly constants provided in advance. In RL, often the "true values" depend on predicted values themselves: they come from the model.

For instance, when you form a TD target, you use a reward, which is a constant, and the discounted value of the next state, which comes from the model. Notice, this value is also not a true value, which is going to cause all sorts of problems that we'll address in the next chapter. But what I also want you to notice now is that the predicted value comes from the neural network. You have to make this predicted value a constant. In PyTorch, you do this only by calling the *detach* method. Please look at the two previous boxes and understand these points. They're vital for the reliable implementation of DRL algorithms.

The second issue that I want to raise before we move on is the way terminal states are handled when using OpenAI Gym environments. The OpenAI Gym step, which is used to interact with the environment, returns after every step a handy flag indicating whether the agent just landed on a terminal state. This flag helps the agent force the value of terminal states to zero, which, as you remember from chapter 2, is a requirement to keep the value functions from diverging. You know the value of life after death is nil.

The tricky part is that some OpenAI Gym environments, such as the cart-pole, have a wrapper code that artificially terminates an episode after some time steps. In CartPole-v0, the time step limit is 200, and in CartPole-v1 it is 500. This wrapper code helps to prevent agents from taking too long to complete an episode, which can be useful, but it can get you in trouble. Think about it: what do you think the value of having the pole straight up in time step 500 would be? I mean, if the pole is straight up, and you get +1 for every step, then the true value of straight-up is infinite. Yet, since at

What's the value of this state?

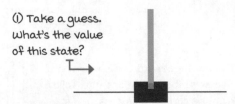

① Take a guess. What's the value of this state?

② HINT: This state looks pretty good to me! The cart-pole seems to be under control in a straight-up position. Perhaps the best action is to push right, but it doesn't seem like a critical state. Both actions are probably similarly valued.

time step 500 your agent times out, and a terminal flag is passed to the agent, you'll bootstrap on zero if you're not careful. This is bad. I cannot stress this enough. There is a handful of ways you can handle this issue, and here are the two common ones. Instead of bootstrapping on zero, bootstrap on the value of the next state as predicted by the network, if either you (1) reach the time step limit for the environment or (2) find the key "TimeLimit.truncated" in the info dictionary. Let me show you the second way.

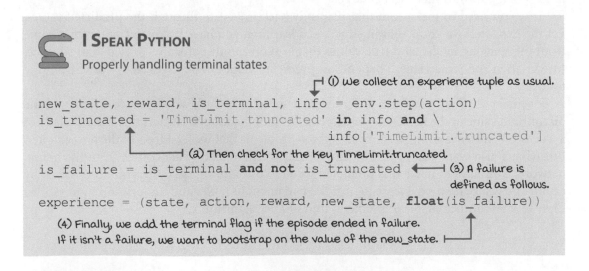

I Speak Python
Properly handling terminal states

① We collect an experience tuple as usual.

```
new_state, reward, is_terminal, info = env.step(action)
is_truncated = 'TimeLimit.truncated' in info and \
                        info['TimeLimit.truncated']
is_failure = is_terminal and not is_truncated
experience = (state, action, reward, new_state, float(is_failure))
```

② Then check for the key TimeLimit.truncated.

③ A failure is defined as follows.

④ Finally, we add the terminal flag if the episode ended in failure. If it isn't a failure, we want to bootstrap on the value of the new_state.

Fifth decision point: Selecting an exploration strategy

Another thing we need to decide is which policy improvement step to use for our generalized policy iteration needs. You know this from chapters 6 and 7, in which we alternate a policy evaluation method, such as MC or TD, and a policy improvement method that accounts for exploration, such as decaying e-greedy.

In chapter 4, we surveyed many different ways to balance the exploration-exploitation trade-off, and almost any of those techniques would work fine. But in an attempt to keep it simple, we're going to use an epsilon-greedy strategy on our NFQ implementation.

But, I want to highlight the implication of the fact that we're training an off-policy learning algorithm here. What that means is that there are two policies: a policy that generates behavior, which in this case is an epsilon-greedy policy, and a policy that we're learning about, which is the greedy (an ultimately optimal) policy.

One interesting fact of off-policy learning algorithms you studied in chapter 6 is that the policy generating behavior can be virtually anything. That is, it can be anything as long as it has broad support, which means it must ensure enough exploration of all state-action pairs. In our NFQ implementation, I use an epsilon-greedy strategy that selects an action randomly 50% of the time during training. However, when evaluating the agent, I use the action greedy with respect to the learned action-value function.

I Speak Python

Epsilon-greedy exploration strategy

```python
class EGreedyStrategy():
    <...>
    def select_action(self, model, state):
        with torch.no_grad():
            q_values = model(state).cpu().detach()
            q_values = q_values.data.numpy().squeeze()

        if np.random.rand() > self.epsilon:
            action = np.argmax(q_values)
        else:
            action = np.random.randint(len(q_values))

    <...>
    return action
```

(1) The select_action function of the epsilon-greedy strategy' starts by pulling out the Q-values for state s.

(2) I make the values "Numpy friendly" and remove an extra dimension.

(3) Then, get a random number and, if greater than epsilon, act greedily.

(4) Otherwise, act randomly in the number of actions.

(5) NOTE: I always query the model to calculate stats. But, you shouldn't do that if your goal is performance!

Sixth decision point: Selecting a loss function

A loss function is a measure of how well our neural network predictions are. In supervised learning, it's more straightforward to interpret the loss function: given a batch of predictions and their corresponding true values, the loss function computes a distance score indicating how well the network has done in this batch.

There are many different ways for calculating this distance score, but I continue to keep it simple in this chapter and use one of the most common ones: MSE (mean squared error, or L2 loss). Still, let me restate that one challenge in reinforcement learning, as compared to supervised learning, is that our "true values" use predictions that come from the network.

MSE (or L2 loss) is defined as the average squared difference between the predicted and true values; in our case, the predicted values are the predicted values of the action-value function that come straight from the neural network: all good. But the true values are, yes, the TD targets, which depend on a prediction also coming from the network, the value of the next state.

Circular dependency of the action-value function

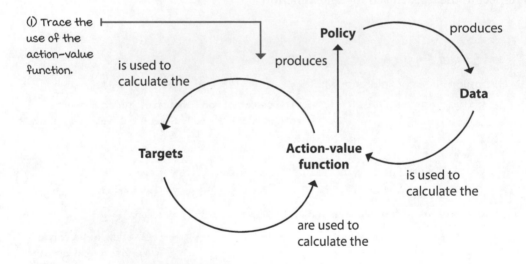

As you may be thinking, this circular dependency is bad. It's not well behaved because it doesn't respect several of the assumptions made in supervised learning problems. We'll cover what these assumptions are later in this chapter, and the problems that arise when we violate them in the next chapter.

Seventh decision point: Selecting an optimization method

Gradient descent is a stable optimization method given a couple of assumptions: data must be independent and identically distributed (IID), and targets must be stationary. In reinforcement learning, however, we cannot ensure any of these assumptions hold, so choosing a robust optimization method to minimize the loss function can often make the difference between convergence and divergence.

If you visualize a loss function as a landscape with valleys, peaks, and planes, an optimization method is the hiking strategy for finding areas of interest, usually the lowest or highest point in that landscape.

A classic optimization method in supervised learning is called *batch gradient descent*. The batch gradient descent algorithm takes the entire dataset at once, calculates the gradient of the given dataset, and steps toward this gradient a little bit at a time. Then, it repeats this cycle until convergence. In the landscape analogy, this gradient represents a signal telling us the direction we need to move. Batch gradient descent isn't the first choice of researchers because it isn't practical to process massive datasets at once. When you have a considerable dataset with millions of samples, batch gradient descent is too slow to be practical. Moreover, in reinforcement learning, we don't even have a dataset in advance, so batch gradient descent isn't a practical method for our purpose either.

An optimization method capable of handling smaller batches of data is called mini-batch gradient descent. In mini-batch gradient descent, we use only a fraction of the data at a time.

Batch gradient descent

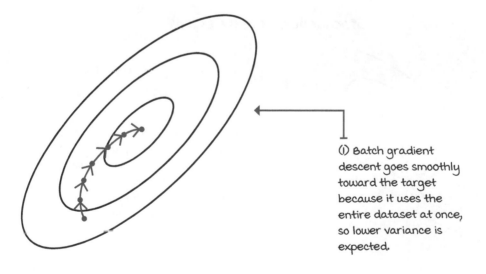

(1) Batch gradient descent goes smoothly toward the target because it uses the entire dataset at once, so lower variance is expected.

We process a mini-batch of samples to find its loss, then backpropagate to compute the gradient of this loss, and then adjust the weights of the network to make the network better at predicting the values of that mini-batch. With mini-batch gradient descent, you can control the size of the mini-batches, which allows the processing of large datasets.

Mini-batch gradient descent

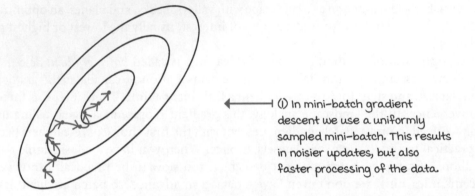

(1) In mini-batch gradient descent we use a uniformly sampled mini-batch. This results in noisier updates, but also faster processing of the data.

At one extreme, you can set the size of your mini-batch to the size of your dataset, in which case, you're back at batch gradient descent. At the other extreme, you can set the mini-batch size to a single sample per step. In this case, you're using an algorithm called *stochastic gradient descent*.

Stochastic gradient descent

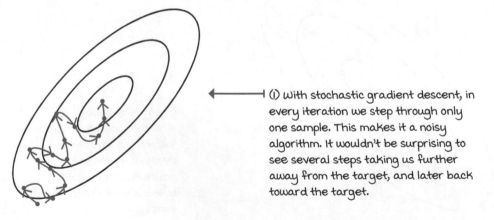

(1) With stochastic gradient descent, in every iteration we step through only one sample. This makes it a noisy algorithm. It wouldn't be surprising to see several steps taking us further away from the target, and later back toward the target.

The larger the batch, the lower the variance the steps of the optimization method have. But use a batch too large, and learning slows down considerably. Both extremes are too slow in practice. For these reasons, it's common to see mini-batch sizes ranging from 32 to 1024.

Zig-zag pattern of mini-batch gradient descent

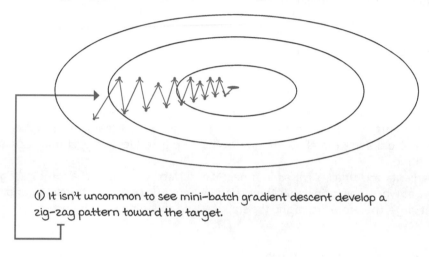

(1) It isn't uncommon to see mini-batch gradient descent develop a zig-zag pattern toward the target.

An improved gradient descent algorithm is called *gradient descent with momentum*, or *momentum* for short. This method is a mini-batch gradient descent algorithm that updates the network's weights in the direction of the moving average of the gradients, instead of the gradient itself.

Mini-batch gradient descent vs. momentum

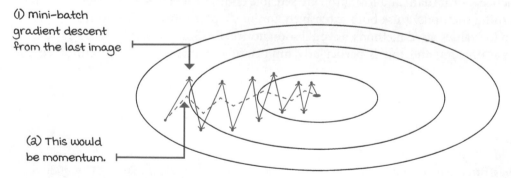

(1) mini-batch gradient descent from the last image

(2) This would be momentum.

An alternative to using momentum is called *root mean square propagation* (RMSprop). Both RMSprop and momentum do the same thing of dampening the oscillations and moving more directly towards the goal, but they do so in different ways.

While momentum takes steps in the direction of the moving average of the gradients, RMSprop takes the safer bet of scaling the gradient in proportion to a moving average of the magnitude of gradients. It reduces oscillations by merely scaling the gradient in proportion to the square root of the moving average of the square of the gradients or, more simply put, in proportion to the average magnitude of recent gradients.

MIGUEL'S ANALOGY

Optimization methods in value-based deep reinforcement learning

To visualize RMSprop, think of the steepness change of the surface of your loss function. If gradients are high, such as when going downhill, and the surface changes to a flat valley, where gradients are small, the moving average magnitude of gradients is higher than the most recent gradient; therefore, the size of the step is reduced, preventing oscillations or overshooting.

If gradients are small, such as in a near-flat surface, and they change to a significant gradient, as when going downhill, the average magnitude of gradients is small, and the new gradient large, therefore increasing the step size and speeding up learning.

A final optimization method I'd like to introduce is called *adaptive moment estimation* (Adam). Adam is a combination of RMSprop and momentum. The Adam method steps in the direction of the velocity of the gradients, as in momentum. But, it scales updates in proportion to the moving average of the magnitude of the gradients, as in RMSprop. These properties make Adam as an optimization method a bit more aggressive than RMSprop, yet not as aggressive as momentum.

In practice, both Adam and RMSprop are sensible choices for value-based deep reinforcement learning methods. I use both extensively in the chapters ahead. However, I do prefer RMSprop for value-based methods, as you'll soon notice. RMSprop is stable and less sensitive to hyperparameters, and this is particularly important in value-based deep reinforcement learning.

0001   A BIT OF HISTORY

Introduction of the NFQ algorithm

NFQ was introduced in 2005 by Martin Riedmiller in a paper called "Neural Fitted Q Iteration – First Experiences with a Data Efficient Neural Reinforcement Learning Method." After 13 years working as a professor at a number of European universities, Martin took a job as a research scientist at Google DeepMind.

It's in the Details
The full neural fitted Q-iteration (NFQ) algorithm

Currently, we've made the following selections:

- Approximate the action-value function $Q(s,a;\theta)$.
- Use a state-in-values-out architecture (nodes: 4, 512,128, 2).
- Optimize the action-value function to approximate the optimal action-value function $q*(s,a)$.
- Use off-policy TD targets ($r + \gamma*max\_a'Q(s',a';\theta)$) to evaluate policies.
- Use an epsilon-greedy strategy (epsilon set to 0.5) to improve policies.
- Use mean squared error (MSE) for our loss function.
- Use RMSprop as our optimizer with a learning rate of 0.0005.

NFQ has three main steps:

1. Collect E experiences: (s, a, r, s', d) tuples. We use 1024 samples.
2. Calculate the off-policy TD targets: $r + \gamma*max\_a'Q(s',a';\theta)$.
3. Fit the action-value function $Q(s,a;\theta)$ using MSE and RMSprop.

This algorithm repeats steps 2 and 3 *K* number of times before going back to step 1. That's what makes it fitted: the nested loop. We'll use 40 fitting steps *K*.

NFQ

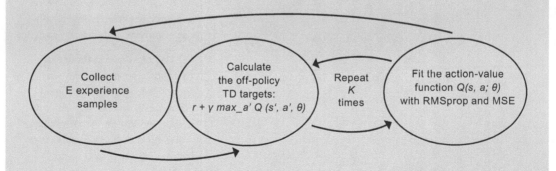

TALLY IT UP
NFQ passes the cart-pole environment

Although NFQ is far from a state-of-the-art, value-based deep reinforcement learning method, in a somewhat simple environment, such as the cart-pole, NFQ shows a decent performance.

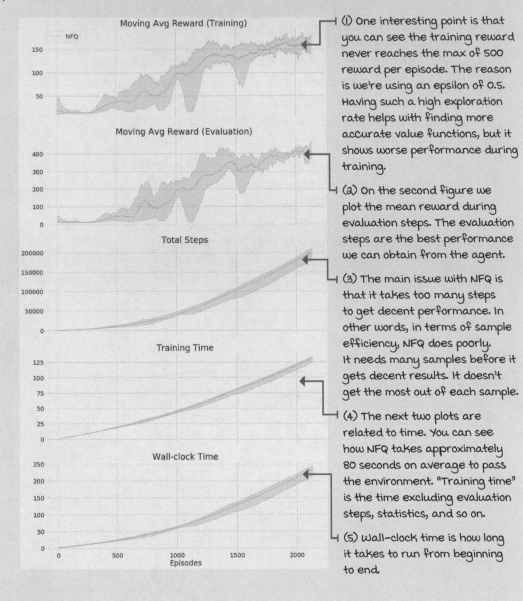

(1) One interesting point is that you can see the training reward never reaches the max of 500 reward per episode. The reason is we're using an epsilon of 0.5. Having such a high exploration rate helps with finding more accurate value functions, but it shows worse performance during training.

(2) On the second figure we plot the mean reward during evaluation steps. The evaluation steps are the best performance we can obtain from the agent.

(3) The main issue with NFQ is that it takes too many steps to get decent performance. In other words, in terms of sample efficiency, NFQ does poorly. It needs many samples before it gets decent results. It doesn't get the most out of each sample.

(4) The next two plots are related to time. You can see how NFQ takes approximately 80 seconds on average to pass the environment. "Training time" is the time excluding evaluation steps, statistics, and so on.

(5) Wall-clock time is how long it takes to run from beginning to end.

Things that could (and do) go wrong

There are two issues with our algorithm. First, because we're using a powerful function approximator, we can generalize across state-action pairs, which is excellent, but that also means that the neural network adjusts the values of all similar states at once.

Now, think about this for a second: our target values depend on the values for the next state, which we can safely assume are similar to the states we are adjusting the values of in the first place. In other words, we're creating a non-stationary target for our learning updates. As we update the weights of the approximate Q-function, the targets also move and make our most recent update outdated. Thus, training becomes unstable quickly.

Non-stationary target

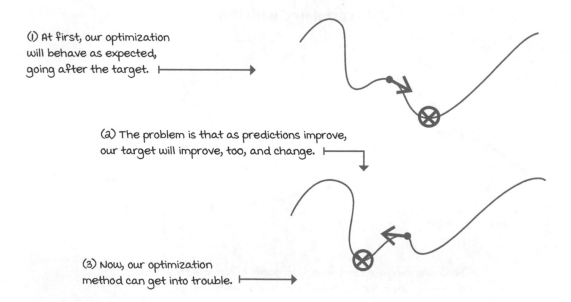

① At first, our optimization will behave as expected, going after the target. ⊢——————▶

② The problem is that as predictions improve, our target will improve, too, and change. ⊢

③ Now, our optimization method can get into trouble. ⊢——————▶

Second, in NFQ, we batched 1024 experience samples collected online and update the network from that mini-batch. As you can imagine, these samples are correlated, given that most of these samples come from the same trajectory and policy. That means the network learns from mini-batches of samples that are similar, and later uses different mini-batches that are also internally correlated, but likely different from previous mini-batches, mainly if a different, older policy collected the samples.

All this means that we aren't holding the IID assumption, and this is a problem because optimization methods assume the data samples they use for training are independent and identically distributed. But we're training on almost the exact opposite: samples on our distribution are not independent because the outcome of a new state *s* is dependent on our current state *s*.

And, also, our samples aren't identically distributed because the underlying data generating process, which is our policy, is changing over time. That means we don't have a fixed data distribution. Instead, our policy, which is responsible for generating the data, is changing and hopefully improving periodically. Every time our policy changes, we receive new and likely different experiences. Optimization methods allow us to relax the IID assumption to a certain degree, but reinforcement learning problems go all the way, so we need to do something about this, too.

Data correlated with time

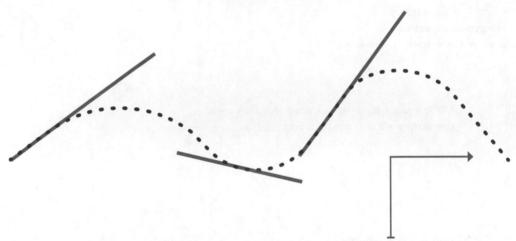

(i) Imagine we generate these data points in a single trajectory. Say the y-axis is the position of the cart along the track, and the x-axis is the step of the trajectory. You can see how likely it is data points at adjacent time steps will be similar, making our function approximator likely to overfit to that local region.

In the next chapter, we look at ways of mitigating these two issues. We start by improving NFQ with the algorithm that arguably started the deep reinforcement learning revolution, DQN. We then follow by exploring many of the several improvements proposed to the original DQN algorithm over the years. We also look at double DQN in the next chapter, and then in chapter 10, we look at dueling DQN and PER.

Summary

In this chapter, we gave a high-level overview of how sampled feedback interacts with sequential and evaluative feedback. We did so while introducing a simple deep reinforcement learning agent that approximates the Q-function, that in previous chapters, we would represent in tabular form, with a lookup table. This chapter was an introduction to value-based deep reinforcement learning methods.

You learned the difference between high-dimensional and continuous state and action spaces. The former indicates a large number of values that make up a single state; the latter hints at at least one variable that can take on an infinite number of values. You learned that decision-making problems could be both high-dimensional and continuous variables, and that makes the use of non-linear function approximation intriguing.

You learned that function approximation isn't only beneficial for estimating expectations of values for which we only have a few samples, but also for learning the underlying relationships in the state and action dimensions. By having a good model, we can estimate values for which we never received samples and use all experiences across the board.

You had an in-depth overview of different components commonly used when building deep reinforcement learning agents. You learned you could approximate different kinds of value functions, from the state-value function $v(s)$ to the action-value $q(s, a)$. And, you can approximate these value functions using different neural network architectures; we explored the state-action pair in, value out, to the more efficient state-in, values out. You learned about using the same objective we used for Q-learning, using the TD target for off-policy control. And, you know there are many different targets you can use to train your network. You surveyed exploration strategies, loss functions, and optimization methods. You learned that deep reinforcement learning agents are susceptible to the loss and optimization methods we select. You learned about RMSprop and Adam as the stable options for optimization methods.

You learned to combine all of these components into an algorithm called neural fitted Q-iteration. You learned about the issues commonly occurring in value-based deep reinforcement learning methods. You learned about the IID assumption and the stationarity of the targets. You learned that not being careful with these two issues can get us into trouble.

By now, you

- Understand what it is to learn from feedback that is sequential, evaluative, and sampled

- Can solve reinforcement learning problems with continuous state-spaces

- Know about the components and issues in value-based DRL methods

TWEETABLE FEAT
Work on your own and share your findings

Here are several ideas on how to take what you've learned to the next level. If you'd like, share your results with the rest of the world and make sure to check out what others have done, too. It's a win-win situation, and hopefully, you'll take advantage of it.

- **#gdrl_ch08_tf01:** After tabular reinforcement learning, and before deep reinforcement learning, there are a couple things to explore. With this hashtag, explore and share results for state discretization and tile coding techniques. What are those? Are there any other techniques that we should know about?

- **#gdrl_ch08_tf02:** The other thing I'd like you to explore is the use of linear function approximation, instead of deep neural networks. Can you tell us how other function approximation techniques compare? What techniques show promising results?

- **#gdrl_ch08_tf03:** In this chapter, I introduced gradient descent as the type of optimization method we use for the remainder of the book. However, gradient descent is not the only way to optimize a neural network; did you know? Either way, you should go out there and investigate other ways to optimize a neural network, from black-box optimization methods, such as genetic algorithms, to other methods that aren't as popular. Share your findings, create a Notebook with examples, and share your results.

- **#gdrl_ch08_tf04:** I started this chapter with a better way for doing Q-learning with function approximation. Equally important to knowing a better way is to have an implementation of the simplest way that didn't work. Implement the minimal changes to make Q-learning work with a neural network: that is, Q-learning with online experiences as you learned in chapter 6. Test and share your results.

- **#gdrl_ch08_tf05:** In every chapter, I'm using the final hashtag as a catchall hashtag. Feel free to use this one to discuss anything else that you worked on relevant to this chapter. There's no more exciting homework than that which you create for yourself. Make sure to share what you set yourself to investigate and your results.

Write a tweet with your findings, tag me @mimoralea (I'll retweet), and use the particular hashtag from the list to help interested folks find your results. There are no right or wrong results; you share your findings and check others' findings. Take advantage of this to socialize, contribute, and get yourself out there! We're waiting for you!

Here's a tweet example:

"Hey, @mimoralea. I created a blog post with a list of resources to study deep reinforcement learning. Check it out at <link>. #gdrl_ch01_tf01"

I'll make sure to retweet and help others find your work.

More stable
value-based methods | 9

In this chapter

- You will improve on the methods you learned in the previous chapter by making them more stable and therefore less prone to divergence.

- You will explore advanced value-based deep reinforcement learning methods, and the many components that make value-based methods better.

- You will solve the cart-pole environment in a fewer number of samples, and with more reliable and consistent results.

In the last chapter, you learned about value-based deep reinforcement learning. NFQ, the algorithm we developed, is a simple solution to the two most common issues value-based methods face: first, the issue that data in RL isn't independent and identically distributed. It's probably the exact opposite. The experiences are dependent on the policy that generates them. And, they aren't identically distributed since the policy changes throughout the training process. Second, the targets we use aren't stationary, either. Optimization methods require fixed targets for robust performance. In supervised learning, this is easy to see. We have a dataset with premade labels as constants, and our optimization method uses these fixed targets for stochastically approximating the underlying data-generating function. In RL, on the other hand, targets such as the TD target use the reward and the discounted predicted return from the landing state as a target. But this predicted return comes from the network we're optimizing, which changes every time we execute the optimization steps. This issue creates a moving target that creates instabilities in the training process.

The way NFQ addresses these issues is through the use of batching. By growing a batch, we have the opportunity of optimizing several samples at the same time. The larger the batch, the more the opportunity for collecting a diverse set of experience samples. This somewhat addresses the IID assumption. NFQ addresses the stationarity of target requirements by using the same mini-batch in multiple sequential optimization steps. Remember that in NFQ, every E episode, we "fit" the neural network to the same mini-batch K times. That K allows the optimization method to move toward the target more stably. Gathering a batch and fitting the model for multiple iterations is similar to the way we train supervised learning methods, in which we gather a dataset and train for multiple epochs.

NFQ does an okay job, but we can do better. Now that we know the issues, we can address them using better techniques. In this chapter, we explore algorithms that address not only these issues, but other issues that you learn about making value-based methods more stable.

DQN: Making reinforcement learning more like supervised learning

The first algorithm that we discuss in this chapter is called *deep Q-network* (DQN). DQN is one of the most popular DRL algorithms because it started a series of research innovations that mark the history of RL. DQN claimed for the first time superhuman level performance on an Atari benchmark in which agents learned from raw pixel data from mere images.

Throughout the years, there have been many improvements proposed to DQN. And while these days DQN in its original form is not a go-to algorithm, with the improvements, many of which you learn about in this book, the algorithm still has a spot among the best-performing DRL agents.

Common problems in value-based deep reinforcement learning

We must be clear and understand the two most common problems that consistently show up in value-based deep reinforcement learning: the violations of the IID assumption, and the stationarity of targets.

In supervised learning, we obtain a full dataset in advance. We preprocess it, shuffle it, and then split it into sets for training. One crucial step in this process is the shuffling of the dataset. By doing so, we allow our optimization method to avoid developing overfitting biases; reduce the variance of the training process; speed up convergence; and overall learn a more general representation of the underlying data-generating process. In reinforcement learning, unfortunately, data is often gathered online; as a result, the experience sample generated at time step *t+1* correlates with the experience sample generated at time step *t*. Moreover, as the policy is to improve, it changes the underlying data-generating process changes, too, which means that new data is locally correlated and not evenly distributed.

 BOIL IT DOWN

Data isn't independently and identically distributed (IID)

The first problem is non-compliance with the IID assumption of the data. Optimization methods have been developed with the assumption that samples in the dataset we train with are independent and identically distributed.

We know, however, our samples aren't independent, but instead, they come from a sequence, a time series, a trajectory. The sample at time step *t+1* is dependent on the sample at time step *t*. Samples are correlated, and we can't prevent that from happening; it's a natural consequence of online learning.

But samples are also not identically distributed because they depend on the policy that generates the actions. We know the policy is changing through time, and for us that's a good thing. We want policies to improve. But that also means the distribution of samples (state-action pairs visited) will change as we keep improving.

Also, in supervised learning, the targets used for training are fixed values on your dataset; they're fixed throughout the training process. In reinforcement learning in general, and even more so in the extreme case of online learning, targets move with every training step of the network. At every training update step, we optimize the approximate value function and therefore change the shape of the function, possibly the entire value function. Changing the value function means that the target values change as well, which, in turn, means the targets used are no longer valid. Because the targets come from the network, even before we use them, we can assume targets are invalid or biased at a minimum.

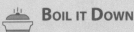

BOIL IT DOWN
Non-stationarity of targets

The problem of the non-stationarity of targets is depicted. These are the targets we use to train our network, but these targets are calculated using the network itself. As a result, the function changes with every update, in turn changing the targets.

Non-stationarity of targets

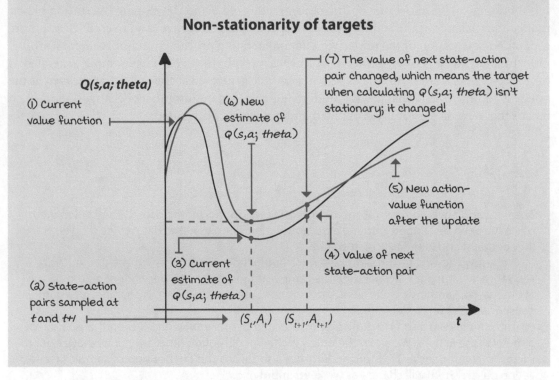

In NFQ, we lessen this problem by using a batch and fitting the network to a small fixed dataset for multiple iterations. In NFQ, we collect a small dataset, calculating targets, and optimize the network several times before going out to collect more samples. By doing this on a large batch of samples, the updates to the neural network are composed of many points across the function, additionally making changes even more stable.

DQN is an algorithm that addresses the question, how do we make reinforcement learning look more like supervised learning? Consider this question for a second, and think about the tweaks you would make to make the data look IID and the targets fixed.

Using target networks

A straightforward way to make target values more stationary is to have a separate network that we can fix for multiple steps and reserve it for calculating more stationary targets. The network with this purpose in DQN is called the *target network*.

Q-function optimization without a target network

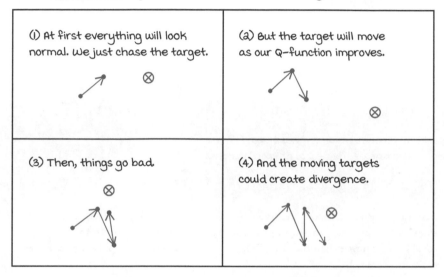

① At first everything will look normal. We just chase the target.

② But the target will move as our Q-function improves.

③ Then, things go bad.

④ And the moving targets could create divergence.

Q-function approximation with a target network

① Suppose we freeze the target for a few steps.

② That way, the optimizer can make stable progress toward it.

③ We eventually update the target, and repeat.

④ This allows the algorithm to make stable progress.

By using a target network to fix targets, we mitigate the issue of "chasing your own tail" by artificially creating several small supervised learning problems presented sequentially to the agent. Our targets are fixed for as many steps as we fix our target network. This improves our chances of convergence, but not to the optimal values because such things don't exist with non-linear function approximation, but convergence in general. But, more importantly, it substantially reduces the chance of divergence, which isn't uncommon in value-based deep reinforcement learning methods.

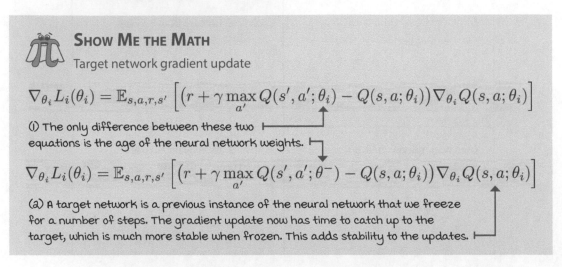

SHOW ME THE MATH
Target network gradient update

$$\nabla_{\theta_i} L_i(\theta_i) = \mathbb{E}_{s,a,r,s'} \left[\left(r + \gamma \max_{a'} Q(s', a'; \theta_i) - Q(s, a; \theta_i) \right) \nabla_{\theta_i} Q(s, a; \theta_i) \right]$$

① The only difference between these two
equations is the age of the neural network weights.

$$\nabla_{\theta_i} L_i(\theta_i) = \mathbb{E}_{s,a,r,s'} \left[\left(r + \gamma \max_{a'} Q(s', a'; \theta^-) - Q(s, a; \theta_i) \right) \nabla_{\theta_i} Q(s, a; \theta_i) \right]$$

② A target network is a previous instance of the neural network that we freeze
for a number of steps. The gradient update now has time to catch up to the
target, which is much more stable when frozen. This adds stability to the updates.

It's important to note that in practice we don't have two "networks," but instead, we have two instances of the neural network weights. We use the same model architecture and frequently update the weights of the target network to match the weights of the online network, which is the network we optimize on every step. "Frequently" here means something different depending on the problem, unfortunately. It's common to freeze these target network weights for 10 to 10,000 steps at a time, again depending on the problem. (That's time steps, not episodes. Be careful there.) If you're using a convolutional neural network, such as what you'd use for learning in Atari games, then a 10,000-step frequency is the norm. But for more straightforward problems such as the cart-pole environment, 10–20 steps is more appropriate.

By using target networks, we prevent the training process from spiraling around because we're fixing the targets for multiple time steps, thus allowing the online network weights to move consistently toward the targets before an update changes the optimization problem, and a new one is set. By using target networks, we stabilize training, but we also slow down learning because you're no longer training on up-to-date values; the frozen weights of the target network can be lagging for up to 10,000 steps at a time. It's essential to balance stability and speed and tune this hyperparameter.

I SPEAK PYTHON

Use of the target and online networks in DQN

```python
def optimize_model(self, experiences):
    states, actions, rewards, \
        next_states, is_terminals = experiences
    batch_size = len(is_terminals)
```

(1) Notice how we now query a target network to get the estimate of the next state.

```python
    q_sp = self.target_model(next_states).detach()
```

(2) We grab the maximum of those values, and make sure to treat terminal states appropriately.

```python
    max_a_q_sp = q_sp.max(1)[0].unsqueeze(1)
    max_a_q_sp *= (1 - is_terminals)
```

(3) Finally, we create the TD targets.

```python
    target_q_sa = rewards + self.gamma * max_a_q_sp
```

(4) Query the current "online" estimate.

```python
    q_sa = self.online_model(states).gather(1, actions)
```

(5) Use those values to create the errors.

```python
    td_error = q_sa - target_q_sa
    value_loss = td_error.pow(2).mul(0.5).mean()
    self.value_optimizer.zero_grad()
    value_loss.backward()
    self.value_optimizer.step()
```

(6) Calculate the loss, and optimize the online network.

```python
def interaction_step(self, state, env):
    action = self.training_strategy.select_action(
                self.online_model, state)
```

(7) Notice how we use the online model for selecting actions.

```python
    new_state, reward, is_terminal, _ = env.step(action)
    <...>
    return new_state, is_terminal
```

(8) This is how the target network (lagging network) gets updated with the online network (up-to-date network).

```python
def update_network(self):
    for target, online in zip(
                    self.target_model.parameters(),
                    self.online_model.parameters()):
        target.data.copy_(online.data)
```

Using larger networks

Another way you can lessen the non-stationarity issue, to some degree, is to use larger networks. With more powerful networks, subtle differences between states are more likely to be detected. Larger networks reduce the aliasing of state-action pairs; the more powerful the network, the lower the aliasing; the lower the aliasing, the less apparent correlation between consecutive samples. And all of this can make target values and current estimates look more independent of each other.

By "aliasing" here I refer to the fact that two states can look like the same (or quite similar) state to the neural network, but still possibly require different actions. State aliasing can occur when networks lack representational power. After all, neural networks are trying to find similarities to generalize; their job is to find these similarities. But, too small of a network can cause the generalization to go wrong. The network could get fixated with simple, easy to find patterns.

One of the motivations for using a target network is that they allow you to differentiate between correlated states more easily. Using a more capable network helps your network learn subtle differences, too.

But, a more powerful neural network takes longer to train. It needs not only more data (interaction time) but also more compute (processing time). Using a target network is a more robust approach to mitigating the non-stationary problem, but I want you to know all the tricks. It's favorable for you to know how these two properties of your agent (the size of your networks, and the use of target networks, along with the update frequency), interact and affect final performance in similar ways.

 BOIL IT DOWN

Ways to mitigate the fact that targets in reinforcement learning are non-stationary

Allow me to restate that to mitigate the non-stationarity issue we can

1. Create a target network that provides us with a temporarily stationary target value.
2. Create large-enough networks so that they can "see" the small differences between similar states (like those temporally correlated).

Target networks work and work well, and have been proven to work multiple times. The technique of "larger networks" is more of a hand-wavy solution than something scientifically proven to work every time. Feel free to experiment with this chapter's Notebook. You'll find it easy to change values and test hypotheses.

Using experience replay

In our NFQ experiments, we use a mini-batch of 1,024 samples, and train with it for 40 iterations, alternating between calculating new targets and optimizing the network. These 1,024 samples are temporally correlated because most of them belong to the same trajectory, and the maximum number of steps in a cart-pole episode is 500. One way to improve on this is to use a technique called *experience replay*. Experience replay consists of a data structure, often referred to as a replay buffer or a replay memory, that holds experience samples for several steps (much more than 1,024 steps), allowing the sampling of mini-batches from a broad set of past experiences. Having a replay buffer allows the agent two critical things. First, the training process can use a more diverse mini-batch for performing updates. Second, the agent no longer has to fit the model to the same small mini-batch for multiple iterations. Adequately sampling a sufficiently large replay buffer yields a slow-moving target, so the agent can now sample and train on every time step with a lower risk of divergence.

0001 **A Bit of History**
Introduction of experience replay

Experience replay was introduced by Long-Ji Lin in a paper titled "Self-Improving Reactive Agents Based On Reinforcement Learning, Planning and Teaching," believe it or not, published in *1992*! That's right, 1992! Again, that's when neural networks were referred to as "connectionism"... Sad times!

After getting his PhD from CMU, Dr. Lin moved through several technical roles in many different companies. Currently, he's a Chief Scientist at Signifyd, leading a team that works on a system to predict and prevent online fraud.

There are multiple benefits to using experience replay. By sampling at random, we increase the probability that our updates to the neural network have low variance. When we used the batch in NFQ, most of the samples in that batch were correlated and similar. Updating with similar samples concentrates the changes on a limited area of the function, and that potentially overemphasizes the magnitude of the updates. If we sample uniformly at random from a substantial buffer, on the other hand, chances are that our updates to the network are better distributed all across, and therefore more representative of the true value function.

Using a replay buffer also gives the impression our data is IID so that the optimization method is stable. Samples appear independent and identically distributed because of the sampling from multiple trajectories and even policies at once.

By storing experiences and later sampling them uniformly, we make the data entering the optimization method look independent and identically distributed. In practice, the replay buffer needs to have considerable capacity to perform optimally, from 10,000 to 1,000,000 experiences depending on the problem. Once you hit the maximum size, you evict the oldest experience before inserting the new one.

DQN with a replay buffer

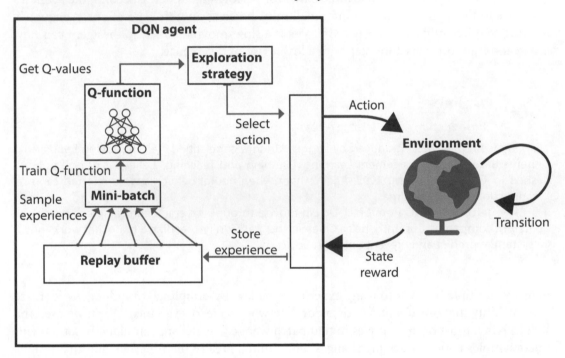

Unfortunately, the implementation becomes a little bit of a challenge when working with high-dimensional observations, because poorly implemented replay buffers hit a hardware memory limit quickly in high-dimensional environments. In image-based environments, for instance, where each state representation is a stack of the four latest image frames, as is common for Atari games, you probably don't have enough memory on your personal computer to naively store 1,000,000 experience samples. For the cart-pole environment, this isn't so much of a problem. First, we don't need 1,000,000 samples, and we use a buffer of size 50,000 instead. But also, states are represented by four-element vectors, so there isn't so much of an implementation performance challenge.

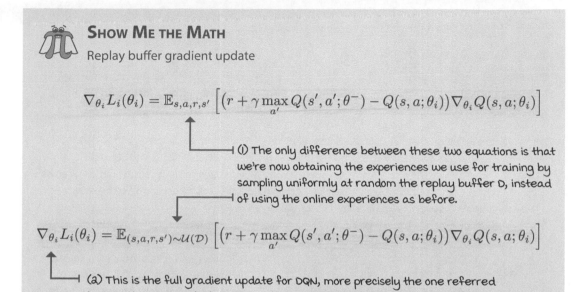

SHOW ME THE MATH
Replay buffer gradient update

$$\nabla_{\theta_i} L_i(\theta_i) = \mathbb{E}_{s,a,r,s'} \left[\left(r + \gamma \max_{a'} Q(s', a'; \theta^-) - Q(s, a; \theta_i) \right) \nabla_{\theta_i} Q(s, a; \theta_i) \right]$$

(1) The only difference between these two equations is that we're now obtaining the experiences we use for training by sampling uniformly at random the replay buffer D, instead of using the online experiences as before.

$$\nabla_{\theta_i} L_i(\theta_i) = \mathbb{E}_{(s,a,r,s') \sim \mathcal{U}(\mathcal{D})} \left[\left(r + \gamma \max_{a'} Q(s', a'; \theta^-) - Q(s, a; \theta_i) \right) \nabla_{\theta_i} Q(s, a; \theta_i) \right]$$

(2) This is the full gradient update for DQN, more precisely the one referred to as Nature DQN, which is DQN with a target network and a replay buffer.

Nevertheless, by using a replay buffer, your data looks more IID and your targets more stationary than in reality. By training from uniformly sampled mini-batches, you make the RL experiences gathered online look more like a traditional supervised learning dataset with IID data and fixed targets. Sure, data is still changing as you add new and discard old samples, but these changes are happening slowly, and so they go somewhat unnoticed by the neural network and optimizer.

BOIL IT DOWN
Experience replay makes the data look IID, and targets somewhat stationary

The best solution to the problem of data not being IID is called *experience replay*.

The technique is simple, and it's been around for decades: As your agent collects experiences tuples $e_t=(S_t,A_t,R_{t+1},S_{t+1})$ online, we insert them into a data structure, commonly referred to as the *replay buffer D*, such that $D=\{e_1, e_2, ..., e_M\}$. M, the size of the replay buffer, is a value often between 10,000 to 1,000,000, depending on the problem.

We then train the agent on mini-batches sampled, usually uniformly at random, from the buffer, so that each sample has equal probability of being selected. Though, as you learn in the next chapter, you could possibly sample with another distribution. Just beware because it isn't that straightforward. We'll discuss details in the next chapter.

I SPEAK PYTHON

A simple replay buffer

```python
class ReplayBuffer():
    def __init__(self,
                 m_size=50000,
                 batch_size=64):
        self.ss_mem = np.empty(shape=(m_size), dtype=np.ndarray)
        self.as_mem = np.empty(shape=(m_size), dtype=np.ndarray)
        <...>
```

(1) This is a simple replay buffer with a default maximum size of 50,000, and a default batch size of 64 samples.

(2) We initialize five arrays to hold states, actions, reward, next states, and done flags. Shortened for brevity.

(3) We initialize several variables to do storage and sampling.

```python
        self.m_size, self.batch_size = m_size, batch_size
        self._idx, self.size = 0, 0

    def store(self, sample):
        s, a, r, p, d = sample
        self.ss_mem[self._idx] = s
        self.as_mem[self._idx] = a
        <...>
        self._idx += 1
        self._idx = self._idx % self.m_size

        self.size += 1
        self.size = min(self.size, self.m_size)

    def sample(self, batch_size=None):
        if batch_size == None:
            batch_size = self.batch_size
        idxs = np.random.choice(
            self.size, batch_size, replace=False)
        experiences = np.vstack(self.ss_mem[idxs]), \
                      np.vstack(self.as_mem[idxs]), \
                      np.vstack(self.rs_mem[idxs]), \
                      np.vstack(self.ps_mem[idxs]), \
                      np.vstack(self.ds_mem[idxs])
        return experiences

    def __len__(self):
        return self.size
```

(4) When we store a new sample, we begin by unwrapping the sample variable, and then setting each array's element to its corresponding value.

(5) Again removed for brevity

(6) _idx points to the next index to modify, so we increase it, and also make sure it loops back after reaching the maximum size (the end of the buffer).

(7) Size also increases with every new sample stored, but it doesn't loop back to 0; it stops growing instead.

(8) In the sample function, we begin by determining the batch size. We use the default of 64 if nothing else was passed.

(9) Sample batch_size ids from 0 to size.

(10) Then, extract the experiences from the buffer using the sampled ids.

(11) And return those experiences.

(12) This is a handy function to return the correct size of the buffer when len(buffer) is called.

Using other exploration strategies

Exploration is a vital component of reinforcement learning. In the NFQ algorithm, we use an epsilon-greedy exploration strategy, which consists of acting randomly with epsilon probability. We sample a number from a uniform distribution (0, 1). If the number is less than the hyperparameter constant, called epsilon, your agent selects an action uniformly at random (that's including the greedy action); otherwise, it acts greedily.

For the DQN experiments, I added to chapter 9's Notebook some of the other exploration strategies introduced in chapter 4. I adapted them to use them with neural networks, and they are reintroduced next. Make sure to check out all Notebooks and play around.

I Speak Python
Linearly decaying epsilon-greedy exploration strategy

```python
class EGreedyLinearStrategy():
    <...>
    def _epsilon_update(self):
        self.epsilon = 1 - self.t / self.max_steps
        self.epsilon = (self.init_epsilon - self.min_epsilon) * \
                            self.epsilon + self.min_epsilon
        self.epsilon = np.clip(self.epsilon,
                               self.min_epsilon,
                               self.init_epsilon)
        self.t += 1
        return self.epsilon

    def select_action(self, model, state):
        self.exploratory_action = False
        with torch.no_grad():
            q_values = model(state).cpu().detach()
            q_values = q_values.data.numpy().squeeze()
        if np.random.rand() > self.epsilon:
            action = np.argmax(q_values)
        else:
            action = np.random.randint(len(q_values))

        self._epsilon_update()
        self.exploratory_action = action != np.argmax(q_values)
        return action
```

(1) In a linearly decaying epsilon-greedy strategy, we start with a high epsilon value and decay its value in a linear fashion.

(2) We clip epsilon to be between the initial and the minimum value.

(3) This is a variable holding the number of times epsilon has been updated.

(4) In the select_action method, we use a model and a state.

(5) For logging purposes, I always extract the q_values.

(6) We draw the random number from a uniform distribution and compare it to epsilon.

(7) If higher, we use the argmax of the q_values; otherwise, a random action.

(8) Finally, we update epsilon, set a variable for logging purposes, and return the action selected.

I SPEAK PYTHON

Exponentially decaying epsilon-greedy exploration strategy

```python
class EGreedyExpStrategy():
    <...>


    def _epsilon_update(self):
        self.epsilon = max(self.min_epsilon,
                           self.decay_rate * self.epsilon)
        return self.epsilon

# def _epsilon_update(self):
#     self.decay_rate = 0.0001
#     epsilon = self.init_epsilon * np.exp( \
#                           -self.decay_rate * self.t)
#     epsilon = max(epsilon, self.min_epsilon)
#     self.t += 1
#     return epsilon


    def select_action(self, model, state):
        self.exploratory_action = False
        with torch.no_grad():
            q_values = model(state).cpu().detach()
            q_values = q_values.data.numpy().squeeze()

        if np.random.rand() > self.epsilon:
            action = np.argmax(q_values)
        else:
            action = np.random.randint(len(q_values))
        self._epsilon_update()

        self.exploratory_action = action != np.argmax(q_values)
        return action
```

(1) In the exponentially decaying strategy, the only difference is that now epsilon is decaying in an exponential curve.

(2) This is yet another way to exponentially decay epsilon, this one uses the exponential function. The epsilon values will be much the same, but the decay rate will have to be a different scale.

(3) This select_action function is identical to the previous strategy. One thing I want to highlight is that I'm querying the q_values every time only because I'm collecting information to show to you. But if you care about performance, this is a bad idea. A faster implementation would only query the network after determining that a greedy action is being called for.

(4) exploratory_action here is a variable used to calculate the percentage of exploratory actions taken per episode. Only used for logging information.

I SPEAK PYTHON

Softmax exploration strategy

```python
class SoftMaxStrategy():
    <...>
    def _update_temp(self):
        temp = 1 - self.t / (self.max_steps * self.explore_ratio)
        temp = (self.init_temp - self.min_temp) * \
```

(1) In the softmax strategy, we use a temperature parameter, `temp + self.min_temp` which, the closer the value is to 0, the more pronounced the differences in the values will become, making action selection more greedy. The temperature is decayed linearly.

```python
        temp = np.clip(temp, self.min_temp, self.init_temp)
        self.t += 1
        return temp
```

(2) Here, after decaying the temperature linearly, we clip its value to make sure it's in an acceptable range.

```python
    def select_action(self, model, state):
        self.exploratory_action = False
        temp = self._update_temp()
        with torch.no_grad():
```

(3) Notice that in the softmax strategy we really have no chance of avoiding extracting the q_values from the model. After all, actions depend directly on the values.

```python
            q_values = model(state).cpu().detach()
            q_values = q_values.data.numpy().squeeze()
```

(4) After extracting the values, we want to accentuate their differences (unless temp equals 1).

```python
            scaled_qs = q_values/temp
```

(5) We normalize them to avoid an overflow in the exp operation.

```python
            norm_qs = scaled_qs - scaled_qs.max()
            e = np.exp(norm_qs)
            probs = e / np.sum(e)
            assert np.isclose(probs.sum(), 1.0)
```

(6) Calculate the exponential.
(7) Convert to probabilities.

(8) Finally, we use the probabilities to select an action. Notice how we pass the probs variable to the p function argument.

```python
        action = np.random.choice(np.arange(len(probs)),
                                  size=1, p=probs)[0]
```

(9) And as before: Was the action the greedy or exploratory?

```python
        self.exploratory_action = action != np.argmax(q_values)
        return action
```

IT'S IN THE DETAILS

Exploration strategies have an impactful effect on performance

(1) In NFQ, we used epsilon-greedy with a constant value of 0.5. Yes! That's 50% of the time we acted greedily, and 50% of the time, we chose uniformly at random. Given that there are only two actions in this environment, the actual probability of choosing the greedy action is 75%, and the chance of selecting the non-greedy action is 25%. Notice that in a large action space, the probability of selecting the greedy action would be smaller. In the Notebook, I output this effective probability value under "ex 100." That means "ratio of exploratory action over the last 100 steps."

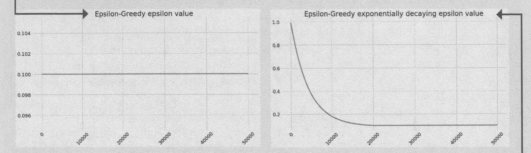

(2) In DQN and all remaining value-based algorithms in this and the following chapter, I use the exponentially decaying epsilon-greedy strategy. I prefer this one because it's simple and it works well. But other, more advanced, strategies may be worth trying. I noticed that even a small difference in hyperparameters makes a significant difference in performance. Make sure to test that yourself.

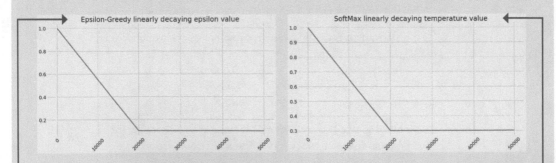

(3) The plots in this box are the decaying schedules of all the different exploration strategies available in chapter 9's Notebook. I highly encourage you to go through it and play with the many different hyperparameters and exploration strategies. There's more to deep reinforcement learning than just the algorithms.

IT'S IN THE DETAILS
The full deep Q-network (DQN) algorithm

Our DQN implementation has components and settings similar to our NFQ:

- Approximate the action-value function $Q(s,a; \theta)$.
- Use a state-in-values-out architecture (nodes: 4, 512,128, 2).
- Optimize the action-value function to approximate the optimal action-value function $q^*(s,a)$.
- Use off-policy TD targets ($r + gamma*max\_a'Q(s',a'; \theta)$) to evaluate policies.
- Use mean squared error (MSE) for our loss function.
- Use RMSprop as our optimizer with a learning rate of 0.0005.

Some of the differences are that in the DQN implementation we now

- Use an exponentially decaying epsilon-greedy strategy to improve policies, decaying from 1.0 to 0.3 in roughly 20,000 steps.
- Use a replay buffer with 320 samples min, 50,000 max, and mini-batches of 64.
- Use a target network that updates every 15 steps.

DQN has three main steps:

1. Collect experience: ($S_t, A_t, R_{t+1}, S_{t+1}, D_{t+1}$), and insert it into the replay buffer.
2. Randomly sample a mini-batch from the buffer, and calculate the off-policy TD targets for the whole batch: $r + gamma*max\_a'Q(s',a'; \theta)$.
3. Fit the action-value function $Q(s,a; \theta)$ using MSE and RMSprop.

0001 **A BIT OF HISTORY**
Introduction of the DQN algorithm

DQN was introduced in 2013 by Volodymyr "Vlad" Mnih in a paper called "Playing Atari with Deep Reinforcement Learning." This paper introduced DQN with experience replay. In 2015, another paper came out, "Human-level control through deep reinforcement learning." This second paper introduced DQN with the addition of target networks; it's the full DQN version you just learned about.

Vlad got his PhD under Geoffrey Hinton (one of the fathers of deep learning), and works as a research scientist at Google DeepMind. He's been recognized for his DQN contributions, and has been included in the 2017 MIT Technology Review 35 Innovators under 35 list.

╫╫╫ TALLY IT UP

DQN passes the cart-pole environment

The most remarkable part of the results is that NFQ needs far more samples than DQN to solve the environment; DQN is more sample efficient. However, they take about the same time, both training (compute) and wall-clock time.

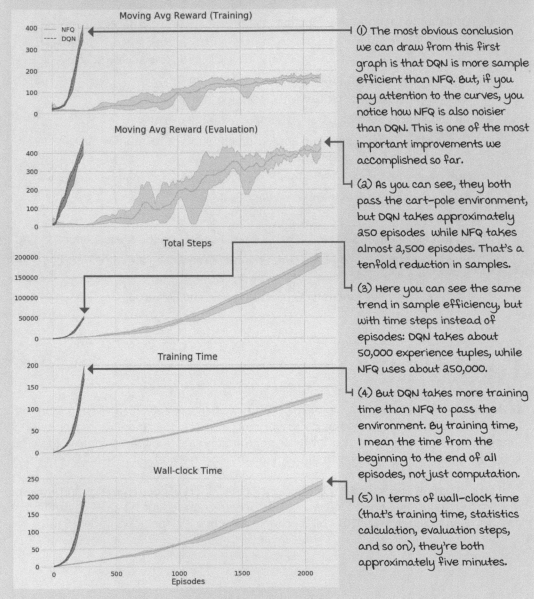

(1) The most obvious conclusion we can draw from this first graph is that DQN is more sample efficient than NFQ. But, if you pay attention to the curves, you notice how NFQ is also noisier than DQN. This is one of the most important improvements we accomplished so far.

(2) As you can see, they both pass the cart-pole environment, but DQN takes approximately 250 episodes while NFQ takes almost 2,500 episodes. That's a tenfold reduction in samples.

(3) Here you can see the same trend in sample efficiency, but with time steps instead of episodes: DQN takes about 50,000 experience tuples, while NFQ uses about 250,000.

(4) But DQN takes more training time than NFQ to pass the environment. By training time, I mean the time from the beginning to the end of all episodes, not just computation.

(5) In terms of wall-clock time (that's training time, statistics calculation, evaluation steps, and so on), they're both approximately five minutes.

Double DQN: Mitigating the overestimation of action-value functions

In this section, we introduce one of the main improvements to DQN that have been proposed throughout the years, called *double deep Q-networks* (double DQN, or DDQN). This improvement consists of adding double learning to our DQN agent. It's straightforward to implement, and it yields agents with consistently better performance than DQN. The changes required are similar to the changes applied to Q-learning to develop double Q-learning; however, there are several differences that we need to discuss.

The problem of overestimation, take two

As you can probably remember from chapter 6, Q-learning tends to overestimate action-value functions. Our DQN agent is no different; we're using the same off-policy TD target, after all, with that max operator. The crux of the problem is simple: We're taking the max of estimated values. Estimated values are often off-center, some higher than the true values, some lower, but the bottom line is that they're off. The problem is that we're always taking the max of these values, so we have a preference for higher values, even if they aren't correct. Our algorithms show a positive bias, and performance suffers.

 MIGUEL'S ANALOGY

The issue with overoptimistic agents, and people

I used to like super-positive people until I learned about double DQN. No, seriously, imagine you meet a very optimistic person; let's call her DQN. DQN is extremely optimistic. She's experienced many things in life, from the toughest defeat to the highest success. The problem with DQN, though, is she expects the sweetest possible outcome from every single thing she does, regardless of what she actually does. Is that a problem?

One day, DQN went to a local casino. It was the first time, but lucky DQN got the jackpot at the slot machines. Optimistic as she is, DQN immediately adjusted her value function. She thought, "Going to the casino is quite rewarding (the value of $Q(s,a)$ should be high) because at the casino you can go to the slot machines (next state s') and by playing the slot machines, you get the jackpot [$max\_a' Q(s', a')$]".

But, there are multiple issues with this thinking. To begin with, DQN doesn't play the slot machines every time she goes to the casino. She likes to try new things too (she explores), and sometimes she tries the roulette, poker, or blackjack (tries a different action). Sometimes the slot machine area is under maintenance and not accessible (the environment transitions her somewhere else). Additionally, most of the time when DQN plays the slot machines, she doesn't get the jackpot (the environment is stochastic). After all, slot machines are called bandits for a reason, not those bandits, the other—never mind.

Separating action selection from action evaluation

One way to better understand positive bias and how we can address it when using function approximation is by unwrapping the *max* operator in the target calculations. The *max* of a Q-function is the same as the Q-function of the *argmax* action.

REFRESH MY MEMORY

What's an argmax, again?

The argmax function is defined as the arguments of the maxima. The argmax action-value function, argmax Q-function, *argmax_a Q(s,a)* is the *index* of the action with the maximum value at the given state *s*.

For example, if you have a *Q(s)* with values *[−1, 0 , −4, −9]* for actions 0–3, the *max_a Q(s, a)* is *0*, which is the maximum value, and the *argmax_a Q(s, a)* is *1* which is the index of the maximum value.

Let's unpack the previous sentence with the max and argmax. Notice that we made pretty much the same changes when we went from Q-learning to double Q-learning, but given that we're using function approximation, we need to be cautious. At first, this unwrapping might seem like a silly step, but it helps me understand how to mitigate this problem.

SHOW ME THE MATH

Unwrapping the argmax

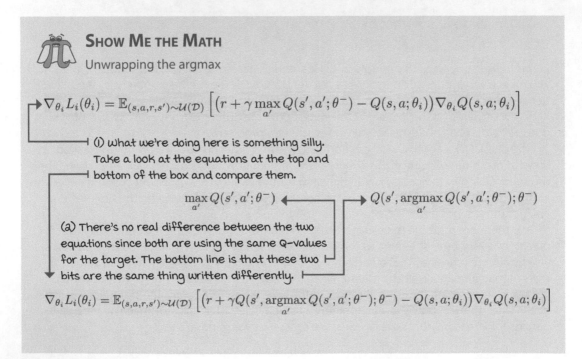

$$\nabla_{\theta_i} L_i(\theta_i) = \mathbb{E}_{(s,a,r,s') \sim \mathcal{U}(\mathcal{D})} \left[(r + \gamma \max_{a'} Q(s', a'; \theta^-) - Q(s, a; \theta_i)) \nabla_{\theta_i} Q(s, a; \theta_i) \right]$$

(1) What we're doing here is something silly. Take a look at the equations at the top and bottom of the box and compare them.

$$\max_{a'} Q(s', a'; \theta^-) \longleftarrow \qquad \longrightarrow Q(s', \operatorname*{argmax}_{a'} Q(s', a'; \theta^-); \theta^-)$$

(2) There's no real difference between the two equations since both are using the same Q-values for the target. The bottom line is that these two bits are the same thing written differently.

$$\nabla_{\theta_i} L_i(\theta_i) = \mathbb{E}_{(s,a,r,s') \sim \mathcal{U}(\mathcal{D})} \left[(r + \gamma Q(s', \operatorname*{argmax}_{a'} Q(s', a'; \theta^-); \theta^-) - Q(s, a; \theta_i)) \nabla_{\theta_i} Q(s, a; \theta_i) \right]$$

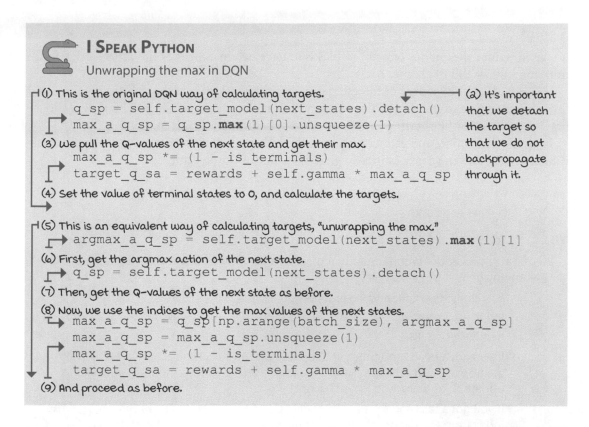

I SPEAK PYTHON

Unwrapping the max in DQN

(1) This is the original DQN way of calculating targets.

```
q_sp = self.target_model(next_states).detach()
max_a_q_sp = q_sp.max(1)[0].unsqueeze(1)
```

(2) It's important that we detach the target so that we do not backpropagate through it.

(3) We pull the Q-values of the next state and get their max.

```
max_a_q_sp *= (1 - is_terminals)
target_q_sa = rewards + self.gamma * max_a_q_sp
```

(4) Set the value of terminal states to 0, and calculate the targets.

(5) This is an equivalent way of calculating targets, "unwrapping the max."

```
argmax_a_q_sp = self.target_model(next_states).max(1)[1]
```

(6) First, get the argmax action of the next state.

```
q_sp = self.target_model(next_states).detach()
```

(7) Then, get the Q-values of the next state as before.

(8) Now, we use the indices to get the max values of the next states.

```
max_a_q_sp = q_sp[np.arange(batch_size), argmax_a_q_sp]
max_a_q_sp = max_a_q_sp.unsqueeze(1)
max_a_q_sp *= (1 - is_terminals)
target_q_sa = rewards + self.gamma * max_a_q_sp
```

(9) And proceed as before.

All we're saying here is that taking the *max* is like asking the network, "What's the value of the highest-valued action in state *s*?"

But, we are really asking two questions with a single question. First, we do an *argmax*, which is equivalent to asking, "Which action is the highest-valued action in state *s*?"

And then, we use that action to get its value, equivalent to asking, "What's the value of this action (which happens to be the highest-valued action) in state *s*?"

One of the problems is that we are asking both questions to the same Q-function, which shows bias in the same direction in both answers. In other words, the function approximator will answer, "I think this one is the highest-valued action in state *s*, and this is its value."

A solution

A way to reduce the chance of positive bias is to have two instances of the action-value function, the way we did in chapter 6.

If you had another source of the estimates, you could ask one of the questions to one and the other question to the other. It's somewhat like taking votes, or like an "I cut, you choose first" procedure, or like getting a second doctor's opinion on health matters.

In double learning, one estimator selects the index of what it believes to be the highest-valued action, and the other estimator gives the value of this action.

REFRESH MY MEMORY
Double learning procedure

We did this procedure with tabular reinforcement learning in chapter 6 under the double Q-learning agent. It goes like this:

- You create two action-value functions, Q_A and Q_B.

- You flip a coin to decide which action-value function to update. For example, Q_A on heads, Q_B on tails.

- If you got a heads and thus get to update Q_A: You select the action *index* to evaluate from Q_B, and *evaluate* it using the estimate Q_A predicts. Then, you proceed to update Q_A as usual, and leave Q_B alone.

- If you got a tails and thus get to update Q_B, you do it the other way around: get the index from Q_A, and get the value estimate from Q_B. Q_B gets updated, and Q_A is left alone.

However, implementing this double-learning procedure exactly as described when using function approximation (for DQN) creates unnecessary overhead. If we did so, we'd end up with four networks: two networks for training (Q_A, Q_B) and two target networks, one for each online network.

Additionally, it creates a slowdown in the training process, since we'd be training only one of these networks at a time. Therefore, only one network would improve per step. This is certainly a waste.

Doing this double-learning procedure with function approximators may still be better than not doing it at all, despite the extra overhead. Fortunately for us, there's a simple modification to the original double-learning procedure that adapts it to DQN and gives us substantial improvements without the extra overhead.

A more practical solution

Instead of adding this overhead that's a detriment to training speed, we can perform double learning with the other network we already have, which is the target network. However, instead of training both the online and target networks, we continue training only the online network, but use the target network to help us, in a sense, cross-validate the estimates.

We want to be cautious as to which network to use for action selection and which network to use for action evaluation. Initially, we added the target network to stabilize training by avoiding chasing a moving target. To continue on this path, we want to make sure we use the network we're training, the online network, for answering the first question. In other words, we use the online network to find the index of the best action. Then, we use the target network to ask the second question, that is, to evaluate the previously selected action.

This is the ordering that works best in practice, and it makes sense why it works. By using the target network for value estimates, we make sure the target values are frozen as needed for stability. If we were to implement it the other way around, the values would come from the online network, which is getting updated at every time step, and therefore changing continuously.

Selecting action, evaluating action

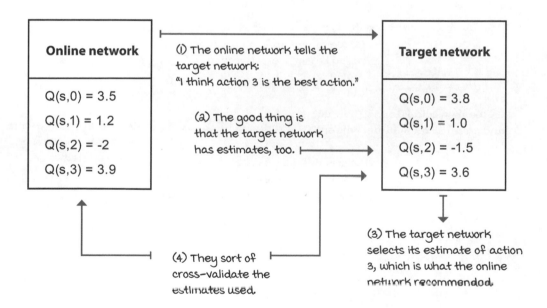

Online network

Q(s,0) = 3.5

Q(s,1) = 1.2

Q(s,2) = -2

Q(s,3) = 3.9

① The online network tells the target network:
"I think action 3 is the best action."

② The good thing is that the target network has estimates, too.

Target network

Q(s,0) = 3.8

Q(s,1) = 1.0

Q(s,2) = -1.5

Q(s,3) = 3.6

③ The target network selects its estimate of action 3, which is what the online network recommended.

④ They sort of cross-validate the estimates used.

0001 A BIT OF HISTORY

Introduction of the double DQN algorithm

Double DQN was introduced in 2015 by Hado van Hasselt, shortly after the release of the 2015 version of DQN. (The 2015 version of DQN is sometimes referred to as Nature DQN—because it was published in the Nature scientific journal, and sometimes as Vanilla DQN—because it is the first of many other improvements over the years.)

In 2010, Hado also authored the double Q-learning algorithm (double learning for the tabular case), as an improvement to the Q-learning algorithm. This is the algorithm you learned about and implemented in chapter 6.

Double DQN, also referred to as DDQN, was the first of many improvements proposed over the years for DQN. Back in 2015 when it was first introduced, DDQN obtained state-of-the-art (best at the moment) results in the Atari domain.

Hado obtained his PhD from the University of Utrecht in the Netherlands in artificial intelligence (reinforcement learning). After a couple of years as a postdoctoral researcher, he got a job at Google DeepMind as a research scientist.

SHOW ME THE MATH

DDQN gradient update

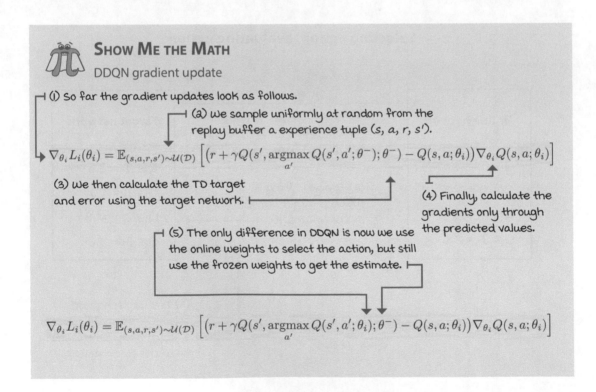

(1) So far the gradient updates look as follows.

(2) We sample uniformly at random from the replay buffer a experience tuple (s, a, r, s').

$$\nabla_{\theta_i} L_i(\theta_i) = \mathbb{E}_{(s,a,r,s') \sim \mathcal{U}(\mathcal{D})} \left[\left(r + \gamma Q(s', \underset{a'}{\operatorname{argmax}} Q(s', a'; \theta^-); \theta^-) - Q(s, a; \theta_i) \right) \nabla_{\theta_i} Q(s, a; \theta_i) \right]$$

(3) We then calculate the TD target and error using the target network.

(4) Finally, calculate the gradients only through the predicted values.

(5) The only difference in DDQN is now we use the online weights to select the action, but still use the frozen weights to get the estimate.

$$\nabla_{\theta_i} L_i(\theta_i) = \mathbb{E}_{(s,a,r,s') \sim \mathcal{U}(\mathcal{D})} \left[\left(r + \gamma Q(s', \underset{a'}{\operatorname{argmax}} Q(s', a'; \theta_i); \theta^-) - Q(s, a; \theta_i) \right) \nabla_{\theta_i} Q(s, a; \theta_i) \right]$$

I SPEAK PYTHON
Double DQN

```python
def optimize_model(self, experiences):
    states, actions, rewards, \
        next_states, is_terminals = experiences
    batch_size = len(is_terminals)
```

① In Double DQN, we use the online network to get the index of the highest-valued action of the next state, the argmax. Note we don't detach the argmax because they're not differentiable. The max(1)[1] returned the index of the max, which is already "detached."

```python
    #argmax_a_q_sp = self.target_model(next_states).max(1)[1]
    argmax_a_q_sp = self.online_model(next_states).max(1)[1]
```

② Then, extract the Q-values of the next state according to the target network.

```python
    q_sp = self.target_model(next_states).detach()
```

③ We then index the Q-values provided by the target network with the action indices provided by the online network.

```python
    max_a_q_sp = q_sp[np.arange(batch_size), argmax_a_q_sp]
```

④ Then set up the targets as usual.

```python
    max_a_q_sp = max_a_q_sp.unsqueeze(1)
    max_a_q_sp *= (1 - is_terminals)
    target_q_sa = rewards + (self.gamma * max_a_q_sp)
```

⑤ Get the current estimates. Note this is where the gradients are flowing through.

```python
    q_sa = self.online_model(states).gather(1, actions)
    td_error = q_sa - target_q_sa
    value_loss = td_error.pow(2).mul(0.5).mean()
    self.value_optimizer.zero_grad()
    value_loss.backward()
    self.value_optimizer.step()
```

⑥ Calculate the loss, and step the optimizer.

```python
def interaction_step(self, state, env):
    action = self.training_strategy.select_action(
                         self.online_model, state)
```

⑦ Here we keep using the online network for action selection.

```python
    new_state, reward, is_terminal, _ = env.step(action)
    return new_state, is_terminal
```

```python
def update_network(self):
    for target, online in zip(
                    self.target_model.parameters(),
                    self.online_model.parameters()):
        target.data.copy_(online.data)
```

⑧ Updating the target network is still the same as before.

A more forgiving loss function

In the previous chapter, we selected the L2 loss, also known as *mean square error* (MSE), as our loss function, mostly for its widespread use and simplicity. And, in reality, in a problem such as the cart-pole environment, there might not be a good reason to look any further. However, because I'm teaching you the ins and outs of the algorithms and not only "how to hammer the nail," I'd also like to make you aware of the different knobs available so you can play around when tackling more challenging problems.

MSE is a ubiquitous loss function because it's simple, it makes sense, and it works well. But, one of the issues with using MSE for reinforcement learning is that it penalizes large errors more than small errors. This makes sense when doing supervised learning because our targets are the true value from the get-go, and are fixed throughout the training process. That means we're confident that, if the model is very wrong, then it should be penalized more heavily than if it's just wrong.

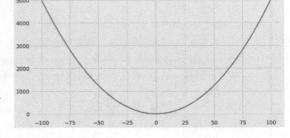

But as stated now several times, in reinforcement learning, we don't have these true values, and the values we use to train our network are dependent on the agent itself. That's a mind shift. Besides, targets are constantly changing; even when using target networks, they still change often. In reinforcement learning, being very wrong is something we expect and welcome. At the end of the day, if you think about it, we aren't "training" agents; our agents learn on their own. Think about that for a second.

A loss function not as unforgiving, and also more robust to outliers, is the *mean absolute error*, also known as MAE or L1 loss. MAE is defined as the average absolute difference between the predicted and true values, that is, the predicted action-value function and the TD target. Given that MAE is a linear function as opposed to quadratic such as MSE, we can expect MAE to be more successful at treating large errors the same way as small errors. This can come in handy in our case because we expect our action-value function to give wrong values at some point during training, particularly at the beginning. Being more resilient to outliers often implies errors have less effect, as compared to MSE, in terms of changes to our network, which means more stable learning.

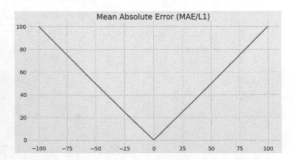

Now, on the flip side, one of the helpful things of MSE that MAE doesn't have is the fact that its gradients decrease as the loss goes to zero. This feature is helpful for optimization methods because it makes it easier to reach the optima: lower gradients mean small changes to the network. But luckily for us, there's a loss function that's somewhat a mix of MSE and MAE, called the Huber loss.

The *Huber loss* has the same useful property as MSE of quadratically penalizing the errors near zero, but it isn't quadratic all the way out for huge errors. Instead, the Huber loss is quadratic (curved) near-zero error, and it becomes linear (straight) for errors larger than a preset threshold. Having the best of both worlds makes the Huber loss robust to outliers, just like MAE, and differentiable at 0, just like MSE.

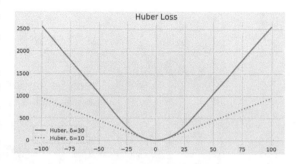

The Huber loss uses a hyperparameter, δ, to set this threshold in which the loss goes from quadratic to linear, basically, from MSE to MAE. If δ is zero, you're left precisely with MAE, and if δ is infinite, then you're left precisely with MSE. A typical value for δ is 1, but be aware that your loss function, optimization, and learning rate interact in complex ways. If you change one, you may need to tune several of the others. Check out the Notebook for this chapter so you can play around.

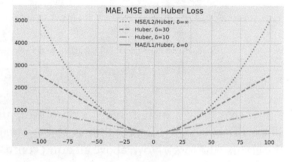

Interestingly, there are at least two different ways of implementing the Huber loss function. You could either compute the Huber loss as defined, or compute the MSE loss instead, and then set all gradients larger than a threshold to a fixed magnitude value. You clip the magnitude of the gradients. The former depends on the deep learning framework you use, but the problem is that some frameworks don't give you access to the δ hyperparameter, so you're stuck with δ set to 1, which doesn't always work, and isn't always the best. The latter, often referred to as *loss clipping,* or better yet *gradient clipping,* is more flexible and, therefore, what I implement in the Notebook.

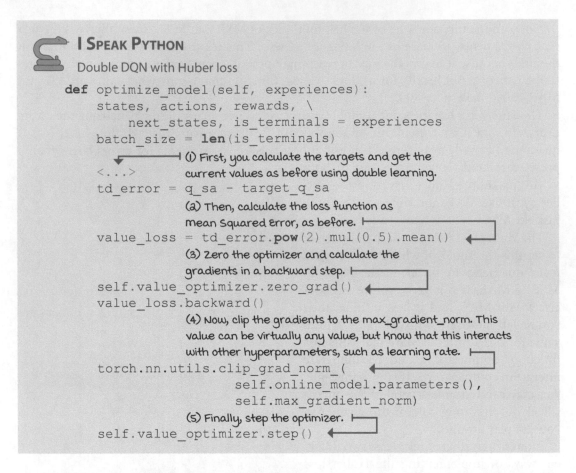

I Speak Python

Double DQN with Huber loss

```python
def optimize_model(self, experiences):
    states, actions, rewards, \
        next_states, is_terminals = experiences
    batch_size = len(is_terminals)
```

① First, you calculate the targets and get the
current values as before using double learning.

```python
    <...>
    td_error = q_sa - target_q_sa
```

② Then, calculate the loss function as
mean squared error, as before.

```python
    value_loss = td_error.pow(2).mul(0.5).mean()
```

③ Zero the optimizer and calculate the
gradients in a backward step.

```python
    self.value_optimizer.zero_grad()
    value_loss.backward()
```

④ Now, clip the gradients to the max_gradient_norm. This
value can be virtually any value, but know that this interacts
with other hyperparameters, such as learning rate.

```python
    torch.nn.utils.clip_grad_norm_(
                    self.online_model.parameters(),
                    self.max_gradient_norm)
```

⑤ Finally, step the optimizer.

```python
    self.value_optimizer.step()
```

Know that there's such a thing as *reward clipping*, which is different than *gradient clipping*. These are two very different things, so beware. One works on the rewards and the other on the errors (the loss). Now, above all don't confuse either of these with *Q-value clipping*, which is undoubtedly a mistake.

Remember, the goal in our case is to prevent gradients from becoming too large. For this, we either make the loss linear outside a given absolute TD error threshold or make the gradient constant outside a max gradient magnitude threshold.

In the cart-pole environment experiments that you find in the Notebook, I implement the Huber loss function by using the gradient clipping technique. That is, I calculate MSE and then clip the gradients. However, as I mentioned before, I set the hyperparameter setting for the maximum gradient values to infinity. Therefore, it's effectively using good-old MSE. But, please, experiment, play around, explore! The Notebooks I created should help you learn almost as much as the book. Set yourself free over there.

ॐ **IT'S IN THE DETAILS**

The full double deep Q-network (DDQN) algorithm

DDQN is almost identical to DQN, but there are still several differences:

- Approximate the action-value function $Q(s,a;\theta)$.
- Use a state-in-values-out architecture (nodes: 4, 512, 128, 2).
- Optimize the action-value function to approximate the optimal action-value function $q*(s,a)$.
- Use off-policy TD targets ($r + gamma*max\_a'Q(s',a';\theta)$) to evaluate policies.

Notice that we now

- Use an adjustable Huber loss, which, since we set the max_gradient_norm variable to "float('inf')," we're effectively using mean squared error (MSE) for our loss function.
- Use RMSprop as our optimizer with a learning rate of 0.0007. Note that before we used 0.0005 because without double learning (vanilla DQN), several seeds fail if we train with a learning rate of 0.0007. Perhaps stability? In DDQN, on the other hand, training with a higher learning rate works best.

In DDQN we're still using

- An exponentially decaying epsilon-greedy strategy (from 1.0 to 0.3 in roughly 20,000 steps) to improve policies.
- A replay buffer with 320 samples min, 50,000 max, and a batch of 64.
- A target network that freezes for 15 steps and then updates fully.

DDQN, similar to DQN, has the same three main steps:

1. Collect experience: $(S_t, A_t, R_{t+1}, S_{t+1}, D_{t+1})$, and insert it into the replay buffer.
2. Randomly sample a mini-batch from the buffer and calculate the off-policy TD targets for the whole batch: $r + gamma*max\_a'Q(s',a';\theta)$.
3. Fit the action-value function $Q(s,a;\theta)$ using MSE and RMSprop.

The bottom line is that the DDQN implementation and hyperparameters are *identical* to those of DQN, except that we now use double learning and therefore train with a slightly higher learning rate. The addition of the Huber loss doesn't change anything because we're "clipping" gradients to a max value of infinite, which is equivalent to using MSE. However, for many other environments you'll find it useful, so tune this hyperparameter.

TALLY IT UP
DDQN is more stable than NFQ or DQN

DQN and DDQN have similar performance in the cart-pole environment. However, this is a simple environment with a smooth reward function. In reality, DDQN should always give better performance.

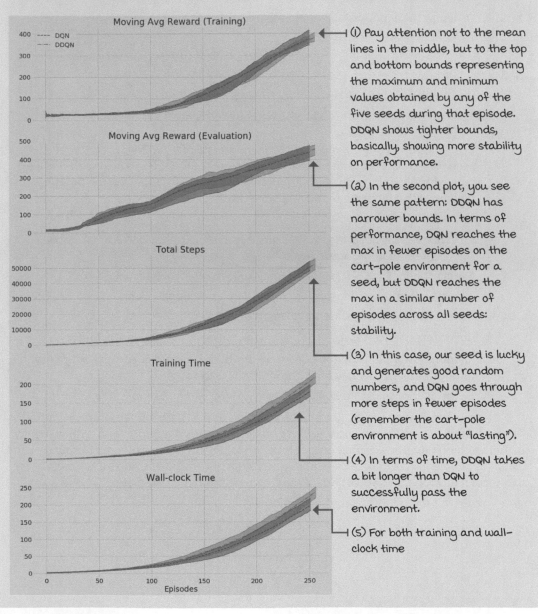

(1) Pay attention not to the mean lines in the middle, but to the top and bottom bounds representing the maximum and minimum values obtained by any of the five seeds during that episode. DDQN shows tighter bounds, basically, showing more stability on performance.

(2) In the second plot, you see the same pattern: DDQN has narrower bounds. In terms of performance, DQN reaches the max in fewer episodes on the cart-pole environment for a seed, but DDQN reaches the max in a similar number of episodes across all seeds: stability.

(3) In this case, our seed is lucky and generates good random numbers, and DQN goes through more steps in fewer episodes (remember the cart-pole environment is about "lasting").

(4) In terms of time, DDQN takes a bit longer than DQN to successfully pass the environment.

(5) For both training and wall-clock time

Things we can still improve on

Surely our current value-based deep reinforcement learning method isn't perfect, but it's pretty solid. DDQN can reach superhuman performance in many of the Atari games. To replicate those results, you'd have to change the network to take images as input (a stack of four images to be able to infer things such as direction and velocity from the images), and, of course, tune the hyperparameters.

Yet, we can still go a little further. There are at least a couple of other improvements to consider that are easy to implement and impact performance in a positive way.

The first improvement requires us to reconsider the current network architecture. As of right now, we have a naive representation of the Q-function on our neural network architecture.

 REFRESH MY MEMORY

Current neural network architecture

We're literately "making reinforcement learning look like supervised learning." But, we can, and should, break free from this constraint, and think out of the box.

State-in-values-out architecture

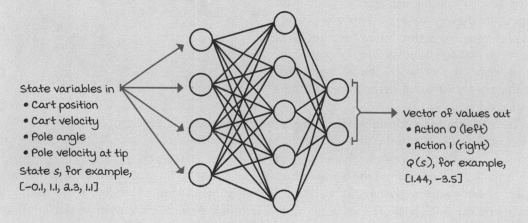

Is there any better way of representing the Q-function? Think about this for a second while you look at the images on the next page.

The images on the right are bar plots representing the estimated action-value function Q, state-value function V, and action-advantage function A for the cart-pole environment with a state in which the pole is near vertical.

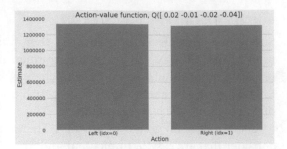

Notice the different functions and values and start thinking about how to better architect the neural network so that data is used more efficiently. As a hint, let me remind you that the Q-values of a state are related through the V-function. That is, the action-value function Q has an essential relationship with the state-value function V, because of both actions in $Q(s)$ are indexed by the same state s (in the example to the right s=[0.02, −0.01, −0.02, −0.04]).

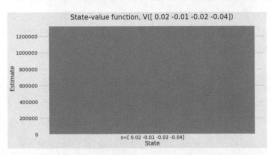

The question is, could you learn anything about $Q(s, 0)$ if you're using a $Q(s, 1)$ sample? Look at the plot showing the action-advantage function $A(s)$ and notice how much easier it is for you to eyeball the greedy action with respect to these estimates than when using the plot with the action-value function $Q(s)$. What can you do about this? In the next chapter, we look at a network architecture called the *dueling network* that helps us exploit these relationships.

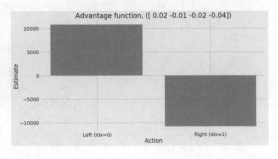

The other thing to consider improving is the way we sample experiences from the replay buffer. As of now, we pull samples from the buffer uniformly at random, and I'm sure your intuition questions this approach and suggests we can do better, and we can.

Humans don't go around the world remembering random things to learn from at random times. There's a more systematic way in which intelligent agents "replay memories." I'm pretty sure my dog chases rabbits in her sleep. Certain experiences are more important than others to our goals. Humans often replay experiences that caused them unexpected joy or pain. And it makes sense, and you need to learn from these experiences to generate more or less of them. In the next chapter, we look at ways of prioritizing the sampling of experiences to get the most out of each sample, when we learn about the prioritized experience replay (PER) method.

Summary

In this chapter, you learned about the widespread issues with value-based deep reinforcement learning methods. The fact that online data isn't stationary, and it also isn't independent and identically distributed as most optimization methods expect, creates an enormous amount of problems value-based methods are susceptible to.

You learned to stabilize value-based deep reinforcement learning methods by using a variety of techniques that have empirical results in several benchmarks, and you dug deep on these components that make value-based methods more stable. Namely, you learned about the advantages of using target networks and replay buffers in an algorithm known as DQN (nature DQN, or vanilla DQN). You learned that by using target networks, we make the targets appear stationary to the optimizer, which is good for stability, albeit by sacrificing convergence speed. You also learned that by using replay buffers, the online data looks more IID, which, you also learned, is a source of significant issues in value-based bootstrapping methods. These two techniques combined make the algorithm sufficiently stable for performing well in several deep reinforcement learning tasks.

However, there are many more potential improvements to value-based methods. You implemented a straightforward change that has a significant impact on performance, in general. You added a double-learning strategy to the baseline DQN agent that, when using function approximation, is known as the DDQN agent, and it mitigates the issues of overestimation in off-policy value-based methods.

In addition to these new algorithms, you learned about different exploration strategies to use with value-based methods. You learned about linearly and exponentially decaying epsilon-greedy and softmax exploration strategies, this time, in the context of function approximation. Also, you learned about different loss functions and which ones make more sense for reinforcement learning and why. You learned that the Huber loss function allows you to tune between MSE and MAE with a single hyperparameter, and it's one of the preferred loss functions used in value-based deep reinforcement learning methods.

By now, you

- Understand why using online data for training neural network with optimizers that expect stationary and IID data is a problem in value-based DRL methods

- Can solve reinforcement learning problems with continuous state-spaces with algorithms that are more stable and therefore give more consistent results

- Have an understanding of state-of-the-art, value-based, deep reinforcement learning methods and can solve complex problems

TWEETABLE FEAT

Work on your own and share your findings

Here are several ideas on how to take what you have learned to the next level. If you'd like, share your results with the rest of the world and make sure to check out what others have done, too. It's a win-win situation, and hopefully, you'll take advantage of it.

- **#gdrl_ch09_tf01:** In this and the next chapter, we test the algorithms only in the cart-pole environment. Find a couple other environments and test the agents in those, for instance, the lunar lander environment here: https://gym.openai.com/envs/#box2d, and the mountain car environment here: https://gym.openai.com/envs/#classic_control. Did you have to make any changes to the agents, excluding hyperparameters, to make the agents work in these environments? Make sure to find a single set of hyperparameters that solve all environments. To clarify, I mean you use a single set of hyperparameters, and train an agent from scratch in each environment, not a single trained agent that does well in all environments.

- **#gdrl_ch09_tf02:** In this and the next chapter, we test the algorithms in environments that are continuous, but low dimensional. You know what a high-dimensional environment is? Atari environments. Look them up here (the non "ram"): https://gym.openai.com/envs/#atari. Now, modify the networks, replay buffer, and agent code in this chapter so that the agent can solve image-based environments. Beware that this isn't a trivial task, and training will take a while, from many hours to several days.

- **#gdrl_ch09_tf03:** I mentioned that value-based methods are sensitive to hyperparameters. In reality, there's something called the "deadly triad," that basically tells us using neural networks with bootstrapping and off-policy is bad. Investigate!

- **#gdrl_ch09_tf04:** In every chapter, I'm using the final hashtag as a catchall hashtag. Feel free to use this one to discuss anything else that you worked on relevant to this chapter. There's no more exciting homework than that which you create for yourself. Make sure to share what you set yourself to investigate and your results.

Write a tweet with your findings, tag me @mimoralea (I'll retweet), and use the particular hashtag from the list to help interested folks find your results. There are no right or wrong results; you share your findings and check others' findings. Take advantage of this to socialize, contribute, and get yourself out there! We're waiting for you!

Here's a tweet example:

"Hey, @mimoralea. I created a blog post with a list of resources to study deep reinforcement learning. Check it out at <link>. #gdrl_ch01_tf01"

I'll make sure to retweet and help others find your work.

Sample-efficient value-based methods | 10

In this chapter

- You will implement a deep neural network architecture that exploits some of the nuances that exist in value-based deep reinforcement learning methods.

- You will create a replay buffer that prioritizes experiences by how surprising they are.

- You will build an agent that trains to a near-optimal policy in fewer episodes than all the value-based deep reinforcement learning agents we've discussed.

> 66 *Intelligence is based on how efficient a species became at doing the things they need to survive.* 99
>
> — CHARLES DARWIN
> ENGLISH NATURALIST, GEOLOGIST, AND BIOLOGIST
> BEST KNOWN FOR HIS CONTRIBUTIONS TO THE SCIENCE OF EVOLUTION

In the previous chapter, we improved on NFQ with the implementation of DQN and DDQN. In this chapter, we continue on this line of improvements to previous algorithms by presenting two additional techniques for improving value-based deep reinforcement learning methods. This time, though, the improvements aren't so much about stability, although that could easily be a by-product. But more accurately, the techniques presented in this chapter improve the sample-efficiency of DQN and other value-based DRL methods.

First, we introduce a functional neural network architecture that splits the Q-function representation into two streams. One stream approximates the V-function, and the other stream approximates the A-function. V-functions are per-state values, while A-functions express the distance of each action from their V-functions.

This is a handy fact for designing RL-specialized architectures that are capable of squeezing information from samples coming from all action in a given state into the V-function for that same state. What that means is that a single experience tuple can help improve the value estimates of all the actions in that state. This improves the sample efficiency of the agent.

The second improvement we introduce in this chapter is related to the replay buffer. As you remember from the previous chapter, the standard replay buffer in DQN samples experiences uniformly at random. It's crucial to understand that sampling uniformly at random is a good thing for keeping gradients proportional to the true data-generating underlying distribution, and therefore keeping the updates unbiased. The issue is, however, that if we could devise a way for prioritizing experiences, we could use the samples that are the most promising for learning. Therefore, in this chapter, we introduce a different technique for sampling experiences that allows us to draw samples that appear to provide the most information to the agent for actually making improvements.

Dueling DDQN: A reinforcement-learning-aware neural network architecture

Let's now dig into the details of this specialized neural network architecture called the *dueling network architecture*. The dueling network is an improvement that applies only to the network architecture and not the algorithm. That is, we won't make any changes to the algorithm, but the only modifications go into the network architecture. This property allows dueling networks to be combined with virtually any of the improvements proposed over the years to the original DQN algorithm. For instance, we could have a dueling DQN agent, and a dueling double DQN agent (or the way I'm referring to it—dueling DDQN), and more. Many of these improvements are just plug-and-play, which we take advantage of in this chapter. Let's now implement a dueling architecture to be used in our experiments and learn about it while building it.

Reinforcement learning isn't a supervised learning problem

In the previous chapter, we concentrated our efforts on making reinforcement learning look more like a supervised learning problem. By using a replay buffer, we made online data, which is experienced and collected sequentially by the agent, look more like an independent and identically distributed dataset, such as those commonly found in supervised learning.

We also made targets look more static, which is also a common trait of supervised learning problems. This surely helps stabilize training, but ignoring the fact that reinforcement learning problems are problems of their own isn't the smartest approach to solving these problems.

One of the subtleties value-based deep reinforcement learning agents have, and that we will exploit in this chapter, is in the way the value functions relate to one another. More specifically, we can use the fact that the state-value function $V(s)$ and the action-value function $Q(s, a)$ are related to each other through the action-advantage function $A(s, a)$.

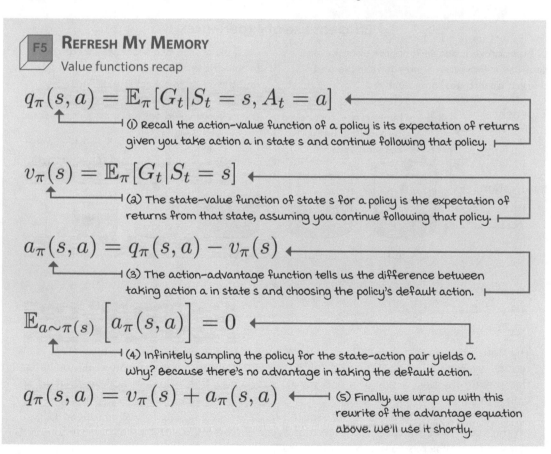

REFRESH MY MEMORY

Value functions recap

$$q_\pi(s, a) = \mathbb{E}_\pi[G_t | S_t = s, A_t = a]$$

(1) Recall the action-value function of a policy is its expectation of returns given you take action a in state s and continue following that policy.

$$v_\pi(s) = \mathbb{E}_\pi[G_t | S_t = s]$$

(2) The state-value function of state s for a policy is the expectation of returns from that state, assuming you continue following that policy.

$$a_\pi(s, a) = q_\pi(s, a) - v_\pi(s)$$

(3) The action-advantage function tells us the difference between taking action a in state s and choosing the policy's default action.

$$\mathbb{E}_{a \sim \pi(s)}\left[a_\pi(s, a)\right] = 0$$

(4) Infinitely sampling the policy for the state-action pair yields 0. Why? Because there's no advantage in taking the default action.

$$q_\pi(s, a) = v_\pi(s) + a_\pi(s, a)$$

(5) Finally, we wrap up with this rewrite of the advantage equation above. We'll use it shortly.

Nuances of value-based deep reinforcement learning methods

The action-value function *Q(s, a)* can be defined as the sum of the state-value function *V(s)* and the action-advantage function *A(s, a)*. This means that we can decompose a Q-function into two components: one that's shared across all actions, and another that's unique to each action; or, to say it another way, a component that is dependent on the action and another that isn't.

Currently, we're learning the action-value function *Q(s, a)* for each action separately, but that's inefficient. Of course, there's a bit of generalization happening because networks are internally connected. Therefore, information is shared between the nodes of a network. But, when learning about $Q(s, a_1)$, we're ignoring the fact that we could use the same information to learn something about $Q(s, a_2)$, $Q(s, a_3)$, and all other actions available in state s. The fact is that *V(s)* is common to all actions $a_1, a_2, a_3, ..., a_N$.

Efficient use of experiences

(1) By approximating Q–functions directly, we squeeze information from each sample and dump it all into the same bucket.

(2) If we create two separate streams: one to collect the common information ($V(s)$), and the other to collect the differences between the actions ($A(s,a1)$ and $A(s,a2)$), the network could get more accurate faster.

Experience tuple ⊢

(Technically, these buckets are connected through the network, but stay with me . . .)

Information ⊢

Information in the $V(s)$ bucket gets used by all $A(s,a)$.

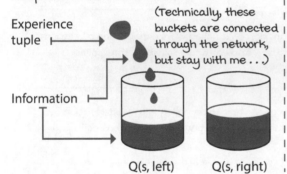

Q(s, left)   Q(s, right)   V(s)   A(s, left)   A(s, right)

 ### BOIL IT DOWN

The action-value function *Q(s, a)* depends on the state-value function *V(s)*

The bottom line is that the values of actions depend on the values of states, and it would be nice to leverage this fact. In the end, taking the worst action in a good state could be better than taking the best action in a bad state. You see how "the values of actions depend on values of states"?

The dueling network architecture uses this dependency of the action-value function *Q(s, a)* on the state-value function *V(s)* such that every update improves the state-value function *V(s)* estimate, which is common to all actions.

Advantage of using advantages

Now, let me give you an example. In the cart-pole environment, when the pole is in the upright position, the values of the left and right actions are virtually the same. It doesn't matter what you do when the pole is precisely upright (for the sake of argument, assume the cart is precisely in the middle of the track and that all velocities are 0). Going either left or right should have the same value in this perfect state.

However, it does matter what action you take when the pole is tilted 10 degrees to the right, for instance. In this state, pushing the cart to the right to counter the tilt, is the best action the agent can take. Conversely, going left, and consequently, pronouncing the tilt is probably a bad idea.

Notice that this is what the action-advantage function $A(s, a)$ represents: how much better than average is taking this particular action a in the current state s?

Relationship between value functions

State s=[0.02, -0.01, -0.02, -0.04]

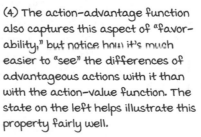

(1) The state on the left is a pretty good state because the pole is almost in the upright position and the cart somewhat in the middle of the track. On the other hand, the state on the right isn't as good because the pole is falling over to the right.

State s=[-0.16, -1.97, 0.24, 3.01]

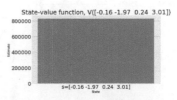

State-value function, V([0.02 -0.01 -0.02 -0.04])

(2) The state-value function captures this "goodness" of the situation. The state on the left is 10 times more valuable than the one on the right (at least according to a highly trained agent).

State-value function, V([-0.16 -1.97 0.24 3.01])

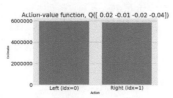
Action-value function, Q([0.02 -0.01 -0.02 -0.04])

(3) The action-value function doesn't capture this relationship directly, but instead it helps determine several favorable actions to take. On the left, it isn't clear what to do, while on the right, it's obvious you should move the cart right.

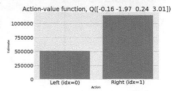
Action-value function, Q([-0.16 -1.97 0.24 3.01])

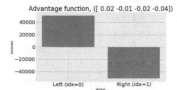
Advantage function, ([0.02 -0.01 -0.02 -0.04])

(4) The action-advantage function also captures this aspect of "favorability," but notice how it's much easier to "see" the differences of advantageous actions with it than with the action-value function. The state on the left helps illustrate this property fairly well.

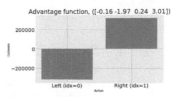
Advantage function, ([-0.16 -1.97 0.24 3.01])

A reinforcement-learning-aware architecture

The dueling network architecture consists of creating two separate estimators, one of the state-value function $V(s)$, and the other of the action-advantage function $A(s, a)$. Before splitting up the network, though, you want to make sure your network shares internal nodes. For instance, if you're using images as inputs, you want the convolutions to be shared so that feature-extraction layers are shared. In the cart-pole environment, we share the hidden layers.

After sharing most of the internal nodes and layers, the layer before the output layers splits into two streams: a stream for the state-value function $V(s)$, and another for the action-advantage function $A(s, a)$. The V-function output layer always ends in a single node because the value of a state is always a single number. The output layer for the Q-function, however, outputs a vector of the same size as the number of actions. In the cart-pole environment, the output layer of the action-advantage function stream has two nodes, one for the left action, and the other for the right action.

Dueling network architecture

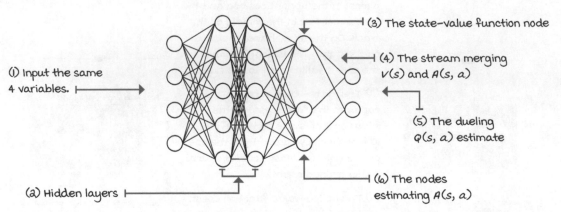

(1) Input the same 4 variables.

(2) Hidden layers

(3) The state-value function node

(4) The stream merging $V(s)$ and $A(s, a)$

(5) The dueling $Q(s, a)$ estimate

(6) The nodes estimating $A(s, a)$

0001 A BIT OF HISTORY

Introduction of the dueling network architecture

The Dueling neural network architecture was introduced in 2015 in a paper called "Dueling Network Architectures for Deep Reinforcement Learning" by Ziyu Wang when he was a PhD student at the University of Oxford. This was arguably the first paper to introduce a custom deep neural network architecture designed specifically for value-based deep reinforcement learning methods.

Ziyu is now a research scientist at Google DeepMind, where he continues to contribute to the field of deep reinforcement learning.

Building a dueling network

Building the dueling network is straightforward. I noticed that you could split the network anywhere after the input layer, and it would work just fine. I can imagine you could even have two separate networks, but I don't see the benefits of doing that. In general, my recommendation is to share as many layers as possible and split only in two heads, a layer before the output layer.

I SPEAK PYTHON
Building the dueling network

(1) The dueling network is similar to the regular network. We need variables for the number of nodes in the input and output layers, the shape of the hidden layers, and the activation function, the way we did before.

```python
class FCDuelingQ(nn.Module):
    def __init__(self,
                 input_dim,
                 output_dim,
                 hidden_dims=(32,32),
                 activation_fc=F.relu):
        super(FCDuelingQ, self).__init__()
        self.activation_fc = activation_fc
```

(2) Next, we create the input layer and "connect" it to the first hidden layer. Here the input_dim variable is the number of input nodes, and hidden_dims[0] is the number of nodes of the first hidden layer. nn.Linear creates a layer with inputs and outputs.

```python
        self.input_layer = nn.Linear(input_dim,
                                     hidden_dims[0])
```

(3) Here we create the hidden layers by creating layers as defined in the hidden_dims variable. For example, a value of (64, 32, 16) will create a layer with 64 input nodes and 32 output nodes, and then a layer with 32 input nodes and 16 output nodes.

```python
        self.hidden_layers = nn.ModuleList()
        for i in range(len(hidden_dims)-1):
            hidden_layer = nn.Linear(
                hidden_dims[i], hidden_dims[i+1])
            self.hidden_layers.append(hidden_layer)
```

(4) Finally, we build the two output layers, both "connected" to the last hidden layer. The value_output has a single node output, and the advantage_output has output_dim nodes. In the cart-pole environment, that number is two.

```python
        self.value_output = nn.Linear(hidden_dims[-1], 1)
        self.advantage_output = nn.Linear(
            hidden_dims[-1], output_dim)
```

Reconstructing the action-value function

First, let me clarify that the motivation of the dueling architecture is to create a new network that improves on the previous network, but without having to change the underlying control method. We need changes that aren't disruptive and that are compatible with previous methods. We want to swap the neural network and be done with it.

For this, we need to find a way to aggregate the two outputs from the network and reconstruct the action-value function *Q(s, a)*, so that any of the previous methods could use the dueling network model. This way, we create the dueling DDQN agent when using the dueling architecture with the DDQN agent. A dueling network and the DQN agent would make the dueling DQN agent.

SHOW ME THE MATH
Dueling architecture aggregating equations

(1) The Q-function is parameterized by theta, alpha, and beta. Theta represents the weights of the shared layers, alpha the weights of the action-advantage function stream, and beta the weights of the state-value function stream.

$$Q(s, a; \theta, \alpha, \beta) = V(s; \theta, \beta) + A(s, a; \theta, \alpha)$$

$$Q(s, a; \theta, \alpha, \beta) = V(s; \theta, \beta) + \left(A(s, a; \theta, \alpha) - \frac{1}{|\mathcal{A}|} \sum_{a'} A(s, a'; \theta, \alpha) \right)$$

(2) But because we cannot uniquely recover the Q from V and A, we use the above equation in practice. This removes one degree of freedom from the Q-function. The action-advantage and state-value functions lose their true meaning by doing this. But in practice, they're off-centered by a constant and are now more stable when optimizing.

But, how do we join the outputs? Some of you are thinking, add them up, right? I mean, that's the definition that I provided, after all. Though, several of you may have noticed that there is no way to recover *V(s)* and *A(s, a)* uniquely given only *Q(s, a)*. Think about it; if you add +10 to *V(s)* and remove it from *A(s, a)* you obtain the same *Q(s, a)* with two different values for *V(s)* and *A(s, a)*.

The way we address this issue in the dueling architecture is by subtracting the mean of the advantages from the aggregated action-value function *Q(s, a)* estimate. Doing this shifts *V(s)* and *A(s, a)* off by a constant, but also stabilizes the optimization process.

While estimates are off by a constant, they do not change the relative rank of *A(s, a)*, and therefore *Q(s, a)* also has the appropriate rank. All of this, while still using the same control algorithm. Big win.

I SPEAK PYTHON

The forward pass of a dueling network

```
class FCDuelingQ(nn.Module):
    <...>
    def forward(self, state):
```

(1) Notice that this is the same class as before. I removed the code for building of the network for brevity.

(2) In the forward pass, we start by making sure the input to the network, the 'state,' is of the expected type and shape. We do this because sometimes we input batches of states (training), sometimes single states (interacting). Sometimes these are NumPy vectors.

```
        x = state
        if not isinstance(x, torch.Tensor):
            x = torch.tensor(x,
                             device=self.device,
                             dtype=torch.float32)
            x = x.unsqueeze(0)
```

(3) At this point, we've prepped the input (again single or batch of states) variable *x* to what the network expects. we pass the variable *x* to the input layer, which, remember, takes in input_dim variables and outputs hidden_dim[0] variables; those will then pass through the activation function.

```
        x = self.activation_fc(self.input_layer(x))
```

(4) We use that output as the input for our first hidden layer. We pass the variable *x*, which you can think of as the current state of a pulse wave that goes from the input to the output of the network, sequentially to each hidden layer and the activation function.

```
        for hidden_layer in self.hidden_layers:
            x = self.activation_fc(hidden_layer(x))
```

(5) *x* now contains the values that came out of the last hidden layer and its respective activation. We use those as the input to the advantage_output and the value_output layers. Since *v* is a single value that will be added to *a*, we expand it.

```
        a = self.advantage_output(x)
        v = self.value_output(x)
        v = v.expand_as(a)
```

(6) Finally, we add *v* and *a* and subtract the mean of *a* from it. That's our *Q(s, ·)* estimate, containing the estimates of all actions for all states.

```
        q = v + a - a.mean(1, keepdim=True).expand_as(a)
        return q
```

Continuously updating the target network

Currently, our agent is using a target network that can be outdated for several steps before it gets a big weight update when syncing with the online network. In the cart-pole environment, that's merely ~15 steps apart, but in more complex environments, that number can rise to tens of thousands.

Full target network update

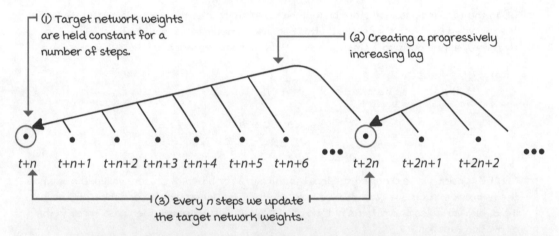

(1) Target network weights are held constant for a number of steps.

(2) Creating a progressively increasing lag

t+n   t+n+1   t+n+2 t+n+3 t+n+4   t+n+5   t+n+6   t+2n   t+2n+1   t+2n+2

(3) Every *n* steps we update the target network weights.

There are at least a couple of issues with this approach. On the one hand, we're freezing the weights for several steps and calculating estimates with progressively increasing stale data. As we reach the end of an update cycle, the likelihood of the estimates being of no benefit to the training progress of the network is higher. On the other hand, every so often, a huge update is made to the network. Making a big update likely changes the whole landscape of the loss function all at once. This update style seems to be both too conservative and too aggressive at the same time, if that's possible.

We got into this issue because we wanted our network not to move too quickly and therefore create instabilities, and we still want to preserve those desirable traits. But, can you think of other ways we can accomplish something similar but in a smooth manner? How about slowing down the target network, instead of freezing it?

We can do that. The technique is called *Polyak Averaging*, and it consists of mixing in online network weights into the target network on every step. Another way of seeing it is that, every step, we create a new target network composed of a large percentage of the target network weights and a small percentage of the online network weights. We add ~1% of new information every step to the network. Therefore, the network always lags, but by a much smaller gap. Additionally, we can now update the network on each step.

Show Me the Math

Polyak averaging

← (1) Instead of making the target network equal to the online network every *N* time steps, keep it frozen in the mean time.

(2) Why not mix the target network with a tiny bit of the online network more frequently, perhaps every time step?

$$\theta_i^- = \tau\theta_i + (1 - \tau)\theta_i^-$$

(3) Here tau is the mixing factor.

(4) Since we're doing this with a dueling network, all parameters, including the ones for the action-advantage and state-value stream, will be mixed in.

$$\alpha_i^- = \tau\alpha_i + (1 - \tau)\alpha_i^-$$
$$\beta_i^- = \tau\beta_i + (1 - \tau)\beta_i^-$$

I Speak Python

Mixing in target and online network weights

```python
class DuelingDDQN():
    <...>
    def update_network(self, tau=None):
```

(1) This is the same dueling DDQN class, but with most of the code removed for brevity.

(2) *tau* is a variable representing the ratio of the online network that will be mixed into the target network. A value of 1 is equivalent to a full update.

```python
        tau = self.tau if tau is None else tau
        for target, online in zip(
                self.target_model.parameters(),
                self.online_model.parameters()):
```

(3) zip takes iterables and returns an iterator of tuples.

(4) Now, we calculate the ratios we're taking from the target and online weights.

```python
            target_ratio = (1.0 - self.tau) * target.data
            online_ratio = self.tau * online.data
```

(5) Finally, we mix the weights and copy the new values into the target network.

```python
            mixed_weights = target_ratio + online_ratio
            target.data.copy_(mixed_weights)
```

What does the dueling network bring to the table?

Action-advantages are particularly useful when you have many similarly valued actions, as you've seen for yourself. Technically speaking, the dueling architecture improves policy evaluation, especially in the face of many actions with similar values. Using a dueling network, our agent can more quickly and accurately compare similarly valued actions, which is something useful in the cart-pole environment.

Function approximators, such as a neural network, have errors; that's expected. In a network with the architecture we were using before, these errors are potentially different for all of the state-actions pairs, as they're all separate. But, given the fact that the state-value function is the component of the action-value function that's common to all actions in a state, by using a dueling architecture, we reduce the function error and error variance. This is because now the error in the component with the most significant magnitude in similarly valued actions (the state-value function $V(s)$) is now the same for all actions.

If the dueling network is improving policy evaluation in our agent, then a fully trained dueling DDQN agent should have better performance than the DDQN when the left and right actions have almost the same value. I ran an experiment by collecting the states of 100 episodes for both, the DDQN and the dueling DDQN agents. My intuition tells me that if one agent is better than the other at evaluating similarly valued actions, then the better agent should have a smaller range along the track. This is because a better agent should learn the difference between going left and right, even when the pole is exactly upright. Warning! I didn't do ablation studies, but the results of my hand-wavy experiment suggest that the dueling DDQN agent is indeed able to evaluate in those states better.

State-space visited by fully trained cart-pole agents

(1) I'm not going to draw any conclusions here. But, notice the states visited by fully trained DDQN and dueling DDQN agents across five seeds.

Range of state-variable values for DDQN   Range of state-variable values for DuelingDDQN

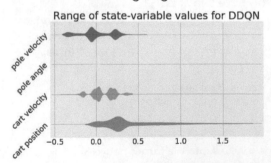 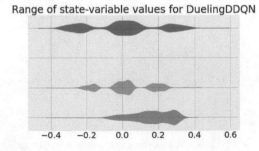

(a) See how the fully trained DDQN agents on the left visit cart positions that are far to the right, all the way to over 1.5 units, while the fully trained dueling DDQN agents trained with the same hyperparameters stay near the center. Could this suggest a better policy evaluation for dueling DDQN agents? Think about it, and experiment yourself.

It's in the Details

The dueling double deep Q-network (dueling DDQN) algorithm

Dueling DDQN is almost identical to DDQN, and DQN, with only a few tweaks. My intention is to keep the differences of the algorithms to a minimal while still showing you the many different improvements that can be made. I'm certain that changing only a few hyperparameters by a little bit has big effects in performance of many of these algorithms; therefore, I don't optimize the agents. That being said, now let me go through the things that are still the same as before:

- Network outputs the action-value function $Q(s,a; \theta)$.
- Optimize the action-value function to approximate the optimal action-value function $q^*(s,a)$.
- Use off-policy TD targets ($r + gamma^*max\_a'Q(s',a'; \theta)$) to evaluate policies.
- Use an adjustable Huber loss, but still with the max_gradient_norm variable set to float('inf'). Therefore, we're using MSE.
- Use RMSprop as our optimizer with a learning rate of 0.0007.
- An exponentially decaying epsilon-greedy strategy (from 1.0 to 0.3 in roughly 20,000 steps) to improve policies.
- A greedy action selection strategy for evaluation steps.
- A replay buffer with 320 samples min, 50,000 max, and a batch of 64.

We replaced

- The neural network architecture. We now use a state-in-values-out dueling network architecture (nodes: 4, 512,128, 1; 2, 2).
- The target network that used to freeze for 15 steps and update fully now uses Polyak averaging: every time step, we mix in 0.1 of the online network and 0.9 of the target network to form the new target network weights.

Dueling DDQN is the same exact algorithm as DDQN, but a different network:

1. Collect experience: ($S_t, A_t, R_{t+1}, S_{t+1}, D_{t+1}$), and insert into the replay buffer.
2. Pull a batch out of the buffer and calculate the off-policy TD targets: $R + gamma^*max\_a'Q(s',a'; \theta)$, using double learning.
3. Fit the action-value function $Q(s,a; \theta)$, using MSE and RMSprop.

One cool thing to notice is that all of these improvements are like Lego™ blocks for you to get creative. Maybe you want to try dueling DQN, without the double learning; maybe you want the Huber loss to clip gradients; or maybe you like the Polyak averaging to mix 50:50 every 5 time steps. It's up to you! Hopefully, the way I've organized the code will give you the freedom to try things out.

⦚⦚⦚⦚ TALLY IT UP
Dueling DDQN is more data efficient than all previous methods

Dueling DDQN and DDQN have similar performance in the cart-pole environment. Dueling DDQN is slightly more data efficient. The number of samples DDQN needs to pass the environment is higher than that of dueling DDQN. However, dueling DDQN takes slightly longer than DDQN.

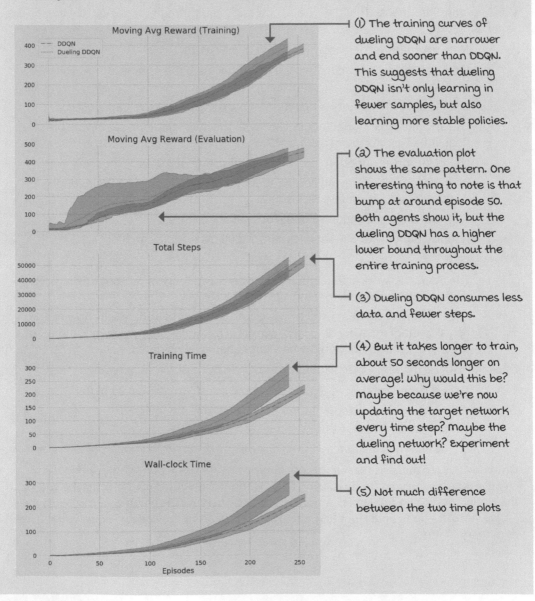

(1) The training curves of dueling DDQN are narrower and end sooner than DDQN. This suggests that dueling DDQN isn't only learning in fewer samples, but also learning more stable policies.

(2) The evaluation plot shows the same pattern. One interesting thing to note is that bump at around episode 50. Both agents show it, but the dueling DDQN has a higher lower bound throughout the entire training process.

(3) Dueling DDQN consumes less data and fewer steps.

(4) But it takes longer to train, about 50 seconds longer on average! Why would this be? Maybe because we're now updating the target network every time step? Maybe the dueling network? Experiment and find out!

(5) Not much difference between the two time plots

PER: Prioritizing the replay of meaningful experiences

In this section, we introduce a more intelligent experience replay technique. The goal is to allocate resources for experience tuples that have the most significant potential for learning. *prioritized experience replay* (PER) is a specialized replay buffer that does just that.

A smarter way to replay experiences

At the moment, our agent samples experience tuples from the replay buffer uniformly at random. Mathematically speaking, this feels right, and it is. But intuitively, this seems like an inferior way of replaying experiences. Replaying uniformly at random allocates resources to unimportant experiences. It doesn't feel right that our agent spends time and compute power "learning" things that have nothing to offer to the current state of the agent

But, let's be careful here: while it's evident that uniformly at random isn't good enough, it's also the case that human intuition might not work well in determining a better learning signal. When I first implemented a prioritized replay buffer, before reading the PER paper, my first thought was, "Well, I want the agent to get the highest cumulative discounted rewards possible; I should have it replay experiences with high reward only." Yeah, that didn't work. I then realized agents also need negative experiences, so I thought, "Aha! I should have the agent replay experiences with the highest reward magnitude! Besides, I love using that 'abs' function!" But that didn't work either. Can you think why these experiments didn't work? It makes sense that if I want the agent to learn to experience rewarding states, I should have it replay those the most so that it learns to get there. Right?

 MIGUEL'S ANALOGY

Human intuition and the relentless pursuit of happiness

I love my daughter. I love her so much. In fact, so much that I want her to experience only the good things in life. No, seriously, if you're a parent, you know what I mean.

I noticed she likes chocolate a lot, or as she would say, "a bunch," so, I started opening up to giving her candies every so often. And then more often than not. But, then she started getting mad at me when I didn't think she should get a candy.

Too much high-reward experiences, you think? You bet! Agents (maybe even humans) need to be reminded often of good and bad experiences alike, but they also need mundane experiences with low-magnitude rewards. In the end, none of these experiences give you the most learning, which is what we're after. Isn't that counterintuitive?

Then, what's a good measure of "important" experiences?

What we're looking for is to learn from experiences with unexpected value, surprising experiences, experiences we thought should be valued this much, and ended up valued that much. That makes more sense; these experiences bring reality to us. We have a view of the world, we anticipate outcomes, and when the difference between expectation and reality is significant, we know we need to learn something from that.

In reinforcement learning, this measure of surprise is given by the TD error! Well, technically, the *absolute* TD error. The TD error provides us with the difference between the agent's current estimate and target value. The current estimate indicates the value our agent thinks it's going to get for acting in a specific way. The target value suggests a new estimate for the same state-action pair, which can be seen as a reality check. The absolute difference between these values indicates how far off we are, how unexpected this experience is, and how much new information we received, which makes it a good indicator for learning opportunity.

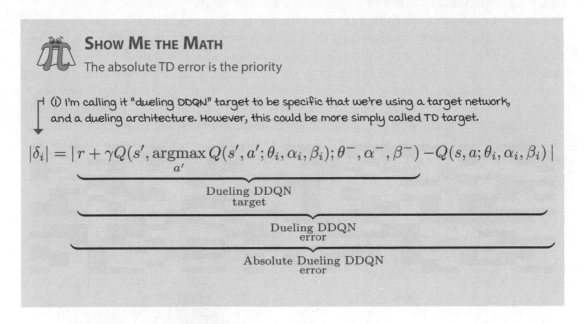

SHOW ME THE MATH

The absolute TD error is the priority

(i) I'm calling it "dueling DDQN" target to be specific that we're using a target network, and a dueling architecture. However, this could be more simply called TD target.

$$|\delta_i| = |\, \underbrace{\overbrace{r + \gamma Q(s', \underset{a'}{\mathrm{argmax}}\, Q(s', a'; \theta_i, \alpha_i, \beta_i); \theta^-, \alpha^-, \beta^-)}^{\text{Dueling DDQN target}} - Q(s, a; \theta_i, \alpha_i, \beta_i)}_{\text{Dueling DDQN error}}\, |$$

Absolute Dueling DDQN error

The TD error isn't the perfect indicator of the highest learning opportunity, but maybe the best reasonable proxy for it. In reality, the best criterion for learning the most is inside the network and hidden behind parameter updates. But, it seems impractical to calculate gradients for all experiences in the replay buffer every time step. The good things about the TD error are that the machinery to calculate it is in there already, and of course, the fact that the TD error is still a good signal for prioritizing the replay of experiences.

Greedy prioritization by TD error

Let's pretend we use TD errors for prioritizing experiences are follows:

- Take action *a* in state *s* and receive a new state *s'*, a reward *r*, and a done flag *d*.

- Query the network for the estimate of the current state $Q(s, a; \theta)$.

- Calculate a new target value for that experience as *target = r + gamma*max_a'Q (s',a'; θ)*.

- Calculate the absolute TD error as *atd_err = abs(Q(s, a; θ) – target)*.

- Insert experience into the replay buffer as a tuple *(s, a, r, s', d, atd_err)*.

- Pull out the top experiences from the buffer when sorted by *atd_err*.

- Train with these experiences, and repeat.

There are multiple issues with this approach, but let's try to get them one by one. First, we are calculating the TD errors twice: we calculate the TD error before inserting it into the buffer, but then again when we train with the network. In addition to this, we're ignoring the fact that TD errors change every time the network changes because they're calculated using the network. But, the solution can't be updating all of the TD errors every time step. It's simply not cost effective.

A workaround for both these problems is to update the TD errors only for experiences that are used to update the network (the replayed experiences) and insert new experiences with the highest magnitude TD error in the buffer to ensure they're all replayed at least once.

However, from this workaround, other issues arise. First, a TD error of zero in the first update means that experience will likely never be replayed again. Second, when using function approximators, errors shrink slowly, and this means that updates concentrate heavily in a small subset of the replay buffer. And finally, TD errors are noisy.

For these reasons, we need a strategy for sampling experiences based on the TD errors, but stochastically, not greedily. If we sample prioritized experiences stochastically, we can simultaneously ensure all experiences have a chance of being replayed, and that the probabilities of sampling experiences are monotonic in the absolute TD error.

 BOIL IT DOWN

TD errors, priorities, and probabilities

The most important takeaway from this page is that TD errors aren't enough; we'll use TD errors to calculate priorities, and from priorities we calculate probabilities.

Sampling prioritized experiences stochastically

Allow me to dig deeper into why we need stochastic prioritization. In highly stochastic environments, learning from experiences sampled greedily based on the TD error may lead us to where the noise takes us.

TD errors depend on the one-step reward and the action-value function of the next state, both of which can be highly stochastic. Highly stochastic environments can have higher variance TD errors. In such environments, we can get ourselves into trouble if we let our agents strictly follow the TD error. We don't want our agents to get fixated with surprising situations; that's not the point. An additional source of noise in the TD error is the neural network. Using highly non-linear function approximators also contributes to the noise in TD errors, especially early during training when errors are the highest. If we were to sample greedily solely based on TD errors, much of the training time would be spent on the experiences with potentially inaccurately large magnitude TD error.

Boil it Down
Sampling prioritized experiences stochastically

TD errors are noisy and shrink slowly. We don't want to stop replaying experiences that, due to noise, get a TD error value of zero. We don't want to get stuck with noisy experiences that, due to noise, get a significant TD error. And, we don't want to fixate on experiences with an initially high TD error.

0001 A Bit of History
Introduction of the prioritized experience replay buffer

The paper "Prioritized Experience Replay" was introduced simultaneously with the dueling architecture paper in 2015 by the Google DeepMind folks.

Tom Schaul, a Senior Research Scientist at Google DeepMind, is the main author of the PER paper. Tom obtained his PhD in 2011 from the Technical University of Munich. After two years as a postdoc at New York University, Tom joined DeepMind Technologies, which six months later would be acquired by Google and turned into what today is Google DeepMind.

Tom is a core developer of the PyBrain framework, a modular machine learning library for Python. PyBrain was probably one of the earlier frameworks to implement machine learning, reinforcement learning and black-box optimization algorithms. He's also a core developer of PyVGDL, a high-level video game description language built on top of pygame.

Proportional prioritization

Let's calculate priorities for each sample in the buffer based on TD errors. A first approach to do so is to sample experiences in proportion to their absolute TD error. We can use the absolute TD error of each experience and add a small constant, epsilon, to make sure zero TD error samples still have a chance of being replayed.

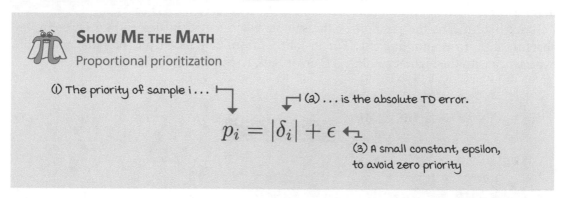

We scale this priority value by exponentiating it to alpha, a hyperparameter between zero and one. That allows us to interpolate between uniform and prioritized sampling. It allows us to perform the stochastic prioritization we discussed.

When alpha is zero, all values become one, therefore, an equal priority. When alpha is one, all values stay the same as the absolute TD error; therefore, the priority is proportional to the absolute TD error—a value in between blends the two sampling strategies.

These scaled priorities are converted to actual probabilities only by dividing their values by the sum of the values. Then, we can use these probabilities for drawing samples from the replay buffer.

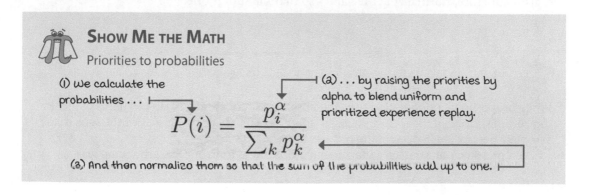

Rank-based prioritization

One issue with the proportional-prioritization approach is that it's sensitive to outliers. That means experiences with much higher TD error than the rest, whether by fact or noise, are sampled more often than those with low magnitudes, which may be an undesired side effect.

A slightly different experience prioritization approach to calculating priorities is to sample them using the rank of the samples when sorted by their absolute TD error.

Rank here means the position of the sample when sorted in descending order by the absolute TD error—nothing else. For instance, prioritizing based on the rank makes the experience with the highest absolute TD error rank 1, the second rank 2, and so on.

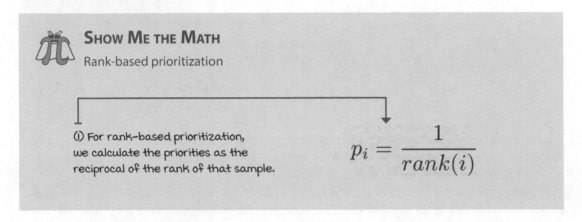

SHOW ME THE MATH
Rank-based prioritization

(i) For rank-based prioritization, we calculate the priorities as the reciprocal of the rank of that sample.

$$p_i = \frac{1}{rank(i)}$$

After we rank them by TD error, we calculate their priorities as the reciprocal of the rank. And again, for calculating priorities, we proceed by scaling the priorities with alpha, the same as with the proportional strategy. And then, we calculate actual probabilities from these priorities, also, as before, normalizing the values so that the sum is one.

BOIL IT DOWN
Rank-based prioritization

While proportional prioritization uses the absolute TD error and a small constant for including zero TD error experiences, rank-based prioritization uses the reciprocal of the rank of the sample when sorted in descending order by absolute TD error.

Both prioritization strategies then create probabilities from priorities the same way.

Prioritization bias

Using one distribution for estimating another one introduces bias in the estimates. Because we're sampling based on these probabilities, priorities, and TD errors, we need to account for that.

First, let me explain the problem in more depth. The distribution of the updates must be from the same distribution as its expectation. When we update the action-value function of state s and an action a, we must be cognizant that we always update with targets.

Targets are samples of expectations. That means the reward and state at the next step could be stochastic; there could be many possible different rewards and states when taking action a in a state s.

If we were to ignore this fact and update a single sample more often than it appears in that expectation, we'd create a bias toward this value. This issue is particularly impactful at the end of training when our methods are near convergence.

The way to mitigate this bias is to use a technique called *weighted importance sampling*. It consists of scaling the TD errors by weights calculated with the probabilities of each sample.

What weighted importance sampling does is change the magnitude of the updates so that it appears the samples came from a uniform distribution.

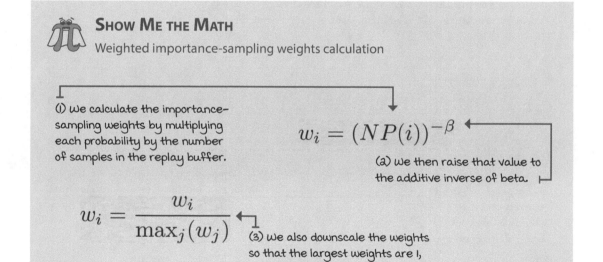

SHOW ME THE MATH

Weighted importance-sampling weights calculation

① We calculate the importance-sampling weights by multiplying each probability by the number of samples in the replay buffer.

$$w_i = (NP(i))^{-\beta}$$

② We then raise that value to the additive inverse of beta.

$$w_i = \frac{w_i}{\max_j(w_j)}$$

③ We also downscale the weights so that the largest weights are 1, and everything else is lower.

To do weighted importance-sampling effectively with a prioritized replay buffer, we add a convenient hyperparameter, beta, that allows us to tune the degree of the corrections. When beta is zero, there's no correction; when beta is one, there's a full correction of the bias.

Additionally, we want to normalize the weights by their max so that the max weight becomes one, and all other weights scale down the TD errors. This way, we keep TD errors from growing too much and keep training stable.

These importance-sampling weights are used in the loss function. Instead of using the TD errors straight in the gradient updates, in PER, we multiply them by the importance-sampling weights and scale all TD errors down to compensate for the mismatch in the distributions.

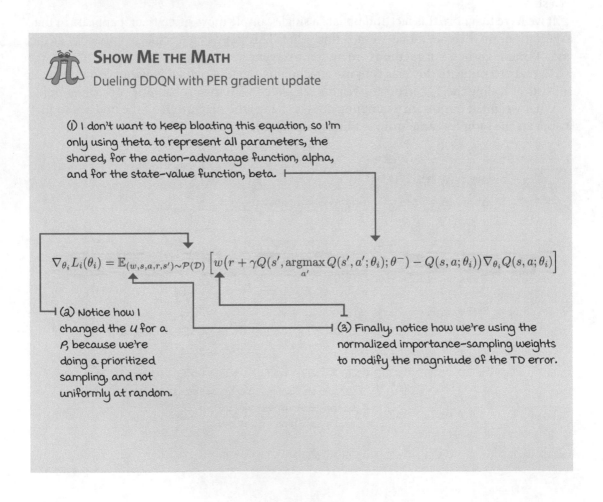

SHOW ME THE MATH

Dueling DDQN with PER gradient update

(1) I don't want to keep bloating this equation, so I'm only using theta to represent all parameters, the shared, for the action-advantage function, alpha, and for the state-value function, beta.

$$\nabla_{\theta_i} L_i(\theta_i) = \mathbb{E}_{(w,s,a,r,s') \sim \mathcal{P}(\mathcal{D})} \left[w\big(r + \gamma Q(s', \underset{a'}{\mathrm{argmax}}\, Q(s', a'; \theta_i); \theta^-) - Q(s, a; \theta_i)\big) \nabla_{\theta_i} Q(s, a; \theta_i) \right]$$

(2) Notice how I changed the U for a P, because we're doing a prioritized sampling, and not uniformly at random.

(3) Finally, notice how we're using the normalized importance-sampling weights to modify the magnitude of the TD error.

I SPEAK PYTHON
Prioritized replay buffer 1/2

```python
class PrioritizedReplayBuffer():
    <...>
    def store(self, sample):
```

(1) The store function of the PrioritizedReplayBuffer class is straightforward. The first thing we do is calculate the priority for the sample. Remember, we set the priority to the maximum. The following code shows 1 as default; then it's overwritten with the max value.

```python
        priority = 1.0
        if self.n_entries > 0:
            priority = self.memory[
                :self.n_entries,
                self.td_error_index].max()
```

(2) With the priority and sample (experience) in hand, we insert it into the memory.

```python
        self.memory[self.next_index,
                    self.td_error_index] = priority
        self.memory[self.next_index,
                    self.sample_index] = np.array(sample)
```

(3) We increase the variable that indicates the number of experiences in the buffer, but we need to make sure the buffer doesn't increase beyond the max_samples.

```python
        self.n_entries = min(self.n_entries + 1,
                                          self.max_samples)
```

(4) This next variable indicates the index at which the next experience will be inserted. This variable loops back around from max_samples to 0 and goes back up.

```python
        self.next_index += 1
        self.next_index = self.next_index % self.max_samples


    def update(self, idxs, td_errors):
```

(5) The update function takes an array of experiences ids, and new TD error values. Then, we insert the absolute TD errors into the right place.

```python
        self.memory[idxs,
                    self.td_error_index] = np.abs(td_errors)
```

(6) If we're doing rank-based sampling, we additionally sort the array. Notice that arrays are sub-optimal for implementing a prioritized replay buffer, mainly because of this sort that depends on the number of samples. Not good for performance.

```python
        if self.rank_based:
            sorted_arg = self.memory[:self.n_entries,
                    self.td_error_index].argsort()[::-1]
            self.memory[:self.n_entries] = self.memory[
                                          sorted_arg]
```

I Speak Python

Prioritized replay buffer 2/2

```python
class PrioritizedReplayBuffer():
    <...>
    def sample(self, batch_size=None):
```

(1) Calculate the batch_size, anneal 'beta,' and remove zeroed rows from entries.

```python
        batch_size = self.batch_size if batch_size == None \
                                      else batch_size
        self._update_beta()
        entries = self.memory[:self.n_entries]
```

(2) We now calculate priorities. If it's a rank-based prioritization, it's one over the rank (we sorted these in the update function). Proportional is the absolute TD error plus a small constant epsilon to avoid zero priorities.

```python
        if self.rank_based:
            priorities = 1/(np.arange(self.n_entries) + 1)
        else: # proportional
            priorities = entries[:, self.td_error_index] + EPS
```

(3) Now, we go from priorities to probabilities. First, we blend with uniform, then probs.

```python
        scaled_priorities = priorities**self.alpha
        pri_sum = np.sum(scaled_priorities)
        probs = np.array(scaled_priorities/pri_sum,
                                          dtype=np.float64)
```

(4) We then calculate the importance-sampling weights using the probabilities.

```python
        weights = (self.n_entries * probs)**-self.beta
```

(5) Normalize the weights. The maximum weight will be 1.

```python
        normalized_weights = weights/weights.max()
```

(6) We sample indices of the experiences in the buffer using the probabilities.

```python
        idxs = np.random.choice(self.n_entries,
                          batch_size, replace=False, p=probs)
```

(7) Get the samples out of the buffer.

```python
        samples = np.array([entries[idx] for idx in idxs])
```

(8) Finally, stack the samples by ids, weights, and experience tuples, and return them.

```python
        samples_stacks = [np.vstack(batch_type) for \
    batch_type in np.vstack(samples[:, self.sample_index]).T]
        idxs_stack = np.vstack(idxs)
        weights_stack = np.vstack(normalized_weights[idxs])
        return idxs_stack, weights_stack, samples_stacks
```

I SPEAK PYTHON
Prioritized replay buffer loss function 1/2

```
class PER():
    <...>
```
(1) As I've pointed out on other occasions, this is part of the code. These are snippets that I feel are worth showing here.

```
    def optimize_model(self, experiences):
```
(2) One thing to notice is that now we have ids and weights coming along with the experiences.

```
        idxs, weights, \
        (states, actions, rewards,
                    next_states, is_terminals) = experiences
        <...>
```
(3) We calculate the target values, as before.
```
        argmax_a_q_sp = self.online_model(next_states).max(1)[1]
        q_sp = self.target_model(next_states).detach()
        max_a_q_sp = q_sp[np.arange(batch_size), argmax_a_q_sp]
        max_a_q_sp = max_a_q_sp.unsqueeze(1)
        max_a_q_sp *= (1 - is_terminals)
        target_q_sa = rewards + (self.gamma * max_a_q_sp)
```
(4) We query the current estimates: nothing new.
```
        q_sa = self.online_model(states).gather(1, actions)
```
(5) We calculate the TD errors, the same way.
```
        td_error = q_sa - target_q_sa
```

(6) But, now the loss function has TD errors downscaled by the weights.
```
        value_loss = (weights * td_error).pow(2).mul(0.5).mean()
```

(7) We continue the optimization as before.
```
        self.value_optimizer.zero_grad()
        value_loss.backward()
        torch.nn.utils.clip_grad_norm_(
                            self.online_model.parameters(),
                            self.max_gradient_norm)
        self.value_optimizer.step()
```

(8) And we update the priorities of the replayed batch using the absolute TD errors.
```
        priorities = np.abs(td_error.detach().cpu().numpy())
        self.replay_buffer.update(idxs, priorities)
```

I Speak Python

Prioritized replay buffer loss function 2/2

```python
class PER():
    <...>
```

(1) This is the same PER class, but we're now in the train function.

```python
    def train(self, make_env_fn, make_env_kargs, seed, gamma,
              max_minutes, max_episodes, goal_mean_100_reward):
        <...>
```

(2) Inside the episode loop

```python
        for episode in range(1, max_episodes + 1):
            <...>
```

(3) Inside the time step loop

```python
            for step in count():
                state, is_terminal = \
                            self.interaction_step(state, env)
                <...>
```

(4) Every time step during training time

```python
                if len(self.replay_buffer) > min_samples:
```

(5) Look how we pull the experiences from the buffer.

```python
                    experiences = self.replay_buffer.sample()
```

(6) From the experiences, we pull the idxs, weights, and experience tuple. Notice how we load the samples variables into the GPU.

```python
                    idxs, weights, samples = experiences
                    experiences = self.online_model.load(
                                                    samples)
```

(7) Then, we stack the variables again. Note that we did that only to load the samples into the GPU and have them ready for training.

```python
                    experiences = (idxs, weights) + \
                                                (experiences,)
```

(8) Then, we optimize the model (this is the function in the previous page).

```python
                    self.optimize_model(experiences)
```

(9) And, everything proceeds as usual.

```python
                if np.sum(self.episode_timestep) % \
                        self.update_target_every_steps == 0:
                    self.update_network()

                if is_terminal:
                    break
```

IT'S IN THE DETAILS

The dueling DDQN with the prioritized replay buffer algorithm

One final time, we improve on all previous value-based deep reinforcement learning methods. This time, we do so by improving on the replay buffer. As you can imagine, most hyperparameters stay the same as the previous methods. Let's go into the details. These are the things that are still the same as before:

- Network outputs the action-value function $Q(s,a;\theta)$.
- We use a state-in-values-out dueling network architecture (nodes: 4, 512,128, 1; 2, 2).
- Optimize the action-value function to approximate the optimal action-value function $q*(s, a)$.
- Use off-policy TD targets ($r + gamma*max\_a'Q(s',a'; \theta)$) to evaluate policies.
- Use an adjustable Huber loss with max_gradient_norm variable set to float('inf'). Therefore, we're using MSE.
- Use RMSprop as our optimizer with a learning rate of 0.0007.
- An exponentially decaying epsilon-greedy strategy (from 1.0 to 0.3 in roughly 20,000 steps) to improve policies.
- A greedy action selection strategy for evaluation steps.
- A target network that updates every time step using Polyak averaging with a tau (the mix-in factor) of 0.1.
- A replay buffer with 320 samples minimum and a batch of 64.

Things we've changed:

- Use weighted important sampling to adjust the TD errors (which changes the loss function).
- Use a prioritized replay buffer with proportional prioritization, with a max number of samples of 10,000, an alpha (degree of prioritization versus uniform—1 is full priority) value of 0.6, a beta (initial value of beta, which is bias correction—1 is full correction) value of 0.1 and a beta annealing rate of 0.99992 (fully annealed in roughly 30,000 time steps).

PER is the same base algorithm as dueling DDQN, DDQN, and DQN:

1. Collect experience: (S_t, A_t, R_{t+1}, S_{t+1}, D_{t+1}), and insert into the replay buffer.
2. Pull a batch out of the buffer and calculate the off-policy TD targets: $R + gamma*max\_a'Q(s',a'; \theta)$, using double learning.
3. Fit the action-value function $Q(s,a;\theta)$, using MSE and RMSprop.
4. Adjust TD errors in the replay buffer.

ꟼꟼꟼꟼ TALLY IT UP
PER improves data efficiency even more

The prioritized replay buffer uses fewer samples than any of the previous methods. And as you can see it in the graphs below, it even makes things look more stable. Maybe?

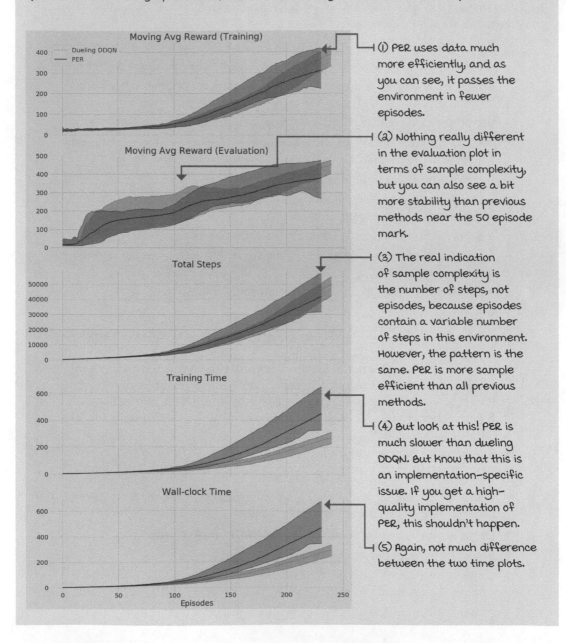

(1) PER uses data much more efficiently, and as you can see, it passes the environment in fewer episodes.

(2) Nothing really different in the evaluation plot in terms of sample complexity, but you can also see a bit more stability than previous methods near the 50 episode mark.

(3) The real indication of sample complexity is the number of steps, not episodes, because episodes contain a variable number of steps in this environment. However, the pattern is the same. PER is more sample efficient than all previous methods.

(4) But look at this! PER is much slower than dueling DDQN. But know that this is an implementation-specific issue. If you get a high-quality implementation of PER, this shouldn't happen.

(5) Again, not much difference between the two time plots.

Summary

This chapter concludes a survey of value-based DRL methods. In this chapter, we explored ways to make value-based methods more data efficient. You learned about the dueling architecture, and how it leverages the nuances of value-based RL by separating the $Q(s, a)$ into its two components: the state-value function $V(s)$ and the action-advantage function $A(s, a)$. This separation allows every experience used for updating the network to add information to the estimate of the state-value function $V(s)$, which is common to all actions. By doing this, we arrive at the correct estimates more quickly, reducing sample complexity.

You also looked into the prioritization of experiences. You learned that TD errors are a good criterion for creating priorities and that from priorities, you can calculate probabilities. You learned that we must compensate for changing the distribution of the expectation we're estimating. Thus, we use importance sampling, which is a technique for correcting the bias.

In the past three chapters, we dove headfirst into the field of value-based DRL. We started with a simple approach, NFQ. Then, we made this technique more stable with the improvements presented in DQN and DDQN. Then, we made it more sample-efficient with dueling DDQN and PER. Overall, we have a pretty robust algorithm. But, as with everything, value-based methods also have cons. First, they're sensitive to hyperparameters. This is well known, but you should try it for yourself; change any hyperparameter. You can find more values that don't work than values that do. Second, value-based methods assume they interact with a Markovian environment, that the states contain all information required by the agent. This assumption dissipates as we move away from bootstrapping and value-based methods in general. Last, the combination of bootstrapping, off-policy learning, and function approximators are known conjointly as "the deadly triad." While the deadly triad is known to produce divergence, researchers still don't know exactly how to prevent it.

By no means am I saying that value-based methods are inferior to the methods we survey in future chapters. Those methods have issues of their own, too. The fundamental takeaway is to know that value-based deep reinforcement learning methods are well known to diverge, and that's their weakness. How to fix it is still a research question, but sound practical advice is to use target networks, replay buffers, double learning, sufficiently small learning rates (but not too small), and maybe a little bit of patience. I'm sorry about that; I don't make the rules.

By now, you

- Can solve reinforcement learning problems with continuous state spaces

- Know how to stabilize value-based DRL agents

- Know how to make value-based DRL agents more sample efficient

TWEETABLE FEAT
Work on your own and share your findings

Here are several ideas on how to take what you've learned to the next level. If you'd like, share your results with the rest of the world and make sure to check out what others have done, too. It's a win-win situation, and hopefully, you'll take advantage of it.

- **#gdrl_ch10_tf01:** The replay buffers used in this and the previous chapter are sufficient for the cart-pole environment and other low-dimensional environments. However, you likely noticed that the prioritized buffer becomes the bottleneck for any more complex environment. Try rewriting all replay buffer code by yourself to speed it up. Do not look up other's code on this yet; try making the replay buffers faster. In the prioritized buffer, you can see that the bottleneck is the sorting of the samples. Find ways to make this portion faster, too.

- **#gdrl_ch10_tf02:** When trying to solve high-dimensional environments, such as Atari games, the replay buffer code in this and the previous chapter becomes prohibitively slow, and totally unpractical. Now what? Research how others solve this problem, which is a blocking issue for prioritized buffers. Share your findings and implement the data structures on your own. Understand them well, and create a blog post explaining the benefits of using them, in detail.

- **#gdrl_ch10_tf03:** In the last two chapters, you've learned about methods that can solve problems with high-dimensional and continuous state spaces, but how about action spaces? It seems lame that these algorithms can only select one action at a time, and these actions have discrete values. But wait, can DQN-like methods only solve problems with discrete action spaces of size one? Investigate and tell us!

- **#gdrl_ch10_tf04:** In every chapter, I'm using the final hashtag as a catchall hashtag. Feel free to use this one to discuss anything else that you worked on relevant to this chapter. There's no more exciting homework than that which you create for yourself. Make sure to share what you set yourself to investigate and your results.

Write a tweet with your findings, tag me @mimoralea (I'll retweet), and use the particular hashtag from the list to help interested folks find your results. There are no right or wrong results; you share your findings and check others' findings. Take advantage of this to socialize, contribute, and get yourself out there! We're waiting for you!

Here's a tweet example:

"Hey, @mimoralea. I created a blog post with a list of resources to study deep reinforcement learning. Check it out at <link>. #gdrl_ch01_tf01"

I'll make sure to retweet and help others find your work.

Policy-gradient and actor-critic methods | 11

In this chapter

- You will learn about a family of deep reinforcement learning methods that can optimize their performance directly, without the need for value functions.

- You will learn how to use value function to make these algorithms even better.

- You will implement deep reinforcement learning algorithms that use multiple processes at once for very fast learning.

> 66 *There is no better than adversity. Every defeat, every heartbreak, every loss, contains its own seed, its own lesson on how to improve your performance the next time.* 99
>
> — MALCOLM X
> AMERICAN MUSLIM MINISTER AND
> HUMAN RIGHTS ACTIVIST

In this book, we've explored methods that can find optimal and near-optimal policies with the help of value functions. However, all of those algorithms learn value functions when what we need are policies.

In this chapter, we explore the other side of the spectrum and what's in the middle. We start exploring methods that optimize policies directly. These methods, referred to as *policy-based* or *policy-gradient* methods, parameterize a policy and adjust it to maximize expected returns.

After introducing foundational policy-gradient methods, we explore a combined class of methods that learn both policies and value functions. These methods are referred to as actor-critic because the policy, which selects actions, can be seen as an actor, and the value function, which evaluates policies, can be seen as a critic. Actor-critic methods often perform better than value-based or policy-gradient methods alone on many of the deep reinforcement learning benchmarks. Learning about these methods allows you to tackle more challenging problems.

These methods combine what you learned in the previous three chapters concerning learning value functions and what you learn about in the first part of this chapter, about learning policies. Actor-critic methods often yield state-of-the-art performance in diverse sets of deep reinforcement learning benchmarks.

Policy-based, value-based, and actor-critic methods

(1) For the last three chapters, you were here.

(2) You're here for the next two sections . . .

(3) . . . and here through the end of the chapter.

Policy-based　**Actor-critic**　**Value-based**

REINFORCE: Outcome-based policy learning

In this section, we begin motivating the use of policy-based methods, first with an introduction; then we discuss several of the advantages you can expect when using these kinds of methods; and finally, we introduce the simplest policy-gradient algorithm, called *REINFORCE*.

Introduction to policy-gradient methods

The first point I'd like to emphasize is that in policy-gradient methods, unlike in value-based methods, we're trying to maximize a performance objective. In value-based methods, the main focus is to learn to evaluate policies. For this, the objective is to minimize a loss between predicted and target values. More specifically, our goal is to match the true action-value function of a given policy, and therefore, we parameterized a value function and minimized the mean squared error between predicted and target values. Note that we didn't have true target values, and instead, we used actual returns in Monte Carlo methods or predicted returns in bootstrapping methods.

In policy-based methods, on the other hand, the objective is to maximize the performance of a parameterized policy, so we're running gradient ascent (or executing regular gradient descent on the negative performance). It's rather evident that the performance of an agent is the expected total discounted reward from the initial state, which is the same thing as the expected state-value function from all initial states of a given policy.

SHOW ME THE MATH
Value-based vs. policy-based methods objectives

(1) In value-based methods, the objective is to minimize the loss function, which is the mean squared error between the true Q-function and the parameterized Q-function.

$$L_i(\theta_i) = \mathbb{E}_{s,a}\left[\left(q_\pi(s,a) - Q(s,a;\theta_i)\right)^2\right]$$

$$J_i(\theta_i) = \mathbb{E}_{s_0 \sim p_0}\left[v_{\pi_{\theta_i}}(s_0)\right]$$

(2) In policy-based methods, the objective is to maximize a performance measure, which is the true value-function of the parameterized policy from all initial states.

ŘŁ WITH AN RL ACCENT
Value-based vs. policy-based vs. policy-gradient vs. actor-critic methods

Value-based methods: Refers to algorithms that learn value functions and only value functions. Q-learning, SARSA, DQN, and company are all value-based methods.

Policy-based methods: Refers to a broad range of algorithms that optimize policies, including black-box optimization methods, such as genetic algorithms.

Policy-gradient methods: Refers to methods that solve an optimization problem on the gradient of the performance of a parameterized policy, methods you'll learn in this chapter.

Actor-critic methods: Refers to methods that learn both a policy and a value function, primarily if the value function is learned with bootstrapping and used as the score for the stochastic policy gradient. You learn about these methods in this and the next chapter.

Advantages of policy-gradient methods

The main advantage of learning parameterized policies is that policies can now be any learnable function. In value-based methods, we worked with discrete action spaces, mostly because we calculate the maximum value over the actions. In high-dimensional action spaces, this max could be prohibitively expensive. Moreover, in the case of continuous action spaces, value-based methods are severely limited.

Policy-based methods, on the other hand, can more easily learn stochastic policies, which in turn has multiple additional advantages. First, learning stochastic policies means better performance under partially observable environments. The intuition is that because we can learn arbitrary probabilities of actions, the agent is less dependent on the Markov assumption. For example, if the agent can't distinguish a handful of states from their emitted observations, the best strategy is often to act randomly with specific probabilities.

Learning stochastic policies could get us out of trouble

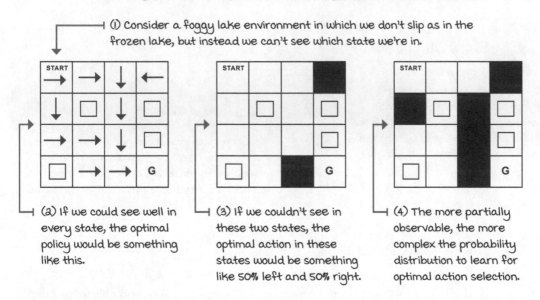

(1) Consider a foggy lake environment in which we don't slip as in the frozen lake, but instead we can't see which state we're in.

(2) If we could see well in every state, the optimal policy would be something like this.

(3) If we couldn't see in these two states, the optimal action in these states would be something like 50% left and 50% right.

(4) The more partially observable, the more complex the probability distribution to learn for optimal action selection.

Interestingly, even though we're learning stochastic policies, nothing prevents the learning algorithm from approaching a deterministic policy. This is unlike value-based methods, in which, throughout training, we have to force exploration with some probability to ensure optimality. In policy-based methods with stochastic policies, exploration is embedded in the learned function, and converging to a deterministic policy for a given state while training is possible.

Another advantage of learning stochastic policies is that it could be more straightforward for function approximation to represent a policy than a value function. Sometimes value functions are too much information for what's truly needed. It could be that calculating the exact value of a state or state-action pair is complicated or unnecessary.

Learning policies could be an easier, more generalizable problem to solve

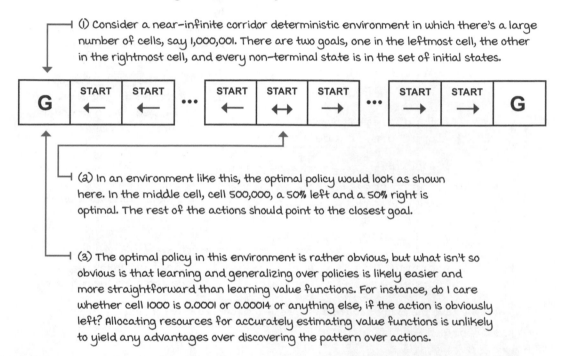

(1) Consider a near-infinite corridor deterministic environment in which there's a large number of cells, say 1,000,001. There are two goals, one in the leftmost cell, the other in the rightmost cell, and every non-terminal state is in the set of initial states.

(2) In an environment like this, the optimal policy would look as shown here. In the middle cell, cell 500,000, a 50% left and a 50% right is optimal. The rest of the actions should point to the closest goal.

(3) The optimal policy in this environment is rather obvious, but what isn't so obvious is that learning and generalizing over policies is likely easier and more straightforward than learning value functions. For instance, do I care whether cell 1000 is 0.0001 or 0.00014 or anything else, if the action is obviously left? Allocating resources for accurately estimating value functions is unlikely to yield any advantages over discovering the pattern over actions.

A final advantage to mention is that because policies are parameterized with continuous values, the action probabilities change smoothly as a function of the learned parameters. Therefore, policy-based methods often have better convergence properties. As you remember from previous chapters, value-based methods are prone to oscillations and even divergence. One of the reasons for this is that tiny changes in value-function space may imply significant changes in action space. A significant difference in actions can create entirely unusual new trajectories, and therefore create instabilities.

In value-based methods, we use an aggressive operator to change the value function; we take the maximum over Q-value estimates. In policy based methods, we instead follow the gradient with respect to stochastic policies, which only progressively and smoothly changes the actions. If you directly follow the gradient of the policy, you're guaranteed convergence to, at least, a local optimum.

I Speak Python
Stochastic policy for discrete action spaces 1/2

```python
class FCDAP(nn.Module):
    def __init__(self,
                 input_dim,
                 output_dim,
                 hidden_dims=(32,32),
                 init_std=1,
                 activation_fc=F.relu):
        super(FCDAP, self).__init__()
        self.activation_fc = activation_fc

        self.input_layer = nn.Linear(
            input_dim, hidden_dims[0])

        self.hidden_layers = nn.ModuleList()
        for i in range(len(hidden_dims)-1):
            hidden_layer = nn.Linear(
                hidden_dims[i], hidden_dims[i+1])
            self.hidden_layers.append(hidden_layer)

        self.output_layer = nn.Linear(
            hidden_dims[-1], output_dim)
```

(1) This class, FCDAP stands for fully connected discrete-action policy.

(2) The parameters allow you to specify a fully connected architecture, activation function, and weight and bias max magnitude.

(3) The __init__ function creates a linear connection between the input and the first hidden layer.

(4) Then, it creates connections across all hidden layers.

(5) Last, it connects the final hidden layer to the output nodes, creating the output layer.

(6) Here we have the method that takes care of the forward functionality.

```python
    def forward(self, state):
        x = state
        if not isinstance(x, torch.Tensor):
            x = torch.tensor(x, dtype=torch.float32)
            x = x.unsqueeze(0)
```

(7) First, we make sure the state is of the type of variable and shape we expect before we can pass it through the network.

(8) Next, we pass the properly formatted state into the input layer and then through the activation function.

```python
        x = self.activation_fc(self.input_layer(x))
```

(9) Then, we pass the output of the first activation through the sequence of hidden layers and respective activations.

```python
        for hidden_layer in self.hidden_layers:
            x = self.activation_fc(hidden_layer(x))
```

(10) Finally, we obtain the output, which are logits, preferences over actions.

```python
        return self.output_layer(x)
```

I SPEAK PYTHON

Stochastic policy for discrete action spaces 2/2

```python
    return self.output_layer(x)
```
(11) This line repeats the last line on the previous page.

```python
def full_pass(self, state):
```
(12) Here we do the full forward pass. This is a handy function to obtain probabilities, actions, and everything needed for training.

```python
    logits = self.forward(state)
```
(13) The forward pass returns the logits, the preferences over actions.

```python
    dist = torch.distributions.Categorical(logits=logits)
```
(14) Next, we sample the action from the probability distribution.

```python
    action = dist.sample()
```
(15) Then, calculate the log probability of that action and format it for training.

```python
    logpa = dist.log_prob(action).unsqueeze(-1)
```
(16) Here we calculate the entropy of the policy.

```python
    entropy = dist.entropy().unsqueeze(-1)
```
(17) And in here, for stats, we determine whether the policy selected was exploratory or not.

```python
    is_exploratory = action != np.argmax( \
                                 logits.detach().numpy())
```
(18) Finally, we return an action that can be directly passed into the environment, the flag indicating whether the action was exploratory, the log probability of the action, and the entropy of the policy.

```python
    return action.item(), is_exploratory.item(), \
                                        logpa, entropy
```
(19) This is a helper function for when we only need sampled action.

```python
def select_action(self, state):
    logits = self.forward(state)
    dist = torch.distributions.Categorical(logits=logits)
    action = dist.sample()
    return action.item()
```
(20) And this one is for selecting the greedy action according to the policy.

```python
def select_greedy_action(self, state):
    logits = self.forward(state)
    return np.argmax(logits.detach().numpy())
```

Learning policies directly

One of the main advantages of optimizing policies directly is that, well, it's the right objective. We learn a policy that optimizes the value function directly, without learning a value function, and without taking into account the dynamics of the environment. How is this possible? Let me show you.

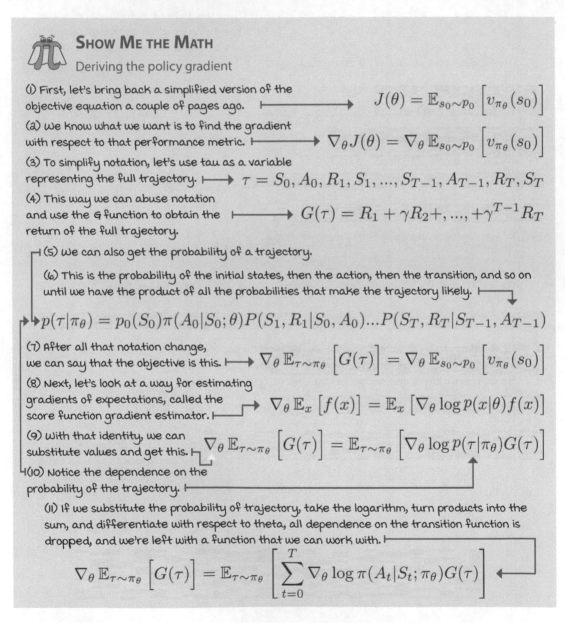

SHOW ME THE MATH

Deriving the policy gradient

(1) First, let's bring back a simplified version of the objective equation a couple of pages ago. ⊢──────▶ $J(\theta) = \mathbb{E}_{s_0 \sim p_0} \left[v_{\pi_\theta}(s_0) \right]$

(2) We know what we want is to find the gradient with respect to that performance metric. ⊢──────▶ $\nabla_\theta J(\theta) = \nabla_\theta \mathbb{E}_{s_0 \sim p_0} \left[v_{\pi_\theta}(s_0) \right]$

(3) To simplify notation, let's use tau as a variable representing the full trajectory. ⊢──────▶ $\tau = S_0, A_0, R_1, S_1, ..., S_{T-1}, A_{T-1}, R_T, S_T$

(4) This way we can abuse notation and use the G function to obtain the return of the full trajectory. ⊢──────▶ $G(\tau) = R_1 + \gamma R_2 +, ..., + \gamma^{T-1} R_T$

(5) We can also get the probability of a trajectory.

(6) This is the probability of the initial states, then the action, then the transition, and so on until we have the product of all the probabilities that make the trajectory likely. ⊢

$$p(\tau | \pi_\theta) = p_0(S_0) \pi(A_0 | S_0; \theta) P(S_1, R_1 | S_0, A_0) ... P(S_T, R_T | S_{T-1}, A_{T-1})$$

(7) After all that notation change, we can say that the objective is this. ⊢──────▶ $\nabla_\theta \mathbb{E}_{\tau \sim \pi_\theta} \left[G(\tau) \right] = \nabla_\theta \mathbb{E}_{s_0 \sim p_0} \left[v_{\pi_\theta}(s_0) \right]$

(8) Next, let's look at a way for estimating gradients of expectations, called the score function gradient estimator. ⊢──────▶ $\nabla_\theta \mathbb{E}_x \left[f(x) \right] = \mathbb{E}_x \left[\nabla_\theta \log p(x | \theta) f(x) \right]$

(9) With that identity, we can substitute values and get this. ⊢ $\nabla_\theta \mathbb{E}_{\tau \sim \pi_\theta} \left[G(\tau) \right] = \mathbb{E}_{\tau \sim \pi_\theta} \left[\nabla_\theta \log p(\tau | \pi_\theta) G(\tau) \right]$

(10) Notice the dependence on the probability of the trajectory. ⊢

(11) If we substitute the probability of trajectory, take the logarithm, turn products into the sum, and differentiate with respect to theta, all dependence on the transition function is dropped, and we're left with a function that we can work with. ⊢

$$\nabla_\theta \mathbb{E}_{\tau \sim \pi_\theta} \left[G(\tau) \right] = \mathbb{E}_{\tau \sim \pi_\theta} \left[\sum_{t=0}^{T} \nabla_\theta \log \pi(A_t | S_t; \pi_\theta) G(\tau) \right] \longleftarrow$$

Reducing the variance of the policy gradient

It's useful to have a way to compute the policy gradient without knowing anything about the environment's transition function. This algorithm increases the log probability of all actions in a trajectory, proportional to the goodness of the full return. In other words, we first collect a full trajectory and calculate the full discounted return, and then use that score to weight the log probabilities of every action taken in that trajectory: $A_t, A_{t+1}, \ldots, A_{T-1}$.

Let's use only rewards that are a consequence of actions

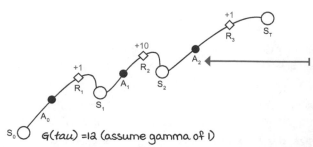

(1) This is somewhat counterintuitive because we're increasing the likelihood of action A_a in the same proportion as action A_o, even if the return after A_o is greater than the return after A_a. We know we can't go back in time and current actions aren't responsible for past reward. We can do something about that.

$G(tau) = 12$ (assume gamma of 1)

SHOW ME THE MATH

Reducing the variance of the policy gradient

(1) This is the gradient we try to estimate in the REINFORCE algorithm coming up next.

$$\nabla_\theta J(\theta) = \mathbb{E}_{\tau \sim \pi_\theta} \left[\sum_{t=0}^{T} G_t(\tau) \nabla_\theta \log \pi_\theta (A_t | S_t) \right]$$

(2) All this says is that we sample a trajectory.

(3) Then, for each step in the trajectory, we calculate the return from that step.

(4) And use that value as the score to weight the log probability of the action taken at that time step.

0001 **A BIT OF HISTORY**

Introduction of the REINFORCE algorithm

Ronald J. Williams introduced the REINFORCE family of algorithms in 1992 in a paper titled "Simple Statistical Gradient-Following Algorithms for Connectionist Reinforcement Learning."

In 1906, he coauthored a paper with Geoffrey Hinton et al. called "Learning representations by back-propagating errors," triggering growth in artificial neural network (ANN) research at the time.

I SPEAK PYTHON

REINFORCE 1/2

```python
class REINFORCE():
    <...>
```

(1) This is the REINFORCE algorithm. When you see the `<...>`, that means code was removed for simplicity. Go to the chapter's Notebook for the complete code.

```python
    def optimize_model(self):
        T = len(self.rewards)
        discounts = np.logspace(0, T, num=T, base=self.gamma,
                                endpoint=False)
```

(2) First, we calculate the discounts as with all Monte Carlo methods. The logspace function with these parameters returns the series of per time step gammas; for example, [1, 0.99, 0.9801, . . .].

```python
        returns = np.array(
            [np.sum(discounts[:T-t] * self.rewards[t:]) \
                for t in range(T)])
```

(3) Next, we calculate the sum of discounted returns for all time steps.

(4) To emphasize, this is the returns for every time step in the episode, from the initial state at time step 0, to one before the terminal T-1.

(5) Notice here that we're using the mathematically correct policy-gradient update, which isn't what you commonly find out there. The extra discount assumes that we're trying to optimize the expect discounted return from the initial state, so returns later in an episode get discounted.

```python
        <...>
        policy_loss = -(discounts * returns * \
                        self.logpas).mean()
```

(6) This is policy loss; it's the log probability of the actions selected weighted by the returns obtained after that action was selected. Notice that because PyTorch does gradient descent by default and the performance is something we want to maximize, we use the negative mean of the performance to flip the function. Think about it as doing gradient ascent on the performance. Also, we account for discounted policy gradients, so we multiply the returns by the discounts.

```python
        self.policy_optimizer.zero_grad()
        policy_loss.backward()
        self.policy_optimizer.step()
```

(7) In these three steps, we first zero the gradients in the optimizer, then do a backward pass, and then step in the direction of the gradient.

(8) This function obtains an action to be passed to the environment and all variables required for training.

```python
    def interaction_step(self, state, env):
        action, is_exploratory, logpa, _ = \
                            self.policy_model.full_pass(state)
        new_state, reward, is_terminal, _ = env.step(action)
        <...>
        return new_state, is_terminal
```

I Speak Python

REINFORCE 2/2

```python
class REINFORCE():
    <...>
```

(9) Still exploring functions of the REINFORCE class

(10) The train method is the entry point for training the agent.

```python
    def train(self, make_env_fn, make_env_kargs, seed, gamma,
              max_minutes, max_episodes, goal_mean_100_reward):
        for episode in range(1, max_episodes + 1):
```

(11) We begin by looping through the episodes.

```python
            state, is_terminal = env.reset(), False
            <...>
            self.logpas, self.rewards = [], []
```

(12) For each new episode, we initialize the variables needed for training and stats.

(13) Then, do the following for each time step.

```python
            for step in count():
                state, is_terminal = \
                    self.interaction_step(state, env)
```

(14) First, we collect experiences until we hit a terminal state.

```python
                if is_terminal:
                    break
```

(15) Then, we run one optimization step with the batch of all time steps in the episode.

```python
            self.optimize_model()

    def evaluate(self, eval_policy_model,
                 eval_env, n_episodes=1,
                 greedy=True):
        rs = []
        for _ in range(n_episodes):
            <...>
            for _ in count():

                if greedy:
                    a = eval_policy_model.\
                        select_greedy_action(s)
                else:
                    a = eval_policy_model.select_action(s)
                s, r, d, _ = eval_env.step(a)
            <...>
        return np.mean(rs), np.std(rs)
```

(16) Another thing I want you to see is the way I select the policy during evaluation. Instead of selecting a greedy policy, I sample from the learned stochastic policy. The correct thing to do here depends on the environment, but sampling is the safe bet.

VPG: Learning a value function

The REINFORCE algorithm you learned about in the previous section works well in simple problems, and it has convergence guarantees. But because we're using full Monte Carlo returns for calculating the gradient, its variance is a problem. In this section, we discuss a few approaches for dealing with this variance in an algorithm called *vanilla policy gradient* or *REINFORCE with baseline*.

Further reducing the variance of the policy gradient

REINFORCE is a principled algorithm, but it has a high variance. You probably remember from the discussion in chapter 5 about Monte Carlo targets, but let's restate. The accumulation of random events along a trajectory, including the initial state sampled from the initial state distribution—transition function probabilities, but now in this chapter with stochastic policies—is the randomness that action selection adds to the mix. All this randomness is compounded inside the return, making it a high-variance signal that's challenging to interpret.

One way for reducing the variance is to use partial returns instead of the full return for changing the log probabilities of actions. We already implemented this improvement. But another issue is that action log probabilities change in the proportion of the return. This means that, if we receive a significant positive return, the probabilities of the actions that led to that return are increased by a large margin. And if the return is of significant negative magnitude, then the probabilities are decreased by of large margin.

However, imagine an environment such as the cart-pole, in which all rewards and returns are positive. In order to accurately separate okay actions from the best actions, we need a lot of data. The variance is, otherwise, hard to muffle. It would be handy if we could, instead of using noisy returns, use something that allows us to differentiate the values of actions in the same state. Recall?

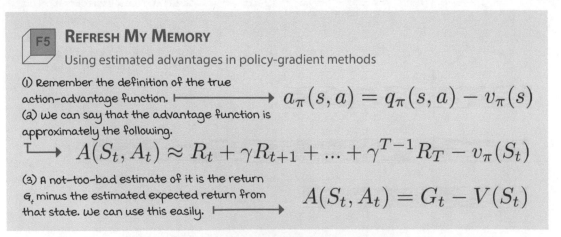

Learning a value function

As you see on the previous page, we can further reduce the variance of the policy gradient by using an estimate of the action-advantage function, instead of the actual return. Using the advantage somewhat centers scores around zero; better-than-average actions have a positive score, worse-than-average, a negative score. The former decreases the probabilities, and the latter increases them.

We're going to do exactly that. Let's now create two neural networks, one for learning the policy, the other for learning a state-value function, V. Then, we use the state-value function and the return for calculating an estimate of the advantage function, as we see next.

Two neural networks, one for the policy, one for the value function

Policy network   **Value network**

(1) The policy network we use for the cart-pole environment is the same one we use in REINFORCE: a four-node input layer, and a two-node output layer. I provide more details on the experiments later.

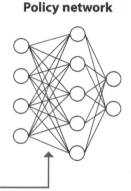

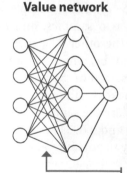

(2) The value network we use for the cart-pole environment is four-node input as well, representing the state, and a one-node output representing the value of that state. This network outputs the expected return from the input state. More details soon.

ŘŁ **WITH AN RL ACCENT**

REINFORCE, vanilla policy gradient, baselines, actor-critic

Some of you with prior DRL exposure may be wondering, is this a so-called "actor-critic"? It's learning a policy and a value-function, so it seems it should be. Unfortunately, this is one of those concepts where the "RL accent" confuses newcomers. Here's why.

First, according to one of the fathers of RL, Rich Sutton, policy-gradient methods approximate the gradient of the performance measure, whether or not they learn an approximate value function. However, David Silver, one of the most prominent figures in DRL, and a former student of Sutton, disagrees. He says that policy-based methods don't additionally learn a value function, only actor-critic methods do. But, Sutton further explains that only methods that learn the value function using bootstrapping should be called actor critic, because it's bootstrapping that adds bias to the value function, and thus makes it a "critic." I like this distinction; therefore, REINFORCE and VPG, as presented in this book, aren't considered actor-critic methods. But beware of the lingo, it's not consistent.

Encouraging exploration

Another essential improvement to policy-gradient methods is to add an entropy term to the loss function. We can interpret entropy in many different ways, from the amount of information one can gain by sampling from a distribution to the number of ways one can order a set.

The way I like to think of entropy is straight-forward. A uniform distribution, which has evenly distributed samples, has high entropy, in fact, the highest it can be. For instance, if you have two samples, and both can be drawn with a 50% chance, then the entropy is the highest it can be for a two-sample set. If you have four samples, each with a 25% chance, the entropy is the same, the highest it can be for a four-sample set. Conversely, if you have two samples, and one has a 100% chance and the other 0%, then the

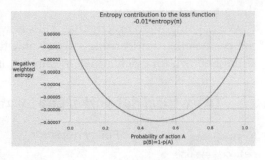

entropy is the lowest it can be, which is always zero. In PyTorch, the natural log is used for calculating the entropy instead of the binary log. This is mostly because the natural log uses Euler's number, e, and makes math more "natural." Practically speaking, however, there's no difference and the effects are the same. The entropy in the cart-pole environment, which has two actions, is between 0 and 0.6931.

The way to use entropy in policy-gradient methods is to add the negative weighted entropy to the loss function to encourage having evenly distributed actions. That way, a policy with evenly distributed actions, which yields the highest entropy, contributes to minimizing the loss. On the other hand, converging to a single action, which means entropy is zero, doesn't reduce the loss. In that case, the agent had better converge to the optimal action.

SHOW ME THE MATH
Losses to use for VPG

(1) This is the loss for the value function. It's simple, the mean squared Monte Carlo error. $\longmapsto$
$$L_v(\phi) = \frac{1}{N} \sum_{n=0}^{N} \left[\left(G_t - V(S_t; \phi) \right)^2 \right]$$

(2) The loss of the policy is this.

(3) The estimated advantage

(4) Log probability of the action taken

(5) The weighted entropy term

$$L_\pi(\theta) = -\frac{1}{N} \sum_{n=0}^{N} \left[\left(G_t - V(S_t; \phi) \right) \log \pi(A_t | S_t; \theta) + \beta H(\pi(S_t; \theta)) \right]$$

(8) Negative because we're minimizing

(7) mean over the samples

(6) Entropy is good

I SPEAK PYTHON

State-value function neural network model

```python
class FCV(nn.Module):

    def __init__(self,
                 input_dim,
                 hidden_dims=(32,32),
                 activation_fc=F.relu):
        super(FCV, self).__init__()
        self.activation_fc = activation_fc

        self.input_layer = nn.Linear(input_dim,
                                     hidden_dims[0])

        self.hidden_layers = nn.ModuleList()
        for i in range(len(hidden_dims)-1):
            hidden_layer = nn.Linear(
                hidden_dims[i], hidden_dims[i+1])
            self.hidden_layers.append(hidden_layer)

        self.output_layer = nn.Linear(
            hidden_dims[-1], 1)

    def forward(self, state):
        x = state
        if not isinstance(x, torch.Tensor):
            x = torch.tensor(x, dtype=torch.float32)
            x = x.unsqueeze(0)

        x = self.activation_fc(self.input_layer(x))
        for hidden_layer in self.hidden_layers:
            x = self.activation_fc(hidden_layer(x))

        return self.output_layer(x)
```

(1) This is the state-value function neural network. It's similar to the Q-function network we used in the past.

(2) Notice I left handy hyperparameters for you to play around with, so go ahead and do so.

(3) Here we create linear connections between the input nodes and the first hidden layer.

(4) Here we create the connections between the hidden layers.

(5) Here we connect the last hidden layer to the output layer, which has only one node, representing the value of the state.

(6) This is the forward-pass function.

(7) This is formatting the input as we expect it.

(8) Doing a full forward pass . . .

(9) . . . and returning the value of the state.

I Speak Python

Vanilla policy gradient a.k.a. REINFORCE with baseline

```
class VPG():  ◄——┤ ① This is the VPG algorithm. I removed quite a bit of code, so if you
    <...>     ◄——┤ want the full implementation, head to the chapter's Notebook.


    def optimize_model(self):
        T = len(self.rewards)
        discounts = np.logspace(0, T, num=T, base=self.gamma,
                                endpoint=False)
    ——► returns = np.array(
[np.sum(discounts[:T-t] * self.rewards[t:]) for t in range(T)])
```

② Very handy way for calculating the sum of discounted rewards from time step 0 to T

③ I want to emphasize that this loop is going through all steps from 0, then 1, 2, 3 all the way to the terminal state *T*, and calculating the return from that state, which is the sum of discounted rewards from that state at time step t to the terminal state *T*.

```
        value_error = returns - self.values
        policy_loss = -(
          discounts * value_error.detach() * self.logpas).mean()
```

④ First, calculate the value error; then use it to score the log probabilities of the actions. Then, discount these to be compatible with the discounted policy gradient. Then, use the negative mean.

```
        entropy_loss = -self.entropies.mean()
        loss = policy_loss + \
                      self.entropy_loss_weight * entropy_loss
```

⑤ Calculate the entropy, and add a fraction to the loss.

```
        self.policy_optimizer.zero_grad()
        loss.backward()
        torch.nn.utils.clip_grad_norm_(
                          self.policy_model.parameters(),
                          self.policy_model_max_grad_norm)
        self.policy_optimizer.step()  ◄——┤ ⑦ We step the optimizer.
```

⑥ Now, we optimize the policy. Zero the optimizer, do the backward pass, then clip the gradients, if desired.

⑧ Last, we optimize the value-function neural network.

```
        value_loss = value_error.pow(2).mul(0.5).mean()
        self.value_optimizer.zero_grad()
        value_loss.backward()
        torch.nn.utils.clip_grad_norm_(
                            self.value_model.parameters(),
                            self.value_model_max_grad_norm)
        self.value_optimizer.step()
```

A3C: Parallel policy updates

VPG is a pretty robust method for simple problems; it is, for the most part, unbiased because it uses an unbiased target for learning both the policy and value function. That is, it uses Monte Carlo returns, which are complete actual returns experienced directly in the environment, without any bootstrapping. The only bias in the entire algorithm is because we use function approximation, which is inherently biased, but since the ANN is only a baseline used to reduce the variance of the actual return, little bias is introduced, if any at all.

However, biased algorithms are necessarily a thing to avoid. Often, to reduce variance, we add bias. An algorithm called *asynchronous advantage actor-critic* (A3C) does a couple of things to further reduce variance. First, it uses *n*-step returns with bootstrapping to learn the policy and value function, and second, it uses concurrent actors to generate a broad set of experience samples in parallel. Let's get into the details.

Using actor-workers

One of the main sources of variance in DRL algorithms is how correlated and non-stationary online samples are. In value-based methods, we use a replay buffer to uniformly sample mini-batches of, for the most part, independent and identically distributed data. Unfortunately, using this experience-replay scheme for reducing variance is limited to off-policy methods, because on-policy agents cannot reuse data generated by previous policies. In other words, every optimization step requires a fresh batch of on-policy experiences.

Instead of using a replay buffer, what we can do in on-policy methods such as the policy-gradient algorithms we learn about in this chapter, is have multiple workers generating experience in parallel and asynchronously updating the policy and value function. Having multiple workers generating experience on multiple instances of the environment in parallel decorrelates the data used for training and reduces the variance of the algorithm.

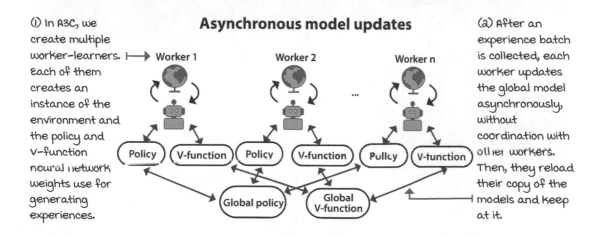

Asynchronous model updates

(1) In A3C, we create multiple worker-learners. ⊢→ Each of them creates an instance of the environment and the policy and v-function neural network weights use for generating experiences.

(2) After an experience batch is collected, each worker updates the global model asynchronously, without coordination with other workers. Then, they reload their copy of the models and keep at it.

Worker 1   Worker 2   Worker n

Policy   V-function   Policy   V-function   Policy   V-function

Global policy   Global V-function

I SPEAK PYTHON

A3C worker logic 1/2

```python
class A3C():
    <...>
    def work(self, rank):
```

(1) This is the A3C agent.

(2) As usual, these are snippets. You know where to find the working code.

(3) This is the work function each worker loops around in. The rank parameter is used as an ID for workers.

```python
        local_seed = self.seed + rank
        env = self.make_env_fn(
            **self.make_env_kargs,
            seed=local_seed)
```

(4) See how we create a unique seed per worker. We want diverse experiences.

(5) We create a uniquely seeded environment for each worker.

```python
        torch.manual_seed(local_seed)
        np.random.seed(local_seed)
        random.seed(local_seed)
```

(6) We also use that unique seed for PyTorch, NumPy and Python.

```python
        nS = env.observation_space.shape[0]
        nA = env.action_space.n
```

(7) Handy variables

(8) Here we create a local policy model. See how we initialize its weights with the weights of a shared policy network. This network allow us to synchronize the agents periodically.

```python
        local_policy_model = self.policy_model_fn(nS, nA)
        local_policy_model.load_state_dict(
                    self.shared_policy_model.state_dict())
```

(9) We do the same thing with the value model. Notice we don't need nA for output dimensions.

```python
        local_value_model = self.value_model_fn(nS)
        local_value_model.load_state_dict(
                    self.shared_value_model.state_dict())
```

(10) We start the training loop, until the worker is signaled to get out of it.

```python
        while not self.get_out_signal:
            state, is_terminal = env.reset(), False
```

(11) The first thing is to reset the environment, and set the done or is_terminal flag to false.

(12) As you see next, we use *n*-step returns for training the policy and value functions.

```python
            n_steps_start = 0
            logpas, entropies, rewards, values = [], [], [], []

            for step in count(start=1):
```

(13) Let's continue on the next page.

I SPEAK PYTHON

A3C worker logic 2/2

```
for step in count(start=1):
```

(14) I removed eight spaces from the indentation to make it easier to read.

(15) We are in the episode loop. The first thing is to collect a step of experience.

```
        state, reward, is_terminal, is_truncated, \
            is_exploratory = self.interaction_step(
                state, env, local_policy_model,
                local_value_model, logpas,
                entropies, rewards, values)
```

(16) We collect *n*-steps maximum. If we hit a terminal state, we stop there.

```
        if is_terminal or step - n_steps_start == \
                                            self.max_n_steps:

            is_failure = is_terminal and not is_truncated
```

(17) We check if the time wrapper was triggered or this is a true terminal state.

```
            next_value = 0 if is_failure else \
                    local_value_model(state).detach().item()
```

(18) If it's a failure, then the value of the next state is 0; otherwise, we bootstrap.

```
            rewards.append(next_value)
```

(19) Look! I'm being sneaky here and appending the next_value to the rewards. By doing this, the optimization code from VPG remains largely the same, as you'll see soon. Make sure you see it.

```
            self.optimize_model(
                logpas, entropies, rewards, values,
                local_policy_model, local_value_model)
```

(20) Next we optimize the model. We dig into that function shortly.

```
            logpas, entropies, rewards, values = [], [], [], []
            n_steps_start = step
```

(21) We reset the variables after the optimization step and continue.

```
        if is_terminal:
            break
```

(22) And, if the state is terminal, of course exit the episode loop.

```
<...>
```

(23) There is a lot removed.

Using *n*-step estimates

On the previous page, you notice that I append the value of the next state, whether terminal or not, to the reward sequence. That means that the reward variable contains all rewards from the partial trajectory and the state-value estimate of that last state. We can also see this as having the partial return and the predicted remaining return in the same place. The partial return is the sequence of rewards, and the predicted remaining return is a single-number estimate. The only reason why this isn't a return is that it isn't a discounted sum, but we can take care of that as well.

You should realize that this is an *n*-step return, which you learned about in chapter 5. We go out for *n*-steps collecting rewards, and then bootstrap after that *n*th state, or before if we land on a terminal state, whichever comes first.

A3C takes advantage of the lower variance of *n*-step returns when compared to Monte Carlo returns. We use the value function also to predict the return used for updating the policy. You remember that bootstrapping reduces variance, but it adds bias. Therefore, we've added a critic to our policy-gradient algorithm. Welcome to the world of actor-critic methods.

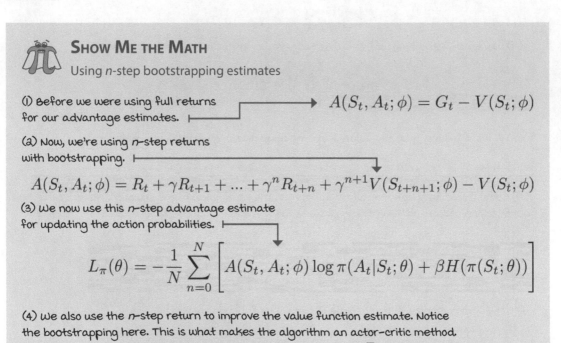

SHOW ME THE MATH
Using *n*-step bootstrapping estimates

① Before we were using full returns for our advantage estimates. $\longmapsto$ $A(S_t, A_t; \phi) = G_t - V(S_t; \phi)$

② Now, we're using *n*-step returns with bootstrapping. $\longmapsto$

$$A(S_t, A_t; \phi) = R_t + \gamma R_{t+1} + \dots + \gamma^n R_{t+n} + \gamma^{n+1} V(S_{t+n+1}; \phi) - V(S_t; \phi)$$

③ We now use this *n*-step advantage estimate for updating the action probabilities. $\longmapsto$

$$L_\pi(\theta) = -\frac{1}{N} \sum_{n=0}^{N} \left[A(S_t, A_t; \phi) \log \pi(A_t | S_t; \theta) + \beta H(\pi(S_t; \theta)) \right]$$

④ We also use the *n*-step return to improve the value function estimate. Notice the bootstrapping here. This is what makes the algorithm an actor-critic method.

$$L_v(\phi) = \frac{1}{N} \sum_{n=0}^{N} \left[\left(R_t + \gamma R_{t+1} + \dots + \gamma^n R_{t+n} + \gamma^{n+1} V(S_{t+n+1}; \phi) - V(S_t; \phi) \right)^2 \right]$$

I SPEAK PYTHON

A3C optimization step 1/2

```python
class A3C():          ←——— (1) A3C, optimization function
    <...>

    def optimize_model(
            self, logpas, entropies, rewards, values,
            local_policy_model, local_value_model):
```

(2) First get the length of the reward. Remember, rewards includes the bootstrapping value.

```python
        T = len(rewards)
        discounts = np.logspace(0, T, num=T, base=self.gamma,
                                endpoint=False)
```

(3) Next, we calculate all discounts up to *n*+1.

```python
        returns = np.array(
    [np.sum(discounts[:T-t] * rewards[t:]) for t in range(T)])
```

(4) This now is the *n*-step predicted return.

```python
        discounts = torch.FloatTensor(
                            discounts[:-1]).unsqueeze(1)
        returns = torch.FloatTensor(returns[:-1]).unsqueeze(1)
```

(5) To continue, we need to remove the extra elements and format the variables as expected.

```python
        value_error = returns - values
```

(6) Now, we calculate the value errors as the predicted return minus the estimated values.

```python
        policy_loss = -(discounts * value_error.detach() * \
                                                logpas).mean()
        entropy_loss = -entropies.mean()
        loss = policy_loss + self.entropy_loss_weight * \
                                                entropy_loss
```

(7) We calculate the loss as before.

```python
        self.shared_policy_optimizer.zero_grad()
        loss.backward()
```

(8) Notice we now zero the shared policy optimizer, then calculate the loss.

```python
        torch.nn.utils.clip_grad_norm_(
                local_policy_model.parameters(),
                self.policy_model_max_grad_norm)
```

(9) Then, clip the gradient magnitude.

```python
        for param, shared_param in zip(
```

(10) Continue on the next page.

I SPEAK PYTHON

A3C optimization step 2/2

```
for param, shared_param in zip(
    local_policy_model.parameters(),
    self.shared_policy_model.parameters()):
```

(11) Okay, so check this out. What we're doing here is iterating over all local and shared policy network parameters.

(12) And what we want to do is copy every gradient from the local to the shared model.

```
    if shared_param.grad is None:
        shared_param._grad = param.grad
```

(13) Once the gradients are copied into the shared optimizer, we run an optimization step.

```
    self.shared_policy_optimizer.step()
```

(14) Immediately after, we load the shared model into the local model.

```
    local_policy_model.load_state_dict(
                self.shared_policy_model.state_dict())
```

(15) Next, we do the same thing but with the state-value network. Calculate the loss.

```
    value_loss = value_error.pow(2).mul(0.5).mean()
```

(16) Zero the shared value optimizer.

```
    self.shared_value_optimizer.zero_grad()
    value_loss.backward()
```

(17) Backpropagate the gradients.

(18) Then, clip them.

```
    torch.nn.utils.clip_grad_norm_(
                local_value_model.parameters(),
                self.value_model_max_grad_norm)
```

(19) Then, copy all the gradients from the local model to the shared model.

```
    for param, shared_param in zip(
                local_value_model.parameters(),
                self.shared_value_model.parameters()):
        if shared_param.grad is None:
            shared_param._grad = param.grad
```

```
    self.shared_value_optimizer.step()
```

(20) Step the optimizer.

(21) Finally, load the shared model into the local variable.

```
    local_value_model.load_state_dict(
                self.shared_value_model.state_dict())
```

Non-blocking model updates

One of the most critical aspects of A3C is that its network updates are asynchronous and lock-free. Having a shared model creates a tendency for competent software engineers to want a blocking mechanism to prevent workers from overwriting other updates. Interestingly, A3C uses an update style called a Hogwild!, which is shown to not only achieve a near-optimal rate of convergence but also outperform alternative schemes that use locking by an order of magnitude.

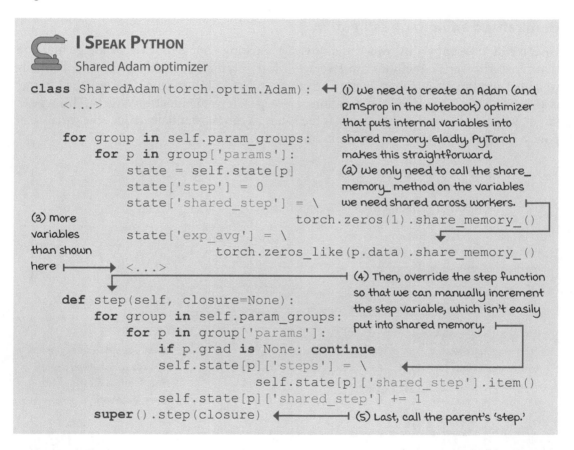

I Speak Python

Shared Adam optimizer

```
class SharedAdam(torch.optim.Adam):         ← (1) We need to create an Adam (and
    <...>                                        RMSprop in the Notebook) optimizer
                                                 that puts internal variables into
    for group in self.param_groups:              shared memory. Gladly, PyTorch
        for p in group['params']:                makes this straightforward.
            state = self.state[p]
            state['step'] = 0                    (2) We only need to call the share_
            state['shared_step'] = \             memory_ method on the variables
                          torch.zeros(1).share_memory_()  we need shared across workers.

            state['exp_avg'] = \
                      torch.zeros_like(p.data).share_memory_()
            <...>
                                                 (4) Then, override the step function
    def step(self, closure=None):                so that we can manually increment
        for group in self.param_groups:          the step variable, which isn't easily
            for p in group['params']:            put into shared memory.
                if p.grad is None: continue
                self.state[p]['steps'] = \
                            self.state[p]['shared_step'].item()
                self.state[p]['shared_step'] += 1
        super().step(closure)         ← (5) Last, call the parent's 'step.'
```

(3) more variables than shown here →

0001 A Bit of History

Introduction of the asynchronous advantage actor-critic (A3C)

Vlad Mnih et al. introduced A3C in 2016 in a paper titled "Asynchronous Methods for Deep Reinforcement Learning." If you remember correctly, Vlad also introduced the DQN agent in two papers, one in 2013 and the other in 2015. While DQN ignited growth in DRL research in general, A3C directed lots of attention to actor-critic methods more precisely.

GAE: Robust advantage estimation

A3C uses *n*-step returns for reducing the variance of the targets. Still, as you probably remember from chapter 5, there's a more robust method that combines multiple *n*-step bootstrapping targets in a single target, creating even more robust targets than a single *n*-step: the λ-target. *Generalized advantage estimation* (GAE) is analogous to the λ-target in TD(λ), but for advantages.

Generalized advantage estimation

GAE is not an agent on its own, but a way of estimating targets for the advantage function that most actor-critic methods can leverage. More specifically, GAE uses an exponentially weighted combination of *n*-step action-advantage function targets, the same way the λ-target is an exponentially weighted combination of *n*-step state-value function targets. This type of target, which we tune in the same way as the λ-target, can substantially reduce the variance of policy-gradient estimates at the cost of some bias.

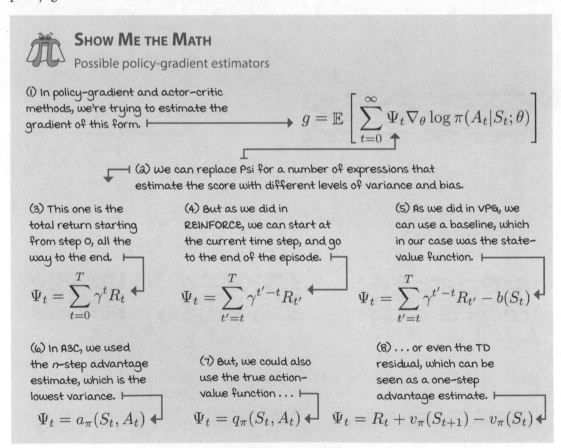

SHOW ME THE MATH

Possible policy-gradient estimators

(1) In policy-gradient and actor–critic methods, we're trying to estimate the gradient of this form.

$$g = \mathbb{E}\left[\sum_{t=0}^{\infty} \Psi_t \nabla_\theta \log \pi(A_t|S_t;\theta) \right]$$

(2) we can replace Psi for a number of expressions that estimate the score with different levels of variance and bias.

(3) This one is the total return starting from step 0, all the way to the end.

$$\Psi_t = \sum_{t=0}^{T} \gamma^t R_t$$

(4) But as we did in REINFORCE, we can start at the current time step, and go to the end of the episode.

$$\Psi_t = \sum_{t'=t}^{T} \gamma^{t'-t} R_{t'}$$

(5) As we did in VPG, we can use a baseline, which in our case was the state-value function.

$$\Psi_t = \sum_{t'=t}^{T} \gamma^{t'-t} R_{t'} - b(S_t)$$

(6) In A3C, we used the *n*-step advantage estimate, which is the lowest variance.

$$\Psi_t = a_\pi(S_t, A_t)$$

(7) But, we could also use the true action-value function...

$$\Psi_t = q_\pi(S_t, A_t)$$

(8) ...or even the TD residual, which can be seen as a one-step advantage estimate.

$$\Psi_t = R_t + v_\pi(S_{t+1}) - v_\pi(S_t)$$

Show Me the Math

GAE is a robust estimate of the advantage function

$$A^1(S_t, A_t; \phi) = R_t + \gamma V(S_{t+1}; \phi) - V(S_t; \phi)$$

$$A^2(S_t, A_t; \phi) = R_t + \gamma R_{t+1} + \gamma^2 V(S_{t+2}; \phi) - V(S_t; \phi)$$

$$A^3(S_t, A_t; \phi) = R_t + \gamma R_{t+1} + \gamma^2 R_{t+2} + \gamma^3 V(S_{t+3}; \phi) - V(S_t; \phi)$$

...

(1) N-step advantage estimates . . .

$$A^n(S_t, A_t; \phi) = R_t + \gamma R_{t+1} + ... + \gamma^n R_{t+n} + \gamma^{n+1} V(S_{t+n+1}; \phi) - V(S_t; \phi)$$

(2) . . . which we can mix to make an estimate analogous to TD lambda, but for advantages.

$$A^{GAE(\gamma, \lambda)}(S_t, A_t; \phi) = \sum_{l=0}^{\infty} (\gamma\lambda)^l \delta_{t+l}$$

(3) Similarly, a lambda of 0 returns the one-step advantage estimate, and a lambda of 1 returns the infinite-step advantage estimate.

$$A^{GAE(\gamma, 0)}(S_t, A_t; \phi) = R_t + \gamma V(S_{t+1}; \phi) - V(S_t; \phi)$$

$$A^{GAE(\gamma, 1)}(S_t, A_t; \phi) = \sum_{l=0}^{\infty} \gamma^l R_{t+l} - V(S_t; \phi)$$

Show Me the Math

Possible value targets

(1) Notice we can use several different targets to train the state-value function neural network used to calculate GAE values.

(2) We could use the reward to go, a.k.a., Monte Carlo returns.

$$y_t = \sum_{t'=t}^{T} \gamma^{t'-t} R_{t'}$$

(3) The n-step bootstrapping target, including the TD target

$$y_t = R_t + \gamma R_{t+1} + ... + \gamma^n R_{t+n} + \gamma^{n+1} V(S_{t+n+1}; \phi)$$

(4) Or the GAE, as a TD(lambda) estimate

$$y_t = A^{GAE(\gamma, \lambda)}(S_t, A_t; \phi) + V(S_t; \phi)$$

0001 A Bit of History

Introduction of the generalized advantage estimations

John Schulman et al. published a paper in 2015 titled "High-dimensional Continuous Control Using Generalized Advantage Estimation," in which he introduces GAE.

John is a research scientist at OpenAI, and the lead inventor behind GAE, TRPO, and PPO, algorithms that you learn about in the next chapter. In 2018, John was recognized by Innovators Under 35 for creating these algorithms, which are to this date state of the art.

I SPEAK PYTHON
GAE's policy optimization step

```python
class GAE():
    <...>                              ← (1) This is the GAE optimize model logic.
    def optimize_model(
            self, logpas, entropies, rewards, values,
            local_policy_model, local_value_model):
```

(2) First, we create the discounted returns, the way we did with A3C.

```python
    T = len(rewards)
    discounts = np.logspace(0, T, num=T, base=self.gamma,
                            endpoint=False)
    returns = np.array(
[np.sum(discounts[:T-t] * rewards[t:]) for t in range(T)])
```

(3) These two lines are creating, first, a NumPy array with all the state values, and second, an array with the *(gamma*lambda)^t*. Note, lambda is often referred to as tau, too. I'm using that.

```python
    np_values = values.view(-1).data.numpy()
    tau_discounts = np.logspace(0, T-1, num=T-1,
                    base=self.gamma*self.tau, endpoint=False)
```

(4) This line creates an array of TD errors: *R_t + gamma * value_t+1 – value_t*, for t=0 to T.

```python
    advs = rewards[:-1] + self.gamma * \
                          np_values[1:] - np_values[:-1]
```

(5) Here we create the GAEs, by multiplying the tau discounts times the TD errors.

```python
    gaes = np.array(
[np.sum(tau_discounts[:T-1-t] * advs[t:]) for t in range(T-1)])

    <...>            ← (6) We now use the gaes to calculate the policy loss.

    policy_loss = -(discounts * gaes.detach() * \
                                            logpas).mean()
    entropy_loss = -entropies.mean()
    loss = policy_loss + self.entropy_loss_weight * \
                                            entropy_loss
```

(7) And proceed as usual.

```python
    value_error = returns - values
    value_loss = value_error.pow(2).mul(0.5).mean()
    <...>
```

A2C: Synchronous policy updates

In A3C, workers update the neural networks asynchronously. But, asynchronous workers may not be what makes A3C such a high-performance algorithm. Advantage actor-critic (A2C) is a synchronous version of A3C, which despite the lower numbering order, was proposed after A3C and showed to perform comparably to A3C. In this section, we explore A2C, along with a few other changes we can apply to policy-gradient methods.

Weight-sharing model

One change to our current algorithm is to use a single neural network for both the policy and the value function. Sharing a model can be particularly beneficial when learning from images because feature extraction can be compute-intensive. However, model sharing can be challenging due to the potentially different scales of the policy and value function updates.

Sharing weights between policy and value outputs

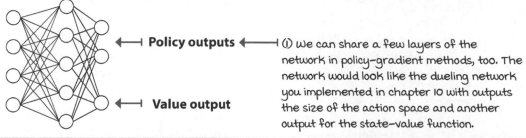

Policy outputs ← (1) We can share a few layers of the network in policy-gradient methods, too. The network would look like the dueling network you implemented in chapter 10 with outputs the size of the action space and another output for the state-value function.

Value output

I Speak Python

Weight-sharing actor-critic neural network model 1/2

```
class FCAC(nn.Module):    ← (1) This is the fully connected actor-critic model.
    def __init__(
        self, input_dim, output_dim,
        hidden_dims=(32,32), activation_fc=F.relu):
```
(2) This is the network instantiation process. This is similar to the independent network model.
```
        super(FCAC, self).__init__()
        self.activation_fc = activation_fc
        self.input_layer = nn.Linear(input_dim, hidden_dims[0])
        self.hidden_layers = nn.ModuleList()
        for i in range(len(hidden_dims)-1):
            hidden_layer = nn.Linear(
                hidden_dims[i], hidden_dims[i+1])
            self.hidden_layers.append(hidden_layer)
        self.value_output_layer = nn.Linear(    ← (3) Continues ...
```

I SPEAK PYTHON

Weight-sharing actor-critic neural network model 2/2

```
self.value_output_layer = nn.Linear(
    hidden_dims[-1], 1)
self.policy_output_layer = nn.Linear(
    hidden_dims[-1], output_dim)
```

(4) Okay. Here's where it's built, both the value output and the policy output connect to the last layer of the hidden layers.

```
def forward(self, state):
    x = state
    if not isinstance(x, torch.Tensor):
        x = torch.tensor(x, dtype=torch.float32)
        if len(x.size()) == 1:
            x = x.unsqueeze(0)
    x = self.activation_fc(self.input_layer(x))
    for hidden_layer in self.hidden_layers:
        x = self.activation_fc(hidden_layer(x))
    return self.policy_output_layer(x), \
           self.value_output_layer(x)
```

(5) The forward pass starts by reshaping the input to match the expected variable type and shape.

(6) And notice how it outputs from the policy and a value layers.

```
def full_pass(self, state):
    logits, value = self.forward(state)
    dist = torch.distributions.Categorical(logits=logits)
    action = dist.sample()
    logpa = dist.log_prob(action).unsqueeze(-1)
    entropy = dist.entropy().unsqueeze(-1)
    action = action.item() if len(action) == 1 \
                           else action.data.numpy()
    is_exploratory = action != np.argmax(
        logits.detach().numpy(), axis=int(len(state)!=1))
    return action, is_exploratory, logpa, entropy, value
```

(7) This is a handy function to get log probabilities, entropies, and other variables at once.

(8) This selects the action or actions for the given state or batch of states.

```
def select_action(self, state):
    logits, _ = self.forward(state)
    dist = torch.distributions.Categorical(logits=logits)
    action = dist.sample()
    action = action.item() if len(action) == 1 \
                           else action.data.numpy()
    return action
```

Restoring order in policy updates

Updating the neural network in a Hogwild!-style can be chaotic, yet introducing a lock mechanism lowers A3C performance considerably. In A2C, we move the workers from the agent down to the environment. Instead of having multiple actor-learners, we have multiple actors with a single learner. As it turns out, having workers rolling out experiences is where the gains are in policy-gradient methods.

Synchronous model updates

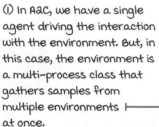

(1) In A2C, we have a single agent driving the interaction with the environment. But, in this case, the environment is a multi-process class that gathers samples from multiple environments at once.

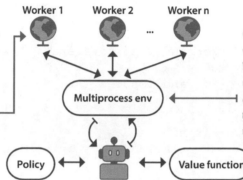

(2) The neural networks now need to process batches of data. This means in A2C we can take advantage of GPUs, unlike A3C in which CPUs are the most important resource.

🐍 I SPEAK PYTHON

Multi-process environment wrapper 1/2

```python
class MultiprocessEnv(object):
    def __init__(self, make_env_fn, make_env_kargs,
                 seed, n_workers):
        self.make_env_fn = make_env_fn
        self.make_env_kargs = make_env_kargs
        self.seed = seed
        self.n_workers = n_workers

        self.pipes = [
                mp.Pipe() for rank in range(self.n_workers)]
```

(1) This is the multi-process environment class, which creates pipes to communicate with the workers, and creates the workers themselves.

(2) Here we create the workers.

```python
        self.workers = [
            mp.Process(target=self.work,
                       args=(rank, self.pipes[rank][1])) \
                            for rank in range(self.n_workers)]
```

(3) Here we start them.

```python
        [w.start() for w in self.workers]
```

I SPEAK PYTHON

Multi-process environment wrapper 2/2

```python
[w.start() for w in self.workers]           ← (4) Continuation

def work(self, rank, worker_end):
    env = self.make_env_fn(            (5) Workers first create the environment.
        **self.make_env_kargs, seed=self.seed + rank)  ←
    while True:    ←               (6) Get in this loop listening for commands.
        cmd, kwargs = worker_end.recv()
        if cmd == 'reset':
            worker_end.send(env.reset(**kwargs))
        elif cmd == 'step':
            worker_end.send(env.step(**kwargs))
        elif cmd == '_past_limit':
            # Another way to check time limit truncation
            worker_end.send(\
                env._elapsed_steps >= env._max_episode_steps)
        else:
            env.close(**kwargs)
            del env
            worker_end.close()
            break
```

(7) Each command calls the respective env function and sends the response back to the parent process.

(8) This is the main step function, for instance.

(9) When called, it broadcasts the command and arguments to workers.

```python
def step(self, actions):
    assert len(actions) == self.n_workers
    [self.send_msg(('step',{'action':actions[rank]}),rank)\
                    for rank in range(self.n_workers)]
    results = []
    for rank in range(self.n_workers):
        parent_end, _ = self.pipes[rank]
        o, r, d, _ = parent_end.recv()
        if d:
            self.send_msg(('reset', {}), rank)
            o = parent_end.recv()
        results.append((o,
                        np.array(r, dtype=np.float),
                        np.array(d, dtype=np.float), _))
    return \
        [np.vstack(block) for block in np.array(results).T]
```

(10) Workers do their part and send back the data, which is collected here.

(11) We automatically reset on done.

(12) Last, append and stack the results by observations, rewards, dones, infos.

I Speak Python

The A2C train logic

```python
class A2C():
    def train(self, make_envs_fn, make_env_fn,
              make_env_kargs, seed, gamma, max_minutes,
              max_episodes, goal_mean_100_reward):
```

(1) This is how we train with the multi-processor environment.

```python
        envs = self.make_envs_fn(make_env_fn,
                    make_env_kargs, self.seed,
                    self.n_workers)
        <...>
```

(2) Here, see how to create, basically, vectorized environments.

(3) Here we create a single model. This is the actor-critic model with policy and value outputs.

```python
        self.ac_model = self.ac_model_fn(nS, nA)
        self.ac_optimizer = self.ac_optimizer_fn(
                    self.ac_model, self.ac_optimizer_lr)
```

```python
        states = envs.reset()
```

(4) Look, we reset the multi-processor environment and get a stack of states back.

```python
        for step in count(start=1):
            states, is_terminals = \
                    self.interaction_step(states, envs)
```

(5) The main thing is we work with stacks now.

```python
            if is_terminals.sum() or \
                    step - n_steps_start == self.max_n_steps:

                past_limits_enforced = envs._past_limit()
                failure = np.logical_and(is_terminals,
                        np.logical_not(past_limits_enforced))

                next_values = self.ac_model.evaluate_state(
                    states).detach().numpy() * (1 - failure)
```

(6) But, at its core, everything is the same.

```python
                self.rewards.append(next_values)
                self.values.append(torch.Tensor(next_values))
                self.optimize_model()
                self.logpas, self.entropies = [], []
                self.rewards, self.values = [], []
                n_steps_start = step
```

I Speak Python

The A2C optimize-model logic

```python
class A2C():                                    ① This is how we optimize the model in A2C.
    def optimize_model(self):
        T = len(self.rewards)
        discounts = np.logspace(0, T, num=T, base=self.gamma,
                                endpoint=False)

        returns = np.array(
                    [[np.sum(discounts[:T-t] * rewards[t:, w])
                      for t in range(T)] \
                      for w in range(self.n_workers)])

        np_values = values.data.numpy()
        tau_discounts = np.logspace(0, T-1, num=T-1,
                        base=self.gamma*self.tau, endpoint=False)
        advs = rewards[:-1] + self.gamma * np_values[1:] \
                                         - np_values[:-1]

        gaes = np.array(
            [[np.sum(tau_discounts[:T-1-t] * advs[t:, w]) \
                for t in range(T-1)]
                for w in range(self.n_workers)])
        discounted_gaes = discounts[:-1] * gaes

        value_error = returns - values
        value_loss = value_error.pow(2).mul(0.5).mean()
        policy_loss = -(discounted_gaes.detach() * \
                                                logpas).mean()

        entropy_loss = -entropies.mean()

        loss = self.policy_loss_weight * policy_loss + \
               self.value_loss_weight * value_loss + \
               self.entropy_loss_weight * entropy_loss

        self.ac_optimizer.zero_grad()
        loss.backward()
        torch.nn.utils.clip_grad_norm_(
            self.ac_model.parameters(),
            self.ac_model_max_grad_norm)
        self.ac_optimizer.step()
```

② The main thing to notice is now we work with matrices with vectors of time steps per worker.

③ Some operations work the same exact way, surprisingly.

④ And for some, we just need to add a loop to include all workers.

⑤ Look how we build a single loss function.

⑥ Finally, we optimize a single neural network.

IT'S IN THE DETAILS

Running all policy-gradient methods in the CartPole-v1 environment

To demonstrate the policy-gradient algorithms, and to make comparison easier with the value-based methods explored in the previous chapters, I ran experiments with the same configurations as in the value-based method experiments. Here are the details:

REINFORCE:

- Runs a policy network with 4-128-64-2 nodes, Adam optimizer, and lr 0.0007.
- Trained at the end of each episode with Monte Carlo returns. No baseline.

VPG (REINFORCE with Monte Carlo baseline):

- Same policy network as REINFORCE, but now we add an entropy term to the loss function with 0.001 weight, and clip the gradient norm to 1.
- We now learn a value function and use it as a baseline, not as a critic. This means MC returns are used without bootstrapping and the value function only reduces the scale of the returns. The value function is learned with a 4-256-128-1 network, RMSprop optimizer, and a 0.001 learning rate. No gradient clippings, though it's possible.

A3C:

- We train the policy and value networks the same exact way.
- We now bootstrap the returns every 50 steps maximum (or when landing on a terminal state). This is an actor-critic method.
- We use eight workers each with copies of the networks and doing Hogwild! updates.

GAE:

- Same exact hyperparameter as the rest of the algorithms.
- Main difference is GAE adds a tau hyperparameter to discount the advantages. We use 0.95 for tau here. Notice that the agent style has the same *n*-step bootstrapping logic, which might not make this a pure GAE implementation. Usually, you see batches of full episodes being processed at once. It still performs pretty well.

A2C:

- A2C does change most of the hyperparameters. To begin with, we have a single network: 4-256-128-3 (2 and 1). Train with Adam, lr of 0.002, gradient norm of 1.
- The policy is weighted at 1.0, value function at 0.6, entropy at 0.001.
- We go for 10-step bootstrapping, eight workers, and a 0.95 tau.

These algorithms weren't tuned independently; I'm sure they could do even better.

ⅢⅢ TALLY IT UP
Policy-gradient and actor-critic methods on the CartPole-v1 environment

(1) I ran all policy-gradient algorithms in the cart-pole environment so that you can more easily compare policy-based and value-based methods.

Moving Avg Reward (Training)

REINFORCE
VPG
A3C
GAE
A2C

400
300
200
100
0

Moving Avg Reward (Evaluation)

500
400
300
200
100
0

Total Steps

100000
80000
60000
40000
20000
0

Training Time

200
150
100
50
0

Wall-clock Time

60
40
20
0

0   100   200   300   400   500   600
Episodes

(2) One of the main things to notice is how VPG is more sample efficient than more complex methods, such as A3C or A2C. This is mostly because these two methods use multiple workers, which initially cost lots of data to get only a bit of progress.

(3) REINFORCE alone is too inefficient to be a practical algorithm.

(4) However, in terms of training time, you can see how REINFORCE uses few resources. Also, notice how algorithms with workers consume much more compute.

(5) Interestingly, in terms of wall-clock time, parallel methods and incredibly fast averaging ~10 seconds to solve cart-pole v1! The 500 steps version. Impressive!

Summary

In this chapter, we surveyed policy-gradient and actor-critic methods. First, we set up the chapter with a few reasons to consider policy-gradient and actor-critic methods. You learned that directly learning a policy is the true objective of reinforcement learning methods. You learned that by learning policies, we could use stochastic policies, which can have better performance than value-based methods in partially observable environments. You learned that even though we typically learn stochastic policies, nothing prevents the neural network from learning a deterministic policy.

You also learned about four algorithms. First, we studied REINFORCE and how it's a straightforward way of improving a policy. In REINFORCE, we could use either the full return or the reward-to-go as the score for improving the policy.

You then learned about vanilla policy gradient, also known as REINFORCE with baseline. In this algorithm, we learn a value function using Monte Carlo returns as targets. Then, we use the value function as a baseline and not as a critic. We don't bootstrap in VPG; instead, we use the reward-to-go, such as in REINFORCE, and subtract the learned value function to reduce the variance of the gradient. In other words, we use the advantage function as the policy score.

We also studied the A3C algorithm. In A3C, we bootstrap the value function, both for learning the value function and for scoring the policy. More specifically, we use n-step returns to improve the models. Additionally, we use multiple actor-learners that each roll out the policy, evaluate the returns, and update the policy and value models using a Hogwild! approach. In other words, workers update lock-free models.

We then learned about GAE, and how this is a way for estimating advantages analogous to TD(λ) and the λ-return. GAE uses an exponentially weighted mixture of all n-step advantages for creating a more robust advantage estimate that can be easily tuned to use more bootstrapping and therefore bias, or actual returns and therefore variance.

Finally, we learned about A2C and how removing the asynchronous part of A3C yields a comparable algorithm without the need for implementing custom optimizers.

By now, you

- Understand the main differences between value-based, policy-based, policy-gradient, and actor-critic methods

- Can implement fundamental policy-gradient and actor-critic methods by yourself

- Can tune policy-gradient and actor-critic algorithms to pass a variety of environments

TWEETABLE FEAT
Work on your own and share your findings

Here are several ideas on how to take what you've learned to the next level. If you'd like, share your results with the rest of the world and make sure to check out what others have done, too. It's a win-win situation, and hopefully, you'll take advantage of it.

- **#gdrl_ch11_tf01:** Earlier in this chapter I talked about a fictitious foggy lake environment, but hey, it's only fictitious because you haven't implemented it, right? Go ahead and implement a foggy lake and also a foggy frozen lake environment. For this one, make sure the observation passed to the agent is different than the actual internal state of the environment. If the agent is in cell 3, for example, the internal state is kept secret, and the agent is only able to observe that it's in a foggy cell. In this case, all foggy cells should emit the same observation, so the agent can't tell where it is. After implementing this environment, test DRL agents that can only learn deterministic policies (such as in previous chapters), and agents that can learn stochastic policies (such as in this chapter). You'll have to do one-hot encoding of the observations to pass into the neural network. Create a Python package with the environment, and a Notebook with interesting tests and results.

- **#gdrl_ch11_tf02:** In this chapter, we're still using the CartPole-v1 environment as a test bed, but you know swapping environments should be straightforward. First, test the same agents in similar environments, such as the LunarLander-v2, or MountainCar-v0. Note what makes it similar is that the observations are low dimensional and continuous, and the actions are low dimensional and discrete. Second, test them in different environments, high dimensional, or continuous observations or actions.

- **#gdrl_ch11_tf03:** In every chapter, I'm using the final hashtag as a catchall hashtag. Feel free to use this one to discuss anything else that you worked on relevant to this chapter. There is no more exciting homework than that which you create for yourself. Make sure to share what you set yourself to investigate and your results.

Write a tweet with your findings, tag me @mimoralea (I'll retweet), and use the particular hashtag from the list to help interested folks find your results. There are no right or wrong results; you share your findings and check others' findings. Take advantage of this to socialize, contribute, and get yourself out there! We're waiting for you!

Here's a tweet example:

"Hey, @mimoralea. I created a blog post with a list of resources to study deep reinforcement learning. Check it out at <link>. #gdrl_ch01_tf01"

I'll make sure to retweet and help others find your work.

In this chapter

- You will learn about more advanced deep reinforcement learning
  methods, which are, to this day, the state-of-the-art algorithmic
  advancements in deep reinforcement learning.

- You will learn about solving a variety of deep reinforcement
  learning problems, from problems with continuous action
  spaces, to problem with high-dimensional action spaces.

- You will build state-of-the-art actor-critic methods from scratch
  and open the door to understanding more advanced concepts
  related to artificial general intelligence.

> *Criticism may not be agreeable, but it is necessary.*
> *It fulfills the same function as pain in the human body.*
> *It calls attention to an unhealthy state of things.*
>
> — WINSTON CHURCHILL
> BRITISH POLITICIAN, ARMY OFFICER, WRITER, AND
> PRIME MINISTER OF THE UNITED KINGDOM

In the last chapter, you learned about a different, more direct, technique for solving deep reinforcement learning problems. You first were introduced to policy-gradient methods in which agents learn policies by approximating them directly. In pure policy-gradient methods, we don't use value functions as a proxy for finding policies, and in fact, we don't use value functions at all. We instead learn stochastic policies directly.

However, you quickly noticed that value functions can still play an important role and make policy-gradient methods better. And so you were introduced to actor-critic methods. In these methods, the agent learns both a policy and a value function. With this approach, you could use the strengths of one function approximation to mitigate the weaknesses of the other approximation. For instance, learning policy can be more straightforward in certain environments than learning a sufficiently accurate value function, because the relationships in action space may be more tightly related than the relationships of values. Still, even though knowing the values of states precisely can be more complicated, a rough approximation can be useful for reducing the variance of the policy-gradient objective. As you explored in the previous chapter, learning a value function and using it as a baseline or for calculating advantages can considerably reduce the variance of the targets used for policy-gradient updates. Moreover, reducing the variance often leads to faster learning.

However, in the previous chapter, we focused on using the value function as a critic for updating a stochastic policy. We used different targets for learning the value function and parallelized the workflows in a few different ways. However, algorithms used the learned value function in the same general way to train the policy, and the policy learned had the same properties, because it was a stochastic policy. We scratched the surface of using a learned policy and value function. In this chapter, we go deeper into the paradigm of actor-critic methods and train them in four different challenging environments: pendulum, hopper, cheetah, and lunar lander. As you soon see, in addition to being more challenging environments, most of these have a continuous action space, which we face for the first time, and it'll require using unique polices models.

To solve these environments, we first explore methods that learn deterministic policies; that is, policies that, when presented with the same state, return the same action, the action that's believed to be optimal. We also study a collection of improvements that make deterministic policy-gradient algorithms one of the state-of-the-art approaches to date for solving deep reinforcement learning problems. We then explore an actor-critic method that, instead of using the entropy in the loss function, directly uses the entropy in the value function equation. In other words, it maximizes the return along with the long-term entropy of the policy. Finally, we close with an algorithm that allows for more stable policy improvement steps by restraining the updates to the policy to small changes. Small changes in policies make policy-gradient methods show steady and often monotonic improvements in performance, allowing for state-of-the-art performance in several DRL benchmarks.

DDPG: Approximating a deterministic policy

In this section, we explore an algorithm called *deep deterministic policy gradient* (DDPG). DDPG can be seen as an approximate DQN, or better yet, a DQN for continuous action spaces. DDPG uses many of the same techniques found in DQN: it uses a replay buffer to train an action-value function in an off-policy manner, and target networks to stabilize training. However, DDPG also trains a policy that approximates the optimal action. Because of this, DDPG is a deterministic policy-gradient method restricted to continuous action spaces.

DDPG uses many tricks from DQN

Start by visualizing DDPG as an algorithm with the same architecture as DQN. The training process is similar: the agent collects experiences in an online manner and stores these online experience samples into a replay buffer. On every step, the agent pulls out a mini-batch from the replay buffer that is commonly sampled uniformly at random. The agent then uses this mini-batch to calculate a bootstrapped TD target and train a Q-function.

The main difference between DQN and DDPG is that while DQN uses the target Q-function for getting the greedy action using an argmax, DDPG uses a target deterministic policy function that is trained to approximate that greedy action. Instead of using the argmax of the Q-function of the next state to get the greedy action as we do in DQN, in DDPG, we directly approximate the best action in the next state using a policy function. Then, in both, we use that action with the Q-function to get the max value.

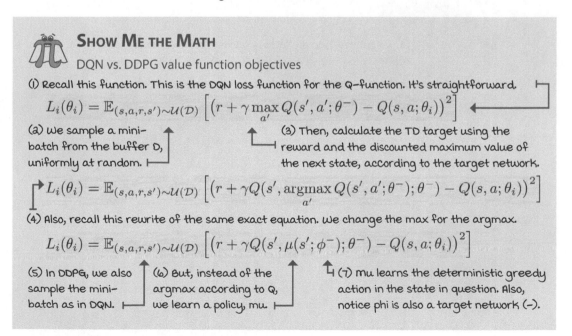

SHOW ME THE MATH

DQN vs. DDPG value function objectives

(1) Recall this function. This is the DQN loss function for the Q-function. It's straightforward.

$$L_i(\theta_i) = \mathbb{E}_{(s,a,r,s') \sim \mathcal{U}(D)} \left[\left(r + \gamma \max_{a'} Q(s', a'; \theta^-) - Q(s, a; \theta_i) \right)^2 \right]$$

(2) We sample a mini-batch from the buffer D, uniformly at random.

(3) Then, calculate the TD target using the reward and the discounted maximum value of the next state, according to the target network.

$$L_i(\theta_i) = \mathbb{E}_{(s,a,r,s') \sim \mathcal{U}(D)} \left[\left(r + \gamma Q(s', \underset{a'}{\arg\max} Q(s', a'; \theta^-); \theta^-) - Q(s, a; \theta_i) \right)^2 \right]$$

(4) Also, recall this rewrite of the same exact equation. We change the max for the argmax.

$$L_i(\theta_i) = \mathbb{E}_{(s,a,r,s') \sim \mathcal{U}(D)} \left[\left(r + \gamma Q(s', \mu(s'; \phi^-); \theta^-) - Q(s, a; \theta_i) \right)^2 \right]$$

(5) In DDPG, we also sample the mini-batch as in DQN.

(6) But, instead of the argmax according to Q, we learn a policy, mu.

(7) mu learns the deterministic greedy action in the state in question. Also, notice phi is also a target network (-).

I SPEAK PYTHON

DDPG's Q-function network

```python
class FCQV(nn.Module):
    def __init__(self,
                 input_dim,
                 output_dim,
                 hidden_dims=(32,32),
                 activation_fc=F.relu):
        super(FCQV, self).__init__()
        self.activation_fc = activation_fc

        self.input_layer = nn.Linear(input_dim, hidden_dims[0])
        self.hidden_layers = nn.ModuleList()
        for i in range(len(hidden_dims)-1):
            in_dim = hidden_dims[i]

            if i == 0:
                in_dim += output_dim

            hidden_layer = nn.Linear(in_dim, hidden_dims[i+1])
            self.hidden_layers.append(hidden_layer)

        self.output_layer = nn.Linear(hidden_dims[-1], 1)

    <...>

    def forward(self, state, action):
        x, u = self._format(state, action)
        x = self.activation_fc(self.input_layer(x))

        for i, hidden_layer in enumerate(self.hidden_layers):

            if i == 0:
                x = torch.cat((x, u), dim=1)

            x = self.activation_fc(hidden_layer(x))

        return self.output_layer(x)
```

(1) This is the Q-function network used in DDPG.

(2) Here we start the architecture as usual.

(3) Here we have the first exception. We increase the dimension of the first hidden layer by the output dimension.

(4) Notice the output of the network is a single node representing the value of the state-action pair.

(5) The forward pass starts as expected.

(6) But we concatenate the action to the states right on the first hidden layer.

(7) Then, continue as expected.

(8) Finally, return the output.

Learning a deterministic policy

Now, the one thing we need to add to this algorithm to make it work is a policy network. We want to train a network that can give us the optimal action in a given state. The network must be differentiable with respect to the action. Therefore, the action must be continuous to make for efficient gradient-based learning. The objective is simple; we can use the expected Q-value using the policy network, mu. That is, the agent tries to find the action that maximizes this value. Notice that in practice, we use minimization techniques, and therefore minimize the negative of this objective.

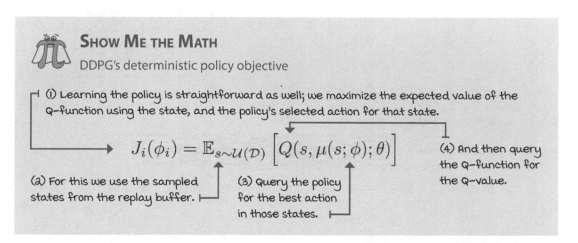

SHOW ME THE MATH

DDPG's deterministic policy objective

(1) Learning the policy is straightforward as well; we maximize the expected value of the Q-function using the state, and the policy's selected action for that state.

$$J_i(\phi_i) = \mathbb{E}_{s \sim \mathcal{U}(\mathcal{D})} \Big[Q(s, \mu(s; \phi); \theta) \Big]$$

(2) For this we use the sampled states from the replay buffer.

(3) Query the policy for the best action in those states.

(4) And then query the Q-function for the Q-value.

Also notice that, in this case, we don't use target networks, but the online networks for both the policy, which is the action selection portion, and the value function (the action evaluation portion). Additionally, given that we need to sample a mini-batch of states for training the value function, we can use these same states for training the policy network.

0001 **A BIT OF HISTORY**

Introduction of the DDPG algorithm

DDPG was introduced in 2015 in a paper titled "Continuous control with deep reinforcement learning." The paper was authored by Timothy Lillicrap (et al.) while he was working at Google DeepMind as a research scientist. Since 2016, Tim has been working as a Staff Research Scientist at Google DeepMind and as an Adjunct Professor at University College London.

Tim has contributed to several other DeepMind papers such as the A3C algorithm, AlphaGo, AlphaZero, Q-Prop, and Starcraft II, to name a few. One of the most interesting facts is that Tim has a background in cognitive science and systems neuroscience, not a traditional computer science path into deep reinforcement learning.

I SPEAK PYTHON

DDPG's deterministic policy network

```python
class FCDP(nn.Module):
    def __init__(self,
                 input_dim,
                 action_bounds,
                 hidden_dims=(32,32),
                 activation_fc=F.relu,
                 out_activation_fc=F.tanh):
        super(FCDP, self).__init__()


        self.activation_fc = activation_fc
        self.out_activation_fc = out_activation_fc
        self.env_min, self.env_max = action_bounds
```

(1) This is the policy network used in DDPG: fully connected deterministic policy.

(2) Notice the activation of the output layer is different this time. We use the tanh activation function to squash the output to (–1, 1).

(3) We need to get the minimum and maximum values of the actions, so that we can rescale the network's output (–1, 1) to the expected range.

```python
        self.input_layer = nn.Linear(input_dim, hidden_dims[0])
        self.hidden_layers = nn.ModuleList()
        for i in range(len(hidden_dims)-1):
            hidden_layer = nn.Linear(hidden_dims[i],
                                     hidden_dims[i+1])
            self.hidden_layers.append(hidden_layer)

        self.output_layer = nn.Linear(hidden_dims[-1],
                                      len(self.env_max))
```

(4) The architecture is as expected: states in, actions out.

```python
    def forward(self, state):
        x = self._format(state)
        x = self.activation_fc(self.input_layer(x))
        for hidden_layer in self.hidden_layers:
            x = self.activation_fc(hidden_layer(x))
        x = self.output_layer(x)
```

(5) The forward pass is also straightforward.

(6) Input

(7) Hidden

(8) Output

(9) Notice, however, that we activate the output using the output activation function.

```python
        x = self.out_activation_fc(x)
```

(10) Also important is that we rescale the action from the –1 to 1 range to the range specific to the environment. The rescale_fn isn't shown here, but you can go to the Notebook for details.

```python
        return self.rescale_fn(x)
```

I SPEAK PYTHON
DDPG's model-optimization step

```python
def optimize_model(self, experiences):

    states, actions, rewards, \
                next_states, is_terminals = experiences
    batch_size = len(is_terminals)
```

(1) The optimize_model function takes in a mini-batch of experiences.

(2) With it, we calculate the targets using the predicted max value of the next state, coming from the actions according to the policy and the values according to the Q-function.

```python
    argmax_a_q_sp = self.target_policy_model(next_states)
    max_a_q_sp = self.target_value_model(next_states,
                                            argmax_a_q_sp)
    target_q_sa = rewards + self.gamma * max_a_q_sp * \
                                            (1 - is_terminals)
```

(3) We then get the predictions, and calculate the error and the loss. Notice where we use the target and online networks.

```python
    q_sa = self.online_value_model(states, actions)
    td_error = q_sa - target_q_sa.detach()
    value_loss = td_error.pow(2).mul(0.5).mean()

    self.value_optimizer.zero_grad()
    value_loss.backward()
    torch.nn.utils.clip_grad_norm_(
                    self.online_value_model.parameters(),
                    self.value_max_grad_norm)
    self.value_optimizer.step()
```

(4) The optimization step is like all other networks.

(5) Next, we get the actions as predicted by the online policy for the states in the mini-batch, then use those actions to get the value estimates using the online value network.

```python
    argmax_a_q_s = self.online_policy_model(states)
    max_a_q_s = self.online_value_model(states,
                                            argmax_a_q_s)
    policy_loss = -max_a_q_s.mean()

    self.policy_optimizer.zero_grad()
    policy_loss.backward()
    torch.nn.utils.clip_grad_norm_(
                    self.online_policy_model.parameters(),
                    self.policy_max_grad_norm)
    self.policy_optimizer.step()
```

(6) Next, we get the policy loss.

(7) Finally, we zero the optimizer, do the backward pass on the loss, clip the gradients, and step the optimizer.

Exploration with deterministic policies

In DDPG, we train deterministic greedy policies. In a perfect world, this type of policy takes in a state and returns the optimal action for that state. But, in an untrained policy, the actions returned won't be accurate enough, yet still deterministic. As mentioned before, agents need to balance exploiting knowledge with exploring. But again, since the DDPG agent learns a deterministic policy, it won't explore on-policy. Imagine the agent is stubborn and always selects the same actions. To deal with this issue, we must explore off-policy. And so in DDPG, we inject Gaussian noise into the actions selected by the policy.

You've learned about exploration in multiple DRL agents. In NFQ, DQN, and so on, we use exploration strategies based on Q-values. We get the values of actions in a given state using the learned Q-function and explore based on those values. In REINFORCE, VPG, and so on, we use stochastic policies, and therefore, exploration is on-policy. That is, exploration is taken care of by the policy itself because it's stochastic; it has randomness. In DDPG, the agent explores by adding external noise to actions, using off-policy exploration strategies.

I Speak Python

Exploration in deterministic policy gradients

```python
class NormalNoiseDecayStrategy():        ← (1) This is the select_action
    def select_action(self, model,           function of the strategy.
                            state, max_exploration=False):
        if max_exploration:                  (2) To maximize exploration, we set the
            noise_scale = self.high ←        noise scale to the maximum action.
        else:
            noise_scale = self.noise_ratio * self.high
                                             (3) Otherwise, we scale the noise down.
        with torch.no_grad():
(4) We get the     greedy_action = model(state).cpu().detach().data
greedy action ⊢▶ greedy_action = greedy_action.numpy().squeeze()
straight from
the network.        (5) Next, we get the Gaussian noise for the action using the scale and 0 mean. ⊢
            noise = np.random.normal(loc=0,
    (6) Add the noise to the action,         scale=noise_scale,
    and clip it to be in range.              size=len(self.high))
            noisy_action = greedy_action + noise
            action = np.clip(noisy_action, self.low, self.high)
(7) Next, we update the noise ratio schedule. This could
be constant, or linear, exponential, and so on.
            self.noise_ratio = self._noise_ratio_update()
        return action                    ◀─── (8) Last, return the action.
```

CONCRETE EXAMPLE
The pendulum environment

The Pendulum-v0 environment consists of an inverted pendulum that the agent needs to swing up, so it stays upright with the least effort possible. The state-space is a vector of three variables (cos(theta), sin(theta), theta dot) indicating the cosine of the angle of the rod, the sine, and the angular speed.

The action space is a single continuous variable from –2 to 2, indicating the joint effort. The joint is that black dot at the bottom of the rod. The action is the effort either clockwise or counterclockwise.

The reward function is an equation based on angle, speed, and effort. The goal is to remain perfectly balanced upright with no effort. In such an ideal time step, the agent receives 0 rewards, the best it can do. The highest cost (lowest reward) the agent can get is approximately –16 reward. The precise equation is *–(theta^2 + 0.1*theta_dt^2 + 0.001*action^2)*.

This is a continuing task, so there's no terminal state. However, the environment times out after 200 steps, which serves the same purpose. The environment is considered unsolved, which means there's no target return. However, –150 is a reasonable threshold to hit.

TALLY IT UP
DDPG in the pendulum environment

(1) On the right you see the results of training DDPG until it reaches –150 reward on the evaluation episodes. We use five seeds here, but the graph is truncated at the point where the first seed's episodes end. As you can see, the algorithm does a good job quickly. Pendulum is a simple environment.

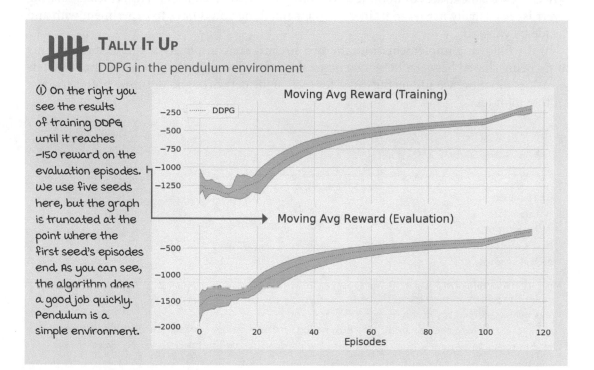

TD3: State-of-the-art improvements over DDPG

DDPG has been one of the state-of-the-art deep reinforcement learning methods for control for several years. However, there have been improvements proposed that make a big difference in performance. In this section, we discuss a collection of improvements that together form a new algorithm called *twin-delayed DDPG* (TD3). TD3 introduces three main changes to the main DDPG algorithm. First, it adds a double learning technique, similar to what you learned in double Q-learning and DDQN, but this time with a unique "twin" network architecture. Second, it adds noise, not only to the action passed into the environment but also to the target actions, making the policy network more robust to approximation error. And, third, it delays updates to the policy network, its target network, and the twin target network, so that the twin network updates more frequently.

Double learning in DDPG

In TD3, we use a particular kind of Q-function network with two separate streams that end on two separate estimates of the state-action pair in question. For the most part, these two streams are totally independent, so one can think about them as two separate networks. However, it'd make sense to share feature layers if the environment was image-based. That way CNN would extract common features and potentially learn faster. Nevertheless, sharing layers is also usually harder to train, so this is something you'd have to experiment with and decide by yourself.

In the following implementation, the two streams are completely separate, and the only thing being shared between these two networks is the optimizer. As you see in the twin network loss function, we add up the losses for each of the networks and optimize both networks on that joint loss.

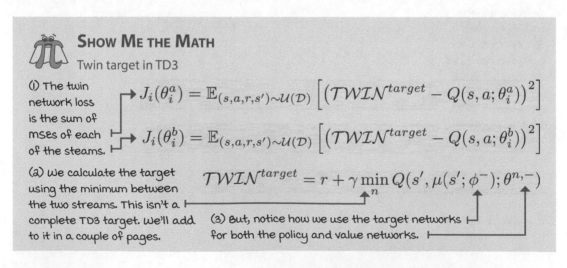

Show Me the Math

Twin target in TD3

(1) The twin network loss is the sum of MSEs of each of the steams.

$$J_i(\theta_i^a) = \mathbb{E}_{(s,a,r,s')\sim\mathcal{U}(\mathcal{D})}\left[\left(\mathcal{TWIN}^{target} - Q(s,a;\theta_i^a)\right)^2\right]$$

$$J_i(\theta_i^b) = \mathbb{E}_{(s,a,r,s')\sim\mathcal{U}(\mathcal{D})}\left[\left(\mathcal{TWIN}^{target} - Q(s,a;\theta_i^b)\right)^2\right]$$

(2) We calculate the target using the minimum between the two streams. This isn't a complete TD3 target. We'll add to it in a couple of pages.

$$\mathcal{TWIN}^{target} = r + \gamma \min_n Q(s', \mu(s';\phi^-); \theta^{n,-})$$

(3) But, notice how we use the target networks for both the policy and value networks.

I SPEAK PYTHON

TD3's twin Q-network 1/2

```python
class FCTQV(nn.Module):
    def __init__(self,
                 input_dim,
                 output_dim,
                 hidden_dims=(32,32),
                 activation_fc=F.relu):
        super(FCTQV, self).__init__()
        self.activation_fc = activation_fc
```

(1) This is the fully connected Twin Q-value network. This is what TD3 uses to approximate the Q-values, with the twin streams.

(2) Notice we have two input layers. Again, these streams are really two separate networks.

```python
        self.input_layer_a = nn.Linear(input_dim + output_dim,
                                       hidden_dims[0])
        self.input_layer_b = nn.Linear(input_dim + output_dim,
                                       hidden_dims[0])
```

(3) Next, we create hidden layers for each of the streams.

```python
        self.hidden_layers_a = nn.ModuleList()
        self.hidden_layers_b = nn.ModuleList()
        for i in range(len(hidden_dims)-1):
            hid_a = nn.Linear(hidden_dims[i], hidden_dims[i+1])
            self.hidden_layers_a.append(hid_a)
            hid_b = nn.Linear(hidden_dims[i], hidden_dims[i+1])
            self.hidden_layers_b.append(hid_b)
```

(4) And we end with two output layers, each with a single node representing the Q-value.

```python
        self.output_layer_a = nn.Linear(hidden_dims[-1], 1)
        self.output_layer_b = nn.Linear(hidden_dims[-1], 1)
```

(5) We start the forward pass, formatting the inputs to match what the network expects.

```python
    def forward(self, state, action):
        x, u = self._format(state, action)
```

(6) Next, we concatenate the state and action and pass them through each stream.

```python
        x = torch.cat((x, u), dim=1)
        xa = self.activation_fc(self.input_layer_a(x))
        xb = self.activation_fc(self.input_layer_b(x))
```

(7) Continues...

```python
        for hidden_layer_a, hidden_layer_b in zip(
                self.hidden_layers_a, self.hidden_layers_b):
```

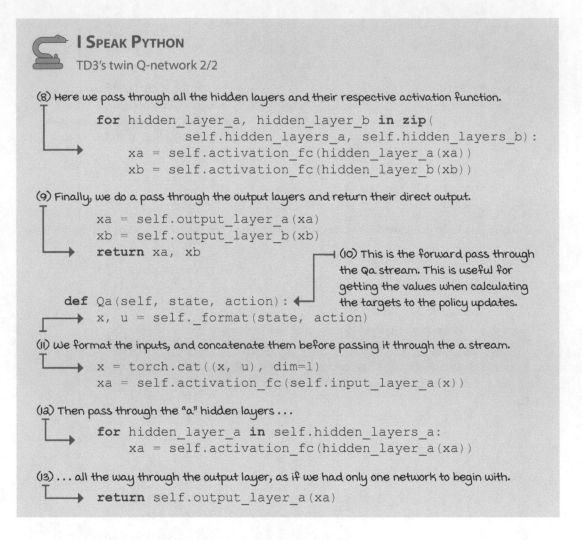

I SPEAK PYTHON

TD3's twin Q-network 2/2

(8) Here we pass through all the hidden layers and their respective activation function.

```
for hidden_layer_a, hidden_layer_b in zip(
            self.hidden_layers_a, self.hidden_layers_b):
    xa = self.activation_fc(hidden_layer_a(xa))
    xb = self.activation_fc(hidden_layer_b(xb))
```

(9) Finally, we do a pass through the output layers and return their direct output.

```
xa = self.output_layer_a(xa)
xb = self.output_layer_b(xb)
return xa, xb
```

(10) This is the forward pass through the Qa stream. This is useful for getting the values when calculating the targets to the policy updates.

```
def Qa(self, state, action):
    x, u = self._format(state, action)
```

(11) We format the inputs, and concatenate them before passing it through the a stream.

```
x = torch.cat((x, u), dim=1)
xa = self.activation_fc(self.input_layer_a(x))
```

(12) Then pass through the "a" hidden layers . . .

```
for hidden_layer_a in self.hidden_layers_a:
    xa = self.activation_fc(hidden_layer_a(xa))
```

(13) . . . all the way through the output layer, as if we had only one network to begin with.

```
return self.output_layer_a(xa)
```

Smoothing the targets used for policy updates

Remember that to improve exploration in DDPG, we inject Gaussian noise into the action used for the environment. In TD3, we take this concept further and add noise, not only to the action used for exploration, but also to the action used to calculate the targets.

Training the policy with noisy targets can be seen as a regularizer because now the network is forced to generalize over similar actions. This technique prevents the policy network from converging to incorrect actions because, early on during training, Q-functions can prematurely inaccurately value certain actions. The noise over the actions spreads that value over a more inclusive range of actions than otherwise.

SHOW ME THE MATH

Target smoothing procedure

(1) Let's consider a clamp function, which basically "clamps" or "clips" a value x between a low l, and a high h.

$$\text{clamp}(x, l, h) = \max(\min(x, h), l)$$

$$a'^{,smooth} = \text{clamp}(\mu(s'; \phi^-) + \text{clamp}(\epsilon, \epsilon\_l), \epsilon\_h), a\_l, a\_h))$$

(2) In TD3, we smooth the action by adding clipped Gaussian noise, ϵ. We first sample ϵ, and clamp it to be between a preset min and max for ϵ. We add that clipped Gaussian noise to the action, and then clamp the action to be between the min and max allowable according to the environment. Finally, we use that smoothed action.

$$\mathcal{TD3}^{target} = r + \gamma \min_n Q(s', a'^{,smooth}; \theta^{n,-})$$

I SPEAK PYTHON

TD3's model-optimization step 1/2

(1) To optimize the TD3 models, we take in a mini-batch of experiences.

```python
def optimize_model(self, experiences):
    states, actions, rewards, \
        next_states, is_terminals = experiences
    batch_size = len(is_terminals)

    with torch.no_grad():
        env_min = self.target_policy_model.env_min
        env_max = self.target_policy_model.env_max
        a_ran = env_max - env_min
        a_noise = torch.randn_like(actions) * \
                        self.policy_noise_ratio * a_ran

        n_min = env_min * self.policy_noise_clip_ratio
        n_max = env_max * self.policy_noise_clip_ratio

        a_noise = torch.max(
                        torch.min(a_noise, n_max), n_min)

        argmax_a_q_sp = self.target_policy_model(
                                        next_states)

        noisy_argmax_a_q_sp = argmax_a_q_sp + a_noise
        noisy_argmax_a_q_sp = torch.max(torch.min(
                    noisy_argmax_a_q_sp, env_max), env_min)
```

(2) We first get the min and max of the environment.

(3) Get the noise and scale it to the range of the actions.

(4) Get the noise clip min and max.

(5) Then, clip the noise.

(6) Get the action from the target policy model.

(7) Then, add the noise to the action, and clip the action, too.

I Speak Python

TD3's model-optimization step 2/2

(8) We use the clamped noisy action to get the max value. ⟶

```
noisy_argmax_a_q_sp = torch.max(torch.min(
                  noisy_argmax_a_q_sp, env_max), env_min)
max_a_q_sp_a, max_a_q_sp_b = \
        self.target_value_model(next_states,
                       noisy_argmax_a_q_sp)
```

(9) Recall we get the max value by getting the minimum predicted value between the two streams, and use it for the target.

```
max_a_q_sp = torch.min(max_a_q_sp_a, max_a_q_sp_b)
target_q_sa = rewards + self.gamma * max_a_q_sp * \
                       (1 - is_terminals)
```

(10) Next, we get the predicted values coming from both of the streams to calculate the errors and the joint loss.

```
q_sa_a, q_sa_b = self.online_value_model(states,
                                    actions)

td_error_a = q_sa_a - target_q_sa
td_error_b = q_sa_b - target_q_sa
value_loss = td_error_a.pow(2).mul(0.5).mean() + \
             td_error_b.pow(2).mul(0.5).mean()
```

```
self.value_optimizer.zero_grad()
value_loss.backward()
torch.nn.utils.clip_grad_norm_(
                self.online_value_model.parameters(),
                self.value_max_grad_norm)
self.value_optimizer.step()
```

(11) Then, we do the standard backpropagation steps for the twin networks.

(12) Notice how we delay the policy updates here. I explain this a bit more on the next page.

```
if np.sum(self.episode_timestep) % \
                self.train_policy_every_steps == 0:
```

(13) The update is similar to DDPG, but using the single stream 'Qa.'

```
argmax_a_q_s = self.online_policy_model(states)
max_a_q_s = self.online_value_model.Qa(
                       states, argmax_a_q_s)
```

(14) But, the loss is the same.

```
policy_loss = -max_a_q_s.mean()
```

(15) Here are the policy optimization steps. The standard stuff.

```
self.policy_optimizer.zero_grad()
policy_loss.backward()
torch.nn.utils.clip_grad_norm_(
                self.online_policy_model.parameters(),
                self.policy_max_grad_norm)
self.policy_optimizer.step()
```

Delaying updates

The final improvement that TD3 applies over DDPG is delaying the updates to the policy network and target networks so that the online Q-function updates at a higher rate than the rest. Delaying these networks is beneficial because often, the online Q-function changes shape abruptly early on in the training process. Slowing down the policy so that it updates after a couple of value function updates allows the value function to settle into more accurate values before we let it guide the policy. The recommended delay for the policy and target networks is every other update to the online Q-function.

The other thing that you may notice in the policy updates is that we must use one of the streams of the online value model for getting the estimated Q-value for the action coming from the policy. In TD3, we use one of the two streams, but the same stream every time.

0001 **A Bit of History**
Introduction of the TD3 agent

TD3 was introduced by Scott Fujimoto et al. in 2018 in a paper titled "Addressing Function Approximation Error in Actor-Critic Methods."

Scott is a graduate student at McGill University working on a PhD in computer science and supervised by Prof. David Meger and Prof. Doina Precup.

Concrete Example
The hopper environment

The hopper environment we use is an open source version of the MuJoCo and Roboschool Hopper environments, powered by the Bullet Physics engine. MuJoCo is a physics engine with a variety of models and tasks. While MuJoCo is widely used in DRL research, it requires a license. If you aren't a student, it can cost you a couple thousand dollars. Roboschool was an attempt by OpenAI to create open source versions of MuJoCo environments, but it was discontinued in favor of Bullet. Bullet Physics is an open source project with many of the same environments found in MuJoCo.

The HopperBulletEnv-v0 environment features a vector with 15 continuous variables as an unbounded observation space, representing the different joints of the hopper robot. It features a vector of three continuous variables bounded between –1 and 1 and representing actions for the thigh, leg, and foot joints. Note that a single action is a vector with three elements at once. The task of the agent is to move the hopper forward, and the reward function reinforces that, also promoting minimal energy cost.

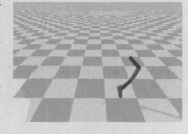

IT'S IN THE DETAILS
Training TD3 in the hopper environment

If you head to the chapter's Notebook, you may notice that we train the agent until it reaches a 1,500 mean reward for 100 consecutive episodes. In reality, the recommended threshold is 2,500. However, because we train using five different seeds, and each training run takes about an hour, I thought to reduce the time it takes to complete the Notebook by merely reducing the threshold. Even at 1,500, the hopper does a decent job of moving forward, as you can see on the GIFs in the Notebook.

Now, you must know that all the book's implementations take a long time because they execute one evaluation episode after every episode. Evaluating performance on every episode isn't necessary and is likely overkill for most purposes. For our purposes, it's okay, but if you want to reuse the code, I recommend you remove that logic and instead check evaluation performance once every 10–100 or so episodes.

Also, take a look at the implementation details. The book's TD3 optimizes the policy and the value networks separately. If you want to train using CNNs, for instance, you may want to share the convolutions and optimize all at once. But again, that would require much tuning.

TALLY IT UP
TD3 in the hopper environment

(i) TD3 does well in the hopper environment, even though this is a challenging one. You can see how the evaluation performance takes off a bit after 1,000 episodes. You should head to the Notebook and enjoy the GIFs. In particular, take a look at the progress of the agent. It's fun to see the progression of the performance.

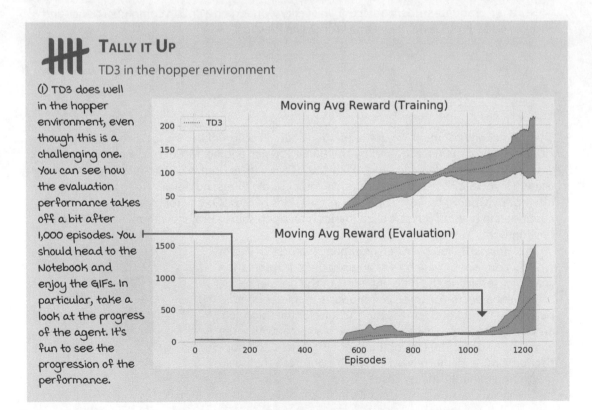

SAC: Maximizing the expected return and entropy

The previous two algorithms, DDPG and TD3, are off-policy methods that train a deterministic policy. Recall, off-policy means that the method uses experiences generated by a behavior policy that's different from the policy optimized. In the cases of DDPG and TD3, they both use a replay buffer that contains experiences generated by several previous policies. Also, because the policy being optimized is deterministic, meaning that it returns the same action every time it's queried, they both use off-policy exploration strategies. On our implementation, they both use Gaussian noise injection to the action vectors going into the environment.

To put it into perspective, the agents that you learned about in the previous chapter learn on-policy. Remember, they train stochastic policies, which by themselves introduce randomness and, therefore, exploration. To promote randomness in stochastic policies, we add an entropy term to the loss function.

In this section, we discuss an algorithm called *soft actor-critic* (SAC), which is a hybrid between these two paradigms. SAC is an off-policy algorithm similar to DDPG and TD3, but it trains a stochastic policy as in REINFORCE, A3C, GAE, and A2C instead of a deterministic policy, as in DDPG and TD3.

Adding the entropy to the Bellman equations

The most crucial characteristic of SAC is that the entropy of the stochastic policy becomes part of the value function that the agent attempts to maximize. As you see in this sectiovn, jointly maximizing the expected total reward and the expected total entropy naturally encourages behavior that's as diverse as possible while still maximizing the expected return.

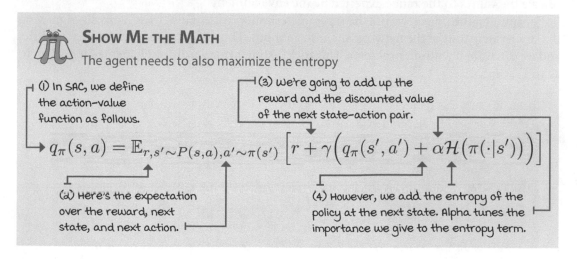

SHOW ME THE MATH
The agent needs to also maximize the entropy

(1) In SAC, we define the action–value function as follows.

(3) We're going to add up the reward and the discounted value of the next state–action pair.

$$q_\pi(s, a) = \mathbb{E}_{r, s' \sim P(s, a), a' \sim \pi(s')} \left[r + \gamma \Big(q_\pi(s', a') + \alpha \mathcal{H}\big(\pi(\cdot|s')\big) \Big) \right]$$

(2) Here's the expectation over the reward, next state, and next action.

(4) However, we add the entropy of the policy at the next state. Alpha tunes the importance we give to the entropy term.

Learning the action-value function

In practice, SAC learns the value function in a way similar to TD3. That is, we use two networks approximating the Q-function and take the minimum estimate for most calculations. A few differences, however, are that, with SAC, independently optimizing each Q-function yields better results, which is what we do. Second, we add the entropy term to the target values. And last, we don't use the target action smoothing directly as we did in TD3. Other than that, the pattern is the same as in TD3.

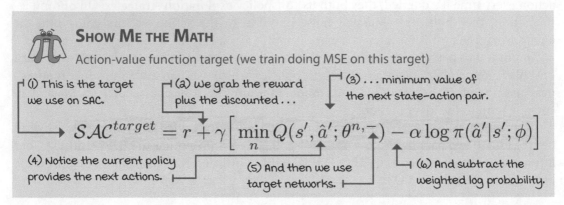

SHOW ME THE MATH

Action-value function target (we train doing MSE on this target)

(1) This is the target we use on SAC.

(2) We grab the reward plus the discounted . . .

(3) . . . minimum value of the next state–action pair.

$$\mathcal{SAC}^{target} = r + \gamma \left[\min_n Q(s', \hat{a}'; \theta^{n,-}) - \alpha \log \pi(\hat{a}'|s'; \phi) \right]$$

(4) Notice the current policy provides the next actions.

(5) And then we use target networks.

(6) And subtract the weighted log probability.

Learning the policy

This time for learning the stochastic policy, we use a squashed Gaussian policy that, in the forward pass, outputs the mean and standard deviation. Then we can use those to sample from that distribution, squash the values with a hyperbolic tangent function tanh, and then rescale the values to the range expected by the environment.

For training the policy, we use the reparameterization trick. This "trick" consists of moving the stochasticity out of the network and into an input. This way, the network is deterministic, and we can train it without problems. This trick is straightforwardly implemented in PyTorch, as you see next.

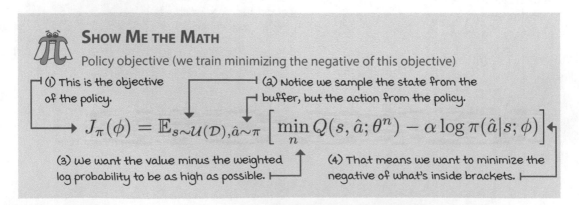

SHOW ME THE MATH

Policy objective (we train minimizing the negative of this objective)

(1) This is the objective of the policy.

(2) Notice we sample the state from the buffer, but the action from the policy.

$$J_\pi(\phi) = \mathbb{E}_{s \sim \mathcal{U}(\mathcal{D}), \hat{a} \sim \pi} \left[\min_n Q(s, \hat{a}; \theta^n) - \alpha \log \pi(\hat{a}|s; \phi) \right]$$

(3) We want the value minus the weighted log probability to be as high as possible.

(4) That means we want to minimize the negative of what's inside brackets.

Automatically tuning the entropy coefficient

The cherry on the cake of SAC is that alpha, which is the entropy coefficient, can be tuned automatically. SAC employs gradient-based optimization of alpha toward a heuristic expected entropy. The recommended target entropy is based on the shape of the action space; more specifically, the negative of the vector product of the action shape. Using this target entropy, we can automatically optimize alpha so that there's virtually no hyperparameter to tune related to regulating the entropy term.

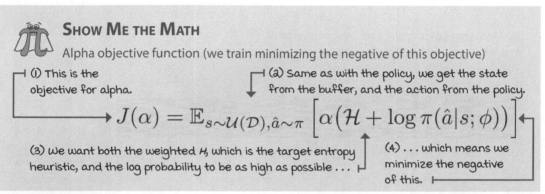

SHOW ME THE MATH

Alpha objective function (we train minimizing the negative of this objective)

(1) This is the objective for alpha.

(2) Same as with the policy, we get the state from the buffer, and the action from the policy.

$$ J(\alpha) = \mathbb{E}_{s \sim \mathcal{U}(\mathcal{D}), \hat{a} \sim \pi} \Big[\alpha \big(\mathcal{H} + \log \pi(\hat{a}|s; \phi) \big) \Big] $$

(3) We want both the weighted $\mathcal{H}$, which is the target entropy heuristic, and the log probability to be as high as possible . . .

(4) . . . which means we minimize the negative of this.

I SPEAK PYTHON

SAC Gaussian policy 1/2

```python
class FCGP(nn.Module):
    def __init__(self,
        <...>
        self.input_layer = nn.Linear(input_dim,
                                     hidden_dims[0])
        self.hidden_layers = nn.ModuleList()
        for i in range(len(hidden_dims)-1):
            hidden_layer = nn.Linear(hidden_dims[i],
                                     hidden_dims[i+1])
            self.hidden_layers.append(hidden_layer)
```

(1) This is the Gaussian policy that we use in SAC.

(2) We start everything the same way as other policy networks: input, to hidden layers.

(3) But the hidden layers connect to the two streams. One represents the mean of the action and the other the log standard deviation.

```python
        self.output_layer_mean = nn.Linear(hidden_dims[-1],
                                           len(self.env_max))

        self.output_layer_log_std = nn.Linear(
                                    hidden_dims[-1],
                                    len(self.env_max))
```

I Speak Python

SAC Gaussian policy 2/2

```python
        self.output_layer_log_std = nn.Linear(
                                        hidden_dims[-1],
                                        len(self.env_max))
```

(4) Same line to help you keep the flow of the code

(5) Here we calculate H, the target entropy heuristic.

```python
        self.target_entropy = -np.prod(self.env_max.shape)
        self.logalpha = torch.zeros(1,
```

(6) Next, we create a variable, initialize to zero,

```python
                                    requires_grad=True,
                                    device=self.device)
        self.alpha_optimizer = optim.Adam([self.logalpha],
                                        lr=entropy_lr)
```

and create an optimizer to optimize the log alpha.

(7) The forward function is what we'd expect.

```python
    def forward(self, state):
        x = self._format(state)
        x = self.activation_fc(self.input_layer(x))
        for hidden_layer in self.hidden_layers:
            x = self.activation_fc(hidden_layer(x))
        x_mean = self.output_layer_mean(x)
        x_log_std = self.output_layer_log_std(x)
        x_log_std = torch.clamp(x_log_std,
                                self.log_std_min,
                                self.log_std_max)
        return x_mean, x_log_std
```

(8) We format the input variables, and pass them through the whole network.

(9) Clamp the log std to -20 to 2, to control the std range to reasonable values.

(10) And return the values.

```python
    def full_pass(self, state, epsilon=1e-6):
        mean, log_std = self.forward(state)
```

(11) In the full pass, we get the mean and log std.

(12) Get a Normal distribution with those values.

```python
        pi_s = Normal(mean, log_std.exp())
```

(13) rsample here does the reparameterization trick.

```python
        pre_tanh_action = pi_s.rsample()
        tanh_action = torch.tanh(pre_tanh_action)
```

(14) Then we squash the action to be in range -1, 1.

```python
        action = self.rescale_fn(tanh_action)
```

(15) Then, rescale to be the environment expected range.

```python
        log_prob = pi_s.log_prob(pre_tanh_action) - torch.log(
                (1 - tanh_action.pow(2)).clamp(0, 1) + epsilon)
```

(16) We also need to rescale the log probability and the mean.

```python
        log_prob = log_prob.sum(dim=1, keepdim=True)
        return action, log_prob, self.rescale_fn(
                                        torch.tanh(mean))
```

I SPEAK PYTHON

SAC optimization step 1/2

```python
def optimize_model(self, experiences):
    states, actions, rewards, \
                    next_states, is_terminals = experiences
    batch_size = len(is_terminals)
```

(1) This is the optimization step in SAC.

(2) First, get the experiences from the mini-batch.

```python
    current_actions, \
            logpi_s, _ = self.policy_model.full_pass(states)
```

(3) Next, we get the current actions, a-hat, and log probabilities of state s.

```python
    target_alpha = (logpi_s + \
                self.policy_model.target_entropy).detach()
    alpha_loss = -(self.policy_model.logalpha * \
                                    target_alpha).mean()
```

(4) Here, we calculate the loss of alpha, and here we step alpha's optimizer.

```python
    self.policy_model.alpha_optimizer.zero_grad()
    alpha_loss.backward()
    self.policy_model.alpha_optimizer.step()
```

(5) This is how we get the current value of alpha.

```python
    alpha = self.policy_model.logalpha.exp()
```

(6) In these lines, we get the Q-values using the online models, and a-hat.

```python
    current_q_sa_a = self.online_value_model_a(
                            states, current_actions)
    current_q_sa_b = self.online_value_model_b(
                            states, current_actions)
```

(7) Then, we use the minimum Q-value estimates.

```python
    current_q_sa = torch.min(current_q_sa_a,
                            current_q_sa_b)
```

(8) Here, we calculate the policy loss using that minimum Q-value estimate.

```python
    policy_loss = (alpha * logpi_s - current_q_sa).mean()
```

(9) On the next page, we calculate the Q-functions loss.

```python
    ap, logpi_sp, _ = self.policy_model.full_pass(
                                    next_states)
```

I SPEAK PYTHON

SAC optimization step 2/2

```
        ap, logpi_sp, _ = self.policy_model.full_pass(
                                                       next_states)
```
(10) To calculate the value loss, we get the predicted next action.

(11) Using the target value models, we calculate the Q-value estimate of the next state-action pair.

```
        q_spap_a = self.target_value_model_a(next_states, ap)
        q_spap_b = self.target_value_model_b(next_states, ap)
        q_spap = torch.min(q_spap_a, q_spap_b) - \
                                               alpha * logpi_sp
```
(12) Get the minimum Q-value estimate, and factor in the entropy.

(13) This is how we calculate the target, using the reward plus the discounted minimum value of the next state along with the entropy.

```
        target_q_sa = (rewards + self.gamma * \
                          q_spap * (1 - is_terminals)).detach()
```

(14) Here we get the predicted values of the state-action pair using the online model.

```
        q_sa_a = self.online_value_model_a(states, actions)
        q_sa_b = self.online_value_model_b(states, actions)
        qa_loss = (q_sa_a - target_q_sa).pow(2).mul(0.5).mean()
        qb_loss = (q_sa_b - target_q_sa).pow(2).mul(0.5).mean()
```
(15) Calculate the loss and optimize each Q-function separately. First, *a*:
```
        self.value_optimizer_a.zero_grad()
        qa_loss.backward()
        torch.nn.utils.clip_grad_norm_(
                    self.online_value_model_a.parameters(),
                    self.value_max_grad_norm)
        self.value_optimizer_a.step()
```
(16) Then, *b*:
```
        self.value_optimizer_b.zero_grad()
        qb_loss.backward()
        torch.nn.utils.clip_grad_norm_(
                    self.online_value_model_b.parameters(),
                    self.value_max_grad_norm)
        self.value_optimizer_b.step()
```
(17) Finally, the policy:
```
        self.policy_optimizer.zero_grad()
        policy_loss.backward()
        torch.nn.utils.clip_grad_norm_(
                        self.policy_model.parameters(),
                        self.policy_max_grad_norm)
        self.policy_optimizer.step()
```

0001 A BIT OF HISTORY
Introduction of the SAC agent

SAC was introduced by Tuomas Haarnoja in 2018 in a paper titled "Soft actor-critic: Off-policy maximum entropy deep reinforcement learning with a stochastic actor." At the time of publication, Tuomas was a graduate student at Berkeley working on a PhD in computer science under the supervision of Prof. Pieter Abbeel and Prof. Sergey Levine, and a research intern at Google. Since 2019, Tuomas is a research scientist at Google DeepMind.

CONCRETE EXAMPLE
The cheetah environment

The HalfCheetahBulletEnv-v0 environment features a vector with 26 continuous variables for the observation space, representing the joints of the robot. It features a vector of 6 continuous variables bounded between −1 and 1, representing the actions. The task of the agent is to move the cheetah forward, and as with the hopper, the reward function reinforces that also, promoting minimal energy cost.

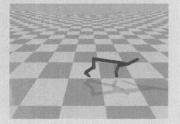

TALLY IT UP
SAC on the cheetah environment

(i) SAC does pretty well on the cheetah environment. In only ~300–600 episodes, it learns to control the robot. Notice that this environment has a recommended reward threshold of 3,000, but at 2,000 the agent does sufficiently well. Also, it already takes a few hours to train.

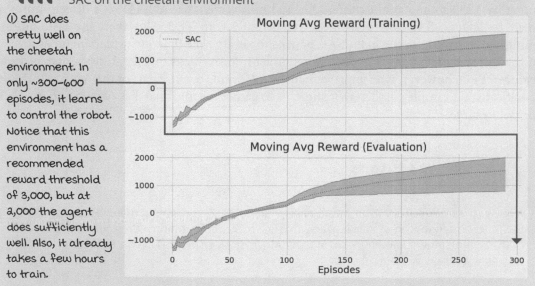

PPO: Restricting optimization steps

In this section, we introduce an actor-critic algorithm called *proximal policy optimization* (PPO). Think of PPO as an algorithm with the same underlying architecture as A2C. PPO can reuse much of the code developed for A2C. That is, we can roll out using multiple environments in parallel, aggregate the experiences into mini-batches, use a critic to get GAE estimates, and train the actor and critic in a way similar to training in A2C.

The critical innovation in PPO is a surrogate objective function that allows an on-policy algorithm to perform multiple gradient steps on the same mini-batch of experiences. As you learned in the previous chapter, A2C, being an on-policy method, cannot reuse experiences for the optimization steps. In general, on-policy methods need to discard experience samples immediately after stepping the optimizer.

However, PPO introduces a clipped objective function that prevents the policy from getting too different after an optimization step. By optimizing the policy conservatively, we not only prevent performance collapse due to the innate high variance of on-policy policy gradient methods but also can reuse mini-batches of experiences and perform multiple optimization steps per mini-batch. The ability to reuse experiences makes PPO a more sample-efficient method than other on-policy methods, such as those you learned about in the previous chapter.

Using the same actor-critic architecture as A2C

Think of PPO as an improvement to A2C. What I mean by that is that even though in this chapter we have learned about DDPG, TD3, and SAC, and all these algorithms have commonality. PPO should not be confused as an improvement to SAC. TD3 is a direct improvement to DDPG. SAC was developed concurrently with TD3. However, the SAC author published a second version of the SAC paper shortly after the first one, which includes several of the features of TD3. While SAC isn't a direct improvement to TD3, it does share several features. PPO, however, is an improvement to A2C, and we reuse part of the A2C code. More specifically, we sample parallel environments to gather the mini-batches of data and use GAE for policy targets.

0001 **A BIT OF HISTORY**
Introduction of the PPO agent

PPO was introduced by John Schulman et al. in 2017 in a paper titled "Proximal Policy Optimization Algorithms." John is a Research Scientist, a cofounding member, and the co-lead of the reinforcement learning team at OpenAI. He received his PhD in computer science from Berkeley, advised by Pieter Abbeel.

Batching experiences

One of the features of PPO that A2C didn't have is that with PPO, we can reuse experience samples. To deal with this, we could gather large trajectory batches, as in NFQ, and "fit" the model to the data, optimizing it over and over again. However, a better approach is to create a replay buffer and sample a large mini-batch from it on every optimization step. That gives the effect of stochasticity on each mini-batch because samples aren't always the same, yet we likely reuse all samples in the long term.

ꙮ I SPEAK PYTHON

Episode replay buffer 1/4

```python
class EpisodeBuffer():          ⟵      ⊢ ① This is the fill of the EpisodeBuffer class.
    def fill(self, envs, policy_model, value_model):
        states = envs.reset()                                        ⟶ ⌐
        we_shape = (n_workers, self.max_episode_steps)  ② Variables
        worker_rewards = np.zeros(shape=we_shape,         to keep
                                  dtype=np.float32)       worker
        worker_exploratory = np.zeros(shape=we_shape,     information
                                      dtype=np.bool)      grouped
        worker_steps = np.zeros(shape=(n_workers),
                                dtype=np.uint16)
        worker_seconds = np.array([time.time(),] * n_workers,
                                  dtype=np.float64)

        buffer_full = False            ⌐                ⊢ ③ Here we enter the main
        while not buffer_full and \    ↓                  loop to fill up the buffer.
                len(self.episode_steps[self.episode_steps>0]) < \
                self.max_episodes/2:
            with torch.no_grad():           ⌐ ④ We start by getting the current
                actions, logpas, \      ⟵ ⌐   actions, log probabilities, and stats.
                are_exploratory = policy_model.np_pass(states)
                values = value_model(states)
        ⑤ We pass the actions to the environments and get the experiences.
        ⌐        next_states, rewards, terminals, \
                                    infos = envs.step(actions)
⑥ Then,
store the       self.states_mem[self.current_ep_idxs,
experiences                 worker_steps] = states
into the        self.actions_mem[self.current_ep_idxs,
replay                      worker_steps] = actions
buffer. ⊢⟶      self.logpas_mem[self.current_ep_idxs,
                            worker_steps] = logpas
```

![snake icon] **I SPEAK PYTHON**

Episode replay buffer 2/4

```python
self.logpas_mem[self.current_ep_idxs,
                worker_steps] = logpas
```

⊢ (7) Same line. Also, I removed spaces to make it easier to read.

(8) We create these two variables for each worker. Remember, workers are inside environments.

```python
worker_exploratory[np.arange(self.n_workers),
                   worker_steps] = are_exploratory
worker_rewards[np.arange(self.n_workers),
               worker_steps] = rewards
```

(9) Here we manually truncate episodes that go for too many steps.

```python
for w_idx in range(self.n_workers):
    if worker_steps[w_idx] + 1 == self.max_episode_steps:
        terminals[w_idx] = 1
        infos[w_idx]['TimeLimit.truncated'] = True
```

(10) We check for terminal states and preprocess them.

```python
if terminals.sum():
    idx_terminals = np.flatnonzero(terminals)
    next_values = np.zeros(shape=(n_workers))
    truncated = self._truncated_fn(infos)
    if truncated.sum():
        idx_truncated = np.flatnonzero(truncated)
        with torch.no_grad():
            next_values[idx_truncated] = value_model(\
                next_states[idx_truncated]).cpu().numpy()
```

⊢ (11) We bootstrap iwhe terminal state was truncated.

```python
states = next_states
worker_steps += 1
```

⊢ (12) We update the states variable and increase the step count.

⊢ (13) Here we process the workers if we have terminals.

```python
if terminals.sum():
    new_states = envs.reset(ranks=idx_terminals)
    states[idx_terminals] = new_states

    for w_idx in range(self.n_workers):
        if w_idx not in idx_terminals:
            continue

    e_idx = self.current_ep_idxs[w_idx]
```

⊢ (14) We process each terminal worker one at a time.

⌇ I Speak Python

Episode replay buffer 3/4

```
e_idx = self.current_ep_idxs[w_idx]
T = worker_steps[w_idx]
self.episode_steps[e_idx] = T
```
(15) Further removed spaces

(16) Here we collect statistics to display and analyze after the fact.

```
self.episode_reward[e_idx] = worker_rewards[w_idx,:T].sum()
self.episode_exploration[e_idx] = worker_exploratory[\
                                     w_idx, :T].mean()
self.episode_seconds[e_idx] = time.time() - \
                                     worker_seconds[w_idx]
```

(17) We append the bootstrapping value to the reward vector. Calculate the predicted returns.

```
ep_rewards = np.concatenate((worker_rewards[w_idx, :T],
                            [next_values[w_idx]]))
ep_discounts = self.discounts[:T+1]
ep_returns = np.array(\
            [np.sum(ep_discounts[:T+1-t] * ep_rewards[t:]) \
                                     for t in range(T)])
self.returns_mem[e_idx, :T] = ep_returns
```

(18) Here we get the predicted values, and also append the bootstrapping value to the vector.

```
ep_states = self.states_mem[e_idx, :T]
with torch.no_grad():
    ep_values = torch.cat((value_model(ep_states),
                          torch.tensor(\
                          [next_values[w_idx]],
                          device=value_model.device,
                          dtype=torch.float32)))
```

(19) Here we calculate the generalized advantage estimators, and save them into the buffer.

```
np_ep_values = ep_values.view(-1).cpu().numpy()
ep_tau_discounts = self.tau_discounts[:T]
deltas = ep_rewards[:-1] + self.gamma * \
                          np_ep_values[1:] - np_ep_values[:-1]
gaes = np.array(\
            [np.sum(self.tau_discounts[:T-t] * deltas[t:]) \
                                     for t in range(T)])
self.gaes_mem[e_idx, :T] = gaes

worker_exploratory[w_idx, :] = 0
worker_rewards[w_idx, :] = 0
worker_steps[w_idx] = 0
worker_seconds[w_idx] = time.time()
```

(20) And start resetting all worker variables to process the next episode.

I Speak Python

Episode replay buffer 4/4

```
                            worker_seconds[w_idx] = time.time()
```

(21) Same line, indentation edited again

```
                            new_ep_id = max(self.current_ep_idxs) + 1
                            if new_ep_id >= self.max_episodes:
                                buffer_full = True
                                break
```

(22) Check which episode is next in queue and break if you have too many.

(23) If buffer isn't full, we set the id of the new episode to the worker.

```
                            self.current_ep_idxs[w_idx] = new_ep_id
```

(24) If we're in these lines, it means the episode is full, so we process the memory for sampling.

```
    ep_idxs = self.episode_steps > 0
    ep_t = self.episode_steps[ep_idxs]
```

(25) Because we initialize the whole buffer at once, we need to remove from the memory everything that isn't a number, in the episode and the steps dimensions.

```
    self.states_mem = [row[:ep_t[i]] for i, \
                    row in enumerate(self.states_mem[ep_idxs])]
    self.states_mem = np.concatenate(self.states_mem)
    self.actions_mem = [row[:ep_t[i]] for i, \
                    row in enumerate(self.actions_mem[ep_idxs])]
    self.actions_mem = np.concatenate(self.actions_mem)
    self.returns_mem = [row[:ep_t[i]] for i, \
                    row in enumerate(self.returns_mem[ep_idxs])]
    self.returns_mem = torch.tensor(np.concatenate(\
                    self.returns_mem), device=value_model.device)
    self.gaes_mem = [row[:ep_t[i]] for i, \
                    row in enumerate(self.gaes_mem[ep_idxs])]
    self.gaes_mem = torch.tensor(np.concatenate(\
                    self.gaes_mem), device=value_model.device)
    self.logpas_mem = [row[:ep_t[i]] for i, \
                    row in enumerate(self.logpas_mem[ep_idxs])]
    self.logpas_mem = torch.tensor(np.concatenate(\
                    self.logpas_mem), device=value_model.device)
```

(26) Finally, we extract the statistics to display.

```
    ep_r = self.episode_reward[ep_idxs]
    ep_x = self.episode_exploration[ep_idxs]
    ep_s = self.episode_seconds[ep_idxs]

    return ep_t, ep_r, ep_x, ep_s
```

(27) And return the stats.

Clipping the policy updates

The main issue with the regular policy gradient is that even a small change in parameter space can lead to a big difference in performance. The discrepancy between parameter space and performance is why we need to use small learning rates in policy-gradient methods, and even so, the variance of these methods can still be too large. The whole point of clipped PPO is to put a limit on the objective such that on each training step, the policy is only allowed to be so far away. Intuitively, you can think of this clipped objective as a coach preventing overreacting to outcomes. Did the team get a good score last night with a new tactic? Great, but don't exaggerate. Don't throw away a whole season of results for a new result. Instead, keep improving a little bit at a time.

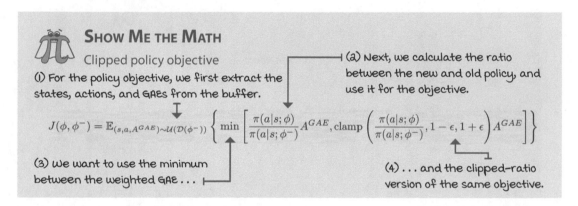

SHOW ME THE MATH
Clipped policy objective

(1) For the policy objective, we first extract the states, actions, and GAEs from the buffer.

(2) Next, we calculate the ratio between the new and old policy, and use it for the objective.

$$J(\phi, \phi^-) = \mathbb{E}_{(s,a,A^{GAE}) \sim \mathcal{U}(\mathcal{D}(\phi^-))} \left\{ \min \left[\frac{\pi(a|s;\phi)}{\pi(a|s;\phi^-)} A^{GAE}, \text{clamp}\left(\frac{\pi(a|s;\phi)}{\pi(a|s;\phi^-)}, 1-\epsilon, 1+\epsilon \right) A^{GAE} \right] \right\}$$

(3) We want to use the minimum between the weighted GAE . . .

(4) . . . and the clipped-ratio version of the same objective.

Clipping the value function updates

We can apply a similar clipping strategy to the value function with the same core concept: let the changes in parameter space change the Q-values only this much, but not more. As you can tell, this clipping technique keeps the variance of the things we care about smooth, whether changes in parameter space are smooth or not. We don't necessarily need small changes in parameter space; however, we'd like level changes in performance and values.

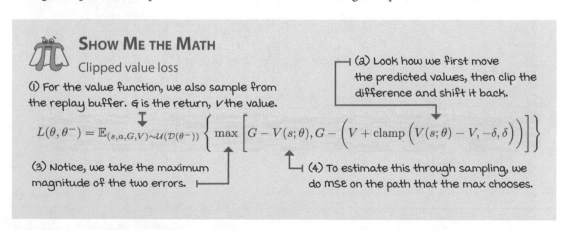

SHOW ME THE MATH
Clipped value loss

(1) For the value function, we also sample from the replay buffer. G is the return, V the value.

(2) Look how we first move the predicted values, then clip the difference and shift it back.

$$L(\theta, \theta^-) = \mathbb{E}_{(s,a,G,V) \sim \mathcal{U}(\mathcal{D}(\theta^-))} \left\{ \max \left[G - V(s;\theta), G - \left(V + \text{clamp}\left(V(s;\theta) - V, -\delta, \delta \right) \right) \right] \right\}$$

(3) Notice, we take the maximum magnitude of the two errors.

(4) To estimate this through sampling, we do MSE on the path that the max chooses.

I SPEAK PYTHON

PPO optimization step 1/3

```python
def optimize_model(self):
```
◄———┤ (1) Now, let's look at those two equations in code.

(2) First, extract the full batch of experiences from the buffer.
```python
    states, actions, returns, \
            gaes, logpas = self.episode_buffer.get_stacks()
```

(3) Get the values before we start optimizing the models.
```python
    values = self.value_model(states).detach()
```

(4) Get the gaes and normalize the batch.
```python
    gaes = (gaes - gaes.mean()) / (gaes.std() + EPS)
    n_samples = len(actions)
```

(5) Now, start optimizing the policy first for at most the preset epochs.
```python
    for i in range(self.policy_optimization_epochs):
```

(6) We sub-sample from the full batch a mini-batch.
```python
        batch_size = int(self.policy_sample_ratio * \
                                            n_samples)
        batch_idxs = np.random.choice(n_samples,
                                      batch_size,
                                      replace=False)
```

(7) Extract the mini-batch using the randomly sampled indices.
```python
        states_batch = states[batch_idxs]
        actions_batch = actions[batch_idxs]
        gaes_batch = gaes[batch_idxs]
        logpas_batch = logpas[batch_idxs]
```

(8) We use the online model to get the predictions.
```python
        logpas_pred, entropies_pred = \
                    self.policy_model.get_predictions( \
                            states_batch, actions_batch)
```

(9) Here we calculate the ratios: log probabilities to ratio of probabilities.
```python
        ratios = (logpas_pred - logpas_batch).exp()
        pi_obj = gaes_batch * ratios
```

(10) Then, calculate the objective and the clipped objective.
```python
        pi_obj_clipped = gaes_batch * ratios.clamp( \
                            1.0 - self.policy_clip_range,
                            1.0 + self.policy_clip_range)
```

I SPEAK PYTHON

PPO optimization step 2/3

```
pi_obj_clipped = gaes_batch * ratios.clamp( \
                        1.0 - self.policy_clip_range,
                        1.0 + self.policy_clip_range)
```

(11) We calculate the loss using the negative of the minimum of the objectives.

```
policy_loss = -torch.min(pi_obj,
                        pi_obj_clipped).mean()
```

(12) Also, we calculate the entropy loss, and weight it accordingly.

```
entropy_loss = -entropies_pred.mean() * \
                        self.entropy_loss_weight
```

(13) Zero the optimizing and start training.

```
self.policy_optimizer.zero_grad()
(policy_loss + entropy_loss).backward()
torch.nn.utils.clip_grad_norm_( \
                self.policy_model.parameters(),
                self.policy_model_max_grad_norm)
self.policy_optimizer.step()
```

(14) After stepping the optimizer, we do this nice trick of ensuring we only optimize again if the new policy is within bounds of the original policy.

```
with torch.no_grad():
    logpas_pred_all, _ = \
        self.policy_model.get_predictions(states,
                                          actions)
```

(15) Here we calculate the KL-divergence of the two policies.

```
kl = (logpas - logpas_pred_all).mean()
```

(16) And break out of the training loop if it's greater than a stopping condition.

```
if kl.item() > self.policy_stopping_kl:
    break
```

(17) Here, we start doing similar updates to the value function.

```
for i in range(self.value_optimization_epochs):
    batch_size = int(self.value_sample_ratio * \
                                        n_samples)
```

(18) We grab the mini-batch from the full batch, as with the policy.

```
batch_idxs = np.random.choice(n_samples,
                              batch_size,
                              replace=False)
states_batch = states[batch_idxs]
```

I SPEAK PYTHON

PPO optimization step 3/3

```
        states_batch = states[batch_idxs]
        returns_batch = returns[batch_idxs]
        values_batch = values[batch_idxs]
```

(19) Get the predicted values according to the model, and calculate the standard loss.

```
        values_pred = self.value_model(states_batch)
        v_loss = (values_pred - returns_batch).pow(2)
```

(20) Here we calculate the clipped predicted values.

```
        values_pred_clipped = values_batch + \
                    (values_pred - values_batch).clamp( \
                            -self.value_clip_range,
                            self.value_clip_range)
```

(21) Then, calculate the clipped loss.

```
        v_loss_clipped = (values_pred_clipped - \
                            returns_batch).pow(2)
```

(22) We use the MSE of the maximum between the standard and clipped loss.

```
        value_loss = torch.max(\
                    v_loss, v_loss_clipped).mul(0.5).mean()
```

(23) Finally, we zero the optimizer, backpropagate the loss, clip the gradient, and step.

```
        self.value_optimizer.zero_grad()
        value_loss.backward()
        torch.nn.utils.clip_grad_norm_( \
                        self.value_model.parameters(),
                        self.value_model_max_grad_norm)
        self.value_optimizer.step()
```

(24) We can do something similar to early stopping, but with the value function.

```
        with torch.no_grad():
            values_pred_all = self.value_model(states)
```

(25) Basically we check for the MSE of the predicted values of the new and old policies.

```
        mse = (values - values_pred_all).pow(2)
        mse = mse.mul(0.5).mean()
        if mse.item() > self.value_stopping_mse:
            break
```

CONCRETE EXAMPLE
The LunarLander environment

Unlike all the other environments we have explored in this chapter, the LunarLander environment features a discrete action space. Algorithms, such as DDPG and TD3, only work with continuous action environments, whether single-variable, such as pendulum, or a vector, such as in hopper and cheetah. Agents such as DQN only work in discrete action-space environments, such as the cart-pole. Actor-critic methods such as A2C and PPO have a big plus, which is that you can use stochastic policy models that are compatible with virtually any action space.

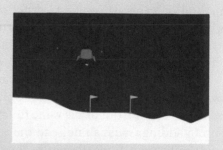

In this environment, the agent needs to select one out of four possible actions on every step. That is 0 for do nothing; or 1 for fire the left engine; or 2 for fire the main engine; or 3 for fire the right engine. The observation space is a vector with eight elements, representing the coordinates, angles, velocities, and whether its legs touch the ground. The reward function is based on distance from the landing pad and fuel consumption. The reward threshold for solving the environment is 200, and the time step limit is 1,000.

╫╫╫ TALLY IT UP
PPO in the LunarLander environment

(i) The environment isn't a difficult environment, and PPO, being a great algorithm, solves it in 10 minutes or so. You may notice the curves aren't continuous. This is because in this algorithm, we only run an evaluation step after each episode batch collection.

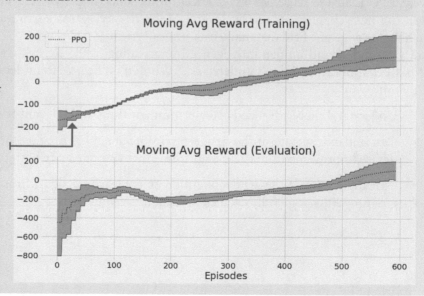

Summary

In this chapter, we surveyed the state-of-the-art actor-critic and deep reinforcement learning methods in general. You first learned about DDPG methods, in which a deterministic policy is learned. Because these methods learn deterministic policies, they use off-policy exploration strategies and update equations. For instance, with DDPG and TD3, we inject Gaussian noise into the action-selection process, allowing deterministic policies to become exploratory.

In addition, you learned that TD3 improves DDPG with three key adjustments. First, TD3 uses a double-learning technique similar to that of DDQN, in which we "cross-validate" the estimates coming out of the value function by using a twin Q-network. Second, TD3, in addition to adding Gaussian noise to the action passed into the environment, also adds Gaussian noise to target actions, to ensure the policy does not learn actions based on bogus Q-value estimates. Third, TD3 delays the updates to the policy network, so that the value networks get better estimates before we use them to change the policy.

We then explored an entropy-maximization method called SAC, which consists of maximizing a joint objective of the value function and policy entropy, which intuitively translates into getting the most reward with the most diverse policy. The SAC agent, similar to DDPG and TD3, learns in an off-policy way, which means these agents can reuse experiences to improve policies. However, unlike DDPG and TD3, SAC learns a stochastic policy, which implies exploration can be on-policy and embedded in the learned policy.

Finally, we explored an algorithm called PPO, which is a more direct descendant of A2C, being an on-policy learning method that also uses an on-policy exploration strategy. However, because of a clipped objective that makes PPO improve the learned policy more conservatively, PPO is able to reuse past experiences for its policy-improvement steps.

In the next chapter, we review several of the research areas surrounding DRL that are pushing the edge of a field that many call *artificial general intelligence* (AGI). AGI is an opportunity to understand human intelligence by recreating it. Physicist Richard Feynman said, "What I cannot create, I don't understand." Wouldn't it be nice to understand intelligence?

By now, you

- Understand more advanced actor-critic algorithms and relevant tricks

- Can implement state-of-the-art deep reinforcement learning methods and perhaps devise improvements to these algorithms that you can share with others

- Can apply state-of-the-art deep reinforcement learning algorithms to a variety of environments, hopefully even environments of your own

TWEETABLE FEAT

Work on your own and share your findings

Here are several ideas on how to take what you've learned to the next level. If you'd like, share your results with the rest of the world and make sure to check out what others have done, too. It's a win-win situation, and hopefully, you'll take advantage of it.

- **#gdrl_ch12_tf01:** Pick a continuous action-space environment and test all of the agents you learned about in this chapter in that same environment. Notice that you'll have to change PPO for this. But, it's worth learning how these algorithms compare.

- **#gdrl_ch12_tf02:** Grab PPO, and add it to the previous chapter's Notebook. Test it in similar environments and compare the results. Notice that this implementation of PPO buffers some experiences before it does any updates. Make sure to adjust the code or hyperparameters to make the comparison fair. How does PPO compare? Make sure to also test on a more challenging environment than cart-pole!

- **#gdrl_ch12_tf03:** There are other maximum-entropy deep reinforcement learning methods, such as soft Q-learning. Find a list of algorithms that implement this maximum-entropy objective, pick one of them, and implement it yourself. Test it and compare your implementation with other agents, including SAC. Create a blog post explaining the pros and cons of these kinds of methods.

- **#gdrl_ch12_tf04:** Test all the algorithms in this chapter in a high-dimensional observation-space environment that also has continuous action space. Check out the car-racing environment (https://gym.openai.com/envs/CarRacing-v0/), for instance. Any other like that one would do. Modify the code so agents learn in these.

- **#gdrl_ch12_tf05:** In every chapter, I'm using the final hashtag as a catchall hashtag. Feel free to use this one to discuss anything else that you worked on relevant to this chapter. There's no more exciting homework than that which you create for yourself. Make sure to share what you set yourself to investigate and your results.

Write a tweet with your findings, tag me @mimoralea (I'll retweet), and use the particular hashtag from the list to help interested folks find your results. There are no right or wrong results; you share your findings and check others' findings. Take advantage of this to socialize, contribute, and get yourself out there! We're waiting for you!

Here's a tweet example:

"Hey, @mimoralea. I created a blog post with a list of resources to study deep reinforcement learning. Check it out at <link>. #gdrl_ch01_tf01"

I'll make sure to retweet and help others find your work.

In this chapter

- You will look back at the algorithms you learned in this book, as well as learn about deep reinforcement learning methods that weren't covered in depth.

- You will learn about advanced deep reinforcement learning techniques that, when combined, allow agents to display more general intelligence.

- You will get my parting advice on how to follow your dreams and contribute to these fabulous fields of artificial intelligence and deep reinforcement learning.

> " *Our ultimate objective is to make programs that learn from their experience as effectively as humans do.* "
>
> — JOHN MCCARTHY
> FOUNDER OF THE FIELD OF ARTIFICIAL INTELLIGENCE
> INVENTOR OF THE LISP PROGRAMMING LANGUAGE

In this book, we have surveyed a wide range of decision-making algorithms and reinforcement learning agents; from the planning methods that you learned about in chapter 3 to the state-of-the-art deep reinforcement learning agents that we covered in the previous chapter. The focus of this book is to teach the ins and outs of the algorithms; however, there's more to DRL than what we covered in this book, and I want you to have some direction going forward.

I designed this chapter to hit a couple of points. In the first section, we recap the entire book. I'd like you to zoom out and look at the big picture again. I want you to see what you've learned so that you can choose for yourself where to go next. I also mention several of the notable types of agents that I couldn't cover before I ran out of pages. But, know that while there are more types of algorithms, what you learned in this book covers the foundational methods and concepts.

After going over what was covered and what wasn't, I introduce several of the more advanced research areas in DRL that may lead to the eventual creation of artificial general intelligence (AGI). I know AGI is a hot topic, and lots of people use it in a deceiving way. Being such an exciting and controversial topic, people use it to get attention. Don't give your energy to those folks; don't be misled; don't get distracted. Instead, focus on what matters, what's right in front of you. And make progress toward your goals, whatever they may be.

I do believe humans can create AGI because we'll keep trying forever. Understanding intelligence and automating tasks is a quest we've been longing for and working on for centuries, and that's never going to change. We try to understand intelligence through philosophy and the understanding of the self. We look for answers about intelligence through introspection. I would argue that most AI researchers are part-time philosophers themselves. They use what they've learned in reinforcement learning to better themselves and the other way around, too.

Also, humans love automation; that's what intelligence has allowed us to do. We're going to continue trying to automate life, and we'll get there. Now, while we can argue whether AGI is the beginning of human-like robots that overtake the world, today, we still cannot train a single agent to play all Atari games at a super-human level. That is, a single trained agent cannot play all games, though a single general-purpose algorithm can be trained independently. But, we should be cautious when considering AGI.

To close the chapter and the book, I provide ideas for you going forward. I receive many questions regarding applying DRL to custom problems, environments of your own. I do this for a living on my full-time job, so I can share my two cents as to how to go about it. I also give career advice for those interested, and a parting message. It's one more chapter: let's do this.

What was covered and what notably wasn't?

This book covers most of the foundations of deep reinforcement learning, from MDPs and their inner workings to state-of-the-art actor-critic algorithms and how to train them in complex environments. Deep reinforcement learning is an active research field in which new algorithms are published every month. The field is advancing at a rapid pace, and it's unfortunately not possible to provide high-quality explanations for everything there is in a single book.

Thankfully, most of the things left out are advanced concepts that aren't required in most applications. That doesn't mean that they aren't relevant; I highly recommend you continue the journey of learning DRL. You can count on me to help along the way; I'm easy to find. For now, though, of the things left out of this book, I only consider two essential; they're model-based deep reinforcement learning methods and derivative-free optimization methods.

In this section, we quickly review the algorithms and methods that you learned about in this book and touch on these two essential methods that were notably missing.

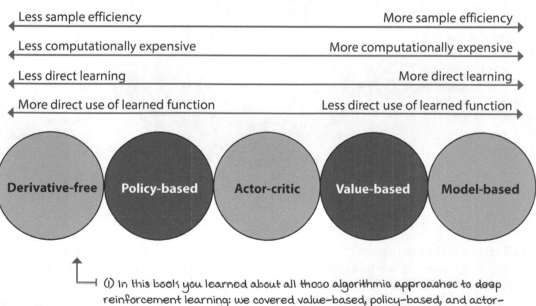

Comparison of different algorithmic approaches to deep reinforcement learning

① In this book you learned about all those algorithmic approaches to deep reinforcement learning: we covered value-based, policy-based, and actor-critic methods in depth. And later in this chapter, I introduce model-based and derivative-free methods to paint the full picture for you.

Markov decision processes

The first two chapters were an introduction to the field of reinforcement learning and to the way we describe the problems we're trying to solve. MDPs are an essential concept to have in mind, and even if they look simple and limited, they're powerful. There's much more we could have explored in this area. The thing I want you to take from these concepts is the ability to think of problems as MDPs. Practice this yourself. Think about a problem, and break it down into states, observations, actions, and all the components that would make that problem an MDP.

The transition function of the frozen lake environment

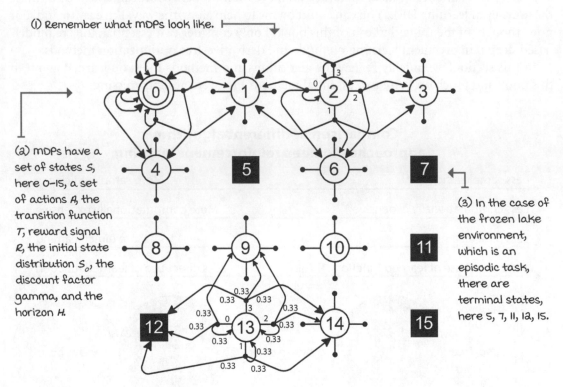

(1) Remember what MDPs look like.

(2) MDPs have a set of states S, here 0–15, a set of actions A, the transition function T, reward signal R, the initial state distribution S_0, the discount factor gamma, and the horizon H.

(3) In the case of the frozen lake environment, which is an episodic task, there are terminal states, here 5, 7, 11, 12, 15.

You'll notice that even though it seems the world is non-stationary and non-Markovian, we can transform some of the things that make it seem that way, and then see the world as an MDP. Do the probability distributions of the real world change, or is it that we don't have enough data to determine the actual distributions? Does the future depend on past states, or is the state space so high-dimensional that we can't conceive all history of the world being part of a single state? Again, as an exercise, think of problems and try to fit them into this MDP framework. It may turn out to be useful if you want to apply DRL to your problems.

Planning methods

In the third chapter, we discussed methods that help you find optimal policies of problems that have MDPs available. These methods, such as value iteration and policy iteration, iteratively compute the optimal value functions, which in turn allow extracting optimal policies quickly. Policies are nothing but universal plans—a plan for every situation.

Policy evaluation on the always-left policy on the SWF environment

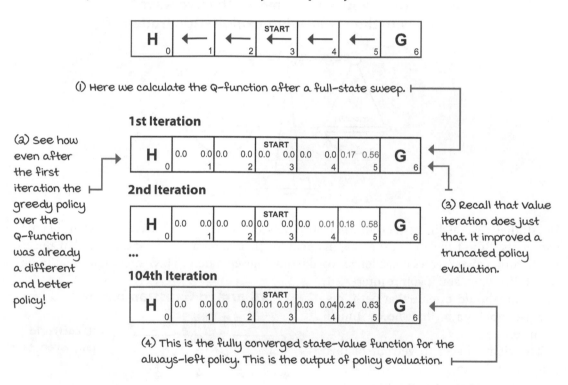

(1) Here we calculate the Q-function after a full-state sweep.

(2) See how even after the first iteration the greedy policy over the Q-function was already a different and better policy!

(3) Recall that value iteration does just that. It improved a truncated policy evaluation.

(4) This is the fully converged state-value function for the always-left policy. This is the output of policy evaluation.

The two most important takeaways from this section are first. These algorithms isolate sequential decision-making problems. There's no uncertainty because they require the MDP, and there's no complexity because they only work for discrete state and action spaces. Second, there's a general pattern to see here; we're interested in evaluating behaviors, perhaps as much as we're interested in improving them. This realization was something I didn't get for some time. To me, improving, optimizing sounded more interesting, so policy evaluation methods didn't get my attention. But you later understand that if you get evaluation right, improving is a piece of cake. The main challenge is usually evaluating policies accurately and precisely. But, if you have the MDP, you calculate these values correctly and straightforwardly.

Bandit methods

The fourth chapter was about learning from evaluative feedback. In this case, we learned about the uncertainty aspect of reinforcement learning by taking the MDP away. We hide the MDP, but make the MDP super simple; a single-state single-step horizon MDP, in which the challenge is to find the optimal action or action distribution in the fewest number of episodes; that is, minimizing total regret.

In chapter 4, you learned more effective ways for dealing with the exploration-exploitation trade-off

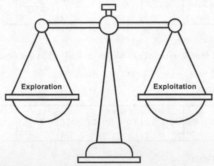

We studied several different exploration strategies and tested them in a couple of bandit environments. But at the end of the day, my goal for that chapter was to show you that uncertainty on its own creates a challenge worth studying separately. There are a few great books about this topic, and if you're interested in it, you should pursue that path; it's a reasonable path that needs much attention.

The right nugget to get out of this chapter and into reinforcement learning is that reinforcement learning is challenging because we don't have access to the MDP, as in the planning methods in chapter 3. Not having the MDP creates uncertainty, and we can only solve uncertainty with exploration. Exploration strategies are the reason why our agents can learn on their own, by trial-and-error learning, and it's what makes this field exciting.

10-armed Gaussian bandits

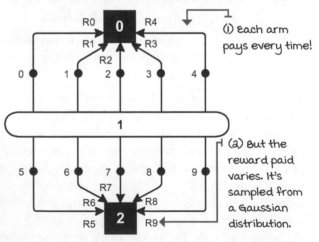

Tabular reinforcement learning

Chapters 5, 6, and 7 are all about mixing the sequential and uncertain aspects of reinforcement learning. Sequential decision-making problems under uncertainty are at the core of reinforcement learning when presented in a way that can be more easily studied; that is, without the complexity of large and high-dimensional state or action spaces.

Chapter 5 was about evaluating policies, chapter 6 was about optimizing policies, and chapter 7 was about advanced techniques for evaluating and optimizing policies. To me, this is the core of reinforcement learning, and learning these concepts well helps you understand deep reinforcement learning more quickly. Don't think of DRL as something separate from tabular reinforcement learning; that's the wrong thinking. Complexity is only one dimension of the problem, but it's the same exact problem. You often see top, deep reinforcement learning–research labs releasing papers solving problems in discrete state and action spaces. There's no shame in that. That's often the smart approach, and you should have that in mind when you experiment. Don't start with the highest-complexity problem; instead, isolate, then tackle, and finally, increase complexity.

In these three chapters, we covered a wide variety of algorithms. We covered evaluation methods such as first-visit and every-visit Monte Carlo prediction, temporal-difference prediction, n-step TD, and TD(λ). We also covered control methods such as first-visit and every-visit Monte Carlo control, SARSA, Q-learning, double Q-learning, and more advanced methods, such as SARSA(λ) and Q(λ) both with replacing and also with accumulating traces. We also covered model-based approaches, such as Dyna-Q and trajectory sampling.

Deep reinforcement learning is part of the larger field of reinforcement learning

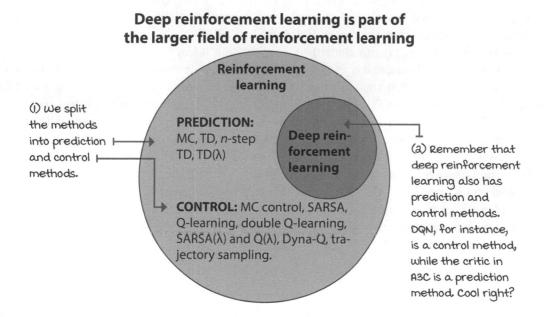

Value-based deep reinforcement learning

Chapters 8, 9, and 10 are all about the nuances of value-based deep reinforcement learning methods. We touched on neural fitted Q-iteration (NFQ), deep Q-networks (DQN), double deep Q-networks (DDQN), dueling architecture in DDQN (dueling DDQN), and prioritized experience replay (PER). We started with DQN and added improvements to this baseline method one at a time. We tested all algorithms in the cart-pole environment.

There are many more improvements that one can implement to this baseline algorithm, and I recommend you try that. Check out an algorithm called Rainbow, and implement some of the improvements to DQN not in this book. Create a blog post about it and share it with the world. Techniques you learn when implementing value-based deep reinforcement learning methods are essential to other deep reinforcement learning approaches, including learning critics in actor-critic methods. There are a many improvements and techniques to discover. Keep playing around with these methods.

Policy-based and actor-critic deep reinforcement learning

Chapter 11 was an introduction to policy-based and actor-critic methods. Policy-based was a new approach to reinforcement learning at that point in the book, so we introduced the concepts in a straightforward algorithm known as REINFORCE, which only parameterizes the policy. For this, we approximated the policy directly and didn't use any value function at all. The signal that we use to optimize the policy in REINFORCE is the Monte Carlo return, the actual returns experienced by the agent during an episode.

We then explored an algorithm that learns a value function to reduce the variance of the MC return. We called this algorithm vanilla policy gradient (VPG). The name is somewhat arbitrary, and perhaps a better name would have been *REINFORCE with Baseline*. Nevertheless, it's important to note that this algorithm, even though it learns a value function, is not an actor-critic method because it uses the value function as a baseline and not as a critic. The crucial insight here is that we don't use the value function for bootstrapping purposes, and because we also train the value-function model using MC returns, there's minimal bias in it. The only bias in the algorithm is the bias introduced by the neural network, nothing else.

Then, we covered more advanced actor-critic methods that do use bootstrapping. A3C, which uses *n*-step returns; GAE, which is a form of lambda return for policy updates; and A2C, which uses synchronous updates to the policy. Overall, these are state-of-the-art methods, and you should know that they're reliable methods that are still widely used. One of the main advantages and unique characteristics of A3C, for instance, is that it only needs CPUs, and can train faster than other methods, if you lack a GPU.

Advanced actor-critic techniques

Even though A3C, GAE, and A2C, are actor-critic methods, they don't use the critic in unique ways. In chapter 12, we explored methods that do. For instance, many people consider DDPG and TD3 actor-critic methods, but they fit better as value-based methods for continuous action spaces. If you look at the way A3C uses the actor and the critic, for instance, you find substantial differences in DDPG. Regardless, DDPG and TD3 are state-of-the-art methods, and whether actor-critic or not, it doesn't make much of a difference when solving a problem. The main caveat is that these two methods can only solve continuous action-space environments. They could be high-dimensional action spaces, but the actions must be continuous. Other methods, such as A3C, can solve both continuous and discrete action spaces.

SAC is an animal of its own. The only reason why it follows after DDPG and TD3 is because SAC uses many of the same techniques as DDPG and TD3. But the unique characteristic of SAC is that it's an entropy-maximization method. The value function maximizes not only the return but also the entropy of the policy. These kinds of methods are promising, and I wouldn't be surprised to see new state-of-the-art methods that derive from SAC.

Finally, we looked at another exciting kind of actor-critic method with PPO. PPO is an actor-critic method, and you probably notice that because we reused much of the code from A3C. The critical insight with PPO is the policy update step. In short, PPO improves the policy a bit at a time; we make sure the policy doesn't change too much with an update. You can think of it as a conservative policy-optimization method. PPO can be easily applied to both continuous and discrete action spaces, and PPO is behind some of the most exciting results in DRL, such as OpenAI Five, for instance.

We covered many great methods throughout these chapters, but more importantly, we covered the foundational methods that allow you to understand the field going forward. Many of the algorithms out there derive from the algorithms we covered in this book, with a few exceptions, namely, model-based deep reinforcement learning methods, and derivative-free optimization methods. In the next two sections, I give insights into what these methods are so that you can continue your journey exploring deep reinforcement learning.

DRL algorithms in this book

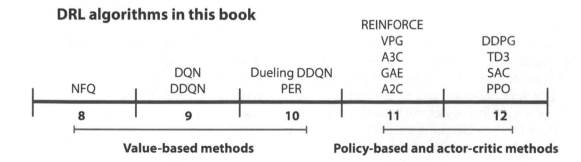

Model-based deep reinforcement learning

In chapter 7, you learned about model-based reinforcement learning methods such as Dyna-Q and trajectory sampling. Model-based deep reinforcement learning is, at its core, what you'd expect; the use of deep learning techniques for learning the transition, the reward function, or both, and then using that for decision making. As with the methods you learned about in chapter 7, one of the significant advantages of model-based deep reinforcement learning is sample efficiency; model-based methods are the most sample efficient in reinforcement learning.

**Model-based reinforcement
learning algorithms to have in mind**

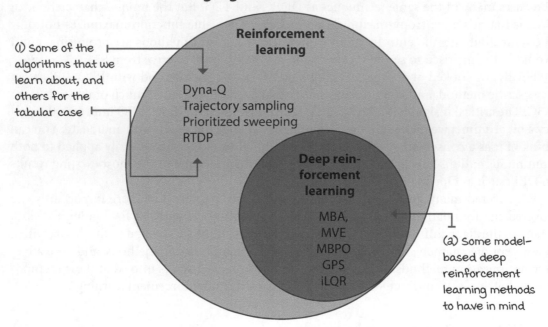

(1) Some of the algorithms that we learn about, and others for the tabular case

Reinforcement learning

Dyna-Q
Trajectory sampling
Prioritized sweeping
RTDP

Deep rein-forcement learning

MBA,
MVE
MBPO
GPS
iLQR

(2) Some model-based deep reinforcement learning methods to have in mind

In addition to sample efficiency, another inherent advantage of using model-based methods is transferability. Learning a model of the dynamics of the world can help you achieve different related tasks. For instance, if you train an agent to control a robotic arm to reach an object, a model-based agent that learns how the environment reacts to the agent's attempts to move toward the object might more easily learn to pick up that object in a later task. Notice that, in this case, learning a model of the reward function isn't useful for transfer. However, learning how the environment reacts to its motion commands is transferable knowledge that can allow the accomplishment of other tasks. Last time I checked, the laws of physics hadn't been updated for hundreds of years—talk about a slow-moving field!

A couple of other pluses worth mentioning follow. First, learning a model is often a supervised-learning task, which is much more stable and well-behaved than reinforcement learning. Second, if we have an accurate model of the environment, we can use theoretically grounded algorithms for planning, such as trajectory optimization, model-predictive control, or even heuristic search algorithms, such as Monte Carlo tree search. Last, by learning a model, we make better use of experiences overall because we extract the most information from the environment, which means more possibilities for better decisions.

But it isn't all roses; model-based learning is also challenging. There are a few disadvantages to have in mind when using model-based methods. First, learning a model of the dynamics of an environment, in addition to a policy, a value function, or both, is more computationally expensive. And if you were to learn only a model of the dynamics, then the compounding of model error from the model would make your algorithm impractical.

Not all aspects of the dynamics are directly beneficial to the policy. We covered this issue when arguing for learning a policy directly instead of learning a value function. Imagine a pouring task; if you need first to learn fluid dynamics, the viscosity of fluids, and fluid flow when you only want to pick up a cup and pour, then we're overcomplicating the task. Trying to learn a model of the environment is more complicated than learning the policy directly.

It's essential to recall that deep learning models are data hungry. As you know, to get the best out of a deep neural network, you need lots of data, and this is a challenge for model-based deep reinforcement learning methods. The problem compounds with the fact that it's also hard to estimate model uncertainty in neural networks. And so, given that a neural network tries to generalize, regardless of model uncertainty, you can end up with long-term predictions that are total garbage.

This issue makes the argument that model-based methods are the most sample efficient questionable because you may end up needing more data to learn a useful model than the data you need for learning a good policy under model-free methods. However, if you have that model, or acquire the model independently of the task, then you can reuse that model for other tasks. Additionally, if you were to use "shallow" models, such as Gaussian processes, or Gaussian mixture models, then we're back at square one, having model-based methods as the most sample efficient.

I'd like you to move from this section, knowing that it isn't about model-based versus model-free. And even though you can combine model-based and model-free methods and get attractive solutions, at the end of the day, engineering isn't about that either, the same way that it isn't a matter of value-based versus policy-based, and it also isn't actor-critic. You don't want to use a hammer when you need a screwdriver. My job is to describe what each type of algorithm is suitable for, but it's up to you to use that knowledge the right way. Of course, explore, have fun, that matters, but, when it's time to solve a problem, pick wisely.

Derivative-free optimization methods

Deep learning is the use of multi-layered function approximators to learn a function. A traditional deep learning use case goes as follows. First, we create a parametric model that mirrors a function of interest. Then, we define an objective function to know how wrong the model is at any given time. Next, we iteratively optimize the model by calculating where to move the parameters, using backpropagation. And finally, we update the parameters, using gradient descent.

Backpropagation and gradient descent are practical algorithms for optimizing neural networks. These methods are valuable for finding the lowest or highest point of a function within a given range; for instance, a local optimum of the loss or objective function. But, interestingly, they aren't the only way of optimizing parametric models, such as deep neural networks, and, more importantly, they aren't always the most effective.

Derivative-free optimization, such as genetic algorithms or evolution strategies, is a different model-optimization technique that has gotten attention from the deep reinforcement learning community in recent years. Derivative-free methods, which are also known as gradient-free, black-box, and zeroth-order methods, don't require derivatives and can be useful in situations in which gradient-based optimization methods suffer. Gradient-based optimization methods suffer when optimizing discrete, discontinuous, or multi-model functions, for instance.

Derivative-free methods can be useful and straightforward in many cases. Even randomly perturbing the weights of a neural network, if given enough compute, can get the job done. The main advantage of derivative-free methods is that they can optimize an arbitrary function. They don't need gradients to work. Another advantage is that these methods are straightforward to parallelize. It's not uncommon to hear hundreds or thousands of CPUs used with derivative-free methods. On the flip side, it's good that they're easy to parallelize because they're sample inefficient. Being black-box optimization methods, they don't exploit the structure of the reinforcement learning problem. They ignore the sequential nature of reinforcement learning problems, which can otherwise give valuable information to optimization methods.

Derivative-free methods are an extreme case

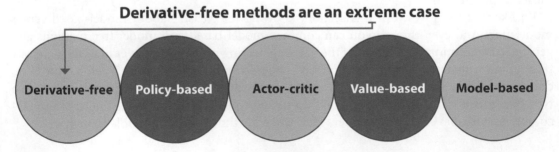

MIGUEL'S ANALOGY

How derivative-free methods work

To get an intuitive sense of how gradient-based and gradient-free methods compare, imagine for a second the game of Hot and Cold. Yeah, that game kids play in which one kid, the hunter, is supposed to find a hidden object of interest, while the rest of the kids, who know where the object is, yell "cold" if the hunter is far from the object, and "hot" if the hunter is close to it. In this analogy, the location of the hunter is the parameters of the neural network. The hidden object of interest is the global optimum, which is either the lowest value of the loss function to minimize or the highest value of the objective function to maximize. The intent is to optimize the distance between the hunter and the object. For this, in the game, you use the kids yelling "cold" or "hot" to optimize the hunter's position.

Here's when this analogy gets interesting. Imagine you have kids who, in addition to yelling "cold" or "hot," get louder as the hunter gets closer to the object. You know, kids get excited too quickly and can't keep a secret. As you hear them go from saying "cold" softly to getting louder every second, you know, as the hunter, you're walking in the right direction. The distance can be minimized using that "gradient" information. The use of this information for getting to the object of interest is what gradient-based methods do. If the information comes in a continuous form, meaning the kids yell a couple of times per second, and get louder or softer and go from yelling "cold" to yelling "hot" with distance, then you can use the increase or decrease in the magnitude of the information, which is the gradient, to get to the object. Great!

On the other hand, imagine the kids yelling the information are mean, or maybe just not perfect. Imagine they give discontinuous information. For instance, they may not be allowed to say anything while the hunter is in certain areas. They go from "softly cold" to nothing for a while to "softly cold" again. Or perhaps, imagine the object is right behind the middle of a long wall. Even if the hunter gets close to the object, the hunter won't be able to reach the object with gradient information. The hunter would be close to the object, so the right thing to yell is "hot," but in reality, the object is out of reach behind a wall. In all these cases, perhaps a gradient-based optimization approach isn't the best strategy, and gradient-free methods, even if moving randomly, may be better for finding the object.

A gradient-free method approach could be as simple as that. The hunter would pick a random place to go and ignore "gradient" information while getting there, then check with the yelling kids, and then try another random position. After getting an idea of a few random positions, say, 10, the hunter would take the top 3 and try random variations from those 3 that are apparently better locations. In this case, gradient information isn't useful.

Trust me, this analogy can keep going, but I'm going to stop it there. The bottom line is gradient-based and gradient-free methods are only strategies for reaching a point of interest. The effectiveness of these strategies depends on the problem at hand.

More advanced concepts toward AGI

In the previous section, we reviewed the foundational concepts of deep reinforcement learning that are covered in this book and touched on the two essential types of methods that we didn't cover in depth. But, as I mentioned before, there are still many advanced concepts that, even though not required for an introduction to deep reinforcement learning, are crucial for devising artificial general intelligence (AGI), which is the ultimate goal for most AI researchers.

In this section, we start by going one step deeper into AGI and argue for some of the traits AI agents need to tackle tasks requiring more-general intelligence. I explain at a high level what these traits are and their intent so that you can continue your journey studying AI and perhaps one day contribute to one of these cutting-edge research fields.

What is AGI, again?

In this book, you've seen many examples of AI agents that seem impressive at first sight. The fact that the same computer program can learn to solve a wide variety of tasks is remarkable. Moreover, after you move on to more complex environments, it's easy to get carried away by these results: AlphaZero learns to play chess, Go, and Shogi. OpenAI Five defeats human teams at the game of Dota2. AlphaStar beats a top professional player at the game of StarCraft II. These are compelling general-purpose algorithms. But do these general-purpose algorithms show any sign of general intelligence? First of all, what is general intelligence?

General intelligence is the ability to combine various cognitive abilities to solve new problems. For artificial general intelligence (AGI), we then expect a computer program to show general intelligence. Okay. Now, let's ask the following question: are any of the algorithms presented in this book, or even state-of-the-art methods such as AlphaZero, OpenAI Five, and AlphaStar, examples of artificial general intelligence? Well, it's not clear, but I'd say no.

You see, on the one hand, many of these algorithms can use "multiple cognitive abilities," including perception and learning for solving a new task, say, playing Pong. If we stick to our definition, the fact that the algorithm uses multiple cognitive abilities to solve new problems is a plus. However, one of the most dissatisfying parts of these algorithms is that none of these trained agents are good at solving new problems unless you train them, which most of the time requires millions of samples before you get any impressive results. In other words, if you train a DQN agent to play Pong from pixels, that trained agent, which can be at superhuman level at Pong, has no clue about how to play a decent game of Breakout and has to train for millions of frames before it shows any skill.

Humans don't have this problem. If you learn to play Pong, I'm pretty sure you can pick up Breakout in like two seconds. Both games have the same task of hitting a ball with a paddle. On the other hand, even the AlphaZero agent, a computer program with the most impressive skills of all time at multiple fundamentally different board games, and that can beat professional players who dedicate their lives at these games, but will never do your laundry.

Certain AI researchers say their goal is to create AI systems that perceive, learn, think, and even feel emotions like humans do. Machines that learn, think, feel, and perhaps even look like people, are most definitely an exciting thought. Other researchers have a more practical approach; they don't necessarily want an AI that thinks like humans unless thinking like a human is a requirement for making a good lunch. And perhaps emotions are what make a great cook, who knows. The point is that while some folks want AGI to delegate, to stop doing mundane tasks, other folks have a more philosophical goal. Creating AGI could be a path to understanding intelligence itself, to understanding the self, and that on its own would be a remarkable accomplishment for humanity.

Either way, every AI researcher would agree that, regardless of the end goal, we still need AI algorithms that display more general and transferable skills. There are many traits that AI systems likely require before they can do more human-like tasks, such as doing the laundry, cooking lunch, or washing the dishes. Interestingly, it's those mundane tasks that are the most difficult to solve for AI. Let's review several of the research areas that are currently pushing the frontier on making deep reinforcement learning and artificial intelligence show signs of general intelligence.

The following sections introduce several of the concepts that you may want to explore further as you keep learning advanced deep reinforcement learning techniques that get the field of AI closer to human-level intelligence. I spend only a few sentences so that you're aware of as many as possible. I intend to show you the door, not what's inside it. It's for you to decide which door to open.

Workforce revolutions

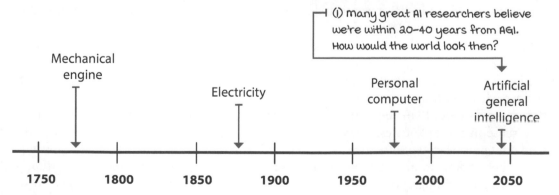

Advanced exploration strategies

One area of research that's showing exciting results has to do with the reward function. Throughout this book, you've seen agents that learn from the reward signal, but interestingly, there's recent research that shows agents can learn without any reward at all. Learning from things other than rewards is an exciting thought, and it may be essential for developing human-like intelligence. If you observe a baby learn, there's much unsupervised and self-supervised learning going on. Sure, at one point in their lives, we reward our children. You know you get an A, you get B; your salary is x, yours is y. But agents aren't always after the rewards we put along their way. What is the reward function of life? Is it career success? Is it to have children? It's not clear.

Now, removing the reward function from the reinforcement learning problem can be a bit scary. If we're not defining the reward function for the agent to maximize, how do we make sure their goals align with ours? How do we make artificial general intelligence that's suitable for the goals of humankind? Maybe it's the case that, to create human-like intelligence, we need to give agents the freedom to choose their destiny. Either way, to me, this is one of the critical research areas to pursue.

Inverse reinforcement learning

There are other ways to learn behavior without a reward function, and even though we often prefer a reward function, learning to imitate a human first can help learn policies with fewer samples. There are a few related fields to look for here. *Behavioral cloning* is the application of supervised learning techniques to learn a policy from demonstrations, often from a human. As the name suggests, there's no reasoning going on here, merely generalization. A related field, called *inverse reinforcement learning*, consists of inferring the reward function from demonstrations. In this case, we're not merely copying the behavior, but we're learning the intentions of another agent. *Inferring intentions* can be a powerful tool for multiple goals. For instance, in multi-agent reinforcement learning, for both adversarial and cooperative settings, knowing what other agents are after can be useful information. If we know what an agent wants to do, and what it wants to do goes against our goals, we can devise strategies for stopping it before it's too late.

But, inverse reinforcement learning allows agents to learn new policies. Learning the reward function from another agent, such as a human, and learning a policy from this learned reward function is a technique often referred to as *apprenticeship learning*. One interesting point to consider when learning about inverse reinforcement learning is that the reward function is often more succinct than the optimal policy. Attempting to learn the reward function can make sense in multiple cases. Techniques that learn policies from demonstrations are also called *imitation learning*, often whether a reward function is inferred before the policy or straight behavioral cloning. A frequent use case for imitation learning is the initialization of agents to a good enough policy. For instance, if an agent has to learn from random behavior, it could take a long time before it learns a good policy. The idea is that imitating a human, even if suboptimal, may lead to optimal policies with fewer interactions with the environment. However, this isn't always the case, and policies pretrained with demonstrations by humans may introduce unwanted bias and prevent agents from finding optimal policies.

Transfer learning

You probably notice that the agent trained on an environment, in general, cannot be transferred to new environments. Reinforcement learning algorithms are general purpose in the sense that the same agent can be trained in different environments, but they don't have general intelligence, and what they learn cannot be straightforwardly transferred to new environments.

Transfer learning is an area of research that looks at ways of transferring knowledge from a set of environments to a new environment. One approach, for instance, that may be intuitive to you if you have a deep learning background, is what's called *fine-tuning*. Similar to reusing the weights of a pretrained network in supervised learning, agents trained in related environments can reuse the features learned by the convolution layers on a different task. If the environments are related, such as Atari games, for instance, several of the features may be transferable. In certain environments, even policies can be transferred.

Sim-to-real transfer learning task is a common need in the real world

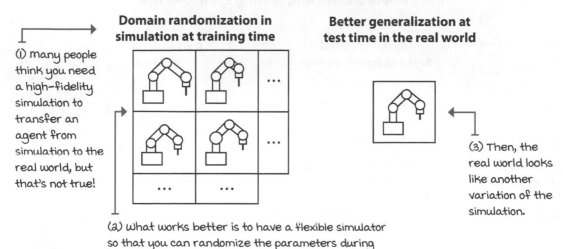

Domain randomization in simulation at training time

Better generalization at test time in the real world

(1) many people think you need a high-fidelity simulation to transfer an agent from simulation to the real world, but that's not true!

(3) Then, the real world looks like another variation of the simulation.

(2) what works better is to have a flexible simulator so that you can randomize the parameters during training, and the agent is forced to generalize better.

The general area of research on making agents learn more general skills is called *transfer learning*. Another frequent use of transfer learning is to transfer policies learned in simulation to the real world. Sim-to-real transfer learning is a common need in robotics, in which training agents controlling robots can be tricky, costly, and dangerous. It's also not as scalable as training in simulation. A common need is to train an agent in simulation and then transfer the policy to the real world. A common misconception is that simulations need to be high-fidelity and realistic for transferring agents from simulation to the real world. There's research suggesting that it's the opposite. It's the variety, the diversity of observations, that makes agents more transferable. Techniques such as domain randomization are at the forefront of this research area and show much promise.

Multi-task learning

A related area of research, called *multi-task learning*, looks at transfer learning from a different perspective. In multi-task learning, the goal is to train on multiple tasks, instead of one, and then transfer to a new task. In this case, model-based reinforcement learning approaches come to mind. In robotics, for instance, learning a variety of tasks with the same robot can help the agent learn a robust model of the dynamics of the environment. The agent learns about gravity, how to move toward the right, or left, and so on. Regardless of the tasks, the model of the dynamics learned can be transferred to a new task.

Multi-task learning consists of training on multiple related tasks and testing on a new one

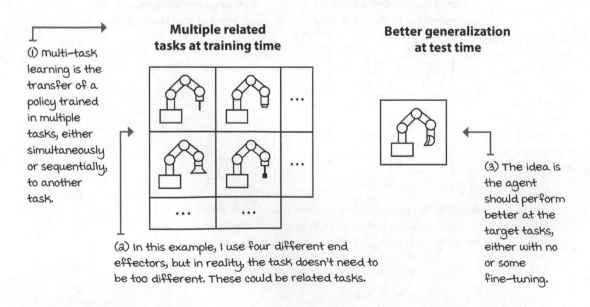

Multiple related tasks at training time

Better generalization at test time

(1) multi-task learning is the transfer of a policy trained in multiple tasks, either simultaneously or sequentially, to another task.

(2) In this example, I use four different end effectors, but in reality, the task doesn't need to be too different. These could be related tasks.

(3) The idea is the agent should perform better at the target tasks, either with no or some fine-tuning.

Curriculum learning

A common use-case scenario for multi-task learning is decomposing a task into multiple tasks sorted by difficulty level. In this case, the agent is put through a curriculum, learning more complicated tasks progressively. *Curriculum learning* makes sense and can be useful when developing scenarios. If you need to create an environment for an agent to solve, it often makes sense for you to create the most straightforward scenario with a dense reward function. By doing this, your agent can quickly show progress toward learning the goal, and this validates that your environment is working well. Then, you can increase the complexity and make the reward function more sparse. After you do this for a handful of scenarios, you naturally create a curriculum that can be used by your agent. Then, you can train your agent in progressively more complex environments, and hopefully, have an agent reach the desired behaviors more quickly.

Meta learning

Another super exciting research area is called *meta learning*. If you think about it, we're hand-coding agents to learn many different tasks. At one point, we become the bottleneck. If we could develop an agent that, instead of learning to solve a challenging task, learns to learn itself, we could remove humans from the equation; well, not quite, but take a step in that direction. Learning to learn is an exciting approach to using experiences from learning multiple tasks to get good at learning itself. It makes intuitive sense. Other exciting research paths coming out of meta learning are automatically discovering neural network architectures and optimization methods. Keep an eye out for these.

Hierarchical reinforcement learning

Often, we find ourselves developing environments that have problems with multiple horizons. For instance, if we want an agent to find the best high-level strategy, but give it only low-level control commands for actions, then the agent needs to learn to go from low-level to high-level action space. Intuitively, there's a hierarchy in the policies for most agents. When I plan, I do so on a higher-level action space. I think about going to the store, not moving my arms to get to the store. *Hierarchical reinforcement learning* enables agents to create a hierarchy of actions internally to tackle long-horizon problems. Agents no longer reason about left-right commands, but more about go here or there.

Multi-agent reinforcement learning

The world wouldn't be as exciting without other agents. In multi-agent reinforcement learning, we look at techniques for having agents learn when there are multiple agents around. One of the main issues that arise, when learning in multi-agent settings, is that as your agent learns, other agents learn too, and therefore change their behavior. The problem is that this change makes the observations non-stationary, because what your agent learns is outdated right after the other agents learn, and so learning becomes challenging.

One exciting approach to cooperative *multi-agent reinforcement learning* is to use actor-critic methods in which the critic uses the full state information of all agents during training. The advantage here is that your agents learn to cooperate through the critic, and we can then use the policy during testing using a more realistic observation space. Sharing the full state may seem unrealistic, but you can think about it as similar to how teams practice. During practice, everything is allowed. Say that you're a soccer player, and you can tell other agents you intend to run on the wing when you make this move, and so on. You get to practice moves with full information during training; then, you can only use your policy with limited information during testing.

Another appealing thought when looking into multi-agent reinforcement learning is that hierarchical reinforcement learning can be thought of as another case of multi-agent reinforcement learning. How so? Think about multiple agents deciding on different horizons. The multiple-horizon structure is similar to the way most companies do business. Folks at the top plan higher-level goals for the next few years and other folks decide on how to get there on a month-to-month and a day-to-day basis. The ones at the top set the goals for those on the bottom. The whole system gets rewarded for the performance of all agents.

Of course, multi-agent reinforcement learning isn't only for the cooperative case but also for the adversarial case, which is perhaps the most exciting. Humans often see competition and adversaries as something inherently unfortunate, but multi-agent reinforcement learning suggests that our adversaries often are the best way to make ourselves better. Underlying many recent reinforcement learning success stories are training techniques that include adversaries: either a previous version of the same agent, such as in self-play, to a whole tournament-like distribution of other agents that form after all the matches—only the best agents survive. Adversaries often make us better, and for better or worse, they might be needed for optimal behavior.

Explainable AI, safety, fairness, and ethical standards

There are a few other critical areas of research that, even though not directly a push for human-level intelligence, are fundamental for the successful development, deployment, and adoption of artificial intelligence solutions.

Explainable artificial intelligence is an area of research that tries to create agents that are more easily understandable by humans. The motives are apparent. A court of law can interrogate any person that breaks the law; however, machine learning models aren't designed to be explainable. To ensure the fast adoption of AI solutions by society, researchers must investigate ways to ease the problem of explainability. To be clear, I don't think this is a requirement. I prefer having an AI give me an accurate prediction in the stock market, whether it can explain to me why or not. However, neither decision is straightforward. In life-or-death decisions involving humans, things become hairy quickly.

Safety is another area of research that should get more attention. It's often the case that AIs fail catastrophically in ways that are too obvious to humans. Also, AIs are vulnerable to attacks that humans aren't. We need to make sure that when AIs are deployed, we know how the systems react to a variety of situations. AIs currently don't have a way to go through classical validation and verification (V&V) of software approaches, and this poses a significant challenge for the adoption of AI.

Fairness is another crucial issue. We need to start thinking about who controls AIs. If a company creates an AI to maximize profits at the expense of society, then what's the point of AI technologies? We already have something similar going on with advertising. Top companies use AI to maximize gains through a form of manipulation. Should these companies be allowed to do this for profit? How about when AIs get better and better? What's the purpose of this, destroy a human through manipulation? These are things that need to be seriously considered.

Finally, AI ethical standards are another issue that has gotten recent attention with the Montreal Declaration for Responsible Development of Artificial Intelligence. These are 10 ethical principles for AI that serve the interests of society, and not merely for-profit companies. These are several of the top fields to have in mind when you're ready to contribute.

What happens next?

While this section marks the end of this book, it should only mark the beginning or continuation of your contributions to the field of AI and DRL. My intention with this book was, not only to get you understanding the basics of DRL, but also to onboard you into this fantastic community. You don't need much other than a commitment to continue the journey. There are many things you could do next, and in this section, I'd like to give you ideas to get you started. Have in mind that the world is a choir needing a wide variety of voice types and talents; your job is to accept the talents given to you, develop them to the best of your abilities, and play your part with all you've got. While I can give you ideas, it's up to you what happens next; the world needs and awaits your voice.

How to use DRL to solve custom problems

There's something super cool about RL algorithms that I want you to have in mind as you learn about other types of agents. The fact is that most RL agents can solve any problem that you choose, as long as you can represent the problem as a correct MDP, the way we discussed in chapter 2. When you ask yourself, "What can X or Y algorithm solve?" the answer is the same problems other algorithms can solve. While in this book, we concentrate on a handful of algorithms, all the agents presented can solve many other environments with some hyperparameter tuning. The need for solving custom environments is something many people want but could take a whole other book to get right. My recommendation is to look at some of the examples available online. For instance, Atari environments use an emulator called Stella in the backend. The environments pass images for observations and actions back and forth between the environment and the emulator. Likewise, MuJoCo and the Bullet Physics simulation engine are the backends that drive continuous-control environments. Take a look at the way these environments work.

Pay attention to how observations are passed from the simulation to the environment and then to the agent. Then, the actions selected by the agent are passed to the environment and then to the simulation engine. This pattern is widespread, so if you want to create a custom environment, investigate how others have done it, and then do it yourself. Do you want to create an environment for an agent to learn to invest in the stock market? Think about which platforms have an API that allows you to do that. Then, you can create different environments using the same API. One environment, for instance, can buy stocks, another buys options, and so on. There are so many potential applications for state-of-the-art deep reinforcement learning methods that it's a shame we have a limited number of quality environments at our disposal. Contributions in this area are undoubtedly welcome. If you want to create an environment and don't find it out there, consider investing the time to create your own and share it with the world.

Going forward

You have learned a lot; there's no doubt about that. But, if you look at the big picture, there's so much more to learn. Now, if you zoom out even further, you realize that there's even more to discover; things nobody has learned before. You see that what the AI community is after is no easy feat; we're trying to understand how the mind works.

The fact is, even other fields, such as Psychology, Philosophy, Economics, Linguistic, Operations Research, Control Theory, and many more, are after the same goal, each from their perspective, and using their language. But the bottom line is that all of these fields would benefit from understanding how the mind works, how humans make decisions, and how to help them make optimal decisions. Here are some ideas for us moving forward.

First, find your motivation, your ambition, and focus. Certain people find the sole desire to explore; to discover facts about the mind is exciting. Others want to leave a better world behind. Whatever your motivation, find it. Find your drive. If you aren't used to reading research papers, you won't enjoy them unless you know your motives. As you find your motivation and drive, you must remain calm, humble, and transparent; you need your drive to focus and work hard toward your goals. Don't let your excitement get in your way. You must learn to keep your motivation in your heart, yet move forward. Our ability to focus is in constant jeopardy from a myriad of readily available distractions. I'm guaranteed to find new notifications on my cell phone every 15 minutes. And we're trained to think that this is a good thing. It isn't. We must get back in control of our lives and be able to concentrate long and hard on something that interests us, that we love. Practice focus.

Second, balance learning and contributions and give yourself time to rest. What do you think would happen if, for the next 30 days, I eat 5,000 calories a day and burn 1,000? What if I, instead, eat 1,000 and burn 5,000? How about I'm an athlete and eat and burn 5,000, but train every day of the week? Right, all of those spell trouble to the body. The same happens with the mind; certain people think they need to learn for years before they can do anything, so they read, watch videos, but don't do anything with it. Others think they no longer need to read any papers; after all, they've already implemented a DQN agent and written a blog post about it. They quickly become obsolete and lack the fuel to think. Some people get those two right, but never include the time to relax, and enjoy their family and reflect. That's the wrong approach. Find a way to balance what you take and what you give, and set time to rest. We're athletes of the mind, too much "fat" in your mind, too much information that you put in without purpose, and you become sluggish and too slow. Too many blog posts without doing any research, and you become outdated, repetitive, and dry. Not enough rest, and you won't plan well enough for the long term.

Also, know that you can't learn everything. Again, we're learning about the mind, and there's much information about it out there. Be wise, and be picky about what you read. Who's the author? What's her background? Still, you can read it but have a higher sense of what you're doing. Try to give often. You should be able to explain things that you learn another way. The quote, "Don't reinvent the wheel," is misleading at best. It would be best if you tried things on your own; that's vital. It's inevitable that if you explore, early on, you may find yourself having a great idea, that you later realize has been worked on before. There's no shame in that; it's more critical for you to keep moving forward than to keep yourself waiting for a eureka moment that solves world hunger. I heard Rich Sutton say something along the lines of "the obvious to you is your biggest contribution." But if you don't allow yourself to "reinvent the wheel," you run the risk of not sharing the "obvious to you," thinking it's probably not worthy. I'm not saying you need to publish a paper about this new algorithm you thought about, Q-learning. I'm asking, please, don't let the fear of doing "worthless" work stop you from experimenting. The bottom line is to keep reading, keep exploring, keep contributing, and let it all sink in. It's a cycle; it's a flow, so keep it going.

Third and last, embrace the process, lose yourself on the path. Your dreams are only a way to get you going, but it's in the going that you live your dreams. Get deep into it; don't just follow what others are doing, and follow your interests. Think critically of your ideas, experiment, gather data, try to understand the results, and detach yourself from the result. Don't bias your experiments, discover facts. If you lose yourself for long enough, you start to specialize, which is good. This field is so vast that being great at everything isn't possible. However, if you follow your interests and intuition for long enough, you automatically spend more time on certain things versus other things. Keep going. Some of us feel a need to stay in the know, and once we start asking questions that have no answers, we feel the need to get back to shore. Don't be afraid to ask hard questions, and work on getting answers. There are no dumb questions; each question is a clue for solving the mystery. Keep asking questions. Keep playing the game, and enjoy it.

Get yourself out there! Now!

Assuming you just finished this book, make sure to get out there right away, think about how to put things together, and contribute something to this amazing community. How about writing a blog post about several of the algorithms not covered in this book that you find interesting? How about investigating some of the advanced concepts discussed in this chapter and sharing what you find? Write a blog post, create a video, and let the world know about it. Become part of the movement; let's find out what intelligence is, let's build intelligent systems, together. It's never the right time unless it's now.

Summary

That's it! You did it! That's a wrap for this book. The ball is in your court.

In the first chapter, I defined deep reinforcement learning as follows: "Deep reinforcement learning is a machine learning approach to artificial intelligence concerned with creating computer programs that can solve problems requiring intelligence. The distinct property of DRL programs is learning through trial and error from feedback that's simultaneously sequential, evaluative, and sampled by leveraging powerful non-linear function approximation."

I mentioned that success to me was that after you complete this book, you should be able to come back to this definition and understand it precisely. I said that you should be able to tell why I used the words that I used, and what each of these words means in the context of deep reinforcement learning.

Did I succeed? Do you intuitively now understand this definition? Now it's your turn to send your reward to the agent behind this book. Was this project a –1, a 0, or a +1? Whatever your comments, I learn, just like DRL agents, from feedback, and I look forward to reading your review and what you have to say. For now, my part is complete.

In this final chapter, we reviewed everything the book teaches, and we also discussed the core methods that we skipped, and some of the advanced concepts that could play a part in the eventual creation of artificial general intelligence agents.

As a parting message, I'd like to first thank you for the opportunity you gave me to share with you my take on the field of deep reinforcement learning. I also want to encourage you to keep going, to concentrate on the day-to-day, to think more about what you can do next, with your current abilities, with your unique talents.

By now, you

- Intuitively understand what deep reinforcement learning is; you know the details of the most critical deep reinforcement learning methods, from the most basic and foundational to the state-of-the-art.

- Have a sense of where to go next because you understand how what we've learned fits into the big picture of the fields of deep reinforcement learning and artificial intelligence.

- Are ready to show us what you've got, your unique talents, and interests. Go, make the RL community proud. Now, it's your turn!

TWEETABLE FEAT

Work on your own and share your findings

Here are several ideas on how to take what you've learned to the next level. If you'd like, share your results with the rest of the world and make sure to check out what others have done, too. It's a win-win situation, and hopefully, you'll take advantage of it.

- **#gdrl_ch13_tf01:** Implement model-based deep reinforcement learning methods.
- **#gdrl_ch13_tf02:** Implement gradient-free deep reinforcement learning methods.
- **#gdrl_ch13_tf03:** Implement a multi-agent environment or agent, and share it.
- **#gdrl_ch13_tf04:** Use advance deep learning techniques not discussed in this book to get better results from deep reinforcement learning agents. To give you an idea, variational autoencoders (VAE) could be a promising way to compress the observation space. This way the agent can learn much quicker. Any other DL technique?
- **#gdrl_ch13_tf05:** Create a list of resources for learning several of the more advance techniques to develop artificial general intelligence, whether mentioned or not.
- **#gdrl_ch13_tf06:** Grab your favorite algorithm from one of the approaches to AGI in this chapter, create a Notebook, and make a blog post explaining the details.
- **#gdrl_ch13_tf07:** Create a list of interesting environments already out there.
- **#gdrl_ch13_tf08:** Create a custom environment that you are passionate about, something unique, maybe a wrapper for AI to play a game, or the stock market, and so on.
- **#gdrl_ch13_tf09:** Update your resume and send it my way, and I'll retweet it. Make sure to include several of the projects that you worked on, DRL related, of course.
- **#gdrl_ch13_tf10:** In every chapter, I'm using the final hashtag as a catchall hashtag. Feel free to use this one to discuss anything else that you worked on relevant to this chapter. There's no more exciting homework than that which you create for yourself. Make sure to share what you set yourself to investigate and your results.

Write a tweet with your findings, tag me @mimoralea (I'll retweet), and use the particular hashtag from the list to help interested folks find your results. There are no right or wrong results; you share your findings and check others' findings. Take advantage of this to socialize, contribute, and get yourself out there! We're waiting for you!

Here's a tweet example:

"Hey, @mimoralea. I created a blog post with a list of resources to study deep reinforcement learning. Check it out at <link>. #gdrl_ch01_tf01"

I'll make sure to retweet and help others find your work.

index

RELATED MANNING TITLES

Deep Reinforcement Learning in Action
by Alexander Zai and Brandon Brown

9781617295430
384 pages, $49.99
March 2020

Deep Learning with Python, Second Edition
by François Chollet

9781617296864
400 page, $59.99
Spring 2021 (estimated)

Deep Learning with PyTorch
by Eli Stevens, Luca Antiga, and Thomas Viehmann
Foreword by Soumith Chintala

978161729526
520 pages, $49.99
July 2020

For ordering information go to www.manning.com